D0597099

ATMASIDDHI
SHASTRA

SHRIMAD RAJCHANDRAJI'S

ATMASIDDHI
SHASTRA

Six Spiritual Truths of the Soul

Concise & Complete Commentary by
PUJYA GURUDEVSHRI RAKESHJI

HarperCollins *Publishers*

First published in India by
HarperCollins *Publishers* 2021
A-75, Sector 57, Noida, Uttar Pradesh 201301, India
www.harpercollins.co.in

2 4 6 8 10 9 7 5 3 1

Copyright © Shrimad Rajchandra Mission Dharampur, 2021
P-ISBN: 9789354894039
E-ISBN: 9789354894046

Shrimad Rajchandra Mission Dharampur
asserts the moral right to be identified as the author of this work.

Printed and bound at
Thomson Press (India) Ltd

This book is produced from independently certified FSC® paper
to ensure responsible forest management.

The Hand who guides me,
The Voice who awakens me,
The Shoulder who uplifts me,
The Countenance that is embedded within me,
The heart of my heart,
The breath of my breath,
The soul of my soul.

Param Krupalu Dev

my God, my Lord, my Bhagwan
Your Grace is immeasurable
to repay is impossible
lifetimes of praise would be too little

forever indebted
eternally in surrender.

BHAGWAN MAHAVIR

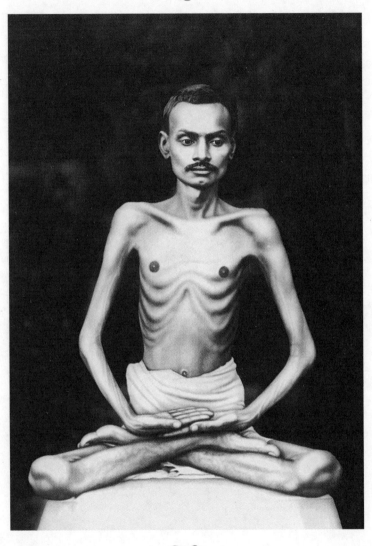

SHRIMAD RAJCHANDRAJI

PUJYA GURUDEVSHRI RAKESHJI

Enlightened Master, spiritual visionary, modern-day mystic and humanitarian leader, Pujya Gurudevshri Rakeshji is the founder of Shrimad Rajchandra Mission Dharampur - a spiritual organisation for inner transformation with 108 centres across five continents, 250 value education children's centres, and over 90 youth groups.

An ardent devotee of Shrimad Rajchandraji, blending theory with experience and the head with the heart, Pujya Gurudevshri provides powerful and practical tools to joyfully tread the journey inward. His mastery of the spiritual principles, illuminating wisdom, pure love, rationality, oratory flair and sparkling wit, captivates people of any age or background. Pujya Gurudevshri reveals the deepest truths embedded in a vast array of scriptures. He has authored inspiring books on spirituality, translated in multiple languages.

His unending flow of compassion has blossomed into Shrimad Rajchandra Love and Care, offering selfless service and bringing joy to the underprivileged. This international initiative enjoys special consultative status in the United Nations Economic and Social Council. Transforming millions globally, inspiring humanity to seek self-realisation, Pujya Gurudevshri is a 21st century spiritual force, while remaining unmoved Himself - the unmoved mover.

प्रधान मंत्री
Prime Minister
MESSAGE

It is heartening to learn that Shrimad Rajchandra Mission, Dharampur is commemorating the 125th anniversary of 'Atmasiddhi Shastra', a spiritual treatise authored by Shrimad Rajchandra Ji.

The endeavour by Shri Rakesh Ji to present the essence of 'Atmasiddhi Shastra' in a lucid manner through its commentary in English is a thoughtful gesture, aimed at the spiritual welfare of the youth.

The profound spiritual wisdom of Shrimad Rajchandra Ji guided generations of seekers to tread the path of self-realisation. The eternal principles immensely benefit the seekers and devotees, contributing towards their spiritual progress and welfare. The expanse and depth of his vision holds a greater relevance for mankind in today's world.

May the global launch of 'Atmasiddhi Shastra' further propagate the richness and depth of the spiritual philosophy of Shrimad Rajchandra Ji.

I wish the publication all success.

(Narendra Modi)

New Delhi
श्रावण 21, शक संवत् 1943
August 12, 2021

SHRI NARENDRA MODI
Hon. Prime Minister of India

THE DALAI LAMA

FOREWORD

Atmasiddhi, a spiritual treatise in verse by the 19th Century Jain master Shrimad Rajchandra, has been an inspiration to many. I am confident that this book kit by my spiritual brother Pujya Gurudevshri will be of great benefit to those wishing to understand and apply the deeper meaning of Jain philosophy.

I am sure there is much in the words gathered here that readers will enjoy and benefit from if they read them, reflect on them and take them to heart.

With my prayers,

12 August 2021
HIS HOLINESS THE DALAI LAMA

"I am pleased to see that the sublime essence of Shrimad Rajchandraji's Atmasiddhi Shastra is now available in a form that appeals to the modern generation. Shri Rakeshji's innovative tribute to this 125-year old spiritual treasure is a laudable step to keep the light of eternal wisdom alive."

Founder - Art of Living Foundation SRI SRI RAVI SHANKAR

"Simple, understandable, and yet profoundly deep, Shrimadji's written works are globally studied and revered. Atmasiddhi Shastra is a contemporary addition to this illustrious library which will appeal to modern spiritual aspirants and consolidate their understanding towards true self realisation."

Spiritual Head - BAPS Swaminarayan Sanstha PUJYA MAHANT SWAMI

"By reading Atmasiddhi Shastra seekers would be provided direction through answers to the most fundamental questions, thereby being blessed and empowered on their journey towards ultimate spiritual fulfilment."

"Celebrating the 125th anniversary of Param Krupalu Bhagwan's composition, Shri Atmasiddhi Shastra, I welcome Pujya Gurudevshri's book Atmasiddhi Shastra which reveals the secrets of the great work. I bow down to it."

"The eternal principles, as explained by Pujya Gurudevshri Rakeshji, will immensely benefit seekers and devotees, contributing towards their spiritual progress and welfare."

"Every verse written by Shrimadji and translated beautifully by Shri Rakeshbhaiji will leave a very deep mark. This book will be well received by all those who wish to walk on this path and attain the timeless wisdom."

"Readers will undoubtedly be transformed through their experience of Atmasiddhi, and the lessons of Shri Atmasiddhi Shastra will live on in a new generation."

"Atmasiddhi Shastra is not just a book, it is the fruit of years of contemplation, self-reflection, meditation and seva by Pujya Gurudevshri Rakeshbhaiji, which have given him the power to see the diamond in the velvet box. As you turn the pages of the book, you set forth on an enriching inward journey. Atmasiddhi Shastra introduces you to yourself."

"All of you should read the book and become a torch light."

"I am sure this book will be useful for the spiritual seekers of all ages and devotees, across the world."

Hon. Chief Minister of Gujarat SHRI VIJAY RUPANI

"Pujya Gurudevshri Rakeshji has redefined what it means to be spiritual. Vanquishing the stubbornness of dogma and the rigidity of rituals by bringing about a paradigm shift in thought process, an inner awakening and a transformation of the heart."

Chairman Emeritus - Tata Sons; Chairman - Tata Trusts RATAN TATA

"Atmasiddhi Shastra is a practical guide to Liberation and freedom from suffering."   Founder - The Chopra Foundation DEEPAK CHOPRA

"I commend all such efforts to promote a deeper appreciation of self-awareness among the youth so that they can live a more purposeful life."

Co-founder - Infosys NANDAN NILEKANI

"Atmasiddhi Shastra has condensed the crux of spirituality, philosophy and science into poetry. A conversation between a Guru and his disciple that takes you on a spiritual adventure."

Chairman - Adani Group GAUTAM ADANI

"The book is filled with deep concepts in simple language and will encourage young readers globally to embark on their path to happiness and enlightenment."   Founder - Sun Pharma DILIP SHANGHVI

"Atmasiddhi Shastra makes one ponder and walk the inner path. It has been my good fortune to be able to delve into this masterpiece. I would recommend it to you as well."

Author, Columnist & Diplomat AMISH TRIPATHI

"Atmasiddhi Shastra is a journey with a well-charted, definite course. Pujya Gurudevshri Rakeshji provides powerful and practical tools to joyfully tread the inward journey."

Chairperson & Co-founder - upGrad RONNIE SCREWVALA

"Atmasiddhi Shastra is an invitation to a spiritual laboratory, where the result is not just inferential, but also experiential. As a scientist and innovator, I believe that a theory is only as relevant as its application."

Former Director General - CSIR & Scientist DR R. A. MASHELKAR

CONTENTS

PROLOGUE

Among rare craftsmen who pave the path of spiritual welfare for the glory of all, is the supremely benevolent and divine Shrimad Rajchandraji. Shrimadji is highly revered for His lofty spiritual state, extraordinary personality, remarkable exposition of Lord Mahavir's teachings and literary genius. Born to Smt. Devba and Shri Ravjibhai on the auspicious day of Kartik Purnima in VS 1924 (November 9, 1867) at Vavania (Gujarat, India), He was pure wisdom incarnate. At the tender age of seven, upon witnessing the burning pyre of an acquaintance, He underwent unprecedented mental churning which led to the attainment of jatismaranjnan - a recollection of several past lives. Then, at the age of 19, He displayed the extraordinary feat of shatavdhan - remaining attentive to 100 activities simultaneously.

Despite a powerful intrinsic sentiment of detachment and burning desire for renunciation, at the age of 20, He was compelled to tie the knot of marriage and engage in business. At the age of 23, He attained self-realisation. After turning 28, He began to spend four to six months a year in the seclusion of forests, mountains and remote places, effortlessly leading an austere life.

On Chaitra Vad Pancham VS 1957 (April 9, 1901) in Rajkot, abiding as ever in the blissful self, He left His mortal body in a state of complete awareness. In a short span of just 33 years, He not only soared high in the spiritual skies but also proved instrumental in directing many others towards the path of enlightenment.

Shrimadji and Gandhiji

Honoured as the spiritual guide of Mahatma Gandhi, Shrimadji had a tremendous formative influence on the father of the nation. Shrimadji shaped Gandhiji's ideas and guided his beliefs. He played a pivotal role in the making of the Mahatma, on the basis of which Gandhiji achieved India's independence and inspired generations across the world. Acknowledging His impact, Gandhiji expresses, "Such was the man who captivated my heart in religious matters as no other man has till now. I have said elsewhere that besides Kavi (Shrimadji), Ruskin and Tolstoy have contributed in forming my intrinsic character; but Kavi has had a more profound effect because I had come in personal and intimate contact with Him."

~ Mahatma Gandhi ~ Modern Review, June 1930

Shrimadji and Gandhiji first met in Mumbai in 1891, when Gandhiji returned from England as a young barrister. Their relationship blossomed over profound interactions for two years in Mumbai. After moving to South Africa, Gandhiji corresponded with Shrimadji through letters. Once, when Gandhiji was faced with a troubling crisis over identity and religion, he resorted to Shrimadji for guidance by penning 27 questions. Shrimadji's answers resolved his doubts.

Even after Shrimadji left His mortal body, Gandhiji contemplated upon His letters and compositions, time and time again. Gandhiji would write about Shrimadji, speak about Him in speeches, discuss Him with close associates, and pay heartfelt tributes to Him.

Shri Atmasiddhi Shastra

Shrimadji created an era of spirituality, carving a path of inner growth for all. The heritage of His literary works has proved invaluable to seekers in their quest of self-discovery. The most significant of these is Shri Atmasiddhi Shastra, which He composed at the age of 28. A testament to Shrimadji's extraordinary state and remarkable creativity, this majestic scriptural composition holds a unique place amongst all His works.

Shri Atmasiddhi Shastra is a journey with a well-charted, definite course. The structure of this composition has been planned with immense care, with each stanza evolving into the next and every verse seamlessly merging into the other. Each thought grows and expands until it has laid before the reader a bird's-eye view of the path to self-realisation. It is the clearest, most cogent outline in the odyssey of the soul, its many pitfalls and final destination. Written in language that simplifies and demystifies complex philosophy, Shri Atmasiddhi Shastra is the guiding light for every struggling soul. It holds hope for the materialist bogged down by practical problems as well as the seeker in conflict with himself. Aspirants thirsting for spiritual upliftment find the highway to inner peace and purity in this text. Through this exhaustive cascade of grace, Shrimadji has imparted teachings capable of ending transmigration.

Inspiration

Shrimadji had written a letter elucidating the six fundamental truths of the soul to His disciple Shri Lalluji Muni in 1894 AD. This letter was sent to Shrimadji's spiritual friend Shri Saubhagyabhai to memorise and repeatedly reflect upon it. As he was an elderly man, Shri Saubhagyabhai found it difficult to memorise the prose and felt that others might face the same challenge. In 1896 AD, when he met Shrimadji in Khambhat, he requested Shrimadji that if a poetic composition similar to the letter was created, it would be beneficial to all seekers and easier to memorise. As a result of this humble request, from Shrimadji's supreme inner purity manifested the inimitable masterpiece Shri Atmasiddhi Shastra, incorporating the six fundamentals in poetic form. The world will indeed remain indebted to Shri Saubhagyabhai for this sacred text. Shrimadji has immortalised him by mentioning his name three times in Shri Atmasiddhi Shastra.

There have been many instances in the past where the great ones have composed scriptures at the requests of others. The question posed by Gommatraja (Chamundray) led Siddhantchakravarti Acharyashri Nemichandraji to compose Gommatsaar and Labdhisaar. At King Kumarpal's request, Kalikaalsarvajna Acharyashri Hemchandrasuriji composed Vitragstav and Yogshastra. Upadhyayshri Yashovijayji Maharaj and Ganishri Devchandraji Maharaj also composed many texts accepting such requests. Similarly, Shri Saubhagyabhai was the key inspiration behind Shri Atmasiddhi Shastra, the crown jewel amongst Shrimadji's writings.

Composition

In the monsoon months of the year 1896, Shrimadji had gone for a retreat to Gujarat. Moving through the jungles of Gujarat, immersed in the self, He reached the town of Nadiad in the Charotar district in October. Shri Ambalalbhai was in His service at that time. On the evening of October 22, after returning from a walk, Shrimadji asked Shri Ambalalbhai for a lantern and began to write. Full of devout humility and modesty, he stood steadfast like a lamp post, holding the lantern and facilitating Shrimadji to write. Thus, with an effortless flow of words, Shrimadji in a single sitting of an hour and a half to two hours, wrote Shri Atmasiddhi Shastra.

All 142 verses were written in one go - no resits, no retakes. Encompassing the nectar obtained from churning the ocean of spiritual scriptures, this unprecedented text could only have been composed in such a short time by one as divine as Shrimadji. Even merely copying these verses requires a longer duration! This event is a testament to His spiritual wealth and poetic prowess. Thus, on the auspicious day of Aso Vad Ekam, VS 1952, Thursday, October 22, 1896, in a room within the Nana Kumbhnath temple in Nadiad, Shrimadji composed this magnum opus. Shri Atmasiddhi Shastra is adequate enough to immortalise Shrimadji's legacy.

Title

This profound spiritual poetic composition is renowned by its glorious name 'Atmasiddhi Shastra'. 'Atma' means soul and 'Siddhi' means establishment or accomplishment. In this composition, Shrimadji has established the truth of the soul by describing the six fundamentals through pure strength of logic and reasoning. Upon contemplating and internalising it, the true seeker is certain to attain self-realisation. Hence the word, 'Atmasiddhi'. In the past hundreds of years, several texts with the word 'siddhi' have been written, in Jain and non-Jain traditions, to establish their viewpoints and opinions. Sarvarthsiddhi, Anekantsiddhi, Siddhivinishchay, Sarvajnasiddhi, etc., have been written in the Jain tradition, whereas Brahmasiddhi, Advaitsiddhi, etc., are well-known Vedant texts.

This composition has been given the status of a shastra - scripture. In Sanskrit, the word 'shastra' is derived as Shasanat Shastram - that which disciplines is called a shastra. It either inspires one to engage in a pursuit or it directs one to refrain from doing something. This supremely beneficial composition provides guidance, inspiration and impetus for spiritual progress. It propounds and encourages one to tread the sacred path of liberation. Hence, it is rightly called shastra. Thus, the title 'Atmasiddhi Shastra' is perfectly apt.

Subject

Shri Atmasiddhi Shastra has emerged from Shrimadji's effortless state of abidance in the self. There is a method to its matter, a careful construction in its composition, a supreme sense in its stanzas. It is divided into 12 sections, comprising 142 verses.

Verses 1-42 deal with the introduction to the principal subject of the text in which Shrimadji throws light on several key points. Shrimadji describes obstacles on the path of liberation, importance of the Sadguru, means to remove defects in seekers, attributes of two types of bigots, and traits of a true seeker.

Verses 43-118 comprise the main subject matter. The six fundamental truths of the soul are elaborated upon in this section - 'the soul exists', 'it is eternal', 'it is the doer of karma', 'it is the receiver of the fruits of karma', 'there is liberation', and 'there is a path of liberation'. The veracity of each fundamental is simply proven through a lively exchange between a Guru and His disciple in the form of doubts and solutions.

Verses 119-142 depict the attainment of enlightenment by the disciple and the conclusion of the text. In nine verses, the exuberant disciple expresses his immense gratitude and reverence towards the Guru. The final fifteen verses serve as a quintessential guide for any spiritual aspirant, pointing out the areas where one could possibly go astray. The concluding section is the pinnacle of the temple of Shri Atmasiddhi Shastra.

Style

Shri Atmasiddhi Shastra carves a special niche for itself through the presentation, in an exceptional question-answer tone. Shrimadji has elucidated the six fundamental truths in the style of a dialogue between a Guru and a disciple. This approach possesses several benefits, aiding the creator to easily reveal the subject to the reader, intrigue his curiosity, provoke a deliberation, and amenably shape his understanding.

This conversational style has been adopted in Jain Canons like Bhagwati Sutra, Jnatadharmakatha, Anuttaroppadikdasha, Vipakasutra, Niryavalika and others. Several texts like Acharyashri Jinbhadraji's Visheshavashyakbhashya, Ganishri Devchandraji's Vicharratnasar too have resorted to this form of delivery. The question-answer mode has been employed in non-Jain texts as well, like Shrimad Bhagavad Gita, Upanishads, Buddhist Tripitak, etc.

Shrimadji has based the discussion of the six fundamentals on logic, not faith. His style of proving the fundamentals is deeply penetrative, heart-touching, appealing, and most importantly, effective. He has used easy Gujarati language and simple couplets in the metre of poetry called doha chhand. Such is the prodigious nature of Shri Atmasiddhi Shastra that it proves extremely beneficial to all, regardless of age, caste or creed. Rising above the petty differences of opinions, and written in a style that can be comprehended by all, this extraordinary text has received an immortal place in spiritual literature.

Worthy Receivers

Since the text depicts the principles of absolute truth and deep essence of spirituality, Shri Atmasiddhi Shastra required special eligibility. Shrimadji chose only four seekers to study the text, and to this effect, instructed Shri Ambalalbhai to make four copies. These four worthy souls were - Shri Saubhagyabhai in Sayla, Shri Lalluji Muni in Khambhat, Shrimadji's business partner Shri Maneklal Ghelabhai Jhaveri in Rangoon, and Shri Ambalalabhai himself. Shrimadji was very particular that Shri Atmasiddhi Shastra should not get into the hands of the unworthy. The sole reason for exercising such caution was to protect the ineligible from the grave harm they could cause themselves due to their inability to grasp the profound spiritual knowledge, and irreverence for the enlightened one. There was nothing but selfless compassion behind giving Shri Atmasiddhi Shastra to only the worthy ones.

The four worthy receivers were hugely influenced by this scripture. They deeply contemplated upon it and eulogised it with immense reverence. The profound study resulted in their state being greatly elevated. This signifies their eligibility as well as Shrimadji's meticulous discerning ability. Moreover, it indicates the miraculous power of Shri Atmasiddhi Shastra to enable aspirants to scale lofty spiritual heights. These nectar-like words can be exceedingly beneficial to devout seekers and hence later, this text was made available to the public in 1905 AD.

Explanations and Translations

Shrimadji has presented the essence of the scriptures in a logical, compact and aphoristic style. Therefore, its explanation is necessary to understand the deeper meaning. It is the great fortune of aspirants that Shrimadji has explained certain verses in His letters. Shri Ambalalbhai wrote the concise meaning of every verse, which was examined by Shrimadji Himself. Shri Maneklal Ghelabhai Jhaveri who was blessed with a copy of Shri Atmasiddhi Shastra, also wrote its meanings during Shrimadji's lifetime. Mahatma Gandhi too had written Shri Atmasiddhi Shastra in English prose. Having received acclaim amongst seekers, more than 30 explanations and commentaries have been written by many eminent saints and scholars on Shri Atmasiddhi Shastra.

Impressed by the importance and popularity of Shri Atmasiddhi Shastra, many scholars have been attracted to undertake its translation. It has been translated into several languages like English, Sanskrit, Hindi, Marathi, Bengali and Kannada. It was Gandhiji's wish that various works of Shrimadji be published in different languages. In 2001, Shri Pratapkumar Toliya published a book, Saptbhashi Atmasiddhi, containing the text in seven languages. The numerous translations have ensured that even those who do not know Gujarati are not deprived of such a supreme spiritual text. The fact that it has been translated into various languages is an indicator of its strength to satiate the thirst of seekers of varied backgrounds.

Divinity Exemplified

When the soul-focused contemplation of great beings takes the shape of a composition, the right words effortlessly arrange themselves into articulate perfection. In this outstanding composition, Shrimadji's expressions flow sequentially and seamlessly. His words are drenched in dispassion and are powerful enough to destroy the suffering of transmigration. Each verse is so captivating, and so filled with sweetness, that its spirit penetrates deeply into the heart and swiftly into the soul.

To elucidate the profound mysteries of the fundamental truths in such a simple, lucid, and understandable manner is possible only for someone endowed with sheer genius as Shrimadji. Through Shri Atmasiddhi Shastra, He has accomplished the laudable task of disseminating the spiritual path to the world. Humanity is grateful to Him for this exceptional text which has emerged from the depths of His experience.

Shri Atmasiddhi Shastra flows from Shrimadji much like the sacred Ganges flows from the majestic Himalayas. It is the purifier of the fallen and the redeemer of the lowly, washing away sins, impurities and sorrows, spreading its cool soothing nectar to seekers. It is supremely beneficial and the bestower of the bliss of liberation. Infinite salutations to the immeasurable benevolence of Shrimadji.

Adoration Prayer

Patit jan pāvani, sur saritā sami, adham uddhārini, Ātmasiddhi,
Janma janmāntaro jāntā jogie, ātmanubhav vade āj didhi;
Bhakt Bhagirath samā, bhāgyashāli mahā, bhavya Saubhāgyani vinatithi,
Chārutar bhuminā nagar Nadiādmā, purna krupā Prabhue kari'ti.

Yād nadini dhare, nām Nadiād pan, charan chumi Mahāpurushonā,
Param Krupāluni charanraj santni, bhaktibhoomi harey chitt saunā;
Sameep rahi ek Ambālāle tahi, bhakti kari deep hāthey dharine,
Eki kalame kari puri Krupālue, Āso Vad Ekame 'Siddhijine.

Shri Atmasiddhi Shastra is like the heavenly river that purifies the downtrodden and uplifts those fallen to the low level; it was brought out of His self-experience by the ascetic, who knew many of His previous births. He extended that utmost favour at Nadiad, in the region of Charotar at the request of the worthy and highly fortunate Shri Saubhagyabhai. Since this stream of spiritual science flowed from the heart of Shrimad Rajchandraji at his request, he is like the king Bhagirath who brought down the river Ganga.

At the banks of a river, the town of Nadiad steals the hearts of all, due to the devotional atmosphere pervading there. It has been sanctified by the footsteps of many great ones including Shrimad Rajchandraji, and hence is a source of attraction for all. Shri Ambalalbhai devotedly held a lamp in the light of which Shri Atmasiddhi Shastra was composed on the auspicious day of Aso Vad Ekam.

Nadiad - Gujarat, India
Aso Vad Ekam, VS 1952
October 22, 1896

ૐ

આનંદવિધિ.

જે સ્વરૂપ સમજ્યા વિના, પામ્યો દુઃખ અનંત,
સમજાવ્યું તે પદ નમું, શ્રી સદ્‌ગુરૂ ભગવંત. ૧

વર્તમાન આ કાળમાં, મોક્ષમાર્ગ બહુ લોપ,
વિચારવા આત્માર્થિને, ભાખ્યો અત્ર અગોપ્ય. ૨

કોઈ ક્રિયા-જડ થઈ રહ્યા, શુષ્ક જ્ઞાનમાં કોઈ,
માને મારગ મોક્ષનો, કરૂણા ઉપજે જોઈ. ૩

બાહ્ય ક્રિયામાં રાચતા, અંતર ભેદ ન કાંઈ,
જ્ઞાનમાર્ગ નિષેધતા, તેહ ક્રિયા જડ આંઈ. ૪

બંધ મોક્ષ છે કલ્પના, ભાખે વાણી માંહી,
વર્તે મોહાવેશમાં, શુષ્ક જ્ઞાની તે આંઈ. ૫

વૈરાગ્યાદિ સફળ તો, જો સહ આતમજ્ઞાન,
તેમ જ આતમજ્ઞાનની, પ્રાપ્તિતણાં નિદાન. ૬

ત્યાગ વિરાગ ન ચિત્તમાં, થાય ન તેને જ્ઞાન,
અટકે ત્યાગ વિરાગમાં, તો ભૂલે નિજ ભાન. ૭

જ્યાં જ્યાં જે જે યોગ્ય છે, તહાં સમજવું તેહ,
ત્યાં ત્યાં તે તે આચરે, આત્માર્થી જન એહ. ૮

સેવે સદ્‌ગુરૂ ચરણને, ત્યાગી દઈ નિજપક્ષ,
પામે તે પરમાર્થને, નિજપદનો લે લક્ષ. ૯

આત્મજ્ઞાન સમદ્રષ્ટિ વિષે ઉપમસંયોગ,
અપૂર્વ વાણી પરમશ્રુત, સદગુરુ લક્ષણ યોગ. ૧૦

પ્રત્યક્ષ સદગુરુ સમ નહીં, પરોક્ષ જિનઉપકાર,
એવો લક્ષ્ય થયા વિના, ઉગે ન આત્મવિચાર. ૧૧

સદગુરુના ઉપદેશવણ, સમજાય ન જિનરૂપ,
સમજ્યા વણ ઉપકાર શો, સમજ્યે જિનસ્વરૂપ. ૧૨

આત્માદિ અસ્તિત્વનાં, જેહ નિરૂપક શાસ્ત્ર,
પ્રત્યક્ષ સદગુરુ યોગ નહિ, ત્યાં આધાર સુપાત્ર. ૧૩

અથવા સદગુરુએ કહ્યાં, જે અવગાહન કાજ,
તે તે નિત્ય વિચારવાં, કરી મતાંતર ત્યાજ. ૧૪

રોકે જીવ સ્વચ્છંદ તો, પામે અવશ્ય મોક્ષ,
પામ્યા એમ અનંત છે, ભાખ્યું જિન નિર્દોષ. ૧૫

પ્રત્યક્ષ સદગુરુ યોગથી, સ્વચ્છંદ તે રોકાય,
અન્ય ઉપાય કર્યા થકી, પ્રાયે બમણો થાય. ૧૬

સ્વચ્છંદ, મત આગ્રહ તજી, વર્તે સદગુરુ લક્ષ,
સમકિત તેને ભાખિયું, કારણ ગણી પ્રત્યક્ષ. ૧૭

માનાદિક શત્રુ મહા, નિજ છંદે ન મરાય,
જાતાં સદગુરુ શરણમાં, અલ્પ પ્રયાસે જાય. ૧૮

જે સદગુરુ ઉપદેશથી, પામ્યો કેવળજ્ઞાન,
ગુરુ રહ્યા છદ્મસ્થ પણ, વિનય કરે ભગવાન. ૧૯

એવો માર્ગ વિનય તણો, ભાખ્યો શ્રી વીતરાગ,
મૂળ હેતુ એ માર્ગનો, સમજે કોઈ સુભાગ્ય. ૨૦

આમાં હુશુરે એ દિવસોને, લાલ બરે જો કાંઈ,
મળ્યાસોહિલ ઇમ્ધ બુકે બ્લબ્વમાંહિ. ૨૧

હોદે મુકુદ્દુ બ્પવે, સામને ઔર વિચાર,
હોય નળાર્થિ બ્પને, આપખોદ લે નિર્ધારે. ૨૨

હોય નળાર્થિ તેહને, ધાખ ન આબબહરે,
તેવ નળાર્થિ બહિલો, આવ્ બુહો નિર્ધરિ. ૨૩

નળાર્થિ બહિલા:

બાહ્ન ત્રોગ ધ્બ ઝાળબાઈ, તો ખાણે છુરે શ્બરે,
આધ્બા નિ્બુબ્ધર્શના, તે ઝુકેમાંગ મમત્ય. ૨૪

એ ત્બિન રેદ ધબાળાને, રામ્બબ્બબ્બાર્બિ બિ્બિ,
ધર્બ્બિ રામ્બ ત્બિન્બં, કેબ્ર્ત રબે બિ્બબુ્ધિ. ૨૫

મ્બબ્ત્બ મ્બહ્બુરે ખેળ્બામાં, બ્બ્ને બ્બ્રિ બિધ્બ
આમ્બર્બ્બરેન્બ ૬૬ બ્બ્ને, બ્બિ માબ્બ્બ્બો બુબ્બ ૨૬

બેબ્બલબ્ગબ્બિળબગ્બ્બમાં, એ બબ્બ્બે બુ્બ્બ્બ્બ્બ,
માન્બ નિબ્બ્બન હેબ્બ્બ્બ્બો, આબ્બ્બ્બ મુક્તિ્બ્બિબ્બ. ૨૭

બ્બ્ગ્બુ બ્બ્બ્બ્બ્બ્બ બ પુ્બ્બ્બ્બ, બ્બ્બ્બ્બ બ્બ્બ આ્બ્બ્બ્બ્બ,
બ્બ્બ્બ બ્બો બ્બબ્બ્બ્બ્બ્બ્બને, બ્બ્બ્બ બ્બેબ્બ્બ્બમ્બ. ૨૮

આબ્બ્બ્બ નિબ્બ્બ્બ્બ્બ બ્બ્બ્બ્બ્બ, મ્બબ્બ્બ બ્બ્બ્બ્બ્બ્બ્બમ્બ,
બ્બ્બ્બ્બ બ્બ્બ્બ્બ્બબ્બ્બ્બ્બ્બ્બ્બ, બ્બ્બ્બ્બ્બ્બ્બ્બ બ્બ્બ. ૨૯

બ્બ્બ્બ્બ્બ્બ્બ્બ બ્બ્બ્બ્બ્બ્બ બ્બ્બ્બ્બ, બ્બ્બ્બ્બ્બ્બ બ્બ્બ્બ્બ્બ્બ બ્બ્બ્બ્બ.
બ્બ્બ્બ્બ્બ્બ્બ બ્બ્બ્બ્બ્બ્બ બ્બ, બ્બ્બ્બ્બ્બ્બ્બ્બ્બ્બ્બ બ્બ્બ્બ્બ્બ્બ. ૩૦

એ દશા બડભાગીમાં, જિજ્ઞાસાવડ જાણ,
પામે નહિ દશામાર્ગને, જાન અધિકારીમાણ. ૩૧

નહિ કષાયે ઉપશાંતના, નહિ અંતર વૈરાગ,
સરળપણું ન મધ્યસ્થતા, એ માર્ગિ કુળતરે. ૩૨

લહ્યા દહ્યાં માર્ગિના, માર્ગ ભવ જાણ,
હવે કહું આત્માર્થિના, આત્મજ્ઞ સુખદાન. ૩૩

આત્માર્થિલક્ષણ.

આત્મજ્ઞાન ત્યાં મુનિપણું, તે સાચા ઉરિધોષ,
બાકી કુળ ગુરે કુળના, આત્માર્થિ નહિ જોષ. ૩૪

પ્રત્યક્ષ સદ્ગુરુ સાંનિને, ગાળે પરમ ઉપકાર,
ત્રણે યોગ એકત્વથી, વર્તે આત્મવિચાર. ૩૫

એક હોયે ત્રણ કાળમાં, પરમાર્થનો પંથ,
પ્રેરેને પરમાર્થને, તે વ્યવહારસમાન. ૩૬

એમ વિચારી અંતરે, શોધે સદ્ગુરુયોગ,
કામ એક આત્માર્થનું, બીજો નહિ મનરોગ. ૩૭

કષાયની ઉપશાંતના, માત્ર મોક્ષઅભિલાષ,
ભવે ખેદ પ્રાણીદયા, ત્યાં આત્માર્થિનિવાસ. ૩૮

દશા ન એવી જ્યાં સુધી, જીવ લહે નહિ જોગ,
મોક્ષમાર્ગ પામે નહિ, મટે ન અંતરરોગ. ૩૯

આવે જ્યાં એવી દશા, સદ્ગુરુબોધ સુહાય,
તે બોધે સુવિચારણા, ત્યાં પ્રગટે સુખદાય. ૪૦

જ્યાં સત્તદે સ્થ દિસાસ્થલા, ત્યાં સત્તદે નિજ્ઞાન,
જે જ્ઞાને સાધે મોક્ષ પદ, પામે પદ નિર્વાણ. ૪૧

ઉપજે ને સ્થ દિસારલા, મોહ ભાર્ગ રાગદ્વે,
ગુરે બિબધ સંવાદથા, લાગ્યું વરદદ આદિ. ૪૨

આત્મા છે તે નિત્ય છે, છે કર્તા નિજ્ઞર્મ,
છે ભોક્તા વલિ મોક્ષ છે, મોક્ષ ઉપાયે સુધર્મ. ૪૩

ષટ્ સ્થાનક સંક્ષેપમાં, ષટ્ દર્શન પણ તેહ,
સામાન્ય પરભાવને, કહ્યાં જ્ઞાનીએ એહ. ૪૪

દોહા.
શિષ્ય ઉવાચ.

નથી દરિસ્થાં આત્મવો, નથી ભળાતું રૂપ,
બીજો પણ અનુભાવ નહીં, તેથી ન જણસ્વરૂપ. ૪૫

આમદા દેખ આત્મા, અધવા ઇંદ્રિ,પ્રાણ,
મિથ્યા ભૂલો માનવો, નહીં ભૂતું એ પ્રાણ. ૪૬

પણ ને આત્મા હોય તો, જણાય તે નહીં કેમ?
જણાય તે તો હોય તો, ઘર ઘર આથી લેમ. ૪૭

માટે છે નહીં આત્મા, મિથ્યા મોક્ષ ઉપાય,
એ અંતર શંકા તણો, સમજાવો સુખદાય. ૪૮

સમાધાન.
સદ્‌ગુરુ ઉવાચ.

ભાસ્યો દેહાધ્યાસથી, આત્મા દેહ સમાન,
પણ તે બન્ને ભિન્ન છે, પ્રગટ લક્ષણે ભાન. ૪૯

કાંઈનો દેહાધિકમથી, આત્મા દેહસમાન,
પણ તે બન્ને ભિન્ન છે, એમ આસને જાણ. ૨૦

જે દ્રવ્ય છે નહિનો, જે ભાળો છે રૂપ,
આત્મદ્રવ્ય અનુભવ કરે, તે છે ભવસ્થૂપ. ૨૧

છે ઇંદ્રિ પ્રત્યેકને, નિજ નિજ વિષયનું જ્ઞાન,
પાંચ ઇંદ્રિના વિષયનું, પણ આત્માનેભાન. ૨૨

દેહ ન જાણે તેહને, જાણે ન ઇંદ્રિ પ્રાણ,
આત્માન સત્તાવડે તેહ પ્રવર્તે જાણ. ૨૩

સર્વ અવસ્થાનેવિષે, ન્યારો સદા જણાય,
પ્રગટ રૂપ ચૈતન્યમય, એ એંધાણ સદાય. ૨૪

ઘટ, પટ આદી જાણ તું, તેથી તેને માન,
જાણનારતે માન નહિ, કહીએ કેવું જ્ઞાન! ૨૫

પરમબુદ્ધિ કૃશ દેહમાં, સ્થૂલ દેહ મતિઅલ્પ,
દેહ હોય જો આત્મા, ઘટે ન આમ વિકલ્પ. ૨૬

જડ ચેતનનો ભિન્ન છે, કેવળ પ્રગટસ્વભાવ,
એકપણું પામે નહીં, ત્રણે કાળ દ્વય ભાવ. ૨૭

આત્માન શંકા કરે, આત્મા પોતે આપ,
શંકાનો કરનાર તે, અચરજ એહ અમાપ. ૨૮

———

છંદ.
શિષ્યબોધ.

આત્માનાં અસ્તિત્વના, આપે કહ્યા પ્રકાર,
સંભવ તેનો થાય છે, અંતર કર્યે વિચાર. ૨૯

બાળ શોધા પામે ત્યાં, આત્મા નહી આવિનાશ,
દેહમોળાષ ઉપજે, દેહ વિભોગે નાશ. ૬૦

અભેદ વસ્તુ દીલાઇ છે, શાને શેહે વલરાશ,
એ અગુલાક્ષ પલાનાં, આત્મા કિમ ભાસે. ૬૧

સમાધાન.
શહ્ગુરૂ ઉવાચ.

દેહ માર સંમોગ છે, પાળિ જ, ડ્યા નશિ,
એવનાં ઉપાત્તિ બે, શીળા અગુલાષ વશે? ૬૨

એના અગુલાષરશેન એા ઉપજન બોહેનું ज્ઞાન,
તે તેથ ઝુદાદિના, પામે ન ર્હે કાળ. ૬૩

જે સંમોગો દેખિએ, તે તે અગુલાષદરસે,
ઉપજે નહિ સંમોગાથી, આત્મા કિમ પ્રસેહ. ૬૪

ઝાઘ એેનલ ઉપજે, એેનાષ જ પામે,
એેવે અગુલાવ હોયને, મોરે કદી ન પામે. ૬૫

કોઇ સંમોગોથા નહી, એેના ઉપરકિ પામે,
નાશ, ન તેનો કોઇપામ, તેથ નિત્ય સેદાહે. ૬૬

ક્રોધાય વઘમેલા, સારાં દિ૪ ની પામે,
પૂર્વજન્મ સંસ્કાર તે, જુષ નિત્રના ત્યાંહે. ૬૭

આત્મા દ્રવ્ય નિત્ય છે, પર્યાયે પલટાય,
બાબાધી વહ અલોધું, જ્ઞાન ઔૌને પામે. ૬૮

અભેદ જ્ઞાન દાબાઇનું, જે બાળી દદ્વાર,
વદવારો તે હાત્તિ નાશ, કર અગુલાદ નિર્ધાર. ૬૯

ક્ષણરે કોઈ વસ્તુનો, ક્ષણવારદીઠ નાશ,
ચેતન પામે નાશ, તો, કેમાં નહીં નરદરા. ૭૦

શંકા
ક્ષણક્ષવાદ

કર્તા જબ ન કર્મનો, ભજન કર્તા કર્મ;
અથવા રાહજ રચ્ચાય કાં, કર્મ જબગોધર્મ ૭૧

આત્મા રાહા અસંગ ને, કરે મ રહિત બંધ,
અથવા ઈશ્વરકેરલા, તેથ બદ્ધઆર્ધ. ૭૨

નાશે મોહે ઉરાહનો, કોઈ ન હેઠ જ્ઞાને;
કર્મજલ્દ કર્તાં જલદં. સાંગાવિ, કાં નારે બીર. ૭૩

સમાધાન-
સદ્દગુરુ ઉવાચ

હોદે ન ચેતનકેરલા, કોણ ગણે તો કર્મ,
જડસ્વભાવ નહિ કેરલા, તુમ્મો દિસ્યાશી ધર્મ ૭૪

જે ચેતન કરતું નહ, નર ધરાં તો કર્મ,
તેથ રાહજ સ્વભાવદનહિ, તેમ નહી જબદ્ધર્મ. ૭૫

કેવલ હોલ અસંગ જો, ભાસન જને ન કેઈ?
અસંગ છે દરશાથધા, પણ જિબલાવે તેઈ. ૭૬

કર્મા ઈશ્વર કોઈ નહિ, ઈશ્વર શુદ્ધ સ્વભાવ,
અથવા જેફઈ ને ગણે, ઈશ્વરદોષ પ્રભાવ. ૭૭

ચેતન જો નિજ ભાનમાં, કર્તા આપ સ્વભાવ,
વર્તેનાહિ નિજભાનમાં, કર્તા કર્મ પ્રભાવ. ૭૮

શિખ્યવાદ.

જય કરમ કરતાં કહ્યો, ખરા નોકરના નહિ સ્નેહે,
શું રાખે જ કરમ કે, કેપદરિણામ સ્નેહે.   ૭૯

કુદરતના ઈશ્વર મળે નો ઝ્રાખવઉં રાખ્યારે;
ઓળ કહે ઈશ્વરનાં, ઈશ્વરરજ્જ બરે.   ૮૦

ઈશ્વર શિખ્ક દેહ વિના, ભાગ્ નોકેમ નહે હોઈ;
ખળ રેણા શકન કરમાં, નોએરસ્નાન નહીં સોઈ.   ૮૧

સમાધાન.
સહ મુકે ઉવાચ.

ભાવ કરમ નિજ કરવના, નાટે મેળવ ઝર,
બખ્યો મન સ્ત્રરણા, ગ્મ ઝ્લ કરે જ્ખર.   ૮૨

ઝેર સુખા સમખે નળી, બય્ખ બાને કેપ દારે;
ઓળ શુકા શકળ કમજ, નોક્રાવઉં જ્ગ્ગે.   ૮૩

આજે બાંકને આઝ્જ્લ, ઓ આધી બેલે;
કરણા વિના ન કાર્ખ ને, તેવ શુકાશ્ળવેણ.   ૮૪

કુદરતના ઈશ્વર ગ્ણા, ઓનાં ગ્ધ બ્ઝર,
કમ રચનાવે દક્ણિાર્ખો, ખ્ને નોગ્ઝ્મ દૂર.   ૮૫

તે તે નોગ્ક વિણ્ચિરા, રઘ્રગ્ક ફખરસ્લાદ,
ગ્ળ્ન ધ્ગ્ન હો શિખ્ય આ, કાષિ સંઘેષો રાવ.   ૮૬

વિભ્રમવાદ.

કર્તા ભોક્તા બદલ છે, પણ તેનો નહિ મોક્ષ,
વાત્મો કાળ અનંત પણ, વર્તમાન છે દોષ.   ૮૭

શુભ કરે ફૂલ ભોગવે, દેવતા ગતિ માંહે,
અશુભ કરે નરકાદિ દુઃખ, કર્મ ચલાવત જાંહે.   ૮૮

સમાધાન.

સદ્‌ગુરૂ ઉવાચ.

એ શુભાશુભ કર્મમાં, બાળ્યાં સઘળાં ખપાળ,
તોય નિવૃત્તિ કરૂંયાં, મારે મોક્ષ રૂપાળ.   ૮૯

વાત્મો કાળ અનંત તે, કર્મ શુભાશુભ ભાય,
તોય શુભાશુભ છોડતાં, ઉપજે મોક્ષ સ્વભાય.   ૯૦

દેહાદિક સંયોગનો, આત્યંતિક વિયોગ,
સિદ્ધ મોક્ષ શાશ્વત પદે, નિજ અનંત સુખ ભોગ.   ૯૧

વિભ્રમવાદ.

હોય કદાપિ મોક્ષપદ, નહિ આવિરોધ ઉપાય;
કર્મો કાળ અનંતનાં, શાથ છેદ્યાં જાય   ૯૨

અથવા મત દર્શનઘણાં, કહે ઉપાય અનેક;
તેમાં મત સાચો કિયો, બને ન એહ વિવેક.   ૯૩

કઈ જાતિમાં મોક્ષ છે, કયા વેષમાં મોક્ષ,
એનો નિશ્ચય ના બને, ઘણા ભેદ એ દોષ.   ૯૪

તેથી એમ જણાય છે, મળે ન મોક્ષ ઉપાય;
જીવાદિ જાણ્યા તણો, શો ઉપકાર જ થાય? ૯૫

પાંચે ઉત્તરથી થયું, સમાધાન સર્વાંગ;
સમજું મોક્ષ ઉપાયનો, ઉદય ઉદય સદ્ભાગ્ય. ૯૬

સમાધાન.
સદ્ગુરુ ઉવાચ.

પાંચે ઉત્તરની થઈ, આત્મા વિષે પ્રતીત,
થાશે મોક્ષોપાયની, સહજ પ્રતીત એ રીત ૯૭

કર્મભાવ અજ્ઞાન છે, મોક્ષભાવ નિજવાસ,
અંધકાર અજ્ઞાનસમ, નાશે જ્ઞાનપ્રકાશ. ૯૮

જે જે કારણ બંધનાં, તેહ બંધનો પંથ;
તે કારણ છેદક દશા, મોક્ષપંથ ભવઅંત. ૯૯

રાગ, દ્વેષ અજ્ઞાન એ, મુખ્ય કર્મની ગ્રંથ,
થાય નિવૃત્તિ જેહથી, તે જ મોક્ષનો પંથ. ૧૦૦

આત્મા સત્ ચૈતન્યમય, સર્વાભાસ રહિત,
જેથી કેવળ પામિયે, મોક્ષપંથ તે રીત ૧૦૧

કર્મ અનંત પ્રકારનાં, તેમાં મુખ્યે આઠ,
તેમાં મુખ્યે મોહનીય, હણાય તે કહું પાઠ. ૧૦૨

કર્મ મોહનીય ભેદ બે, દર્શન ચારિત્ર નામ,
હણે બોધ વીતરાગતા, અચૂક ઉપાય આમ. ૧૦૩

ઇમબંધ ક્રોધાદિથી, હણી સમાધિક લેણ,
સમધા અનુભવ સાધને, ઓમાં શ્યો સંદેહ ? ૧૦૨

ખોલી માદર્શનગળો, આમ્રપ ત્યે દિલધ,
હણો માર્ગ આ સાધિશે, બ્હ્ય તેહના આળખ ૧૦૩

બહુ દહના બહુ મનને, હૂકાં ઇશ દિવાર,
તે દહના રહ્યાંગિગા, માદેરમાર્ગ નિર્ધાર ૧૦૪

ભાતિ, દેહના ભેદનમાંહિ, ઇહ્યો માર્ગ લે હોળો,
સાંધે તે મુકતિ લહે, ઓમાં ભેદ ન કોંય ૧૦૫

ઇબાદિના ઉદેશામાંના, માત્ર મોક્ષ આળિબાપ,
ભાવે ભેદ અંગરદેહ, તે ઇદ્યે નિરાધર ૧૦૬

તે નિરાસ્તુ બ્ધને, ધામે સહ્ગુરુબોધ,
ગો ધામે ષેમશીનને, વહે અંગર શોધિ ૧૦૭

માદેર્શન આમ્રપ નબ, વહે સહ્ગુરુદ્રિધિ,
ભપે ધૂધ ષેમશીનને, ઓમાં ભેદ ન ભદો ૧૦૮

વહે નિજ સ્વભાવનો, અનુભવ લહીજમાં,
ધાતિવર નિજભાવમાં, પરમાર્થે ષેમશીન ૧૦૯

વર્ધમાન ષેમશીન ધર, રાખે ધિધિકમારો,
હ્દે ધામે આહ્દેવનો, ધાગવાગદ્દવાણે ૧૧૦

ઇેવળ નિજ સ્વભાવનું, અષંદ વર્તે ગ્યાન,
કહિયે ઇેવળ ગ્યાન તે, દેવ છ્વાં નિર્વાણ ૧૧૧

કોટિ વર્ષનું સ્વપ્ન પણ, બ્યાગ્ત થતાં શમાંય,
તેમ વિભાવ અભાદિનો, ગ્યાન થતાં દૂર થાય ૧૧૨

ધુરે દેહાધિશા નો, નહિ કર્તા તું કર્મ,
નહિ ભોકતા તું તેહનો, એહ ધર્મનો મર્મ. ૧૧૮

એહ ધર્મ મોકુછે, તું છો મોક્ષસ્વરૂપ,
અનંત દર્શન જ્ઞાન તું, અવ્યાબાધ સ્વરૂપ. ૧૧૯

શુદ્ધબુદ્ધ ચૈતન્યઘન, સ્વયં જ્યોતિ સુખધામ;
બીજું કહિએ કેટલું? કર વિચાર તો પામ. ૧૨૦

નિશ્ચય સર્વે જ્ઞાનિનો, આવી અત્ર શમાશે,
ધરી મૌનતા એમ કહી, સહજ સમાધિમાંહે. ૧૨૮

શિષ્યબોધબીજપ્રાપ્તિ.

સદ્‌ગુરુના ઉપદેશથી, આવ્યું અપૂર્વ ભાન,
નિજપદ નિજમાંહી લહ્યું, દૂર થયું અજ્ઞાન. ૧૧૮

ભાસ્યું નિજ સ્વરૂપ તે, શુદ્ધ ચેતના રૂપ,
અજર અમર અવિનાશી ને, દેહાતીત સ્વરૂપ. ૧૨૦

કર્તા ભોક્તા કર્મનો, વિભાવ વર્તે જ્યાંય,
વૃત્તિ વહી નિજભાવમાં, થયો અકર્તા ત્યાંય. ૧૨૧

અથવા નિજપરિણામ જે, શુદ્ધ ચેતનારૂપ,
કર્તા ભોક્તા તેહનો, નિર્વિકલ્પ સ્વરૂપ. ૧૨૨

મોક્ષ કહ્યો નિજશુદ્ધતા, તે પામે તે પંથ;
સમજાવ્યો સંક્ષેપમાં, સકળ માર્ગ નિર્ગ્રંથ. ૧૨૩

અહો! અહો! શ્રી સદ્‌ગુરુ, કરુણાસિંધુ અપાર,
આ પામર પર પ્રભુ કર્યો, અહો! અહો! ઉપકાર. ૧૨૮

શું મળ્યું મરણ કરે દેહ, આત્માધ મૌલિ;
તે તો મરણુને આવિયો, વર્તે મરણાધીન.   ૧૨૮

આ દેહ તો આત્મા, વળી મરણ આધીન,
દારા, દામનું દમન કર્યું, તેહ મરણનો દીન.   ૧૨૬

બરમ્હાન રામાદિને, જિણ બનાવ્યો આપ,
આ પદ્ધી ગરવ કરવા, એ ઉપકાર અમાપ.   ૧૨૭

૫ શા સુખાનંદને આ અર્થ, આદિ મુક્તિ કાજ,
ગયા આ મેદિત કાવરાો કહો બોધ સુખરાજ.

<hr/>

૬૫ સંહાર

દૈહિન ઘરે શામે છે, આ ઘર સ્થાનક માંહિ,
હિમારાનાં વિસારાય, સંશીધ રહે ન માંહિ.   ૧૨૮

આત્મખ્યાતિ સાધ ધોગાધિ, સદ્ગુરે બોધ સુખળ.
ગરે આસાયમ પદ ગળે, ઔષધ વિમાર ધાન.   ૧૨૯

ને ધસ્તો ધરમાધિલો, કરે મન્ય ઉરિયાધ,
ભવ સ્થિતિ આણા ગાયળ, છે દો ગહિ આત્માર્થ ૧૩૦

નિશ્ચય બળી સાંભળા, સાધિન ગયવાં ગોય,
નિશ્ચય રાખા બહિમાં, સાધિન કરવાં રોગે.   ૧૩૧

ગેદ નિશ્ચય આડૂગાધ, આગમાં ગધા દુરિખ,
આડોગ ને દેહવ્યાર ગહિ, ભને સાધે રહેવ.   ૧૩૨

ગથ માળ ગે કરકના, તે ગહિ સહુદેધવાર,
ભાગ ગળી ગિર રહેવું, તે નિશ્ચય ગળી ઘેવાર.   ૧૩૩

આગળ સાલ દેખાડો, વર્તમાનમાં હોદે,
માર્ગે કાળ ભવિષ્યમાં, માર્ગ જોદ નાંહે હોદે. ૧૩૪

સર્વ બલ છે સિધ્ધસમ, જે સમજે ને જોદે,
રાખ્યું રે આત્મા જિનાથી, નિમિત કરણાનોંદે. ૧૩૬

ઉપાસાનું નાદ બળ, જે ને તેજે નિમિત,
પામે નાંહે જિનત્વને, રહે ઞાણિમાં સ્થિત. ૧૩૬

મુખ્ય ઞાન કહિ આને, અંતર ખુણો ન મોલ,
તે પામર આત્મા કરે, માત્ર ઞાનિનો દોષ. ૧૩૭

દયા,શાંતિ, સમભ, દરમા, સત્યે, ત્યાગ, વૈરાગ્ય,
હોદે મુમુક્ષ ઘટવિષે, એહ સદાયે સુલક્ષ. ૧૩૮

મોલ ભાવ દ્રષે હોદે ત્યાં, અથવા હોદે દશીન,
તે કારણે ઞાનદર્શા, બ્રહી કહિદે ઞાન ૧૩૯

સમય ઞાત તે અંદ્દા, અથવા સ્વદ્રકઞાન,
તે કરણે ઞાનદર્શા, બ્રહી પામા ઞાન. ૧૪૦

સ્થાનક પાંચ વિમાર્ગિને, છઠ્ઠે વર્તે જેહ,
પામે સ્થાનક પાંચમે, એહાં નહિસંદેહ. ૧૪૧

દેહ છતાં જેના દશા, વર્તે દેહાતા,
તે ઞાનના ચરણામાં, હોદંદન પ્રણમાત. ૧૪૨

_____

સાધન જિનદ દશા અતો, કરી રાહ સંહોદ,
બહુરત્નસંહોદપમા. ભાવ્યા નિર્દદોદ.

FOREWORD

Rooted in the ancient wisdom of Jainism, one of the oldest religions of the world, is the timeless path to eternal peace and bliss. More than 2,500 years ago, Jain philosophy was passed on through the genius of one of the greatest spiritual teachers of all time - Lord Mahavir, the 24th Tirthankar. Ever since, several enlightened souls have carried forward His glorious legacy.

In the late 19th century, over 150 years ago, a supreme devotee of the dispassionate Lords, a divine seer, and a self-realised saint, scaled extraordinary spiritual heights and demystified the path to self-discovery - Shrimad Rajchandraji, fondly known as Param Krupalu Dev. An upholder and uplifter of Lord Mahavir's universal path, Shrimadji dispelled the prevalent darkness of delusion, and rediscovered the deepest mysteries of human existence.

Shrimadji was a revolutionary visionary who laid the foundations of spirituality for a new era, an enlightened alchemist who lived in the supreme state of soul consciousness, and a lyrical prodigy who inked the path of liberation in His powerful writings. In a short span of 33 years, He paved the passage to complete purity, and bequeathed the world an invaluable inheritance for the future.

The crown jewel of His philosophical literature, His magnum opus, is the 142-verse poetic masterpiece - Shri Atmasiddhi Shastra. Composed by Shrimadji in a single sitting of about one and a half hours, when He was merely 28 years old, the treatise is a staggering accomplishment, an encyclopedia of spiritual knowledge, the nucleus of all sacred scriptures, and the heart of the inner path. A blend of doctrine and devotion, logic and love, spiritual science and the art of self-realisation, deep insights have been skilfully woven. As the composition evolves, its expression and exposition become piercingly profound, and yet are elucidated in simple, sublime language. Shrimadji flows sequentially, like a stream unsullied, effortlessly penetrating the reader within.

Marking the 125th year of this monumental epic, we invited the world to rekindle the blazing flame of spirituality. Ardent devotee of Shrimadji, enlightened Master, acclaimed author, and founder of Shrimad Rajchandra Mission Dharampur - Pujya Gurudevshri Rakeshji, expounded on Shri Atmasiddhi Shastra through a nine-month journey of illuminating discourses in English. Pujya Gurudevshri has brought a unique potency and universal appeal to the text by authoring a concise and complete commentary in English. Stemming from His experience of the self, and having plumbed the depths of this quintessential scripture, Pujya Gurudevshri's infinite devotion to Shrimadji and His ceaseless compassion have manifested in the form of this book, in the palm of our hands.

This elixir of life is a humble and selfless offering by Pujya Gurudevshri, a painstaking labour of love to spread the treasure of Shrimadji's teachings. But this journey had begun 23 years ago, when He was conferred the PhD degree for His extensive research treatise on Shri Atmasiddhi Shastra. The heartfelt and scholarly exposition of over 3,000 pages was released as a four-volume text in Gujarati, and yet Pujya Gurudevshri had said, "I have only stopped, not finished."

Indeed, His every endeavour is a submission of devotion unto His Lord, His every thought is immersed in the gratitude of His Master's benevolence, and His every heartbeat reverberates with the transcendence of Shrimadji's name. Like a gushing river loses itself as it converges into the mighty ocean, He has dissolved into His Master.

A living, breathing exposition on Shri Atmasiddhi Shastra, this guidebook has been structured to make its deep spiritual richness easy and accessible to read, retain, refer and ruminate. We would like to thank Pujya Gurudveshri profusely for this immeasurable gift He has bestowed on us.

The 142 verses have been divided into 12 chapters, with each section comprising a header, link, verse in Gujarati, transliterated verse in English, word-to-word meaning, short meaning and explanation. Understanding the conventions adopted in this text will provide an insight into the literary approach and rationale. Of primary concern, was maintaining the accuracy, authenticity and fidelity to the original work. He, Him and Himself, have been capitalised when referring to the true Guru, differentiating from the disciple, for the reader's comprehension. Furthermore, all Indian words have been italicised the first time they appear in the verse, to draw attention to the difference in language. The general criteria for determining spellings of Gujarati words is pronunciation - words are spelt as pronounced. One challenge was that some sounds in Gujarati cannot be accurately represented by the English alphabet. Thus, one diacritical mark has been used in the spelling convention to differentiate between the 'a' sound like 'about' and the Gujarati prolonged 'ā' sound as in 'car'. Each verse of the 142 verses has a QR code at its end. Our readers can scan it to view Pujya Gurudevshri's discourse on that verse.

We express our sincere gratitude to all who have contributed to the publication of this book with devotion and dedication. A special mention of Atmarpit Apurvaji, who has assisted Pujya Gurudevshri through the process of its creation.

We pray that this book spreads the path of absolute truth and inexhaustible joy, the unprecedented power of the purest knowledge ends our transmigration, and the highly beneficial words advance aspirants on the highway of spirituality.

May the world be uplifted by the grace of the enlightened ones.

Ashadh Sud Punam,
Gurupurnima,
July 24, 2021

Humbly,
The Trustees,
Shrimad Rajchandra Mission
Dharampur

Introduction

Introduction

Comprising the fundamental truths, completely focused on the soul, Shri Ātmasiddhi Shāstra is an invaluable jewel of spiritual literature. The remarkable and distinctive style in which Shrimadji has composed this scripture is truly a wonder. Each word resounds with spiritual experience and is inundated with heartfelt feelings. Each verse iterates the significance of the soul, leading the seeker towards self-realisation.

Shri Ātmasiddhi Shāstra comprises twelve sections which encompass 142 verses. In the beginning, Shrimadji lays the foundation for the main subject, addressing several vital points before expounding the six fundamental truths. The first introductory section containing 23 verses, can be divided into three parts. In verses 1-8, commencing with the auspicious obeisance, Shrimadji compassionately portrays the fallacy of the deluded ones who have strayed from the path of liberation. Verses 9-14 assert the immense importance, glorious attributes and unparalleled benevolence of a Sadguru. Verses 15-23 advocate the absolute necessity of giving up self-willed behaviour and treading the path of humility. This section serves as a portal to the spiritual treasures embedded in Shri Ātmasiddhi Shāstra.

In the lineage of ancient Indian culture, a tradition prevails whereby an author pays obeisance at the beginning of the text. The subject, purpose and relation are also mentioned. Together, these four constitute the 'anubandh chatushtay'. It means four facts regarding a literary composition. They are as follows:

1. *Mangal* - It is a prayer at the beginning of the text, in which the author pays obeisance to his revered God or benevolent Sadguru to ensure unhindered completion of the auspicious work that he has commenced. The invocation of grace is of paramount importance. Mangal means that which gives happiness or that which causes the dissolution of sins.

2. *Abhidhey Vishay* - This indicates the subject matter addressed in the text. This is essentially stated at the beginning of the text, as no wise reader would want to read a composition without being interested in it.

3. *Prayojan* - This states the purpose of the text. The text is composed keeping in mind a specific goal to be achieved, and this purpose is indicated at the beginning of the text.

4. *Sambandh* - This elucidates the relationship. It is essential to express that the text is not conceived from one's intellectual fancy but is in line with the spiritual teachers of yore. By disclosing the relation, the reader develops faith and reverence for the text, and is able to determine its true value.

Following the ancient tradition of stating the anubandh chatushtay at the beginning, Shrimadji has woven the four topics with proficiency in the opening two verses of the scripture. In the first verse, He has expressed the mangal and the sambandh. In the second verse, He has specified the abhidhey vishay and the prayojan.

VERSE - 1

Obeisance to Sadguru

At the commencement of Shri Ātmasiddhi Shāstra, paying obeisance to His most benevolent Sadguru Bhagwān, Shrimadji says -

જે સ્વરૂપ સમજ્યા વિના, પામ્યો દુઃખ અનંત;
સમજાવ્યું તે પદ નમું, શ્રી સદ્‍ગુરુ ભગવંત. ॥૧॥

Je swaroop samjyā vinā, pāmyo dukh anant;
Samjāvyu te pad namu, Shri Sadguru Bhagwant. ||1||

Je - that; *swaroop* - nature; *samjyā* - understanding; *vinā*- without; *pāmyo* - got; *dukh* - suffering; *anant* - infinite; *samjāvyu* - explained; *te* - that; *pad* - nature; *namu* - bow; *Shri Sadguru* - enlightened Mentor; *Bhagwant* - God

MEANING

Without understanding the true nature of the self, I have undergone infinite suffering. I humbly bow down to the Sadguru who made me understand the true nature of the self.

EXPLANATION

Shrimadji begins this scripture, the holy Gitā of the soul, with the words '*je swaroop*' - that nature. In this verse, 'that' means the self, the nature of the self. The fundamental mistake of the transmigrating soul is ignorance of the nature of the self. Without knowing the self as infinite knowledge-perception-bliss, one suffers, wandering perpetually in countless lifetimes. Not knowing the self's distinctiveness from all objects and feelings, and under the mighty spell of delusion, he establishes the identity of I and mine in the non-self. Due to this ignorance, he believes that the non-self is the source of his happiness, peace and security and hence keeps aspiring for the desired objects, people and circumstances. However, in the process of procuring, indulging and protecting material pleasures, he has experienced only pain and distress.

Despite intending to attain happiness, the soul suffers due to the presence of the fundamental delusion. It tries hard to eliminate suffering but fails due to ignorance of the true cause of suffering. The presence or absence of an external object can never make one happy or sad. Suffering is caused by attachment to the external. The soul, possessing attachments, is trapped in the constant ebb and flow of an uncertain life. Constantly tossed about in the ocean of misery, it has been enduring infinite suffering. It must be noted, the word '*anant*' - infinite, does not mean that suffering will never end, it just denotes the intensity of suffering.

Sorrow need not be a permanent state. The soul can emerge from the throes of infinite sorrow by attaining self-realisation. When one understands the truth about the self, that the soul's nature is pure and complete bliss, suffering will end. Over here, understanding is not limited to merely knowing at the intellectual level, but also reaching the experiential level. It implies the direct experience of the self. To experience the self, one requires the presence of someone who has already experienced the self and can explain it to others. To escape the roaring wildfire-like inferno of infinite sorrow, to end the cycles of birth and death, one needs to take refuge in a Guru. A true Guru is the dispeller of darkness; who has realised the self, remains immersed in it and has the ability to guide others towards attaining it. It is at His lotus feet that the journey of a seeker starts and his infinite suffering ends. Hence, in this verse Shrimadji says, not knowing the true nature of the self, I have suffered infinitely. The one who made me realise that; the one who has severed the root cause of infinite suffering that I would have had to go through in the future, to Him, the benevolent *Shri Sadguru Bhagwān*, I offer my prostrations.

In this verse, Shrimadji has used two expressions for the Sadguru **'Shri'** and **'Bhagwant'**. The word 'Shri' means wealth, and is used to address a wealthy and respectable person. Since Shri Sadguru is self-realised and possesses the wealth of knowledge, the term Shri is appropriate for Him. Likewise, the one endowed with the treasure of supreme virtues is called Bhagwān and so the word Bhagwant is also appropriate for the Sadguru. The Sadguru is Bhagwān because He is divine.

Honouring this enormous importance of the Sadguru, Shrimadji makes an auspicious opening of Shri Ātmasiddhi Shāstra by offering salutations to the Sadguru with utmost gratitude, devotion and elation. Having realised the self through His Sadguru, He establishes the relation with the enlightened ones of yore. Thus, *mangal* and *sambandh* of *anubandh chatushtay* are clearly indicated in this verse.

VERSE - 2

Subject and purpose

Aligning with the ancient traditions of the great composers, Shrimadji paid obeisance to the supremely benevolent *Shri Sadguru Bhagwān* and established the relation in the first verse. In this second verse, He introduces the remaining two aspects of the text: the subject and the purpose. Shrimadji says -

વર્તમાન આ કાળમાં, મોક્ષમાર્ગ બહુ લોપ;
વિચારવા આત્માર્થીને, ભાખ્યો અત્ર અગોપ્ય. ॥૨॥

Vartmān ā kālmā, mokshmārg bahu lop;
Vichārvā ātmārthine, bhākhyo atra agopya. ||2||

Vartmān - present; *ā* - this; *kālmā* - in times; *mokshmārg* - path of liberation; *bahu* - almost; *lop* - disappeared; *vichārvā* - to contemplate; *ātmārthine* - for true seeker; *bhākhyo* - stated; *atra* - here; *agopya* - without concealing

MEANING

In this present era, the path of liberation has almost become extinct. It has been clearly revealed here without concealing, for the contemplation of true seekers.

EXPLANATION

According to Jain scriptures, there are several different regions in the universe. The region in which we currently reside is called *Bharat kshetra*. The current era is called *dusham kāl*, which is the declining time period, when the path of liberation has almost vanished. In the first half of this verse, through the words '**bahu lop**', Shrimadji indicates that in the current period of time, the pure path of liberation is almost lost. However, it is not completely obscured and although difficult, it is not yet impossible to obtain. Possessing an incorrect understanding of dharma, one gets impeded by his own insistences regarding opinions, sects, etc., about the path. Trapped in a maze of external practices, he runs around in circles, losing his way despite walking for miles. Hence, due to this unfortunate reality, Shrimadji proclaims that He will unravel the true path of liberation for the benefit of spiritual seekers.

Thus, Shrimadji indicates that the subject matter of this text is to illuminate the path of liberation, which is almost lost at present. Moreover, He indicates the spiritual purpose of this text with the words, '**vichārvā ātmārthine**' - for aspirants to reflect upon. The immediate objective of the aspirant is to contemplate upon the path of liberation and the ultimate goal is to attain liberation.

Although the path of liberation has already been described in numerous ancient scriptures, they were composed to suit the needs of those times. Shrimadji has composed this scripture keeping present conditions in mind. With utmost divinity, He has unfolded the spiritual essence using such simple language that seekers everywhere can reflect upon it and benefit from the knowledge.

Through the word *'agopya'*, Shrimadji states that the path explained here is the same one illuminated by infinite omniscient ones. He expounds the path as it is, without additions or subtractions and without concealing facts or reservations. He has absolutely no selfish motives or prejudices in this highest endeavour. Hence, this proves to be a testament to the authenticity of the scripture.

Shrimadji's pledge to re-establish the true path kindles hope in this era of darkness. Shri Ātmasiddhi Shāstra serves as a beacon to lead one out from the depths of darkness. All that is required now, is the willingness to be led.

VERSE - 3

Two types of deluded people

Prior to revealing the true path of liberation, Shrimadji points out the prevalent wrong beliefs and conduct regarding it. In this verse, He portrays a tragic picture of why this path seems to have disappeared in the present times. Shrimadji says -

કોઇ ક્રિયાજડ થઈ રહ્યા, શુષ્કજ્ઞાનમાં કોઈ;
માને માર્ગ મોક્ષનો, કરુણા ઉપજે જોઈ. ||૩||

Koi kriyājad thai rahyā, shushkjnānmā koi;
Māney mārag mokshno, karunā upje joi. ||3||

Koi - some; *kriyājad* - lifeless ritualist; *thai rahyā* - have become; *shushkjnānmā* - in dry knowledge; *koi* - some; *māney* - believe; *mārag* - path; *mokshno* - of liberation; *karunā* - compassion; *upje* - arises; *joi* - on seeing

MEANING

While some have become mechanical ritualists, others have become dry intellectualists. Compassion arises for them as they believe themselves to be on the path of liberation.

EXPLANATION

While every religion propounds both theoretical and practical aspects, some people emphasise only metaphysics and others, only rituals. Some believe that liberation can be achieved by merely observing rites, and others through mere theoretical knowledge. In this verse, Shrimadji highlights the two kinds of people who follow the path of liberation with an incorrect understanding: those who are bogged down by rituals and those who pursue superficial scriptural knowledge. He identifies them as '***kriyājaḍ***', the mechanical ritualist and '***shushkjnāni***', the dry intellectualist.

1. Kriyājaḍ - This word is composed of two words, *kriyā* and *jaḍ*. Kriyā means ritual and the word jaḍ means lifeless. Those who find fulfilment in routine practices without understanding the purpose and significance are called kriyājaḍ. A knife that cuts a mango or a bitter gourd does not experience the sweetness or bitterness. Similarly, rituals carried out mechanically, without right understanding or awareness, do not result in an experience of the blissful self. The kriyājaḍ are ignorant of the nature of the self and feel content in external activities. As they consider rituals alone to be the path of liberation, they are said to be pitiable.

2. Shushkjnāni - This word is composed of two words, *shushk* and *jnāni*. Here jnāni does not mean a self-realised one; it refers to the one who only understands the scriptures intellectually. The word shushk means dry words without inner transformation. Guided by delusion, they act contrary to what they speak. Their knowledge can be compared to dry sugarcane that has no juice. In other words, their knowledge does not possess the nectar of self-experience. Since the shushkjnāni have not attained self-realisation and negate pure conduct, they become bereft of the means and drown in the

ocean of transmigration. Instead of striving for the welfare of the self, they cause extreme harm to themselves by insisting on their beliefs as being correct. As they consider studying scriptures alone to be the path of liberation, they too are said to be pitiable.

Mirroring the two above-mentioned behaviours, some believe that only 'doing' leads to liberation, neglecting the study of the true essence, which proves to be a mistake. Similarly, others believe that only 'knowing' leads to liberation and they read religious books, neglecting religious practice, which also proves to be a mistake. Their actions descend to mere mechanical ritualism and their knowledge becomes sheer rote learning. Through actions performed without correct understanding or knowledge sans virtue, they are nowhere near self-realisation. They are both trapped in a maze and yet under the delusion that they are on the path of liberation.

Shrimadji views their pitiable condition and is overwhelmed with compassion. He does not condemn them, instead feels sympathetic to their plight. With patient wisdom, He first focuses on the flaw in their method and then proceeds to set them on the right path. Thus, clearly stating that neither mere rituals nor mere knowledge prove to be beneficial, Shrimadji has compassionately guided all seekers of the path across all times.

VERSE - 4

Characteristics of mechanical ritualist

To ensure the earlier mentioned people realise their folly, Shrimadji explains the traits of *kriyājad* and *shushkjnāni* in the fourth and the fifth verses respectively. In this verse, He describes the nature of the kriyājad, to aid in their identification, helping them to let go of their insistence and move forward on the right path of liberation. Describing the kriyājad, Shrimadji says -

બાહ્ય ક્રિયામાં રાચતા, અંતર્ભેદ ન કાંઈ;
જ્ઞાનમાર્ગ નિષેધતા, તેહ ક્રિયાજડ આંઈ. ||૪||

Bāhya kriyāmā rāchtā, antarbhed na kāi;
Jnānmārg nishedhtā, teh kriyājad āi. ||4||

Bāhya - external; *kriyāmā* - in rituals; *rāchtā* - engrossed; *antarbhed* - inner transformation; *na* - not; *kāi* - any; *jnānmārg* - path of knowledge; *nishedhtā* - negates; *teh* - they; *kriyājad* - mechanical ritualist; *āi* - here

MEANING
Those who are engrossed solely in external rituals without any inner transformation and negate the path of knowledge have been termed here as '*kriyājaď*' - mechanical ritualists.

EXPLANATION
Rituals are religious activities or actions performed to cultivate detachment and gain equanimity. The scriptures prescribe rituals with the sole aim of attaining self-realisation.

The enlightened ones have always advocated several types of rituals, some being worship, chanting and fasting. However, in the present day, it appears that spirituality has been replaced by mere rituals. Steeped in this mad pursuit of rituals, man has lost the value behind values. In other words, he has lost the ability to differentiate between spirituality and an obstinate insistence upon certain practices. Satisfied by outward appearance, he does not delve into inner experience. Thus, in acquiring the shells of action, he has lost the kernels of wisdom. The world is also fascinated by overt actions and considers such people to be religious.

Those who have lost sight of the real purpose of rituals, and are stuck in performing them mechanically, have been termed as *'kriyājad'* by Shrimadji. They mimic a flock of sheep, blindly following tradition without making the effort to understand the true essence of a ritual. They remain engrossed in physical activity and feel content with their effort. Although their observances are meticulous in nature, with great care taken to ensure not a single step is missed, they possess absolutely no inclination towards the journey within. Nevertheless, they feel that their practice of religion is perfect, and falsely believe it will lead them to liberation.

The mechanical ritualists get bogged down in external practices in the name of religion, and hence fail to capture the spirit behind these observances. Untouched by true spirituality, no inner transformation occurs for them. Although they might perform outwardly penance to such an extent that the body shrivels up and withers away, their inner impurities do not die. They fail to realise that the scriptures place more importance on uplifting the soul than bodily acts. The act of fasting is not confined merely to the body; its main purpose is to eliminate likes-dislikes for food. Renunciation is not only changing the attire, but overcoming attachment towards the body. Unfortunately, they possess no inclination to annihilate identification with the body.

Moreover, the kriyājad negate the path of knowledge out of a belief that there is no need for it. They hold that learning and teaching serve no purpose; liberation is possible only by performing rituals. In reality, knowledge of the inner self is very essential. Refuting the path of knowledge negates introspection, reflection, contemplation, self-awareness and meditation, nullifying the possibility of attaining self-realisation.

It is important to note that Shrimadji does not at all reject the need for outer rituals. He disapproves of remaining engrossed in mechanical acts and feeling content with outwardly performed actions without any intention of focusing within. The main purpose of instructing outer rituals is to kindle inwardness. If this does not occur, such activities yield no true benefit whatsoever. Therefore, aimlessly performed outward rituals are considered useless on the path of liberation. If the activities are practised with right understanding and the purpose of self-realisation, then such activities are considered meaningful. Thus, Shrimadji does not reject rituals, instead compassionately points out the irrelevance of mere mechanical indulgence in them.

— ∽⚬∾ —

VERSE - 5

Characteristics of dry intellectualist

After having depicted the nature of a *kriyājad*, Shrimadji, in this verse proceeds to describe that of a *shushkjnāni*. This is to enable those possessing such traits to overcome them and progress in the right way on the path of liberation. Speaking about the shushkjnāni, Shrimadji says -

બંધ મોક્ષ છે કલ્પના, ભાખે વાણી માંહી;
વર્તે મોહાવેશમાં, શુષ્કજ્ઞાની તે આંહી. ॥૫॥

Bandh moksh chhe kalpanā, bhākhe vāni māhi;
Varte   mohāveshmā,   shushkjnāni   te   āhi. ॥5॥

Bandh - bondage; *moksh* - liberation; *chhe* - is; *kalpanā* - imagination; *bhākhe* - states; *vāni* - speech; *māhi* - in; *varte* - acts; *mohāveshmā* - by force of delusion; *shushkjnāni* - dry intellectualist; *te* - they; *āhi* - here

MEANING

Those who speak of bondage and liberation as being imaginary, but behave under the influence of delusion are termed here as '*shushkjnāni*' - dry intellectualists.

EXPLANATION

An equilibrium between knowledge and ritual is necessary on the spiritual path. Those who do not have this understanding tend to follow only one of these and drift from the right path. Their bias towards either knowledge or ritual leads to entanglement in worldly transmigration. In the earlier verse, Shrimadji had described the nature of kriyājad, who are biased towards rituals alone. In this verse, He describes the characteristics of shushkjnāni, who are biased towards knowledge alone.

The shushkjnāni believe that reading, memorising and discussing scriptures are the only worthwhile pursuits in spirituality and do not practise the right activities to turn their focus within. Although they acquire information from the scriptures, they do not apply it in daily living. Content with talking about the self, they ignore experiential knowledge of it. They speak of high philosophy using lofty language, but do not follow this with action. Hence, it is all a mere show without substance, a display devoid of depth, an expression without experience. They strive to establish a position of importance for themselves. Such people are termed as dry intellectualists or barren scholars.

The dry intellectualists interpret the scriptures either on their own without the guidance of a Sadguru or through an ignorant teacher. They read books dealing with the absolute pure nature of the self and conclude: That the soul cannot be polluted, believing the concept of its defilement to be imaginary. That the soul always remains pure and is unblemished by karmic bondage, making the annihilation of karma redundant. That bondage and liberation are figments of imagination, the soul can neither be bound or freed.

From an absolute viewpoint, dry intellectualists are right but it is not the complete truth. The relative viewpoint cannot be ignored. From the relative point of view, the soul resides in the body and is bound by karma. It is transmigrating, not yet liberated. To deny the impure modification, while in the state of bondage is dangerous.

The impractical theorists parrot that bondage and liberation are imaginary but their words are not backed by personal experience. Although they give speeches and exhibit scholastic talents, their conduct is fraught with delusion. Bereft of self-realisation, they are gripped by desires and passions. They are victims of deep infatuations in daily life. Despite their scriptural knowledge, they indulge in sensual pleasures. They get attached to situations that they deem favourable and react with aversion to unfavourable ones. They neither focus on inner transformation nor make any effort to destroy their delusion.

Thus, in summary, the dry intellectualists are only interested in talking about the self, but have no taste of the sweet experience of the blissful soul. Despite constantly memorising and citing definitions they are lost in the darkness of delusion.

VERSE - 6

Benefits of spiritual practices

Having described the nature of mechanical ritualists and dry intellectualists earlier, in this verse, Shrimadji elucidates the benefits of spiritual practices. Aiming to guide both, the *kriyājad* and the *shushkjnāni*, on the path of liberation, Shrimadji says -

વૈરાગ્યાદિ સફળ તો, જો સહ આતમજ્ઞાન;
તેમ જ આતમજ્ઞાનની, પ્રાપ્તિતણાં નિદાન. ||૬||

Vairāgyādi   safal   toh,   jo   sah   ātamjnān;
Tem   ja   ātamjnānni,   prāptitanā   nidān. ||6||

Vairāgyādi - detachment etc.; **safal** - fruitful; **toh** - then; **jo** - if; **sah** - with; **ātamjnān** - self-realisation; **tem** - as well; **ja** - certainly; **ātamjnānni** - of self-realisation; **prāptitanā** - for attainment; **nidān** - means

MEANING

Detachment, etc., are fruitful if accompanied by self-realisation. Moreover, they can serve as the means to attain self-realisation, if practised for the sole purpose of achieving it.

EXPLANATION

In this verse, Shrimadji asserts the value of detachment, etc., before as well as after achieving self-realisation. Detachment, etc., also implies other practices such as renunciation, worship, devotion, charity, compassion, vows and austerity. They are fruitful when accompanied by self-realisation because they assist one to abide in the self, preventing bondage from new karma, shedding past karma in large quantities and eventually leading to the attainment of liberation. The value of zeros without 'one' is as good as nothing. However, they increase the value of the number 'one' manifold, if placed after it. Similarly, when performed with self-realisation these practices become helpful in making rapid progress on the path of liberation. The self-realised one, with the help of these means, reduces the activities of mind, speech and body and puts in effort to obtain the state of absolute purity. Thus, in the first line of this verse, Shrimadji shows the importance of detachment, etc., along with self-realisation on the path of liberation.

Here, Shrimadji highlights the importance of self-realisation by explaining that detachment, etc., are spiritually fruitful only when accompanied by self-realisation. He does not intend to state that detachment, etc., are unnecessary before self-realisation. To clarify this, in the second line of the verse, Shrimadji says that if practised for the sole purpose of attaining self-realisation; detachment, etc., become helpful in cultivating the necessary worthiness and eventually become the cause for self-realisation itself. The practice of detachment, etc., reduces passions, purifies the mind, enhances focus on the self, and enables one to dwell in the awareness of the self. These practices cleanse the heart, which further helps to actualise the teachings of the Sadguru and eventually attain self-realisation. Therefore, the aspirant should earnestly work towards self-realisation by practising detachment, etc., and cultivating the necessary virtues.

If detachment, etc., are not practised with the goal of self-realisation, it may lay the path for suppression, depression and loneliness to occur. It is common for people to experience detachment due to physical pain, emotional stress, loss of dear ones or hurt caused by others. However, as this detachment does not arise out of true understanding of the transitory nature of worldly pleasures, it does not last long. It is actually a feeling of dejection, not true detachment and the attachment within remains intact. The withdrawal of likes-dislikes towards objects and people is detachment; where the outer world seems trivial and one weaves no fantasies around it. Thus, only detachment with true understanding is helpful in the spiritual pursuit.

This verse serves as an implied recommendation to both, the kriyājad and the shushkjnāni. For the kriyājad, who practise detachment superficially, the message is detachment is fruitful if accompanied by self-realisation. For the shushkjnāni, the dry intellectualists who do not practise it at all and simply wax eloquent about their knowledge, the message is detachment is the means to self-realisation and must certainly be practised.

VERSE - 7

Importance of spiritual practices

After having explained the benefits of detachment, etc., before the dawn of self-realisation, Shrimadji now reinforces it here. Explaining the importance of renunciation and detachment to the mechanical ritualists and dry intellectualists, Shrimadji says -

ત્યાગ વિરાગ ન ચિત્તમાં, થાય ન તેને જ્ઞાન;
અટકે ત્યાગ વિરાગમાં, તો ભૂલે નિજભાન. ||૭||

Tyāg virāg na chittmā, thāy na tene jnān;
Atke tyāg virāgmā, toh bhoole nijbhān. ||7||

Tyāg - renunciation; *virāg* - detachment; *na* - not; *chittmā* - in mind; *thāy* - attains; *na* - not; *tene* - him; *jnān* - enlightenment; *atke* - stuck; *tyāg* - renunciation; *virāgmā* - in detachment; *toh* - then; *bhoole* - forgets; *nijbhān* - self-awareness

MEANING

One cannot attain enlightenment without possessing feelings of renunciation and detachment within. One also cannot attain enlightenment if he gets stuck in them, missing self-awareness.

EXPLANATION

As long as one attaches importance to the outer world and finds joy in the objects of desire, he is not inclined to withdraw from them. Turning towards the self becomes impossible as the mind keeps wandering in worldly thoughts. As a countermeasure, this verse elucidates the importance of '*tyāg*' and '*virāg*'. Tyāg means to give up everything that hinders one's spiritual progress. Virāg means to reduce one's attachment towards the world. Therefore, tyāg implies renouncing one's possessions and virāg implies ceasing to accumulate new possessions. Renunciation and detachment are the pre-conditions for self-realisation.

Until the mind is immersed in renunciation and detachment, self-realisation is not possible. Hence, in the first line of this verse, Shrimadji emphasises the word '*chitt*' - the mind. In the absence of renunciation and detachment in the mind, one cannot even cultivate the worthiness to realise the self. The knowledge of scriptures remains dry, merely in memory. When these virtues dawn, they soften the mind and allow knowledge to bloom. Unless the mind is filled with feelings of abandonment towards sensual pleasures and worldly entanglements, one cannot attain spiritual progress. So, the dry intellectualist must understand that self-realisation does not occur until the mind is purified through renunciation and detachment. In other words, they are necessary means for self-realisation.

On the other hand, one might be practising renunciation and detachment but gets trapped in these means, mistaking them to be the end. Using these means, one has to progress towards self-realisation. Forgetting the real objective, if he feels fulfilled by them, he remains bereft of self-realisation despite his efforts. Losing sight of the goal, he is content with his practices and gets attached to them. He dislikes imperfection or defect in his practices yet does not feel pained at his inability to realise the self despite years of asceticism, austerity and worship. Renunciation and detachment without awareness are not only fruitless but also harmful as they lead to ego and insistences. Hence, the mechanical ritualist must understand this and seek his own welfare.

Thus, the *shushkjnāni* must realise that merely speaking about the self is not enough, renunciation and detachment are essential for self-realisation. The *kriyājad* must realise that these are only the means, not the goal. These practices should not remain only at the external level but percolate within. In this manner, Shrimadji warns both, the shushkjnāni and the kriyājad, about their mistakes, with the sole intent of bringing them on the right path.

VERSE - 8

Virtue of prudence

In five verses, Shrimadji described and appropriately addressed the traits of the *kriyājad* and the *shushkjnāni*. In this verse, He indicates that the vehement one-sided beliefs of both mechanical ritualists and dry intellectualists are not beneficial while attaining liberation. Asserting the excellent principle of prudence, the ability to discern, Shrimadji says -

જ્યાં જ્યાં જે જે યોગ્ય છે, તહાં સમજવું તેહ;
ત્યાં ત્યાં તે તે આચરે, આત્માર્થી જન એહ. ||૮||

Jyā jyā je je yogya chhe, tahā samajvu teh;
Tyā tyā te te āchre, ātmārthi jan eh. ||8||

Jyā jyā - wherever; *je je* - whatever; *yogya* - appropriate; *chhe* - is; *tahā* - there; *samajvu* - understand; *teh* - that; *tyā tyā* - there; *te te* - that; *āchre* - follows; *ātmārthi* - true seeker; *jan* - person; *eh* - that

MEANING
One who understands everything in its appropriate context and acts accordingly, is a true seeker.

EXPLANATION
While in different stages of spiritual advancement, the aspirant must assess himself clearly to find his shortcomings in order to make the necessary changes. He should observe himself and decide which tendencies need to be adopted and which

need to be disowned. Only absorbing the advantageous and discarding the detrimental, leads to the growth of virtues in the soul. This ability, to impartially differentiate between the advantageous and the detrimental, is prudence.

Disclosing the right path to both the kriyājad and the shushkjnāni, Shrimadji says that the prudent seeker can discern the appropriate response to a particular situation and act suitably. Wherever there is a need to focus on the self, he puts forth efforts accordingly. Similarly, when the need to practise self-restraint and vows arises, he does the same. A kriyājad pursues rituals without purpose. Instead, he should develop self-awareness, giving up the insistence and pride for the rituals. A shushkjnāni is gratified by possessing barren knowledge. Instead, he should leave behind his deluded behaviour and walk the talk by practising spiritual means like renunciation, detachment and worship. Both the kriyājad and the shushkjnāni must take heed of their drawbacks and undertake the right efforts to eliminate their respective deficiencies.

Such discerning ability arises by itself in an *ātmārthi* - true seeker. He identifies whatever is relevant in all situations and acts accordingly. An ātmārthi has the ability to decide what is appropriate or inappropriate, what to retain and what to discard. Possessing unrelenting determination and unflinching faith, he is aware of his own strengths and weaknesses. Working with dedication and devotion, he is neither lethargic nor impatient in his efforts. Only one with patient perseverance and calm quietness can attain self-realisation.

This verse sets the standard for truth seekers, who should be ready to accept the truth and practise it in every situation. The seeker should possess the discretion to understand what is right and wrong as well as the willingness to adopt the right and discard the wrong. Irrespective of the tradition in which he is brought up, the objective should be to seek truth from whichever direction it comes. For that, one needs to have an open mind. An ātmārthi is capable of thinking clearly and enriching the soul. He understands and follows the truth, activating the process of attaining liberation.

Thus, in this verse, for an easy understanding of the spiritual path, Shrimadji appears to have woven *Āchāryashri Umāswātiji's sutra* - aphorism, *Samyagdarshan-jnān-chāritrāni mokshmārgah* - Right faith, right knowledge and right conduct combine to constitute the path of liberation. An ātmārthi's approach is the union of the three. Here, *samyak darshan* and *samyak jnān* are indicated by *'samajvu'* - understands, and *samyak chāritra* by the word *'āchre'* - follows. Thus Shrimadji, in a unique way, has described that the ātmārthi is on the path of liberation.

— ∽☙∾ —

VERSE - 9

Sadguru is essential

After stating the defining attribute of the true seeker, in verses 9-19, Shrimadji explains the need for a Sadguru, His attributes, greatness, devotion required towards Him and its benefits. In this verse, describing the necessity and benefit of the association of a Sadguru, Shrimadji says -

સેવે સદ્‌ગુરુચરણને, ત્યાગી દઈ નિજપક્ષ;
પામે તે પરમાર્થને, નિજપદનો લે લક્ષ. ||૯||

Seve Sadgurucharanne, tyāgi dai nijpaksh;
Pāmey te parmārthne, nijpadno le laksh. ||9||

Seve - serves; *Sadgurucharanne* - feet of enlightened Mentor; *tyāgi dai* - giving up; *nijpaksh* - own opinions; *pāmey* - attains; *te* - he; *parmārthne* - supreme truth; *nijpadno* - of own self; *le* - attains; *laksh* - focus

MEANING

Giving up his own opinions, one who serves the lotus feet of the Sadguru; understands the supreme truth and focuses on his own self, enabling him to advance towards self-realisation.

EXPLANATION

The primary objective of spiritual pursuit is to attain liberation. However, even a man possessing great understanding is incapable of reaching the goal by himself. One needs an enlightened Mentor to illuminate the way. This verse demonstrates the requirement of taking refuge at the lotus feet of the Sadguru.

Prior to meeting the Sadguru, one may have employed various means in the name of religion. He may have undertaken different activities as per his understanding and choice; may have even met many religious people and adopted their views. However, pursuing religion without the refuge of a Sadguru may lead to a biased and one-sided approach. He either becomes a *kriyājad* or a *shushkjnāni* and renders himself incapable of progressing on the right path. Therefore, one must be prepared to let go of all notions, views, beliefs, likes, dislikes and obstinacy. In other words, the attitude to push one's own opinions and desires must be given up. In the presence of a Sadguru, one needs to shed his ego and completely resign from his insistences. If he is receptive towards the Guru's guidance with an open and clean heart, then and only then, will wisdom dawn upon him.

The very essence of spiritual pursuit emanates from the heart of the Sadguru. He suitably guides the seeker on what to do and how to do it, as He knows the seeker's shortcomings. He imparts subtle knowledge to solve any crisis that may arise on the path. Hence, a seeker should accept with absolute humility that he knows nothing about the path and serve the Sadguru's feet with utmost reverence. This does not merely entail sitting at His feet. Rather, it means to observe Him and adopt His way of thinking, beliefs and conduct. Following the Sadguru does not only mean going to Him but also the readiness to undertake whatever He commands. It is total dedication and complete surrender to His instructions.

One who follows the Sadguru's guidance with steadfastness and earnestness attains the supreme truth. His own beliefs and perspectives are no longer in focus, instead, the true self becomes the point of his focus. He attains the supreme path of liberation and his attention is directed towards the pure nature of the soul. The constant practice of inwardness makes him proficient and he accomplishes the goal of self-realisation.

In this way, after leaving behind his opinions and worshipping the lotus feet of the Sadguru, one certainly attains self-realisation. Treading the path under His guidance is the way to experience the inner bliss. Thus, the importance of a Sadguru has been emphasised in this verse. Saints of all times have unequivocally accepted the need of a Sadguru's refuge to advance on the path of liberation.

VERSE - 10

Qualities of Sadguru

The seeker is safe only if he has a Sadguru as a guide, otherwise there is always the fear of missing the path. For this reason, in this verse, the hallmarks of a Sadguru are enumerated in very simple yet clear words. Shrimadji says -

આત્મજ્ઞાન સમદર્શિતા, વિચરે ઉદયપ્રયોગ;
અપૂર્વ વાણી પરમશ્રુત, સદ્‌ગુરુ લક્ષણ યોગ્ય. ||૧૦||

Ātmajnān samdarshitā, vichre udayprayog;
Apurva vāni paramshrut, Sadguru lakshan yogya. ||10||

Ātmajnān - self-realisation; *samdarshitā* - equanimity; *vichre* - acts; *udayprayog* - operation of past karma; *apurva* - unprecedented; *vāni* - speech; *paramshrut* - supreme knowledge of scriptures; *Sadguru* - enlightened Mentor; *lakshan* - characteristics; *yogya* - true

MEANING

Self-realisation, equanimity, living according to the manifestation of past karma, unprecedented speech, mastery over the scriptures; these are the true characteristics of a Sadguru.

EXPLANATION

The guidance of a Sadguru is imperative for the upliftment of the soul. One sets forth on the path of self-realisation fuelled by the strength of His words. The worship of a Sadguru through the recognition of His inner state leads to spiritual welfare. Just as a lamp is lit by a lamp, the way to truth must come from truth itself. One can never accomplish the desirable fruit of freedom from transmigration without taking the refuge of a Sadguru. Therefore, for the seeker to recognise a Sadguru, Shrimadji describes the attributes of a Sadguru in this verse.

1. *Ātmajnān* - Self-realisation
A Sadguru possesses knowledge of the self. Here, knowledge does not merely mean scriptural knowledge which is information about the self at an intellectual level. It means experiential knowledge of the self. A Sadguru has experienced the pure, blissful self. Since He derives bliss from the self, He is devoid of desires for the non-self. Desirelessness for sensual pleasures is the sign of self-realisation.

2. *Samdarshitā* - Equanimity
Owing to a direct and deep experience of the self, the Sadguru remains untouched in both favourable and unfavourable circumstances. Whether friend or foe, respect or disrespect, pleasure or pain, gain or loss, life or death, He possesses total equanimity. He remains completely balanced and equipoised in every conceivable contrasting situation. No event can cause a reaction and there exists no anxiety whatsoever. He remains perpetually peaceful, calm and stable.

3. *Vichre udayprayog* - Life lived as per past karma
Due to abidance in the self, the Sadguru has no complaints or desires for any situation. The questions arise: What is the basis of His actions? What is the reason behind His activities?

The answer is the fruition of His past karma. The external life of the Sadguru unfolds according to the operation of past karma - much like an actor following a script. Since He accepts these fruits of karma with detachment, new karma is not created and He remains unbound. He does not get trapped in the whirlpool of past karma, thus does not get entangled with likes and dislikes. Even though the Sadguru eats, walks, talks and sleeps just like an ignorant one, He is ever so focused solely on the self.

4. *Apurva vāni* - Unprecedented words
The Sadguru's words reveal subtle spiritual secrets and describe His own sublime experience. As His words emerge from experience, they are extremely powerful and effective. His speech is so attractive and persuasive that it brings one on the path of liberation. His words are filled with such sweetness that the seekers feel a magnetic pull. Flowing naturally with inner conviction, His words are non-contradictory; the ultimate truth and final authority on spirituality. Thus, the Sadguru's speech is unparalleled, exceptional and touches the core of every heart. His unprecedented words give rise to unprecedented feelings in the disciple, bringing about spiritual welfare.

5. *Paramshrut* - Knower of the essence of the scriptures
One who has imbibed the purport of the six schools of philosophy and the essence of all the scriptures is a paramshrut. He possesses complete, consistent devotion to the scriptures and is well-versed with the fundamental truths. He has the ability to appropriately answer all the

wide-ranging questions from myriad seekers. He can satisfy the spiritual needs of every seeker by giving them the right guidance. This expertise is present in the Sadguru.

Thus, Shrimadji describes the attributes of the Sadguru in a short, sweet and effective way, inspiring the earnest aspirant to seek a Sadguru endowed with such virtues. A true Guru can be identified by the presence of these five admirable attributes. One's desired purity and the accomplishment of the goal of self-realisation can only be sought by taking refuge in a Guru who possesses these attributes.

VERSE - 11

Importance of living Sadguru

Having explained the sheer necessity of being in contact with a living Sadguru endowed with the attributes enumerated in the earlier verse, Shrimadji says -

પ્રત્યક્ષ સદ્ગુરુ સમ નહીં, પરોક્ષ જિન ઉપકાર;
એવો લક્ષ થયા વિના, ઊગે ન આત્મવિચાર. ॥૧૧॥

Pratyaksh Sadguru sam nahi, paroksh Jin upkār;
Evo laksh thayā vinā, ugey na ātmavichār. ॥*11*॥

Pratyaksh - living; **Sadguru** - enlightened Mentor; **sam** - same; **nahi** - not; **paroksh** - non-present; **Jin** - omniscient Lord; **upkār** - benevolence; **evo** - such; **laksh** - realisation; **thayā** - occur; **vinā** - without; **ugey** - arise; **na** - not; **ātmavichār** - self-contemplation

MEANING

The benevolence of a living Sadguru is not the same but greater than that of the non-present omniscient Lords, the *Tirthankars*. Until one realises this fact, self-contemplation does not arise within him.

EXPLANATION

When Tirthankars like *Shri Rushabhdev, Shri Mahāvirswāmi,* etc., were present in the physical form, they were called as *pratyaksh Jinas.* After they attain liberation and are not in the physical form any more, they are called *paroksh Jinas.*

The omniscient ones are not present in *Bharat kshetra* any longer. The only way to maintain contact with the paroksh Jinas is through their teachings, inscribed in the *Āgams* - the Jain Canons.

The extraordinary teachings of the Jinas are beneficial. However, without personal guidance, one tends to interpret them according to his intellect. Attempting to understand them on his own, he is incapable of absorbing the underlying meaning and is more than likely to be led astray. Hence, his delusion cannot be destroyed as the essence of the scripture is not understood. Delusion can be dispelled only by a living Sadguru. The paroksh Jinas cannot come and tell a seeker that he has not understood the meaning correctly, nor are they going to guide him personally. Only the pratyaksh Sadguru is capable of this feat. The Sadguru imparts the teachings of the Jinas which are validated by His own experience. In His company, a seeker can progress on the path quickly and easily. Hence, from this perspective, the benevolence of the pratyaksh Sadguru is higher than that of the paroksh Jinas.

A seeker is filled with feelings of great admiration and respect when he beholds the idol of the Jina. However, the idol cannot point out the seeker's faults and shortcomings. This ability is only present in a pratyaksh Sadguru, who can point out his mistakes and enable their corrections. He motivates and persuades the seeker to overcome his flaws. The pratyaksh Sadguru applies different techniques and tactics to bring him on the right path. He resolves the disciple's dilemmas, unravels his conflicts, and annihilates his ignorance.

Until one realises that the pratyaksh Sadguru is more effective and His benevolence is greater than the paroksh Jinas, he remains deprived of spiritual progress. Self-contemplation does not arise in the one who keeps praising the benevolence of the paroksh Jinas while ignoring the supreme benevolence of the pratyaksh Sadguru. Unless the greatness of a pratyaksh Sadguru sets within and His benevolence is accepted with gratitude, the thought of the self does not sprout in the conscience of the disciple. Without genuine contemplation it is not possible to realise the self. A seeker can only start the journey towards self-realisation when firm faith and conviction about the unprecedented importance of the pratyaksh Sadguru dawns within him. With supreme reverence for the pratyaksh Sadguru, inclination towards the self develops, contemplation arises, and the self is realised.

It must be noted that this verse does not aim to diminish the greatness of the Tirthankars in any way. The Jinas have propounded the path of liberation for us, their scriptures are an extraordinary treasure and an invaluable heritage. However, since they are not in physical form, their benevolence is indirect. In the current era, when the Jinas are not present amidst us, there is only one direct recourse left to us - pratyaksh Sadguru. Only a living Sadguru can explain the path of the Jinas to us and simplify dharma for us.

Therefore, even though the state of the pratyaksh Sadguru is not the same as that of the Jinas, the benevolence of the pratyaksh Sadguru is greater because of His physical presence. One must surrender fully at the lotus feet of a pratyaksh Sadguru.

VERSE - 12

Benevolence of Sadguru

Having established the importance of the living Sadguru, now, to highlight His exceptional benevolence, Shrimadji says -

સદ્ગુરુના ઉપદેશ વણ, સમજાય ન જિનરૂપ;
સમજ્યા વણ ઉપકાર શો? સમજ્યે જિનસ્વરૂપ. ||૧૨||

Sadgurunā updesh van, samjāy na Jinroop;
Samjyā van upkār sho? Samjye Jinswaroop. ||12||

Sadgurunā - of enlightened Mentor; ***updesh*** - teachings; ***van*** - without; ***samjāy*** - understand; ***na*** - not; ***Jinroop*** - omniscient state; ***samjyā*** - understanding; ***van*** - without; ***upkār*** - benefit; ***sho*** - what; ***samjye*** - understands; ***Jinswaroop*** - nature of omniscient Lord

MEANING

Without the teachings of a Sadguru, one cannot comprehend the state of the omniscient Lord. Without this understanding, how can one derive any benefit? Through this understanding one can comprehend and attain the state of the omniscient Lord.

EXPLANATION

Those who seek to achieve the goal of liberation need to draw inspiration from the *Jinas*, who have attained that state. Hence, it can be said that the Jinas are the perfect role models for the seekers. These great souls have vanquished attachment and aversion, have fully manifested the infinite virtues of the soul, and are revelling in the purest, dispassionate, blissful state. It is necessary to perfectly comprehend the state of the Jinas in order to achieve it.

If one fails to understand the true state of the Jinas and worships them only because of tradition, the purpose of attaining purity is not served. What benefit could he possibly derive by chanting the Jinas' names and reciting their glory if he does not understand their nature, benevolence and path? Only pure devotion for these great ones can lead to true spiritual benefit, making it imperative to understand the true state of the Jinas. However, an aspirant cannot grasp it by himself. He is unable to comprehend it without the support of a living Sadguru, who provides the necessary insight.

The Sadguru explains the inner state of absolute purity of the Jinas and the way they attained it. Through His teachings, one understands the pure state of the Jinas, a state which is worthy of worship. It is a state which has manifested due to constant abidance in the self. Upon understanding it, one fully realises the divine glory of the Jinas and is immersed in devotion for them. In this way, the true state of the Jinas is understood from the Sadguru. Here the word '*samjāy*' implies that one knows the true state of the Jinas, recognises their unsurpassable excellence and kindles spiritually-rewarding devotion for them.

To understand the Jinas is to understand one's own self. It leads to an inclination for the true self, and with an increase in inwardness, inner purity increases. Eventually by destroying all impurities like attachment and aversion, the soul attains the same state of absolute purity as that of the Jinas. Thus, the supreme benevolence of the Sadguru entails describing the true state of the Jinas. He is the most tangible way to understand the subtleties of the spiritual path. He provides the key with which the seeker unlocks the door to enlightenment. Therefore, Shrimadji repeatedly emphasises the greatness of the living Sadguru.

VERSE - 13

In absence of Sadguru

In verses 11 and 12, Shrimadji clearly stated that taking refuge in the *pratyaksh* Sadguru is the supreme way for attaining self-realisation. In this verse, guiding a qualified seeker who cannot find a pratyaksh Sadguru, Shrimadji says -

આત્માદિ અસ્તિત્વનાં, જેહ નિરૂપક શાસ્ત્ર;
પ્રત્યક્ષ સદ્‌ગુરુ યોગ નહિ, ત્યાં આધાર સુપાત્ર. ॥૧૩॥

Ātmādi   astitvanā,   jeh   nirupak   shāstra;
Pratyaksh Sadguru yog nahi, tyā ādhār supātra. ॥13॥

Ātmādi - soul etc.; *astitvanā* - of existence; *jeh* - that; *nirupak* - explain; *shāstra* - scriptures; *pratyaksh* - living; *Sadguru* - enlightened Mentor; *yog* - association; *nahi* - not; *tyā* - there; *ādhār* - support; *supātra* - deserving souls

MEANING
In the absence of an association with a living Sadguru, the scriptures that expound the existence of the soul, etc., are a support for deserving souls.

EXPLANATION
Through the preceding verses Shrimadji has asserted the greatness of the Sadguru. The qualified one, who possesses the essential qualities of a *mumukshu* - seeker of liberation, should look for guidance in spiritual pursuits from a pratyaksh Sadguru who has experienced the self. However, in the

present era, which is a declining period of spirituality, the company of such an enlightened being is rare. To say it is extremely difficult to find a Sadguru would be an understatement. When faced with such a crisis, it is likely that a seeker would flounder, get confused, lose direction and be led astray by his own doing. Importantly, what must a seeker do if he has not come across an enlightened being? Who should he rely on?

The solution put forth in this verse is that if a seeker does not have a pratyaksh Sadguru, then he should depend on the scriptures - which present the powerful teachings of enlightened beings of the past. Until he meets such a being, he must use the sacred texts for both inspiration and guidance. The scriptures are the voice of the ancient Masters. They contain the wisdom of civilisations, encapsulating the understanding of the soul and the path. They can be relied upon as they have been composed by self-realised beings and are therefore, authentic.

To a worthy seeker, the study of the scriptures - listening, reading and contemplating, can be very helpful to remain steadfast on the spiritual path. Scriptures enable a seeker to determine the true nature of the substance. '*Ātmā*' means the soul, the animate, and '*ādi*' includes inanimate substances. The scriptures that expound the truth about the basic elements - the self and the non-self, are called true scriptures. These scriptures provide explanations to the questions: What is the nature of the soul? What is its beginningless relation with karma? How can that relation be ended? How can new karmic bondage be stopped? How can the existing karma be exhausted? What type of relation do karmic bondage and passions have? What role do the mind's impurities play in this? Besides this, the true scriptures also provide information to the seeker regarding the latent strength of the soul and the means to manifest it. They furnish essential and practical guidance to the seeker.

Thus, in the absence of the Sadguru, the spiritual scriptures that chiefly elucidate the knowledge about the soul act as a support to the worthy seeker. Contemplating the scriptural knowledge helps him increase his levels of calm and detachment. This inspirational knowledge of breaking free from the delusion of body identification and abiding in the pure self, helps him progress on the path. Resorting to the scriptures, he stays vigilant and becomes more qualified to receive the guidance of a living Sadguru when he finds one.

One should bear in mind that the scriptures can definitely support the worthy seeker in the absence of a pratyaksh Sadguru, but they cannot be as helpful in completely destroying delusion as the pratyaksh Sadguru. It is also important to note that self-study cannot bring about a total transformation and can even be dangerous. Hence, a relentless search for a Sadguru should continue endlessly. The scriptures are not a substitute for a Sadguru, but an alternative to follow in His absence. They can never take His place. Thus, the worthy seeker is made well aware that the pratyaksh Sadguru is the supreme refuge and none can be compared to Him.

VERSE - 14

When continuous association is not possible

For the one who is associated with a *pratyaksh* Sadguru, but does not get to be in His company continuously, in such a condition, what should be done? Guiding the course of action in this situation, Shrimadji says -

અથવા સદ્ગુરુએ કહ્યાં, જે અવગાહન કાજ;
તે તે નિત્ય વિચારવાં, કરી મતાંતર ત્યાજ. ||૧૪||

Athvā Sadgurue kahyā, je avgāhan kāj;
Te te nitya vichārvā, kari matāntar tyāj. ||14||

Athvā - or; *Sadgurue* - by enlightened Mentor; *kahyā* - instructed; *je* - which; *avgāhan* - deep study; *kāj* - for; *te te* - those; *nitya* - regularly; *vichārvā* - contemplate; *kari* - doing; *matāntar* - differences of opinion; *tyāj* - giving up

MEANING

Or, one should regularly contemplate upon the scriptures instructed by the Sadguru for deep study, leaving aside his preconceived notions.

EXPLANATION

It is very rare to come across a true Guru and receive His guidance. Even if one is fortunate enough to find a Sadguru, it is difficult to remain in continuous contact with Him. If one is not able to be with Him constantly, the attraction to worldly pleasures may become strong. Therefore, in the absence of the Sadguru's constant association, one must regularly study the scriptures instructed by Him, shedding differences of opinion.

By the word *'avgāhan'*, Shrimadji means to convey the deep study of the scriptures. It means to delve so deep into them that all the mysteries are unravelled. First, the text should be read and after having understood the meaning, one must reflect upon it to grasp the essence. This reflection can include the questions: What did I like? Why did I like it? What did I comprehend? How will I apply this knowledge? In this way, he should study the text in depth and with great enthusiasm. Without restricting the study to merely remembering logical arguments or analogies, he must go over the spiritually beneficial points several times. If a doubt arises, with utmost humility, he must present it to the Sadguru, in order to receive a solution from Him. Thus, avgāhan means - read, reflect, ruminate and reinforce the teachings of the scriptures. This study should be undertaken regularly and persistently so that the seeker remains alert in his spiritual journey.

Engaging in the five forms of self-study, namely - reading, enquiring, repeating, pondering and discussing of the scriptures instructed by the Sadguru can become beneficial on the spiritual path only if one renounces preconceived notions. Inner purification can only occur in an unprejudiced mind that discards all insistences about religions, sects, traditions and customs. The truth can be understood only when one reflects on the scriptures after having given up his stubborn attitude. One must truly renounce all dogmatic opinions and foolhardy beliefs nurtured out of ignorance. The mind must remain uncluttered with a willingness to learn and adopt new teachings. With a keen and open mind, one should accept knowledge from diverse sources by thoroughly understanding their respective viewpoints. If the seeker gives up all differences of opinion and dives deep into the scriptures, as instructed by the Sadguru, he gains spiritual welfare.

Thus, in the beginning of the verse, by using the word *'athvā'* - or, Shrimadji has stated that even when the seeker cannot be constantly with the Sadguru, deep contemplation upon the scriptures should be carried out according to His commands while renouncing prejudiced notions. With the Sadguru in his heart and the scriptures in his hands, the sincere seeker is sure to advance on the path of liberation.

VERSE - 15

Refrain from self-will

Upto verse 14, Shrimadji clearly indicated that the path of liberation is dependent on the *pratyaksh* Sadguru. The next four verses describe the necessity and provide the remedy to eliminate the biggest obstacle that hinders spiritual growth. Conveying the prerequisite for ensuring the attainment of liberation, Shrimadji says -

રોકે જીવ સ્વચ્છંદ તો, પામે અવશ્ય મોક્ષ;
પામ્યા એમ અનંત છે, ભાખ્યું જિન નિર્દોષ. ||૧૫||

Rokey jeev swachhand toh, pāmey avashya moksh;
Pāmyā em anant chhe, bhākhyu Jin nirdosh. ||15||

Rokey - refrains; *jeev* - soul; *swachhand* - self-will; *toh* - then; *pāmey* - attains; *avashya* - surely; *moksh* - liberation; *pāmyā* - attained; *em* - this way; *anant* - infinite; *chhe* - have; *bhākhyu* - stated; *Jin* - omniscient Lord; *nirdosh* - flawless

MEANING

If the soul refrains from self-will, then it can surely attain liberation. The flawless omniscient Lord has stated that infinite souls have attained liberation in this way.

EXPLANATION

The right destination can only be reached by advancing in the right direction. Liberation can only be attained by eliminating the flaws that obstruct one's progress on the path. Unless the seeker starts emptying his mind, the Guru cannot begin His work. The mind must first be receptive to receive His guidance.

The biggest hindrance to the attainment of the path to liberation is a grave flaw called '*swachhand*'. It keeps one engaged in several inappropriate activities and is the cause of transmigration. Hence, the one who yearns to become free from the cycles of birth and death must surely shun swachhand. The one who can do so definitely attains liberation.

Swachhand means self-willed attitude and behaviour. It is the habit of acting according to one's whims and fancies, the inclination to base actions according to moods. Due to swachhand, one is too obstinate about his viewpoints. He likes to partake in whatever appeals to his intellect, behaving in an unrestrained manner. Since swachhand has been nurtured and accumulated over countless lifetimes, it becomes so powerful that it is extremely difficult to relinquish. His clouded intellect prevents him from understanding his own faults, and his attempts at practising religion have also failed because of it. Thus, any religious activity performed with swachhand does not lead to liberation. In the name of religion, the self-willed person may undertake chanting, austerity, studying of scriptures, etc., as per his own imagination and desires; however, not a single one of these practices bring about transformation. Due to his swachhand, he either becomes a *kriyājad* or a *shushkjnāni* and forsakes his welfare.

Employing powerful words like '***toh***' - then, and '***avashya***' - certainly, Shrimadji has conveyed that through the strength of effort, if one eliminates swachhand, then he will certainly attain liberation. As long as one is blinded by swachhand, he cannot view the path of liberation. Only when swachhand is annihilated, he is able to become a true seeker and the pathway to liberation opens. He eventually attains liberation, the absolute state of purity. Thus, in the first line of the verse, Shrimadji has established the certainty of liberation if one destroys the flaw of swachhand, which is very difficult to overcome.

With the annihilation of swachhand, infinite beings have attained liberation in the past and infinite beings will attain it in the future. Thus proclaim the *Jinas*, who are free from the three-fold flaw of likes, dislikes and ignorance. The Jinas have attained the highest level of purity and omniscience. What the flawless, perfect Jinas say is completely true. Hence, one must tread the path by eliminating swachhand, as expounded by the Jinas.

VERSE - 16

Remedy to remove self-will

Having explained earlier that it is beneficial to be free from the grave bondage of *swachhand*, in verse 16, outlining the remedy to remove it, Shrimadji says -

પ્રત્યક્ષ સદ્ગુરુ યોગથી, સ્વચ્છંદ તે રોકાય;
અન્ય ઉપાય કર્યા થકી, પ્રાયે બમણો થાય. ||૧૬||

Pratyaksh Sadguru yogthi, swachhand te rokāy;
Anya upāy karyā thaki, prāye bamno thāy. ||16||

Pratyaksh - living; **Sadguru** - enlightened Mentor; **yogthi** - by association; **swachhand** - self-will; **te** - that; **rokāy** - restrained; **anya** - other; **upāy** - means; **karyā** - doing; **thaki** - by; **prāye** - mostly; **bamno** - double; **thāy** - becomes

MEANING
Self-will can be restrained through the association of a living Sadguru. It is mostly doubled by practising any other means.

EXPLANATION
The will to destroy swachhand arises when one realises that his own impure intellect and desires are hindering spiritual growth. From then on, swachhand pricks the seeker like a thorn and he is keen to eliminate it. In this verse, Shrimadji gives the disciple an unfailing cure to eradicate swachhand. It cannot be destroyed through one's own efforts. Only a

Sadguru can stop it, correct it and disclose the right path. Therefore, if one stays associated with a *pratyaksh* Sadguru and acts in accordance with His instructions, then his greatest flaw, swachhand, is destroyed very easily.

The guidance and training by the Sadguru enable the seeker to eliminate swachhand. He knows where the seeker is likely to fall prey to its trap and keeps him in check. It is His compassion that softens the heart of the seeker and motivates him on the path. His expertise enhances the seeker's abilities and capacities. Just like the sunrays when channelled through a magnifying glass burn paper, the Sadguru channels the seeker's energy in order to burn the flaw of swachhand. All that the seeker needs to do is surrender to Him. Dedication for the Sadguru's commands should pervade every pore of his being. With the firm belief that he is blessed to receive the Sadguru's commands and that they are for his benefit, the seeker should experience joy in following them. Thus, one desirous of eliminating swachhand must give up all his personal opinions and apply all his strength in following the commands of his pratyaksh Sadguru.

Resorting to any means other than the association with a pratyaksh Sadguru, one will not be able to eliminate swachhand. Not only will he fail, but also aggravate the problem. In fact, in most cases doubling its severity. His swachhand erupts, multiplying and becoming manifold. Hence, if he makes efforts to destroy it on his own, it only leads to a higher level of swachhand which is much stronger than what it was earlier. It becomes so strong that it is extremely difficult to get rid of this flaw.

Therefore, Shrimadji states here that swachhand is eliminated only by being associated with a pratyaksh Sadguru. Only by following His commands can it be removed and after that, one certainly attains liberation. Even if one labours to destroy swachhand through his own efforts for eternity, he will not attain self-realisation. In stark contrast, a devout follower of the Sadguru's commands attains omniscience within an *antarmuhurat* - less than 48 minutes. Such being the greatness of the Sadguru, the thoughtful ones follow His commands with single-pointed devotion and attain liberation.

VERSE - 17

Benefit of eliminating self-will

What state does one attain if he eliminates *swachhand* by taking the refuge of a *pratyaksh* Sadguru? Responding to this, Shrimadji says -

સ્વચ્છંદ, મત આગ્રહ તજી, વર્તે સદ્ગુરુલક્ષ;
સમકિત તેને ભાખિયું, કારણ ગણી પ્રત્યક્ષ. ||૧૭||

Swachhand, mat āgrah taji, varte Sadgurulaksh;
Samkit tene bhākhiyu, kāran gani pratyaksh. ||17||

Swachhand - self-will; ***mat*** - opinion; ***āgrah*** - insistence; ***taji*** - giving up; ***varte*** - acts; ***Sadgurulaksh*** - guidance of enlightened Mentor; ***samkit*** - right faith; ***tene*** - that; ***bhākhiyu*** - called; ***kāran*** - cause; ***gani*** - knowing; ***pratyaksh*** - direct

MEANING

Giving up self-will and insistence of opinions, when one acts as per the guidance of a Sadguru, he is said to have right faith; as this is known to be the obvious cause of the right faith.

EXPLANATION

To rectify the mistakes that have been continuously occurring over countless lives, it is absolutely necessary to give up *swachhand* - self-will, and *matāgrah* - insistence of opinions. Due to swachhand, essential reverence and humility towards the Sadguru do not arise. As a result, one remains opposed to the enlightened being and His path. Moreover, due to matāgrah, one does not develop the right faith in the fundamentals. His sectarian perspective, attachment to family religion, and obstinate nature prevent him from grasping the truth. Self-willed behaviour and relentlessly holding on to his opinions do not allow him to seek right guidance.

A true seeker is aware of the harmful outcome of swachhand and matāgrah, and hence does not try to proceed on the path by relying on his own imagination. He seeks the refuge of the Sadguru and follows His directions only. He develops pure love and unwavering faith in Him, and an unprecedented earnestness to live by these instructions. It is the seeker's unflinching conviction that his ultimate welfare lies only in treading the path shown by the Sadguru. The one who has firmly resolved to be in the Sadguru's guidance and also acts accordingly, has attained *samkit* - right faith.

While faith in the pure self arising through a Sadguru is called *vyavhār samkit*, faith in the pure self arising out of direct experience is called *nishchay samkit*. Since, vyavhār samkit is invariably present before the dawn of nishchay samkit, it is considered the cause of nishchay samkit.

Logically, every effect has a cause. The eventual result is inherent in the cause. Therefore, sometimes the cause itself is treated as the result. In other words, the effect is lodged in the cause, prompting the cause to be considered the effect.

Using this rationale, Shrimadji states that moulding one's life according to the Sadguru's instructions is the direct and obvious cause of experiential right faith, therefore this itself is called right faith. Though the feeling of faith towards the Sadguru is not nishchay samkit, it becomes the immediate cause of nishchay samkit - a direct experience of the pure self. Therefore, placing the effect in the cause, the omniscient dispassionate Lord has called it samkit.

VERSE - 18

Vanquishing deadly foes

Presenting an easy and unfailing way to vanquish inner enemies which hinder spiritual growth, Shrimadji says -

માનાદિક શત્રુ મહા, નિજ છંદે ન મરાય;
જાતાં સદ્ગુરુ શરણમાં, અલ્પ પ્રયાસે જાય. ||૧૮||

Mānādik shatru mahā, nij chhande na marāy;
Jātā Sadguru sharanmā, alp prayāse jāy. ||18||

Mānādik - ego etc.; *shatru* - foe; *mahā* - mighty; *nij* - own; *chhande* - efforts; *na* - not; *marāy* - destroyed; *jātā* - going; *Sadguru* - enlightened Mentor; *sharanmā* - in refuge; *alp* - slight; *prayāse* - by effort; *jāy* - go away

MEANING

Mighty enemies like ego, etc., cannot be destroyed through one's own efforts. However, by taking refuge in a Sadguru, they are eliminated with minimal effort.

EXPLANATION

A seeker on the spiritual journey knows that lethal enemies reside within and can take myriad forms. The extent of damage that cannot be caused by external enemies is caused by internal ones. External enemies cause damage to fame, wealth, health or, even life. However, internal enemies affect one's peace and purity. They are the cause for one not to attain liberation and hence, need to be destroyed.

In Jain terminology, defiling instincts called *kashāys* are of four types - anger, ego, deceit and greed. As they are difficult to overcome, they are called the mighty foes. Of these four great internal enemies, ego is the strongest. It is extremely difficult to destroy ego, compared to the other passions. Hence, to show its significance, it is termed as *'mānādik'* - ego, etc., in this verse. An egoistic person harbours the desire for veneration, status, acknowledgement, appreciation. He has an inclination to be seen as a great person and has strong attachments to his opinions. He becomes arrogant due to the obsessive and all-consuming 'I'.

Swachhand is a type of ego, and it is strongest in humans. It does not dissolve as long as the ego is fed and fattened. Logically, that which is fed will increase, not flatten. If one is ill and takes medicine, it is to destroy germs and not feed them. However, if the ego is fed, how will it get destroyed? One needs to decide whether the ego is worth feeding or discarding. One who realises that ego, etc., impede his own worthiness for the attainment of the path, is determined to destroy them.

These deadly enemies cannot be overcome through one's own efforts. They are so deeply entrenched that rooting them out by acting according to one's own will is impossible. Just as a mad elephant cannot be controlled without an elephant trainer, ego cannot be controlled without taking refuge in a Sadguru. This does not just mean to go to Him with folded hands, but to actually humbly follow His guidance. Having the expertise of combating inner enemies, the Sadguru has mastered the art of internal warfare. He imparts deep insights through which flaws like ego get eliminated in a short time. The ego starts melting and swachhand begins to decline. Through this, the elimination of flaws and manifestation of virtues is easily accomplished. By progressing on the path shown by the Sadguru, the journey towards the self becomes easy and free from hindrance.

Thus, it is impossible to attain the path of liberation, which proves to be incomprehensible and imperceptible without the refuge of a Sadguru. He admonishes and prevents the disciple's flaws and hence, only with His help can one embark on the journey and remain steadfast on the path. Great flaws like ego can be destroyed with minimal efforts by following the path directed by the Sadguru. An ocean cannot be crossed by swimming, but the shore can be reached on a ship with a little effort. Similarly, if one dedicates himself totally at the Sadguru's lotus feet, mighty enemies like ego are destroyed with a little effort.

———— ⌒⌇⌒ ————

VERSE - 19

Importance of humility

Only with the help of the Sadguru can one destroy flaws like *swachhand*. Explaining this in verses 15-18, Shrimadji eulogised the greatness of the refuge of the supremely benevolent Sadguru. Depicting the kind of humility a worthy disciple has towards the Sadguru, Shrimadji says -

જે સદ્ગુરુ ઉપદેશથી, પામ્યો કેવળજ્ઞાન;
ગુરુ રહ્યા છદ્મસ્થ પણ, વિનય કરે ભગવાન. ||૧૯||

Je   Sadguru   updeshthi,   pāmyo   kevaljnān;
Guru rahyā chhadmasth pan, vinay karey Bhagwān. ||19||

Je - that; ***Sadguru*** - enlightened Mentor; ***updeshthi*** - by teachings; *pāmyo* - attained; ***kevaljnān*** - omniscience; ***Guru*** - Mentor; *rahyā* - remained; ***chhadmasth*** - not omniscient; ***pan*** - yet; ***vinay*** - reverence; *karey* - does; ***Bhagwān*** - omniscient God

MEANING
A disciple who attains omniscience by imbibing the teachings of the Sadguru, continues to revere the Guru even if the Guru has not attained omniscience.

EXPLANATION
The teachings of the Sadguru unfold the path until the attainment of omniscience, hence the utmost devotion towards the Sadguru is most beneficial to the disciple. His feelings of respect and reverence for the Sadguru develop

while praising, venerating and worshipping Him, bringing about a transformation - beginning with worthiness and culminating into liberation. The Sadguru's divine teachings kindle the light of knowledge in the disciple. He rapidly rises on the path of liberation leading to the attainment of omniscience. Therefore, the enlightened beings expound the supreme benefit of humility.

Realising the significance and magnificence of the Sadguru, the true seeker is quick to learn and follow in His footsteps. The seeker lives a life in accordance with the Sadguru's commands, remaining humble and reverent towards Him. At no point in time does he allow pride or arrogance to blind him to the benevolence of the Sadguru. In acknowledging His importance, the disciple displays maturity and wisdom.

Revealing the zenith of humility in this verse, Shrimadji says that through the Sadguru's teachings the disciple may have attained '*kevaljnān*' - omniscience. However, the Sadguru may yet be a '*chhadmasth*'. It denotes the concealment of the omniscient state. In some cases it might happen that the disciple attains omniscience while the Sadguru is still without it. Even after attaining the finest state of omniscience, which the Sadguru does not yet have, the disciple continues to show reverence towards Him. There are many such instances recorded in Jain scriptures like *Shri Mrugāvati, Shri Pushpchulā, Shri Chandrudrāchārya's* disciple, etc., that exemplify the reverence by the omniscient disciple towards the Sadguru.

If one has become a billionaire through the guidance of a millionaire, he still respects his mentor, even though he is not a billionaire himself. The newly minted billionaire does not forget his mentor's contribution and acknowledges how he was uplifted by his guidance. Similarly, the disciple does not forsake humility and continues to respect the Sadguru, under whose guidance he pursued the spiritual path and attained omniscience. Such is the greatness and paramount importance of humility towards the Sadguru, which has been highlighted here, inspiring one to cultivate it.

VERSE - 20

Path of humility

Shedding more light on the subject of the path of humility, Shrimadji says -

एवो मार्ग विनय तणो, भाख्यो श्री वीतराग;
मूળ हेतु ए मार्गनो, समजे कोई सुभाग्य. ||२०||

Evo mārg vinay tano, bhākhyo Shri Vitrāg;
Mool hetu ae mārgno, samje koi subhāgya. ||20||

Evo - such; *mārg* - path; *vinay* - humility; *tano* - of; *bhākhyo* - stated; *Shri Vitrāg* - dispassionate Lord; *mool* - main; *hetu* - purpose; *ae* - that; *mārgno* - of path; *samje* - understands; *koi* - some; *subhāgya* - fortunate souls

MEANING
Such is the path of humility that has been revealed by the dispassionate Lord. The true significance of that path is understood only by a few fortunate souls.

EXPLANATION
Glorifying the path of humility, Shrimadji here says *'evo'* - such, the way which has been explained in the previous verse. That path of humility has been expounded by the dispassionate Lord who has destroyed all impurities. *'Vinay'* - humility, is the main amongst all virtues. Humility towards the Sadguru is an even more important cause of liberation. From one

virtue of humility, more and more virtues unfold, and eventually, infinite bliss is attained. Therefore, a seeker must follow the supremely benevolent path of humility with the utmost reverence.

The dispassionate Lords have expounded vinay as the root of dharma because the virtue of humility inevitably leads to the goal of liberation. Since it plays such a vital role in spiritual pursuit, the dispassionate Lords have emphasised its importance in the scriptures. In the Jain scriptures like *Shri Uttarādhyayan Sutra* - in 48 verses of its first chapter named *Vinayshrut, Shri Dashvaikālik Sutra* - in the 4 sections of the ninth chapter named *Vinay Samādhi*, and in many other scriptures, the path of humility has been held in great honour.

In Eastern philosophies and especially Indian philosophy, the bond between the Guru and disciple is very sacred. The disciple sees God in the Guru, and the Guru sees potential in the disciple. Although the Guru imparts wisdom to all the disciples, not all are equally capable of benefitting from it. Only those who have the utmost humility are capable of receiving it. The real significance and importance of humility can be realised only by very few. The main purpose of the path of humility can be understood only by a '**subhāgya**' - fortunate one. Only a devout one can comprehend its spiritually beneficial effect. He realises that annihilating *swachhand* is the main purpose of the path of humility and its base is to take refuge in the Sadguru's commands. He is the most fortunate one, who understands that complete surrender to the Sadguru is the easiest way to become free of flaws, manifest virtues and attain the goal. Such a one is also called *sulabhbodhi*, due to his ease in attaining the three jewels of right faith-knowledge-conduct. Those unfortunate ones who do not realise the real significance of the path of humility continue their transmigration.

The word '*subhāgya*' also refers to *Shri Saubhāgyabhāi*, a prime disciple of Shrimadji, upon whose request Shri Ātmasiddhi Shāstra was composed. By using this word, Shrimadji remembers him and glorifies his humility. Shri Saubhāgyabhāi had understood the significance, importance and relevance of the path of humility. Shrimadji has immortalised him by mentioning his name thrice in Shri Ātmasiddhi Shāstra - this verse, verse 96 and a verse which was written after verse 127 but was later deleted.

VERSE - 21

Fate of fake Guru

Shrimadji explained the importance of humility on the part of the disciple. He now expresses a word of caution for an untrue teacher. Shrimadji says -

અસદ્‌ગુરુ એ વિનયનો, લાભ લહે જો કાંઈ;
મહામોહનીય કર્મથી, બૂડે ભવજળ માંહી. ||૨૧||

*Asadguru ae vinayno, lābh lahey jo kāi;
Mahāmohaniy karmathi, budey bhavjal māhi. ||21||*

Asadguru - untrue teacher; *ae* - that; *vinayno* - of reverence; *lābh* - advantage; *lahey* - takes; *jo* - if; *kāi* - any; *mahāmohaniy* - intense deluding; *karmathi* - by karma; *budey* - drowns; *bhavjal* - ocean of worldly existence; *māhi* - in

MEANING
If an untrue teacher takes undue advantage of such reverence, he is bound to drown in the ocean of worldly existence owing to intense deluding karma.

EXPLANATION
The enlightened ones have emphasised the need for reverence towards the Sadguru in the best interest of the seeker. The seeker must follow the supremely beneficial path of humility. However, those who are ignorant of the true traits of the Sadguru and are impressed by feats of external

renunciation, commanding oratory skills, etc., are likely to brand an '**asadguru**' - untrue teacher, as the Sadguru. Surrendering to him, they serve him with complete faith, because devotion to the Sadguru is glorified in the scriptures. The Sadguru is however one who is completely free from within, possessing no desires whatsoever. He does not crave respect, honour or worship. Hence, when someone shows reverence or someone disrespects, He neither likes nor dislikes it. He treats respect and disrespect in the same way. He is totally devoid of ego and expectations.

On the other hand, an asadguru, lacks the attributes of the Sadguru. He does not possess self-realisation, equanimity, living according to past karma, unprecedented speech and mastery over the scriptures. Moreover, he desires worship, seeks name, fame and enjoys being honoured. He is ever-hungry to increase his own status and expects humility, service and provision of comforts from his disciples. Although he is ignorant of the self, he pretends to be an enlightened one. He may be a scholar but claims to possess self-realisation. Deceiving gullible people, tempting them with the false hope of self-realisation or material gains, he gets them to execute his commands as if he were the Sadguru. He entices them by bestowing blessings upon their families, businesses, etc., even using techniques such as astrology to attract them and fulfil his own selfish motives.

A dreadful fate awaits such a person, acquiring *mahāmohaniya* karma - inordinate amount of deluding karma. He creates the maximum possible deluding karma of the magnitude of 70 *kodākodi sāgaropam,* that is 70 x crore x crore sāgaropam - the highest unit of time according to Jain philosophy. This amount is stipulated at 7,000 trillion sāgaropam. Jainism explains sāgaropam through a metaphor. Consider a large pit of eight miles on all sides. It is packed with the tips of hair grown in one to seven days. Once filled, it is emptied by taking out one hair-tip every hundred years. The total time taken in emptying the pit in this manner is called one *palyopam.* 10 x crore x crore palyopam is 1 sāgaropam. He brings about infinite births and continues to wander in the world. He drowns in the ocean of transmigration. Like a boat made of stone, not only does an asadguru sink, but he also makes his disciples sink in the ocean of transmigration.

A true seeker should develop the keen ability to distinguish the Sadguru from an asadguru, in the same way one separates grain from chaff. Often, the external garb of an asadguru is no different from that of the Sadguru. One gets easily trapped due to that, making it even more difficult to recognise a true Sadguru. In this era especially, with the presence of numerous asadgurus, Shrimadji has stressed the importance of finding and identifying the Sadguru. Hence, this verse has been composed with a dual aim: to warn the imposter, the asadguru, of the danger of his actions as well as to caution the seeker to be wary of following an asadguru and search for the Sadguru with the purpose of self-realisation.

VERSE - 22

Necessity of right interpretation

An *asadguru* is one who is ignorant and yet claims to be the Sadguru. The one who wishes to learn the path of liberation from such an asadguru is considered a bigot. Clarifying this point, Shrimadji says -

હોય મુમુક્ષુ જીવ તે, સમજે એહ વિચાર;
હોય મતાર્થી જીવ તે, અવળો લે નિર્ધાર. ||૨૨||

Hoi mumukshu jeev te, samje eh vichār;
Hoi matārthi jeev te, avlo le nirdhār. ||22||

Hoi - is; *mumukshu* - desirous of liberation; *jeev* - soul; *te* - he; *samje* - understands; *eh* - that; *vichār* - concept; *hoi* - is; *matārthi* - bigot; *jeev* - soul; *te* - he; *avlo* - wrong; *le* - takes; *nirdhār* - conclusion

MEANING
The soul desirous of liberation correctly understands the concept of reverence, whereas the bigoted soul misinterprets it and draws wrong conclusions.

EXPLANATION
In this verse, Shrimadji clearly explains the distinction between those who understand the purpose of the path of humility and those who misinterpret it. Mainly, four points seem to be woven here -

Mumukshu - Desirous of liberation

1. A mumukshu understands the unparalleled greatness of the path of humility. He is capable of scrutinising and differentiating between the Sadguru and an asadguru, thus progressing on the path of humility. He is aware that one cannot attain the spiritual goal by following the teachings of an asadguru. Hence, not only does he give up such associations but also remains extremely careful to avoid nurturing or supporting an asadguru's deluded inclinations and activities. Instead, he engages in the reverential service of the Sadguru.

2. In a state of ignorance, one may have donned the robes of a monk. However, after meeting an enlightened being, he realises that, 'I do not possess self-realisation, and without it, real monkhood does not exist therefore I am not a monk but an aspirant.' Hence, admirably, without any fear or guilt, he clearly declares, 'I am not a monk. I am only a seeker of truth, I am a mumukshu.' As he does not crave honour, he does not try to mislead others to believe that he is more than what he really is.

Matārthi - Bigot

3. Unlike the mumukshu monk who curtails his ego and thus remains humble, a matārthi monk is highly opinionated and attached to robes and external rituals. Devoid of any of the inner virtues of a monk and filled to the brim with arrogant beliefs like 'I am a monk', he projects his image as the Sadguru and expects reverence from the naive disciple. Due to this

act of taking undue advantage of others, he wanders through infinite cycles of birth and death.

4. A matārthi considers an asadguru to be the Sadguru due to wrongly-held beliefs. Although the asadguru is merely a Guru for namesake, wandering in ignorance and immersed in the external, the matārthi is attached to his teachings. This is because he is not bothered about internal attributes, just outer appearances. He is impressed by an asadguru's oratory, logic, immense scriptural study and huge following. He firmly takes him as the Guru and reveres him. Thus, a matārthi on one hand considers an asadguru as a Guru and on the other, strengthens his own delusion, self-will and ego.

Hence, Shrimadji states in this verse that a mumukshu desiring freedom from the cycles of birth and death correctly understands the subtle spiritual implication of the path of humility propounded by the dispassionate Lords. Accordingly, he recognises the Sadguru and honourably serves Him. A mumukshu follows His guidance, destroys his flaws like self-will and fulfils his spiritual welfare. On the other hand, a matārthi does not understand the spiritual implication of the path of humility, interprets it incorrectly, and arrives at wrong conclusions. He gets caught in insistences, self-will and false obsessions, becoming either a mechanical ritualist or a dry intellectualist. Through this wrong behaviour he brings spiritual harm to himself.

VERSE - 23

Characteristics of bigot

Depicting the outcome of the behaviour of a bigot, Shrimadji says -

હોય મતાર્થી તેહને, થાય ન આતમલક્ષ;
તેહ મતાર્થી લક્ષણો, અહીં કહ્યાં નિર્પક્ષ. ॥૨૩॥

Hoi matārthi tehne, thāy na ātamlaksh;
Teh matārthi lakshano, ahi kahyā nirpaksh. ॥23॥

Hoi - is; *matārthi* - bigot; ***tehne*** - to him; ***thāy*** - occur; *na* - not; *ātamlaksh* - focus of self; *teh* - that; ***matārthi*** - bigot; ***lakshano*** - attributes; *ahi* - here; ***kahyā*** - stated; ***nirpaksh*** - impartially

MEANING
A bigot will not be inclined to focus on the true self. The attributes of such a bigot are impartially stated here, without any prejudice or selfish motive.

EXPLANATION
Since achieving self-realisation is the sole purpose of a true seeker, he develops reverence for the truth and sets his entire focus on the self. All activities are conducted with awareness of the self. Rituals are not performed for material pleasures, but instead to cultivate virtues. He refrains from getting stuck in mere physical activities or sectarian beliefs. In stark contrast, a *matārthi* does not endeavour to achieve

self-realisation. Considering the means to be the goal, he remains engrossed solely in external rituals, consumed by his own ideology. Passions remain undiminished and worldly interests prevail. He possesses wrong beliefs and a stubborn attitude.

Such deluded matārthis, who value their own style of thinking to be dearer than the truth itself, and remain extremely insistent on their opinions, will never be focused on the self. Where there is self-opinion, there is no truth. Further extending this, where no goal of truth exists, how can there be a possibility of self-realisation? Even further, without self-realisation, how can liberation be attained? The yearning for liberation leads one to focus on the self. It is only after breaking the stronghold of insistence and ego, etc., that he can turn towards the self.

Until there exists focus on the self, one cannot practise dharma in its true sense. He might engage in rituals but they will not prove beneficial to him. These external activities do not lead to inner purity as, consciously or unconsciously, the intention behind them is to gain worldly pleasure and respect. He remains devoid of virtues like detachment, humility and simplicity. He can be compared to the neem tree that grows at the border of a sugarcane field; instead of gaining the sweetness of virtues, he cultivates the bitterness of impurities within him despite practising religious activities. Externally, although he is performing activities of dharma, impure feelings increase karmic bondage. Ironically, by engaging in the same activities through which an ātmārthi achieves liberation, the matārthi increases his transmigration.

To caution the matārthi, Shrimadji in the second line of the verse says the attributes of such a one are described here. By using the phrase, '*ahi kahyā nirpaksh*', He says the characteristics of the religious bigot will be illustrated impartially. He holds no prejudice and does not wish to criticise or condemn these misled souls. It is only out of compassion that arises while observing the damaging results of bigotry, that He will reveal the attributes of a matārthi for his welfare. He has no selfish motive whatsoever, and nor is He targeting any particular sect. He lays out the attributes of the unfortunate matārthi only with the intention that he can recognise and remove these flaws.

This process will aid him to examine and eradicate harmful traits. A matārthi can make a sincere effort to discard these flaws, give up opinionated thoughts and turn towards the right path. Thus, Shrimadji ends the Introduction section, and builds a foundation for the next section - Attributes of a bigot.

Attributes of a Bigot

During the course of transmigration, caused by intense delusion since time immemorial, one has experienced infinite misery. In the dense darkness of the four *gati* - states of existence, he has remained ignorant of the true nature of dharma. At some point in the journey, due to meritorious karma, he had the opportunity to learn something about dharma. However, due to negative impressions prevailing since infinite time, he never fully grasped the overarching importance of the true dharma of realising the self. Through a limited understanding, he either became a *kriyājad* by considering only the external practices to be the path of liberation, or a *shushkjnāni* by believing knowledge of the scriptures to be self-realisation. Thus, despite having received some knowledge of dharma, he has been unable to avert the process of transmigration. Shrimadji now describes the attributes of such unfortunate ones, who lose direction of the path while performing religious activities.

In this section, Shrimadji describes the attributes of a '*matārthi*' - a religious bigot. A matārthi is a deluded fanatic who is absorbed in his own whims, obstinately convinced by his own opinions, and prejudiced against those who hold different opinions. He is totally engrossed in safeguarding his pride and vanity, as well as insisting on the veracity of his sectarian beliefs. Not open to understanding the truth, he misses out on the opportunity to better his spiritual welfare. Instead of imbibing the truth, he firmly holds on to the untruth, ferociously insisting that his belief alone is the truth. This is the main attribute of a matārthi.

In the following ten verses, Shrimadji describes the attributes of a matārthi, who does not possess the right inclination for spiritual welfare. This means that despite performing several religious practices, he has not yet turned in the direction of liberation. While engaging in the means of liberation, he ends up becoming either a kriyājad or a shushkjnāni. These verses serve a practical purpose; enabling one to reflect, introspect and minutely check to understand whether one possesses any of these traits himself. If they are present, he can put in the right effort to remove them so that all his religious practices are successful. In the first five verses 24-28, Shrimadji describes the nature of the kriyājad matārthi - insisting on ritualism; in the next three verses 29-31, He explains the nature of the shushkjnāni matārthi - insisting on intellectualism; and in the last two verses 32-33, giving their common attributes, He concludes this section.

VERSE - 24

Bigot's belief regarding Sadguru

Describing in five verses, the nature of a *kriyājad matārthi* who is under the illusion that he is practising right conduct, Shrimadji throws light on his false beliefs and insistences regarding *Saddev-Sadguru-Saddharma* (True God-Mentor-Religion), the three supreme benevolent factors for spiritual welfare. In this first verse, depicting the matārthi's false belief regarding the Guru, Shrimadji says -

બાહ્યત્યાગ પણ જ્ઞાન નહિ, તે માને ગુરુ સત્ય;
અથવા નિજકુળધર્મના, તે ગુરુમાં જ મમત્વ. ||૨૪||

Bāhyatyāg pan jnān nahi, te māney Guru satya;
Athvā nijkuldharmanā, te Gurumā ja mamatva. ||24||

Bāhyatyāg - external renunciation; *pan* - but; *jnān* - self-realisation; *nahi* - no; *te* - that; *māney* - believes; *Guru* - Mentor; *satya* - true; *athvā* - or; *nijkuldharmanā* - of own family religion; *te* - that; *Gurumā* - in Mentor; *ja* - only; *mamatva* - attachment

MEANING

A bigot whose approach is sectarian, either believes someone who possesses external renunciation but no self-realisation to be a true Guru; or harbours attachment only towards his family Guru.

EXPLANATION

Fulfilment of human birth depends on the association with the Sadguru, as one receives the path of liberation from Him. Aligning with His guidance leads to realisation of the self. Therefore, one desirous of self-realisation seeks an enlightened Sadguru and aspires to accomplish his spiritual goal by following His guidance. In these present times, when spirituality has become rare and there are many false beliefs prevalent regarding who can be considered a true Guru and what should be the true nature of a genuine spiritual guide, Shrimadji describes two types of false notions regarding the Guru -

1. To consider one who does not possess self-realisation to be a Guru, merely because of his feat of external renunciation is the trait of a matārthi. A matārthi is outwardly focused and oblivious of the self, and hence attaches no importance to self-realisation, only to external renunciation. As he himself cannot give up food, clothes, money, etc., he considers anyone who can achieve these feats to be at a high level. Overwhelmed with awe, he believes the renunciate to be great as he has accomplished a lot, and is worthy of being a Guru. He further enmeshes in delusion by offering reverence to such a person. The matārthi fails to realise that if such a Guru has not achieved self-realisation, he himself is ignorant. He has external renunciation but no internal detachment and stability. He visibly refrains from indulging in sense objects, but his mind wanders in them because he has no grip on the nature of the self. However, the matārthi does not realise this. He prefers to

go by rituals, austerities and garbs, insisting on external renunciation and not paying heed to whether the Guru is awakened or not. Accepting such a Guru does not lead to the accomplishment of spiritual welfare.

Does this mean that external renunciation is of no use? Should we not respect monks? The path of renunciation has been stipulated by the omniscient Lords, therefore there is no question of demeaning it. External renunciation is definitely helpful on the path of liberation. It assists in the destruction of attachment and aversion. Although it is necessary, the goal has to be inner purification. Mere external renunciation is not adequate for enlightenment, right understanding of the self is required. Therefore, external renunciation cannot be equated with self-realisation. One can surely respect them as renunciates, but to accept them as Gurus, one needs to ensure that there is self-realisation. If inner transformation to the level of self-realisation is not present, then they do not fit in the definition of the Sadguru.

2. To be attached to the Guru of a religion or sect accepted by one's forefathers, is the trait of a matārthi. The matārthi is so attached to his family tradition that it does not matter to him whether the Guru is self-realised or not. The Guru may not be enlightened, nor even striving for it. He could be ignorant, lax in his practices, living contrary to the Lord's precepts, full of self-will and insistence, harbouring selfish motives, or craving for respect from the community. Despite all this, the matārthi establishes such a one as his Guru.

This does not mean that one has to blindly give up revering one's family Guru. It simply means it is necessary to ascertain whether he has the attributes of the Sadguru or not. His ability to lead seekers across the ocean of transmigration should be verified. It should not be that he is a fraud masquerading as a Guru as such a person is worth rejecting. Hence, only after a detailed examination of whether the Guru possesses self-realisation, should one establish faith in him. This verse does not imply the need of negating reverence for one's family Guru. It strives to point out that revering him solely due to his status as family Guru, without ensuring that he possesses the qualities of the Sadguru, is not spiritually beneficial at all.

The greatest ignorance one can possess is the ignorance of his own self. If the delusion of believing in the wrong Guru is added to that, it causes immense self-harm. Therefore, this verse is a warning which is extremely relevant in current times. Whether it is the skill of a magician or the sweet tone of a salesman, every trick of the trade is used today in the business of being considered a Guru. Naive people fall prey to their messages and consider the false Guru to be the remedy to all problems. One requires an enlightened one to break the chain of births and rebirths. To discover a true Guru, one has to possess the traits of clarity and perseverance. Thus, it is implied here to use prudence in determining the difference between the Sadguru and an *asadguru*, as well as, give up the ignorant Guru and develop faith in the self-realised Guru.

VERSE - 25

Bigot's belief regarding God

Just as the *matārthi* is mistaken when it comes to recognising the Sadguru, he is also mistaken whilst attempting to understand the true nature of *Saddev* - True God. Pointing out his false belief, Shrimadji says -

જે જિનદેહ પ્રમાણ ને, સમવસરણાદિ સિદ્ધિ;
વર્ણન સમજે જિનનું, રોકી રહે નિજ બુદ્ધિ. ||૨૫||

Je Jindeh pramān ne, samavasaranādi siddhi;
Varnan samje Jinnu, roki rahey nij buddhi. ||25||

Je - he; *Jindeh* - omniscient God's body; *pramān* - size; *ne* - and; *samavasaranādi* - holy assembly hall etc.; *siddhi* - splendour; *varnan* - description; *samje* - considers; *Jinnu* - of omniscient God; *roki* - restricts; *rahey* - remains; *nij* - own; *buddhi* - intellect

MEANING

He considers the description of the body of the omniscient God and the glory of the holy assembly hall, etc., to be the true description of the omniscient God, the *Jinas*. He confines his thinking only to external manifestations.

EXPLANATION

After describing the matārthi's wrong beliefs regarding a Guru, Shrimadji now describes his wrong notions regarding God. In the previous verse, He explained who was not a true Guru and how the matārthi establishes faith in him. A noteworthy point here in this verse is, instead of illustrating who is not a true God, He points out the false beliefs of the matārthi regarding the one who is a true God. Despite finding the true God, the matārthi clings to false beliefs due to misunderstanding His true nature.

The Jain scriptures, *Āgams* and *Purāns*, describe the life of the Jinas - omniscient Lords. They depict the lineage, symbol, lifespan and dates of the five major events of their life. They describe the Jina's marvellous physical form, that is, the exceptional characteristics, size, complexion, beauty, strength, etc., of the body. They also detail the Jina's splendour which is the establishment of the *samavasaran*, etc., after the attainment of omniscience. **'Samavasaran'** is the holy assembly hall decorated with jewels created by celestial beings, where the Jina gives sermons. The scriptures portray the Jina's grandeur including *atishay* - special qualities, eight *pratihārya* - attributes endowed by celestial beings. However, the Jina's physical form and splendour of the samavasaran, etc., is not His true nature.

The description of the Jina's external prosperity, physical appearance, special attributes, and the splendour of the samavasaran exists to display His outer glory. They are merely the manifestations of His meritorious karma, and not the actual inner state itself. They remain in existence as long as the meritorious karma exists, ceasing as soon as it is exhausted. These external attributes are not found in the liberated state. His real greatness is that inner state which continues to exist in liberation. That omniscient state, which is pure and unblemished, is His true nature. This is the only real nature of the Jina which must be worshipped. One has only truly worshipped the Jina, if while remembering Him, he brings the virtues of dispassion, desirelessness, tranquillity and uninterrupted bliss of the self to his mind's eye. One cannot truly worship Him if one worships only the external traits and ignores the inner wealth of virtues.

While attempting to describe a king, if one speaks only of the beauty, cleanliness, broad streets or palatial mansions of the capital city, it does not amount to a true description. The real description of a king would be praising his valour, kindness and astuteness, or any special quality he might possess. Although he lives in the capital city, its description cannot be equated with his personal description. Unfortunately, a matārthi considers the Jina's physical form and outer glory such as samavasaran, etc., to be His description. He limits his intellect to accept only the Jina's external grandeur, dazzled by the external pomp and prosperity. So amazed and awestruck by the outer manifestations, he completely overlooks the inner virtues. Believing the external attributes to be the true nature of the Jina, he does not even focus on His inner state of dispassion. How then could he possibly yearn for this state himself? Further, without such intense yearning, how could he make the effort to attain it? How could he abide in the state of complete dispassion without making any effort? Hence, although the matārthi accepts and venerates the true God, he does not attain self-realisation. Consumed by the fanfare of decoration and celebration, he loses the true nature of God.

It can be concluded that to truly take refuge in the Jina, is to take refuge in His pure inner state and make it the goal to achieve in life. One should not be satisfied by simply glorifying His external form and unique attributes like samavasaran, etc., as this amounts to delusion. When we hear the name of a great person, our minds conjure up an image of him. Naturally, along with this greatness, the external personality like the face, height, etc., also appear in our memory. However, our focus remains on his greatness only. Similarly, when we remember and worship the Jina, external manifestations are bound to surface in the mind, but our focus should be on His inner pristine state, totally devoid of both, attachment and aversion.

VERSE - 26

Bigot's disregard for Sadguru

Verse 24 described the prevalence of strong insistence, where due to ignorance, an *asadguru* was believed to be the Sadguru. Now, in verse 26, explaining how a *matārthi* acts, despite being associated with the Sadguru, Shrimadji says -

પ્રત્યક્ષ સદ્ગુરુયોગમાં, વર્તે દૃષ્ટિ વિમુખ;
અસદ્ગુરુને દૃઢ કરે, નિજ માનાર્થે મુખ્ય. ||૨૬||

Pratyaksh Sadguruyogmā, varte drashti vimukh;
Asadgurune dradh karey, nij mānārthe mukhya. ||26||

Pratyaksh - living; ***Sadguruyogmā*** - in association of enlightened Mentor; ***varte*** - behaves; ***drashti*** - view; ***vimukh*** - opposite; ***asadgurune*** - to untrue teacher; ***dradh*** - adhere; ***karey*** - does; ***nij*** - own; ***mānārthe*** - for pride; ***mukhya*** - mainly

MEANING

In the association of a living Sadguru, he behaves with views contrary to His teachings. He overlooks or disregards the Sadguru and strengthens his faith in an untrue teacher, mainly to gratify his own pride.

EXPLANATION

A matārthi is not a real seeker of self-realisation but is a seeker of respect and wants to be considered an *ātmārthi*. Describing the matārthi's nature, in verse 24, Shrimadji explained how he errs while recognising a true Guru. Now, in this verse, He depicts how the matārthi does not avail the opportunity of the association with a true Guru.

Sometimes, as a result of abundant meritorious karma, a matārthi may come across a living Sadguru. He may get a chance to be in His proximity, interact with Him and even serve Him. However, due to his stubborn attitude, he is unable to surrender his mind at the lotus feet of the Sadguru. Although the Sadguru guides him to give up the false notions and prejudices that he possesses, he chooses to disregard Him. Due to lack of a genuine interest in his own spiritual welfare, he is unwilling to walk the path laid forth by the Sadguru. In fact, he acts in exactly the opposite manner due to the influence of wrong logic, doubts, etc. By maintaining views opposite to the Sadguru, he fails to accept His spiritually uplifting teachings that can sever the ties of insistence. Just like an upturned pot in the rain that does not collect even a single drop of water, the matārthi, despite being close to the Sadguru does not imbibe His teachings at all, and instead acts against Him. Without absorbing His guidance, how can there be any scope of bringing about an inner transformation? As a result, he does not benefit spiritually from the Sadguru, and instead ends up making a huge spiritual loss.

Not only does the matārthi ignore the Sadguru's spiritually beneficial teachings and behaves contrary to them, but also follows the asadguru with a fierce determination to safeguard and nurture his pride. To come across an asadguru and to have faith in one are two different things. The former is a result of one's fate, whereas the latter is a result of strengthening one's own faith, which is a wrong present effort. The matārthi firmly adheres to the teachings of such an asadguru, because he views a predominance of characteristics he likes and moreover, his opinions are nourished, giving him importance. He is attracted to the asadguru because he showers him with special attention and feeds his ego. Praising him, the asadguru ignores his flaws. He also gains approval and respect from the people around the asadguru. Therefore, to maintain his pride and position, he strengthens his faith in the asadguru and remains devoted to him.

Pride is such a deadly disease that it leaves no room for true understanding. It is a veil that covers the eyes and prevents one from perceiving reality. The proud man is blinded by his beliefs and boxed in by his prejudices. The asadguru takes advantage of such ignorance and robs him of spiritual welfare. People are often enamoured by the appearance of false Gurus, which belies the truth and is merely a facade meant to deceive gullible seekers. In the eyes of the masses, if someone can predict the future or perform miracles, then he is a Guru worthy of worship and veneration. They firmly believe in such an asadguru to satisfy their ego and desires. Due to his pride and gratification of vanity, the matārthi remains antagonistic towards the Sadguru and staunchly follows the asadguru. By strengthening his false belief, he brings about his own doom.

VERSE - 27

Bigot's belief regarding dharma

In verses 24 to 26, different aspects of false beliefs regarding the nature of the Guru and God were explained. Now, in verses 27 and 28, the prevailing false beliefs regarding the nature of religion are described. In this verse, explaining the false belief regarding scriptures and opinions pertaining to external attire, Shrimadji says -

દેવાદિ ગતિ ભંગમાં, જે સમજે શ્રુતજ્ઞાન;
માને નિજ મત વેષનો, આગ્રહ મુક્તિનિદાન. ||૨૭||

Devādi gati bhangmā, je samje shrutjnān;
Māney nij mat veshno, āgrah muktinidān. ||27||

Devādi - heavenly beings etc.; **gati** - states of existence; **bhangmā** - in classifications; **je** - he; **samje** - understands; **shrutjnān** - scriptural knowledge; **māney** - believes; **nij** - own; **mat** - sect; **veshno** - of external attire; **āgrah** - insistence; **muktinidān** - cause of liberation

MEANING

He believes that scriptural knowledge lies only in the classifications of heavenly beings, etc. He regards the insistence of the external attire of his own sect to be the cause of liberation.

EXPLANATION

An idea is dangerous if one insists it is the best for everyone. This is a characteristic of the bigot, and is called the closed-mind syndrome. The bigot thinks he knows the truth and is so stubborn that he does not hold room for any other opinion at all. He neither thrives nor allows anyone else to thrive, by insisting on the veracity of his own views. His obstinate approach to his religious beliefs deprives him of genuine spiritual welfare. In this verse, two types of false beliefs regarding the nature of dharma held by a *kriyājad matārthi* are explained -

1. Even though a matārthi has been introduced to the true scriptures, he fails to reap the benefit of their teachings because he does not understand their spiritual implications. Scriptures like *Karmagranth, Lokprakāsh, Shatkhandāgam, Gommatsār,* etc., have elaborate descriptions of the classifications of the four states of existence - heavenly beings, hellish beings, animals and humans. These are further sub-divided into 563 types. The four categories of existence, their sub-categories, the nature of each classification - numbers, place, shape, duration, size, etc., and their subtle differences have been explained in great detail.

The true spiritual purpose of these minute descriptions is to make one aware of the ill-fate created by karma when associated with the non-self. They have been provided to impel him to retreat from the impure feelings that are the cause of transmigration and cultivate detachment from the world. The depiction of heavenly beings has not been provided for one to aspire or plan for the celestial abode, it is given to illustrate the transitoriness of sensual pleasures.

It is to prompt the realisation of the suffering endured by wandering in the different states of existence, so that one makes the right effort to arrest bondage and break the cycles of birth and death. To merely memorise the descriptions of the classifications and discuss them as the study of the scriptures, without understanding the spiritual purpose of the enlightened ones, is a form of bigotry. Instead of contemplating and reflecting upon the essence of the scriptures, decreasing interest in sensual pleasures, and developing awareness of the self, the matārthi remains engrossed in the endless pursuit of classifications and remembering numbers. Finding fulfilment in this feat, he gloats, believing that he has gained knowledge and therefore remains bereft of the practice of true spirituality.

2. In the second line of this verse, Shrimadji describes another form of bigotry. A matārthi believes that insisting upon his opinion regarding attire based on his sect or family religion is the cause for liberation. He holds the foolish notion that liberation can only be attained if one belongs to a particular sect and dresses in a specific way, not otherwise. He attaches undue importance to specific clothing and believes that no one can be liberated without donning the attire of his sect. He remains weighed down spiritually, due to such a superficial attitude regarding external attributes.

To associate liberation only with external attire is an indication of sheer ignorance. Liberation is associated with the destruction of attachment and aversion, irrespective of one's outer appearance. Whether one wears ochre clothes or white, wooden footwear or none at all, long braided hair or a shaven head, the only true sign of a monk is detachment from the world. Inner renunciation is the main cause of liberation. Liberation is dependent on the inner state, whereas robes are related to the body. And since it is attained by going beyond the body, how could liberation possibly be dependent on a certain dress? Therefore, one who insists on a particular external attire does not have the right understanding or belief about the path of liberation. He is a matārthi, not an ātmārthi.

Thus, a matārthi does not know the true form of dharma. Adopting a partisan view of his sect, he strongly adheres to it. He remains preoccupied and obsessed with his obstinate ideas, firmly blinded by the grip of his own beliefs. Stubbornly pushing his opinions onto everyone else, he generates friction. So pitiable is his state that he cannot even come near self-realisation.

VERSE - 28

Bigot's belief regarding dharma

In the previous verse, Shrimadji had illustrated the false beliefs about the nature of dharma, regarding scriptures and attire. Now, He explains the wrong notions which prevail regarding the components of dharma, such as vows or restraints. Shrimadji says -

લહું સ્વરૂપ ન વૃત્તિનું, ગ્રહ્યું વ્રત અભિમાન;
ગ્રહે નહીં પરમાર્થને, લેવા લૌકિક માન. ||૨૮||

Lahyu swaroop na vruttinu, grahyu vrat abhimān;
Grahe nahi parmārthne, levā laukik mān. ||28||

Lahyu - understand; *swaroop* - nature; *na* - not; *vruttinu* - of tendencies; *grahyu* - takes; *vrat* - vows; *abhimān* - pride; *grahe* - imbibes; *nahi* - not; *parmārthne* - spiritual significance; *levā* - to gain; *laukik* - worldly; *mān* - respect

MEANING

He does not understand the nature of his tendencies and takes pride in the vows he observes. He is so interested in gaining worldly respect that he does not imbibe the true spiritual significance of vows.

EXPLANATION

There are mainly two types of tendencies: those which lean towards the self and those which lean towards worldliness.

The latter type of tendencies are detrimental to spiritual growth. They taint our thoughts, defile our speech and incite us into doing improper activities. It is necessary for one to wage a spiritual war against these tendencies and aim to vanquish them completely. Spiritual endeavour consists of uprooting impure tendencies and awakening pure dispassionate tendencies. This can be achieved in many ways such as taking vows, practising restraint, austerities and penance. Vows undertaken with the right objective are capable of destroying impure tendencies. They are like the fencing around a farm which prevents cattle from entering and ruining the crop. They prevent impure tendencies and thus enable one to focus within. It is purely for this purpose that the observance of vows has been specified.

It is of utmost necessity that a spiritual aspirant remains aware of the tendencies which govern his activities. Upon recognising his wrong tendencies, he must undertake vows to eliminate them. He needs to then examine whether his impure tendencies have been weakened by practising these vows or if he is entrapped in the pride of vows. Hence, constant vigilance is required to keep the vows aligned to the goal of eradicating impure tendencies. If the spiritual aspirant loses sight of this aspect, the wrong tendencies will continue to simultaneously prevail along with the vows, making the entire practice redundant.

A *matārthi* is one who practises vows only externally, without understanding their spiritual significance or being aware of their effect on his tendencies. Furthermore, he feels proud of his vows, creating karmic bondage. Spiritual progress is related to the purification of tendencies. However, he does not introspect to find out whether the practice leads to the purification of his tendencies or not, bypassing his own growth. The vows are worthwhile only if they aid the analysis of tendencies and the elimination of desires for sensory pleasure. The matārthi neither understands nor desires to understand questions like: What is the nature of my tendencies? What should they be like? What is the difference in my tendencies after the vows? What is the intensity of my attachment and aversion? The matārthi does not bother to introspect, feeling fulfilled upon taking external vows and fuelling his own pride, feeding his passions rather than dispelling them. He is most interested in flaunting his external activities to society and gaining respect. He inflates his own ego by comparing himself to others. This form of ego also makes him prone to criticising others.

The matārthi neither understands the nature of the self nor that of his inner tendencies. He believes that observing external vows is true conduct and chooses to be proud of himself for practising them. Even if he encounters the Sadguru due to the fruition of meritorious karma, and listens to His divine teachings, he does not adopt them as he is fearful of losing the prestige and status he has achieved by practising these vows. Fully aware that his desire to gain respect will remain unfulfilled by imbibing the true teachings, he opts to ignore them. Although the Sadguru does not negate the value of the practice of vows, He recommends that they are performed in the right way. He makes the matārthi aware of their real purpose, questioning whether they were for vanquishing pride, anger, etc., or increasing them. Whether the goal was fame or inner purity.

The matārthi is so overcome by pride that he cannot grasp spirituality or the right meaning of the vows and austerities. In order to maintain his pride, he disregards the very objective of observing vows and austerities. The thorn of ego is so deeply embedded in the mind that it proves extremely difficult to pull out. Even in the name of religion, one ends up nourishing it. Boosting the ego becomes the objective of all spiritual pursuits.

In a world enmeshed in external appearances, humanity is caught up in mere sham and show. There is no substance. Packaging is given such undue importance that the insides remain hollow and empty. Even spirituality has become a fashion statement. Religious practices are now undertaken more for attracting public attention than for blossoming virtues. Vows and austerities have become nothing more than performances that thrive on the applause of the crowd. The matārthi is fascinated by such adulation and hence engages in vows to be recognised as a highly religious person. By doing so he commits two mistakes - wrong belief by associating right practice with only external vows, and wrong conduct by creating impure feelings of pride. Thus, this verse is brimming with a profound message.

VERSE - 29

Bigot forsakes means of liberation

In verses 24-28, Shrimadji explained the characteristics of a *kriyājad matārthi* who is a mechanical ritualist. Now, in verses 29-31, He speaks about the other kind of matārthi - *shushkjnāni*, the dry intellectualist. Explaining the latter's nature in this verse, Shrimadji says -

અથવા નિશ્ચય નય ગ્રહે, માત્ર શબ્દની માંય;
લોપે સદ્‌વ્યવહારને, સાધન રહિત થાય. ॥૨૯॥

Athvā nishchay nay grahe, mātra shabdni māy;
Lopey sadvyavhārne, sādhan rahit thāy. ॥29॥

Athvā - or; *nishchay* - absolute; *nay* - viewpoint; *grahe* - adopts; *mātra* - only; *shabdni* - words; *māy* - in; *lopey* - negates; *sadvyavhārne* - right conduct; *sādhan* - means; *rahit* - without; *thāy* - becomes

MEANING
Alternatively, a bigot only verbally resorts to the absolute point of view. He negates the right conduct and becomes devoid of the means of self-realisation.

EXPLANATION
Dharma needs to be understood from both: the *nishchay naya* - absolute viewpoint, and *vyavhār naya* - relative viewpoint. In the previous five verses, Shrimadji described

the characteristics of those deluded regarding the right conduct, choosing to insist only on the relative viewpoint. Now, in three verses, He explains the characteristics of the second type of matārthi, indicated through the word '*athvā*' - or. In this verse, Shrimadji describes the matārthi who is deluded regarding the absolute viewpoint. Such a matārthi disregards the relative viewpoint and embraces only the absolute viewpoint.

Scriptures like *Samaysār, Yogvāsishtha,* etc., mainly advocate the absolute viewpoint. These texts speak of the inherent purity of the soul saying it cannot be corrupted. They describe the soul to be completely bereft of all attachments and aversions. If understood from the right perspective, they are very helpful in gaining spiritual elevation.

The shushkjnāni matārthi disregards the relative viewpoint, one-sidedly accepting that the soul is always unbound, untouched, the non-doer, but has no such experience of the soul. Hence, the absolute viewpoint remains merely as words on his tongue. Although he engages in discussions regarding the self, spouting statements like, 'I am the eternally pure blissful self', there is no actual experience of the same. An earnest study of the absolute viewpoint in the right manner strengthens the awareness of the self as being a distinct entity separate from the non-self. This is crucial to keep the seeker in an equanimous state in any challenging situation. However, a mere theoretical understanding of such a standpoint can lead to a change in one's language, but it does not bring about an inner transformation. The matārthi uses lofty words regarding the nature of the self, but does not hesitate to act in a deluded manner when faced with favourable or unfavourable situations. He absorbs the absolute viewpoint only in words, but does nothing to purify his tendencies.

If one correctly understands the teachings of the absolute viewpoint intellectually, and applies them appropriately using right conduct, he will certainly achieve the goal. However, instead of engaging in spiritual practices alongside the vision of the absolute, he clings solely to the absolute viewpoint and negates the right means like worship, restraint, detachment and humility. He rejects the means that lead to liberation and remains bereft of spiritual practices.

He strongly believes that inauspicious activities lead to unmeritorious karma and auspicious activities lead to meritorious karma, therefore both are bondage and not worth pursuing. He does not realise that one needs to proceed stepwise on the spiritual path keeping in mind the ultimate goal. Inauspicious activities are eliminated by auspicious activities and these too need to eventually be surpassed to pave way for abidance in the self. Just as climbing the ladder and letting go of it are both required to reach the terrace, one needs to engage in them and go beyond them in order to achieve liberation. However, one cannot begin by giving up auspicious practices while the inauspicious continue to exist. It conveys a dislike and disrespect for the means that are beneficial to one's spiritual progress. One requires a certain alertness to not feel fulfilled by merely performing auspicious activities but by having a proper understanding of their nuances and focusing on the goal while doing them. If they are not undertaken with the right intention and understanding, not an iota of self-awareness is attained, nor are attachment and aversion subverted. It is important to note that this does not imply such practices should be discarded. Whatever means lead to awakening must be undertaken and not forsaken. The opposition of rituals, vows, etc., divulge a wrong understanding of dharma.

Thus, mere knowledge of the true nature of the self as described in the scriptures can hardly get one going on the spiritual path. It entangles one in a maze of words. He may continue to travel in the realm of language but remains lost, as his knowledge is not accompanied by right practices. Hence, he should not dwell in the world of words, finding fulfilment in them. Neither does a menu card satisfy hunger, nor does the formula of water quench thirst. Similarly, one cannot feed on words, substance is required. Hence, when the matārthi views books to be the end of the journey, he loses sight of the goal. By negating the vital means which help one attain the absolute, he wanders in the dense forest of transmigration.

VERSE - 30

Association of bigot

The *shushkjnāni matārthi* gives up the means which are instrumental in bringing about his upliftment. This is further explained in detail in the next two verses. Now, in this verse, describing the fate of those who associate with such ignorant ones, Shrimadji says -

જ્ઞાનદશા પામે નહીં, સાધનદશા ન કાંઈ;
પામે તેનો સંગ જે, તે બૂડે ભવ માંહી. ||૩૦||

Jnāndashā pāmey nahi, sādhandashā na kāi;
Pāmey teno sang je, te budey bhav māhi. ||30||

Jnāndashā - state of self-realisation; *pāmey* - attains; *nahi* - not; *sādhandashā* - state of spiritual practice; *na* - not; *kāi* - any; *pāmey* - attains; *teno* - his; *sang* - company; *je* - those; *te* - they; *budey* - drowns; *bhav* - transmigration; *māhi* - in

MEANING

Neither does he attain the state of self-realisation, nor does he have the state of spiritual practice. Those who stay in his company also drown in the ocean of transmigration.

EXPLANATION

Acquiring knowledge of the self is merely the beginning. The final objective should be to abide in the self. This goal can be achieved by applying scriptural knowledge for purifying one's internal tendencies. It cannot be achieved if the understanding remains only at the verbal level.

The earlier verse described the shushkjnāni matārthi who is deluded regarding the absolute viewpoint. Although he studies texts that primarily expound the absolute viewpoint, he does not understand the author's intention. Resorting to imbibing it only in words, he is neither touched by a corresponding experience, nor does he possess virtues. Hence, he does not attain the true state of enlightenment, becoming knowledgeable only in words, not in terms of experience of the self. The purpose of the absolute viewpoint is to manifest the state of enlightenment with pure self-experience through an inner transformation. However, the matārthi is satisfied with a mere intellectual understanding of the absolute viewpoint and does not make the inner effort to turn towards the self. Hence, he cannot attain the state of self-awareness.

Moreover, due to an incomplete understanding of the absolute viewpoint, he remains totally bereft of the means to attain self-realisation by negating right conduct. Hence, he does not attain the state of spiritual practice which is instrumental in attaining the goal of enlightenment. One cannot satisfy hunger by discarding the means of cooking such as a stove, vessels, etc. Similarly, one cannot reach the state of enlightenment by discarding the means to achieve self-realisation.

Thus, the shushkjnāni matārthi has not attained that effortless state of enlightenment and does not even put in the required effort - spiritual practices to attain this state. Devoid of both, he falls prey to impure feelings like desires, passions, etc., and drowns in the ocean of transmigration.

The irony is that such a matārthi, ensnared in the web of words, believes himself to be an enlightened being. He attracts gullible people with strong logic and an ability to speak well. He misguides unsuspecting people with his oratory skills, inducing them to adopt his one-sided views, rendering them vulnerable to the cycles of birth and death. Those who revere and associate with such doubly-fallen matārthis, who have not reached the state of enlightenment nor even the state of spiritual practice which leads to enlightenment, also drown in the ocean of transmigration. It is impossible for one who can neither swim nor has the means to swim, to save another from drowning. Such ignorant ones drown themselves and are instrumental in drowning others as well.

The shushkjnāni matārthi is deluded by his own illusion of knowledge, believing he can open the door leading to truth. However, he cannot arrive at the truth without first inculcating qualities of detachment, devotion, etc., within himself. Simply mouthing the scriptures does not prove to be enough. To reap the fruit of wisdom, one has to prepare the soil for it first. Only by cultivating the requisite qualities can one reap the fruit of enlightenment. Not only does he fail in this respect, but also infects those unfortunates who come in contact with him with his deluded views.

Thus, this verse stresses the power of association. It can prove to be so dangerous that it is better to be alone than in bad company. The company of such a matārthi can cause immense damage to oneself. Therefore, one should not get trapped in the company of a matārthi, but seek the association of a Sadguru which leads to enlightenment.

VERSE - 31

Bigots stand disqualified

Shrimadji considers the *shushkjnāni*, who is deluded regarding the absolute truth and cannot attain spiritual welfare, to be a *matārthi*. Explaining this, Shrimadji says -

એ પણ જીવ મતાર્થમાં, નિજમાનાદિ કાજ;
પામે નહિ પરમાર્થને, અન્-અધિકારીમાં જ. ||૩૧||

Ae pan jeev matārthmā, nijmānādi kāj;
Pāmey nahi parmārthne, an-adhikārimāj. ||31||

Ae - that; *pan* - also; *jeev* - person; *matārthmā* - in bigotry; *nijmānādi* - own pride etc.; *kāj* - for; *pāmey* - attains; *nahi* - not; *parmārthne* - supreme truth; *an-adhikārimāj* - in unqualified certainly

MEANING

That kind of person is also stuck in bigotry as he wants to satisfy his own pride, etc. He does not attain the supreme truth and is certainly counted amongst the unworthy ones.

EXPLANATION

A dry intellectualist also indulges in bigotry. By remaining occupied with defending his opinions, he misses out on his spiritual welfare and is unable to attain the supreme truth. In the first line of this verse, using the word '*pan*' - also, Shrimadji indicates that just like in the earlier verses 24-28, in which the deluded *kriyājad,* who believes he is practising right conduct, falls in the category of the matārthis; the shushkjnāni, who is deluded about the absolute viewpoint is surely categorised amongst the matārthis.

Since a kriyājad is attached to his own viewpoint, he insists on following his own family Guru and religion, and donning the external attire of his sect. This amounts to behaving like a bigot. Similarly, the shushkjnāni studies spiritual scriptures based on self-will, rote-learns the statements of the absolute viewpoint, and insists upon them without truly letting the spirit of those words touch his heart. Solely to safeguard his own pride and status in society, he does not let go of his opinions and acts in a bigoted manner. Both these types of matārthis believe that they are truly spiritual and lead others to believe the same. The mechanical ritualist cherishes the ego of being labelled devout while the dry intellectualist cherishes the ego of being labelled knowledgeable.

To reach the goal of liberation, one has to sacrifice his ego. It is imperative to learn to forsake pride in one's abilities, activities and achievements. And if not done, it proves to be a limitation that trips one on the spiritual path. When pride is nurtured and allowed to thrive, it grows to become arrogance. Although it is called sweet poison, whether bitter or sweet, it is poison nonetheless. The ignorant soul performs all deeds to nourish his own pride. This is why he does not attain liberation and continues to be entrapped in the cycles of birth and death, enduring infinite sorrow indefinitely. The shushkjnāni matārthi seeks recognition and appreciation for the knowledge he possesses. He endlessly harps about it with immense pride, boasting in front of others to feed his own ego. There exists so much ego within him that it keeps rearing its ugly head.

In order to attain fame, the shushkjnāni matārthi follows the wrong path. Sometimes, even shunning the right path though it is illuminated by the Sadguru, only because of his ego. If he accepted the truth, he would have to admit he was wrong, an act he is averse to as it would be ego-crushing. Caught in a circular loop of biased thoughts, he misses the highway that leads to the supreme truth. Wherever bigotry exists, truth does not, and so he is unable to attain spiritual welfare. He stands unworthy of self-realisation, remaining ineligible, unqualified and undeserving of gaining the supreme essence. Only those who possess an intense desire for inner transformation can attain the supreme truth. It cannot be attained by simply performing rituals, studying scriptures, carrying a label or tag of a particular sect, joining a group or community, or obstinately following an ideology or custom. Only those who want to be free from desires and passions are worthy of attaining the supreme truth.

VERSE - 32

Common attributes of bigots

In verses 24-31, Shrimadji described the distinct characteristics of the two types of *matārthis* - *kriyājad* and *shushkjnāni,* and illustrated that they are both unworthy for the attainment of the supreme truth. Now, in this verse, enumerating the common characteristics of both types of matārthis, Shrimadji says -

નહિ કષાય ઉપશાંતતા, નહિ અંતર વૈરાગ્ય;
સરળપણું ન મધ્યસ્થતા, એ મતાર્થી દુર્ભાગ્ય. ||૩૨||

Nahi kashāy upshāntatā, nahi antar vairāgya;
Saralpanu na madhyasthatā, ae matārthi durbhāgya. ||32||

Nahi - no; *kashāy* - passions; *upshāntatā* - subsidence; *nahi* - no; *antar* - inner; *vairāgya* - detachment; *saralpanu* - straightforwardness; *na* - no; *madhyasthatā* - neutrality; *ae* - that; *matārthi* - bigot; *durbhāgya* - unfortunate

MEANING

Unfortunate is the bigot who has no subsidence of passions, no inner detachment, no straightforwardness and no neutral attitude.

EXPLANATION

The one who does not possess comforts and luxuries of the material world is not the unfortunate one. The true unfortunate one is he who does not possess the attributes to make himself worthy of obtaining the spiritual path. Hence, even if one has attained several outlets of sensual pleasures, he is considered unfortunate if he has not set out on the path of liberation. A matārthi is unfortunate because he cannot attain that spiritual path which brings an end to the cycles of birth-old age-death, despite engaging in religious activities, due to his flaws. Shrimadji explains the common traits of kriyājad and shushkjnāni matārthis by outlining the absence of four principal virtues in them -

1. A matārthi has not decreased his passions. His anger, pride, deceitfulness and greed have not yet been quietened. Due to these strong passions, his mind remains impure, disturbed and constantly fluctuating. The pursuit of spiritual welfare requires a profound and calm mind. One whose mind gets affected by petty events, good or bad, and either swings in the skies of joy or plummets into the depths of despair, cannot pursue the path of liberation.

2. A matārthi lacks inner detachment. His mind keeps rushing towards external objects. Under the spell of delusion, he finds joy in worldly events and is attached to them. Despite a strict adherence to discipline and restraint or engaging in scriptural studies, his worldly desires do not dry up. The pursuit of spiritual welfare requires the fading of attraction and curiosity towards sensual pleasures. The one who finds sweetness in worldly pleasures cannot pursue the path of liberation.

3. A matārthi does not have straightforwardness. He does not have the softness to accept his faults and imbibe virtues. Straightforwardness comes forth by overcoming vanity and deception. A crooked mind creates havoc and

damage. The pursuit of spiritual welfare requires interest and the inclination to cultivate virtues. One who lacks straightforwardness and the ability to accept his flaws cannot pursue the path of liberation.

4. A matārthi does not have the impartial vision which enables one to distinguish between right and wrong. Due to an attachment to his own viewpoints, he insists on his beliefs and calls it steadfastness. He is always embroiled in debates and disputes. The pursuit of spiritual welfare requires an open mind, free from obstinacy and self-opinionated nature. Hence, one who does not have an impartial, neutral attitude that can evaluate and discern things properly, cannot pursue the path of liberation.

Thus, a matārthi remains ineligible and unworthy due to the absence of virtues that qualify one to attain the path of liberation. Until these virtues arise within, he remains incapable of pursuing self-realisation. However, if he properly understands his shortcomings and proceeds to eliminate them, he can achieve spiritual welfare. Here, Shrimadji has given a complete description of a matārthi. This covers all areas of his personality - from the mind full of distractions, to the heart full of desire, and to the character full of prejudices. His quest will indeed be futile as he does not possess the qualities of a true seeker nor the sensibility to determine the right direction. A matārthi's mind is like a feeble straw in the wind with little control. Only one with a steady and pure mind can attain self-realisation.

VERSE - 33

Purpose of explanation

In the previous nine verses 24-32, Shrimadji explained in detail the attributes of those unfortunate ones who strayed from the path while engaging in the means of spiritual welfare. Now, concluding this section, Shrimadji says -

લક્ષણ કહ્યાં મતાર્થીનાં, મતાર્થ જાવા કાજ;
હવે કહું આત્માર્થીનાં, આત્મ-અર્થ સુખસાજ. ||33||

Lakshan kahyā matārthinā, matārth jāvā kāj;
Havey kahu ātmārthinā, ātma-arth sukhsāj. ||33||

Lakshan - attributes; *kahyā* - stated; *matārthinā* - of bigot; *matārth* - bigotry; *jāvā* - removing; *kāj* - for; *havey* - now; *kahu* - will state; *ātmārthinā* - of true seeker; *ātma-arth* - for soul; *sukhsāj* - cause of bliss

MEANING

The characteristics of a bigot have been stated for the purpose of identifying and eliminating bigotry. Now, I will state the characteristics of a true seeker, which are the causes that enable the soul to attain bliss.

EXPLANATION

It is expected that the attributes of an *ātmārthi* would be described in the auspicious Shri Ātmasiddhi Shāstra. However, one might question why the attributes of a *matārthi* are explained here in such great detail. Shrimadji explains that the sole purpose of the elaborate description of a matārthi is to enable the reader of Shri Ātmasiddhi Shāstra to introspect and recognise any such flaws, and to work towards eliminating them.

While in the clutches of bigotry, the ignorance that sets in is such that one becomes unable to recognise his own flaws. In this lethal combination of being caught in the net of bigotry and yet blind to this captivity, he practises obstinacy under the garb of firmness. The signs that help in identifying bigotry are so vividly and accurately portrayed in Shri Ātmasiddhi Shāstra, that if reflected upon without any bias, one can clearly recognise the bigotry within himself. Once these are identified, by reading and contemplating upon them, it becomes possible to give them up. Hence, it is here only for the benefit of the matārthi - to enable him to detect wrong beliefs, rectify his attitude and be cognisant of the real understanding. They have been depicted to warn him from blindly running in circles and guide him to walk the right path.

Thus, it is only with a spiritual intention that Shrimadji describes the attributes of a matārthi, to allow him to get rid of all flaws and thereby uplift his soul. The noble intention is to caution the spiritual seeker of such contrary tendencies that lead him away from the path of liberation. He becomes wary of the pitfalls so that he can avoid them. By knowing where the danger lies, one can steer clear of that territory. Stamping out the hindrances, his mind becomes receptive and his disposition is geared to imbibe the truth. Now, he does not have to chase self-realisation, instead it comes looking for him. Indeed, the description of the matārthi's attributes serve as a lighthouse, saving spiritual aspirants from getting swept away in the undercurrents of mechanical ritualism and dry intellectualism. The attributes of the matārthi are compassionately portrayed to eliminate bigotry, which causes misery.

Now, Shrimadji pledges that He will describe the attributes of an ātmārthi, which lead to true happiness. In the next nine verses, He elaborates the attributes of an ātmārthi, which are instrumental in attaining the infinite bliss of liberation. The characteristics of such truth seekers are highlighted in the next section.

Attributes of a True Seeker

In order to help one eradicate bigotry, the attributes of a *matārthi* were described in verses 24-33. Now, for the purpose of cultivating the virtues of a true seeker, which enable one to experience the endless and unobstructed bliss of the soul, the attributes of an *ātmārthi* have been explained in verses 34-42. An ātmārthi is one who seeks the self or in other words, the one who aims solely to attain self-realisation. Instead of simply stating that an ātmārthi is one who does not have the traits of a matārthi, Shrimadji has perfectly described the ideal mindset of the former, who is desirous of liberation. This is because such a positive description is of great help to a spiritual aspirant, inspiring him to cultivate and further develop the requisite attributes within himself.

When the desire to embrace spiritual welfare arises in one who has been aimlessly wandering in the infinite cycles of birth and death since time immemorial, he begins a deep reflection on the causes and the means that eliminate transmigration. This deliberation becomes so intense that it turns into a deep longing. This in turn leads to a painful yearning for a complete release from transmigration. His attachment to sensual pleasures reduces, with self-realisation now becoming his supreme aim. He only wishes to live at the lotus feet of the Sadguru - the very embodiment of truth. Progressing on the path of upliftment of the self, his main flaw, self-will, which prevailed over infinite lifetimes begins to lose its feisty, iron-like grip over him. This release, prompts his speedy progress in the direction of spiritual welfare. As his interest in the self increases, he delves deeper and deeper until he resides there permanently. Thus, by taking refuge in the Sadguru, gaining the right understanding and living earnestly, he is rapidly able to attain a state of absolute purity.

This section of nine verses can be divided into two parts. In verses 34-36, Shrimadji depicts the ātmārthi's concepts regarding the Sadguru and the path of liberation. These three verses provide an insight into his clarity of thought. Verses 37-42 emphasise the need of worthiness and enumerate the requisite virtues an aspirant must cultivate. He underlines the distinguishing qualities of head and heart that the seeker needs to possess - an open mind, humility, desire to surrender to the Guru and overwhelming need for self-realisation. Thereafter, Shrimadji concisely charts out the journey of an ātmārthi up to liberation in the refuge of a Sadguru.

VERSE - 34

True seeker's belief regarding Sadguru

Describing the *ātmārthi's* belief regarding the most important and fundamental aspect - the nature of the Sadguru, Shrimadji says -

આત્મજ્ઞાન ત્યાં મુનિપણું, તે સાચા ગુરુ હોય;
બાકી કુળગુરુ કલ્પના, આત્માર્થી નહિ જોય. ||૩૪||

Ātmajnān tyā munipanu, Te sāchā Guru hoi;
Bāki kulguru kalpanā, ātmārthi nahi joi. ||34||

Ātmajnān - self-realisation; *tyā* - there; *munipanu* - monkhood;
Te - He; *sāchā* - true; *Guru* - Mentor; *hoi* - is; *bāki* - otherwise;
kulguru - family Mentor; *kalpanā* - delusion; *ātmārthi* - true seeker;
nahi - not; *joi* - accept

MEANING

Self-realisation is essential for monkhood; only such a one is a true Guru. Therefore, an aspirant does not get caught in the delusion of considering a family Guru to be a true Guru.

EXPLANATION

Worldly people are caught in the endless demands of professions, possessions, identities and inclinations. They are not in touch with their true self. What is worse, is their propensity to seek help from false quarters - be it a mere external renunciate or an anointed family Guru. However, this search is never rewarded. An obvious outcome is that the key itself does not fit the door to be opened. Hence, it is essential to first seek the right key. The search for a true Guru is of paramount importance on the path of spiritual pursuit.

It is customary to accept a monk as a Guru. The very idea of external renunciation is so impressive that the layman cannot help but revere a monk. However, in reality, true monkhood is an internal state, not an external one. True monkhood is said to exist only when self-realisation is present. Hence, where there is no self-realisation, there cannot be true monkhood. Not all monks are self-realised. A person might have renounced everything, embraced the external attire of a monk and even adhered to strict vows, but this does not imply that he is self-realised. Until one experiences the true nature of the self, he remains stuck in the grip of wrong belief, despite practising restraint and discipline.

After attaining self-realisation, one becomes only a witness to worldly happenings. Enjoying the bliss of the soul, external desires fade away. Even amidst the adversities of body and circumstances, He remains aware that He is the soul, the body is separate, and happiness is within. As abidance in the self increases and attachment to the world decreases, the true state of monkhood manifests. He now becomes more and more dispassionate, finally striving for the completely pure state. Therefore, it is apparent that one requires self-realisation to be called a true monk, not mere external robes or vows. Only such a one can be called a true Guru. In other words, only one who has experienced the self is a real saint and He alone can be considered a true Guru - self-realisation being the very first attribute of the Sadguru as mentioned in verse 10. This does not imply that one should not respect a monk or someone who has renounced the external, but one should not brand such a person a Guru unless he is self-realised. To believe someone to be a Guru without that person possessing self-realisation will not lead one to the truth.

An ātmārthi is very clear in his beliefs regarding who can be considered a true Guru. He accepts only the one who possesses the experience of the blissful self to be a true Guru. One may possess scriptural knowledge, give lectures, have a high degree of external renunciation, perform severe austerities, or perhaps even be accepted as a family or a sect Guru, but if he is without self-realisation, the ātmārthi does not accept him as the Sadguru. He recognises the futility of worshipping an ignorant Guru of his family tradition. He knows with absolute certainty that the cycles of birth and death cannot be stopped while being sheltered by a Mentor who himself does not possess self-realisation. The ātmārthi does not insist on a particular sect, custom, attire, etc., to be the true one. He does not blindly follow the Guru worshipped by his forefathers. He does not feel guilty or scared of not following the traditions in order to walk on the true path. He fearlessly discards the traditions if they do not fulfil his spiritual needs.

The *matārthi* considers one who has external renunciation or is worshipped by his forefathers to be the Sadguru. In stark contrast, the ātmārthi lays importance on self-realisation and not external renunciation or family beliefs. He accepts only a self-realised one as the Sadguru. Thus, verse 34 has been composed with reference to verse 24 regarding the concept of a Guru. Verse 24 described the matārthi's stubbornness regarding the external renunciate and attachment for his traditional Guru. In contrast, verse 34 describes the ātmārthi's importance for self-realisation and not merely external renunciation. He is convinced that only one who has experienced the self can help him experience the self.

Thus, the primary attitude of an ātmārthi has been attributed to his correct concept of the nature of a true Guru. By entrusting the responsibility of identifying a true Guru to the ātmārthi, Shrimadji has revealed the lofty nature of an ātmārthi's understanding. Without possessing the right discerning vision and a mature ability to examine, it is impossible to identify the Sadguru. The ātmārthi recognises the Sadguru, takes refuge in Him and destroys the chain of transmigration.

VERSE - 35

◇~∽๑

Living Sadguru is a blessing

Having explained what kind of a Guru an *ātmārthi* is devoted to, in this verse, Shrimadji describes the kind of devotion he has for the Guru. Shrimadji says -

પ્રત્યક્ષ સદ્‌ગુરુ પ્રાપ્તિનો, ગણે પરમ ઉપકાર;
ત્રણે યોગ એકત્વથી, વર્તે આજ્ઞાધાર. ||૩૫||

Pratyaksh Sadguru prāptino, ganey param upkār;
Trane   yog   ekatvathi,   varte   ājnādhār. ||35||

Pratyaksh - living; *Sadguru* - enlightened Mentor; *prāptino* - attainment of; *ganey* - considers; *param* - supreme; *upkār* - benefit; *trane* - all three; *yog* - energies of mind, speech, body; *ekatvathi* - in unison; *varte* - acts; *ājnādhār* - as per commands

MEANING

A true seeker considers the attainment of a living Sadguru to be supremely beneficial and follows His commands with the unison of all the three energies of mind, speech and body.

EXPLANATION

It is not enough for a seeker to only aspire for true knowledge. He also needs to seek a Sadguru who can bless him with such knowledge. So powerful is the Sadguru's presence and proximity that just one benevolent look from Him can dry up the vast ocean of material attachment. So enchanting is His oration that it vaporises all desires. Enveloped in the

Sadguru's grace, enlightenment emerges in the worthy disciple as naturally as leaves to a tree and wings to a bird. The main requirement is surrendering to Him with respect and humility.

The attainment of the association with an enlightened one is the fruit of meritorious past karma, whereas the attainment of enlightenment is the fruit of present efforts. However, one cannot put in the right efforts without the teachings of an enlightened one. Unfortunately, one cannot meet an omniscient *Jina* in this era and region. Fortunately, it is possible to meet a living enlightened Sadguru. As a result of the fruition of strong karmic merit of the past, one gains the association of an enlightened one who is endowed with the attributes of a Sadguru. When an ātmārthi meets a Sadguru, he develops immense reverence for Him and surrenders himself to Him.

The ātmārthi understands and feels the worth of the Sadguru's association. For him, the value of the world diminishes and the value of the Sadguru intensifies. So, with immense gratitude, he holds in his heart the enlightened one's benevolence in the highest regard. He considers the association with a living Sadguru to be supremely beneficial as all questions, doubts, curiosity and confusion that cannot be solved by the scriptures are totally resolved by Him. More importantly, that glorious essence which has been elusive since time immemorial, unattainable, a distant dream, despite practising infinite external means is attained in a short time through His grace. By following the Sadguru's guidance, one's uncontrollable flaws are destroyed with very little effort and several virtues like forgiveness, modesty, straightforwardness, etc., blossom easily and quickly. The ātmārthi holds within this indestructible conviction that the supreme benevolence of the living Sadguru is greater than that of anyone else.

The ātmārthi firmly believes that the refuge of the living Sadguru is the simplest and best way to attain the bliss of the self. The only requirement is that one needs to follow His '*ājnā*' - commands, with wholehearted dedication. It is more important to hold inner devotion than to bow the head, fold one's hands, touch His feet or talk sweetly. Only by obeying the Sadguru's ājnā does one become a true disciple. It serves as a barricade, preventing one from the endless cycles of transmigration. If the ājnā is executed with unison of mind-speech-body, then the outcome of the Sadguru's association is that virtues begin to bloom in the disciple. Fortified with the strength of this firm faith, the ātmārthi commences the necessary effort and acts according to the Sadguru's ājnā. The energies of mind-speech-body stand united, only wishing to carry out these commands. Having understood that when these faculties act according to self-will, it leads to bondage, the ātmārthi engages them in following the Sadguru's ājnā and hence fulfils this priceless association.

VERSE - 36

True seeker's belief regarding path of liberation

The *ātmārthi* holds the utmost veneration for the Sadguru who is the supreme pillar of support in the attainment of spirituality. Giving up self-will, he follows the Sadguru's *ājnā* and makes an earnest effort to pursue the path of liberation. Throwing light on the ātmārthi's belief regarding the path of liberation, Shrimadji says -

એક હોય ત્રણ કાળમાં, પરમારથનો પંથ;
પ્રેરે તે પરમાર્થને, તે વ્યવહાર સમંત. ||૩૬||

Ek hoi tran kālmā, parmārathno panth;
Prere te parmārthne, te vyavhār samant. ||36||

Ek - one; *hoi* - is; *tran* - three; *kālmā* - in times; *parmārathno* - of supreme truth; *panth* - path; *prere* - inspires; *te* - that; *parmārthne* - supreme truth; *te* - that; *vyavhār* - practice; *samant* - accepted

MEANING

The absolute path to attain the supreme truth is only one in all three periods of time - past, present and future. Those practices which lead to it should be accepted.

EXPLANATION

In the previous verse, it was stated that the ātmārthi acts in accordance with the Sadguru's commands with the absolute unison of mind-speech-body. The Sadguru's commands are of various forms. If the intention behind them is not fully grasped, it becomes difficult to follow them wholeheartedly. A precise understanding of the path of liberation makes it easier to follow the commands of the Sadguru. Therefore, the ātmārthi's concept about the path of liberation has been described in this verse. As and when the worthiness of an ātmārthi increases, subtle insights and resolutions regarding the path of liberation naturally manifest in him. The right beliefs regarding various aspects of the path take shape in him.

The ātmārthi has a firm conviction that across all three periods of time - past, present and future, the absolute path of liberation is only one, not two. In other words, no variation in the path exists, neither liberation nor the path can ever be altered at any period of time. It remains constant throughout eternity. The one who practises the three jewels, right faith-right knowledge-right conduct, attains the uninterrupted blissful state of liberation which has remained elusive since time immemorial.

The path is undivided, and it is the same in all three periods of time, as well as all places too. The attainment of the supreme truth does not take place in a certain way in the fourth era and another way in the fifth era, it remains absolutely the same across all eras. Although the circumstances of a particular period of time could be inferior or superior for spiritual progress, the path remains the same.

In the same way, it is not true that the attainment of liberation occurs in a particular manner in *Mahāvideh kshetra*, and in another manner in *Bharat kshetra* and *Airāvat kshetra* - regions in Jain cosmology. It is possible that during certain periods of time or in some particular regions there may be either several or fewer means of pursuing the path. However, there is no difference in the path of spirituality whatsoever. The spiritual path is not different in different regions, as it is dependent on the self, which is the same everywhere.

Moreover, it is the same for all beings. The path tread by Lord *Rushabhdev* and the one tread by Lord *Mahāvir* was the same. Which is, to stay absorbed in the self. Thus, the spiritual path of the oneness of faith-knowledge-conduct remains the same at all times. The practices which aid the pursuit of the spiritual path are worth accepting. The means which inspire one to tread the spiritual path should be adopted.

For spiritual pursuit, various faiths and philosophies advocate differing means, rituals and practices. This is because the means to achieve the spiritual path are dependent on several factors including time, place, circumstances and capacity of people, hence naturally different. However, if they lead to the absolute path of liberation, they should be accepted. The external form of spiritual pursuit is activity-based and the absolute path is experience-based. The activities undertaken are helpful in gaining the experience of the self. They are instrumental in abidance in the self, and the depletion of passions. Therefore, such practices have been approved by the enlightened ones and they are certainly worth following.

The ātmārthi respects all the means and practices which are instrumental in attaining the spiritual path. He neither gets confused by different practices nor insists upon the practice he performs. He does not get stuck in the external form. Whether the external behaviour measures up to the ideal is reflected in the manner in which one gets engrossed within and becomes free from passions. Thus, the spiritual path is one in all three periods of time and only those practices that are helpful in attaining it are worth accepting. Such is the faith of the ātmārthi, which is vital on the path.

VERSE - 37

Seek Sadguru with true purpose

In verses 34-36, Shrimadji revealed the *ātmārthi's* clarity of concepts regarding the path of liberation and the one who shows that path, the Sadguru. Explaining what the ātmārthi does thereafter, in this verse Shrimadji says -

એમ વિચારી અંતરે, શોધે સદ્‌ગુરુ યોગ;
કામ એક આત્માર્થનું, બીજો નહિ મનરોગ. ॥૩૭॥

Em vichāri antare, shodhe Sadguru yog;
Kām ek ātmārthnu, bijo nahi mannrog. ||37||

Em - thus; *vichāri* - thinking; *antare* - internally; *shodhe* - searches; *Sadguru* - enlightened Mentor; *yog* - association; *kām* - desire; *ek* - one; *ātmārthnu* - of spiritual welfare; *bijo* - other; *nahi* - no; *mannrog* - mental disease of cravings

MEANING

Thus, thinking internally, the true seeker searches for an association with a Sadguru. He has only one desire, to attain self-realisation and harbours no other mental disease of cravings.

EXPLANATION

It has been previously established that the spiritual path is one and the same in all three periods of time. The practice which propels one on this singular spiritual path is worth following. Since such practice is dependent on a true Guru, it is absolutely essential to be associated with a Sadguru. The ātmārthi is one who wants to pursue the spiritual path. Nobody else other than the living Sadguru has the ability to guide him. One cannot take even a single step forward on the inner journey without a Sadguru. Since the aspiration to realise the true self has arisen in the ātmārthi, he needs the advice and handholding of a Sadguru more than ever before. He has understood that the Sadguru is a living representative of divinity. He has also realised the importance of the Sadguru to accomplish his objective. The ātmārthi has such reverence for His greatness that he believes if he met a self-realised Guru all his flaws would be annihilated; he would become soul-focused and advance on the path. He knows the Sadguru's association will be supremely beneficial.

Thinking this, the ātmārthi who desires spiritual welfare, seeks a living Sadguru and eagerly embarks upon the search for an enlightened one. Through the fruition of strong spiritual merit, when he meets such a one and identifies His divinity, immense devotion arises towards Him. He surrenders his ego at the Sadguru's lotus feet and obeys Him with true dedication. The Sadguru showers blessings on him and through His infinite grace, the ātmārthi begins to succeed in the mighty battle against internal disturbances and external temptations. Earnestly following the Sadguru's commands, the ātmārthi turns towards the self. His deluded vision gradually decreases and spiritual vision gradually increases.

The ātmārthi aspires only for the welfare of his soul. His solitary longing is to attain the blissful self. All his actions are directed towards that goal. If someone aims to become a millionaire, all his acts are concentrated towards making money. So, whether he is working, sleeping, eating and even while dreaming, all his activities are aligned to this goal of making millions. In the same way, the ātmārthi performs his duties, but does not lose sight of his goal of self-realisation.

The ātmārthi's mind is not gripped by the desire for respect, honour, wealth or worldly accomplishments. The desire for prosperity, power, prestige, status, and fame is a disease of the mind. His mind is not afflicted by any such ailment of craving. He has the inner conviction that his happiness, peace and security only lie within him and so there is no need to seek anything in the external. Having resolved that the nature of the self is blissful consciousness, his interest in the truth continues to increase while that in the external world continues to decrease. He wishes to refrain from engaging in fresh worldly initiatives and gaining more possessions. No worldly object or occurrence entices him anymore and neither is he elated by respect nor honour. He remains completely indifferent in such situations. He has absolutely no desire other than the pursuit of the self.

VERSE - 38

Identity of true seeker

Spiritual welfare is the only goal of an *ātmārthi*. Elucidating the nature of a person who yearns for spiritual welfare, explaining the attributes of an ātmārthi, Shrimadji says -

કષાયની ઉપશાંતતા, માત્ર મોક્ષ અભિલાષ;
ભવે ખેદ, પ્રાણીદયા, ત્યાં આત્માર્થ નિવાસ. ||૩૮||

Kashāyni upshāntatā, mātra moksh abhilāsh;
Bhavey khed, prānidayā, tyā ātmārth nivās. ||38||

Kashāyni - of passions; **upshāntatā** - subsidence; **mātra** - only; **moksh** - liberation; **abhilāsh** - desire; **bhavey** - transmigration; **khed** - grief; **prānidayā** - compassion for all beings; **tyā** - there; **ātmārth** - spiritual welfare; **nivās** - abode

MEANING

Search for truth resides where there is subsidence of passions, where liberation is the only desire, where there is grief for the cycles of birth and death, and where there is compassion for all living beings.

EXPLANATION

The inner state of one aspiring for self-realisation has been depicted here. Just as Shrimadji had described the common attributes of *matārthis* in verse 32, He describes the attributes of ātmārthis in this verse. One who does not possess any of the attributes portrayed here cannot be called a seeker of the supreme truth, and until they manifest, cannot even hope to attain this truth. In other words, one who wishes to attain spiritual welfare to end the transmigration ongoing since time infinite and experience unobstructed happiness, must first cultivate the necessary attributes within him. These attributes are stated below -

1. *Kashāyni upshāntatā* - Subsidence of passions

The ātmārthi has weakened passions like anger, pride, deceit and greed. Passions prove to be an obstruction to the manifestation of virtues like forgiveness, humility, straightforwardness and contentment. If one tends to be impulsive, or at the mercy of trivial whims, he ends up causing immense damage to himself. The ātmārthi is aware of this and strives to subdue all his passions by focusing on the self. He remains vigilant to ensure he does not involve himself in triggering situations, and manages to withdraw from them in case passions flare up. As he subjugates the intense feelings of anger and other passions, calmness arises and continues to grow within him. Where the passions have subsided, there exists purity of mind and hence, there is a longing for self-realisation.

2. *Mātra moksh abhilāsh* - Sole desire for liberation

The raging fire of the ātmārthi's desire for liberation sets all other desires ablaze. His life is no longer governed by the desire for comforts and pleasures, and he is not anchored in tendencies of sensual indulgence. He is convinced that the so-called happiness of the world is momentary, impermanent and perishable. So, it cannot be real. He is aware that worldly happiness is only followed by sorrow. That uninterrupted, unobstructed and imperishable happiness lies only in the self. Therefore, his only desire is to attain the bliss of the self and he aspires to achieve this purest state. When an exclusive desire for liberation persists, no worldly desires remain and hence, there is a longing for self-realisation.

3. ***Bhavey khed*** - Grief of transmigration
The ātmārthi understands the irrefutable fact that the world is full of misery, and misery alone. He has wandered aimlessly and suffered hardships in various states of existence. He wants to cross the ocean of birth and death once and for all. He feels remorse for his faults and futile pursuits. His perspective regarding the world, sensual pleasures, and the body takes a paradigm shift. The world appears worthless, undependable and unreliable - sensual pleasures seem to be a disease - the body emerges as merely an association. Such discerning thoughts increase the presence of detachment within him. Where there is grief regarding transmigration, there is no interest in worldliness and hence, there is a longing for self-realisation.

4. ***Prānidayā*** - Compassion for all living beings
The ātmārthi views all living beings with the same lens as he views himself. So, what he wishes for himself, he wishes for others. He harbours feelings of kindness and happiness, wishing that all beings in the universe be happy and no one suffers. He remains alert to prevent any being from

suffering due to him. He becomes sensitive and refrains from hurting others through his mind-speech-body, and instead endeavours to contribute to their happiness. Fuelled by the feeling of compassion, his thinking becomes right, pure, subtle and sharp. Where there is a feeling of compassion, there is softness of heart and hence, there is a longing for self-realisation.

Thus, he who possesses these four virtues is alone worthy of attaining the path to liberation. Whoever has these attributes is a genuine ātmārthi and qualifies to attain the self. The absence of the above-mentioned attributes signifies the absence of the longing for self-realisation. Equipped with these virtues, the ātmārthi ceases to fluctuate, rather advances steadily on the path while keeping his sight on the goal.

VERSE - 39

Need to attain worthiness

Until one attains such a state of worthiness, he is not qualified to attain the experience of the pure self. In this verse, using the method of negative assertion to show the importance of worthiness, Shrimadji says -

દશા ન એવી જ્યાં સુધી, જીવ લહે નહિ જોગ;
મોક્ષમાર્ગ પામે નહીં, મટે ન અંતર રોગ. ||૩૯||

Dashā na evi jyā sudhi, jeev lahey nahi jog;
Mokshmārg pāmey nahi, matey na antar rog. ||39||

Dashā - state; ***na*** - not; ***evi*** - such; ***jyā*** - then; ***sudhi*** - till; ***jeev*** - one; ***lahey*** - takes; ***nahi*** - not; ***jog*** - advantage of association; ***mokshmārg*** - path of liberation; ***pāmey*** - attains; ***nahi*** - not; ***matey*** - cured; ***na*** - not; ***antar*** - inner; ***rog*** - disease

MEANING

As long as the above-mentioned state is not attained, one cannot take advantage of the association with a Sadguru. So, he does not attain the path of liberation and his inner disease of delusion does not get cured.

EXPLANATION

Liberation is impossible without self-realisation and correspondingly self-realisation is impossible without inner worthiness. To become truly worthy, one needs to cultivate the virtues mentioned in verse 38. If the passions have not reduced, all desires except the one for liberation have not disappeared, detachment towards the world has not arisen, and compassion towards all beings has not emerged, one cannot become worthy of self-realisation.

As long as one does not attain the above-mentioned state of true worthiness, he cannot benefit from the Sadguru's association. As a result of meritorious karma, it becomes possible to gain the association of a Sadguru and favourable circumstances to pursue spirituality. However, without true worthiness, His teachings do not bring about a transformation, as they cannot penetrate into a hard and rigid mind. If a worthy seeker gains the association of a Sadguru, he listens, grasps and retains His teachings. He arrives at the right conclusions, experiments with the teachings and attains self-realisation.

In the absence of worthiness, one cannot attain the path of liberation. As the foundation of eligibility has not been laid, all activities like rituals, vows, austerities and scriptural studies are performed in vain. His religious practices prove to be lifeless, like a flower made of paper, which has a good appearance, colour and form but no fragrance. Without making the correct efforts, he is unable to tread the path of liberation and instead goes astray, wandering helplessly due to lack of right direction. Until one develops worthiness, it is not possible to attain the path of liberation in all three periods of time.

The disease of delusion remains uneradicated until one becomes endowed with the attributes of an *ātmārthi*. Cancer, diabetes, blood pressure, etc., are diseases of the body, whereas delusion is a disease of the soul. Bodily diseases last only for a certain period of time. Even an incurable chronic disease lasts only until the end of this life. In stark contrast, the inner disease of delusion continues for lifetimes. The soul has been afflicted with the disease of delusion since infinite time. Due to this delusion, one identifies with the body, indulges in impure feelings and experiences immense suffering. Until one develops worthiness, the inner disease of wrong belief remains uncured. Thus, illustrating the negative impact of unworthiness, Shrimadji has stressed upon the importance of cultivating the virtues of an ātmārthi.

VERSE - 40

Worthiness leads to right thinking

Shrimadji described the state of an unworthy one and established the idea of worthiness through the method of negative assertion. He now establishes the state of a worthy one through the method of positive assertion. Explaining what happens when one attains the state of an *ātmārthi*, Shrimadji says -

આવે જ્યાં એવી દશા, સદ્‌ગુરુબોધ સુહાય;
તે બોધે સુવિચારણા, ત્યાં પ્રગટે સુખદાય. ||૪૦||

Āve jyā evi dashā, Sadgurubodh suhāy;
Te bodhe suvichārnā, tyā pragate sukhdāy. ||40||

Āve - attains; *jyā* - when; *evi* - such; *dashā* - state; *Sadgurubodh* - teachings of enlightened Mentor; *suhāy* - shine forth; *te* - that; *bodhe* - from teachings; *suvichārnā* - right thinking; *tyā* - there; *pragate* - arises; *sukhdāy* - gives bliss

MEANING

When such a state is attained, the teachings of the Sadguru shine forth and start bearing fruit. As a result of these teachings, right thinking arises, which leads to the state of true bliss.

EXPLANATION

As and when the four virtues depicted in verse 38 are acquired, one is ready for self-realisation. A state of calm emerges which keeps one peaceful in the midst of this chaotic world. Not only do the Sadguru's words but also His silence become the source of inspiration for radical changes in his belief and behaviour. When passions like anger have quietened, when the only desire remaining is to attain liberation, when detachment towards the world has arisen, and there is a feeling of compassion for every living being, only then are the Sadguru's teachings rightly understood, bringing about an inner transformation. Therefore, it is said in this verse that only after gaining the state of worthiness do the Sadguru's teachings '**suhāy**' - shine forth to bear fruit.

When the state of ātmārthi arises, the teachings of the Sadguru seem pleasurable and elevating. The ātmārthi listens with immense enthusiasm, inner fondness and an unprecedented reverence. His heart dances with delight. The discourses are not mere entertainment or pastime for him, rather they are a powerful means to spiritual progress. The urge to listen again and again awakens in him. When heard with such deep interest, the Sadguru's teachings get imbibed in his being. So, with the increase of his devout surrendership and detachment, he experiences the uniqueness of the Sadguru's teachings, making him bloom spiritually. The Sadguru's thoughts are mirrored in the mind of the ātmārthi due to the strong connection shared. The Sadguru's words generate the right thoughts within him.

'**Suvichārnā**' means right thinking. It encompasses all thought processes that can coexist with spiritual progress without causing hindrances and create all feelings that immediately or eventually lead to an increase in inner purity. Therefore, suvichārnā includes contemplation, reflection, rumination and meditation since these are helpful in connecting to the self in one way or another. The ātmārthi listens to the teachings about the pure self from the Sadguru and a stream of right thoughts arise in him. As his mind is not filled with prejudices or preconceived notions, noble thoughts and feelings emerge within him. He deliberates upon the Sadguru's teachings, determines the nature of the self with absolute certainty and does a complete turn within.

Thus, when the state of worthiness is attained, the Sadguru's teachings become effective and right thinking is kindled. This thinking takes him towards the state of true happiness. If one remains stuck in worldly or negative thoughts, it becomes a cause of enormous sorrow. However, if right thoughts are harboured, they generate real happiness. Ascending the ladder of right thinking, the ātmārthi withdraws his attention from other associations and focuses on the pure self. Experiencing the pure self as supreme and distinct from the body, he gets immersed in the natural bliss that is beyond the senses.

— ∽⟨∾ —

VERSE - 41

Right thinking leads to liberation

Having explained how the state of right thinking emerges in an *ātmārthi,* now depicting the fruit of right thinking, Shrimadji says -

જ્યાં પ્રગટે સુવિચારણા, ત્યાં પ્રગટે નિજ જ્ઞાન;
જે જ્ઞાને ક્ષય મોહ થઈ, પામે પદ નિર્વાણ. ||૪૧||

Jyā pragate suvichārnā, tyā pragate nij jnān;
Je jnāne kshay moh thai, pāmey pad nirvān. ||41||

Jyā - where; ***pragate*** - arises; ***suvichārnā*** - right thinking; ***tyā*** - there; ***pragate*** - arises; ***nij*** - self; ***jnān*** - realisation; ***je*** - that; ***jnāne*** - by enlightenment; ***kshay*** - annihilation; ***moh*** - delusion; ***thai*** - occurs; ***pāmey*** - attains; ***pad*** - state; ***nirvān*** - liberation

MEANING

When right thinking arises, self-realisation is attained. This enlightenment destroys delusion and leads to the state of liberation.

EXPLANATION

The association with a Sadguru becomes the means that prompts the blossoming of an inner paradise in a worthy seeker's life. Now, it does not take long for the seed lying within him to sprout. Due to his worthiness, he is receptive to the Sadguru's teachings and absorbs them with devotion. He begins from the intellectual level and moves towards the experiential level. With the dawn of right thinking, he goes deeper and deeper within. Hence, right thinking is the wake-up call that stirs the soul from its deep metaphysical slumber.

By constantly reflecting upon the teachings of the Sadguru, the ātmārthi develops the right understanding regarding the pure conscious self, which is an entity distinct from the body. His intense longing for self-realisation encourages him to consciously begin the practice of distinguishing between the self and the non-self. Ignoring the non-self and focusing on the self's true nature changes the direction of his feelings. Repeatedly focusing on his own blissful conscious nature strengthens his interest in the self. Now, an unprecedented importance of the self emerges in him. Disinterest in the world increases, which leads to a decrease in the intensity of *darshanmoh* - faith delusion. As his quest deepens, the fibre of faith delusion weakens and when it eventually breaks completely, he gains self-realisation. So, with the support of the Sadguru's teachings, by solely practising contemplation and meditation, the ātmārthi attains direct experience of the self.

When the ātmārthi gets established in the self, enlightenment emerges in its pristine purity and ever-radiant glory. He enjoys the blissful taste of the nectar of experience as He revels in the self. The sweetness of that experience gets so profoundly imprinted within, that He longs for this nectar to be unceasing, unbroken and uninterrupted. He wishes to constantly remain in the bliss of the abidance in the self. Although the impact of self-realisation is such that *chāritramoh* - conduct delusion, in the form of passions and subsidiary passions has reduced its hold, it continues to hinder the constant abidance in the self. Hence, the enlightened one is ceaselessly engaged in the effort to eliminate and uproot them. The strength of self-realisation gradually vanquishes conduct delusion.

As a result of this constant awareness, He completely annihilates *mohaniya* - deluding karma. After this, the other three *ghāti* - destructive karma, that is *jnānāvarniya* - knowledge obscuring, *darshanāvarniya* - perception obscuring and *antrāya* - obstructing karma, are also annihilated and omniscience manifests. Thereafter when the four *aghāti* - non-destructive karma, that is *vedniya* - feeling pertaining, *nāma* - physique determining, *gotra* - status determining and *āyushya* - lifespan determining karma, are annihilated, the state of liberation is attained. This state, which is completely free of all passions and karma, is called '***nirvān***'. It is the ultimate state, where nothing remains to be accomplished. He experiences infinite bliss, that has a beginning but no end. Thus, liberation follows when one gets engrossed in right thinking based on the Sadguru's teachings due to the emergence of worthiness.

— ❧ —

VERSE - 42

Six truths for right thinking

Shrimadji revealed that the fruit obtained from right thinking is the state of liberation. Now, He refers to the fundamental truths that an *ātmārthi* must know to attain the state of right thinking. Shrimadji says -

ઊપજે તે સુવિચારણા, મોક્ષમાર્ગ સમજાય;
ગુરુશિષ્યસંવાદથી, ભાખું ષટ્પદ આંહી. ॥૪૨॥

Upje te suvichārnā, mokshmārg samjāy;
Gurushishyasamvādthi, bhākhu shatpad āhi. ||42||

Upje - generates; *te* - that; *suvichārnā* - right thinking; *mokshmārg* - path of liberation; *samjāy* - understood; *Gurushishyasamvādthi* - through dialogue between Mentor and disciple; *bhākhu* - state; *shatpad* - six fundamental truths; *āhi* - here

MEANING

In order to ensure right thinking arises and the path of liberation is understood, I state here six aphorisms in the form of a dialogue between a Guru and a disciple.

EXPLANATION

Shrimadji had commenced the description of the attributes of an ātmārthi from verse 34, which He now concludes in this verse. In this section, He clearly explained that the state of an ātmārthi marks the beginning of the spiritual path. As the state arises, he advances in the right direction, and ultimately attains liberation when the state develops completely. He had previously discussed in brief, all the phases of the spiritual pursuit. After portraying a clear picture of the attributes of an ātmārthi, in the closing verse of this section, Shrimadji pledges that He will state the six fundamental truths of the soul.

The purpose behind explaining the six fundamental truths is to prompt the dawn of right thinking and to provide a proper understanding of the path of liberation. When these six fundamental truths are comprehended clearly, false vision is cleared and right vision is gained. It is only by receiving the six fundamental truths from a Sadguru, aptly reflecting upon them, establishing a firm conviction and constantly ruminating over them that one attains self-realisation. Such a self-realised one gradually annihilates all worldly misery and attains the state of complete liberation.

In this verse, Shrimadji has also implied the very purpose of composing Shri Ātmasiddhi Shāstra. This sacred text has been composed in order to expound the concept of gaining self-realisation. Reflection on the self is the root of self-realisation. For this reflection to arise, Shrimadji has made use of simple language while explaining the six fundamental truths, which are supremely important to understand the path to liberation. He has depicted them in the form of a dialogue between a Guru and a disciple.

Shrimadji has employed the dialogue style to make the subject matter of the six fundamental truths easy, interesting and comprehensible to thinkers of all levels. He has embraced this effective conversational style so that all the doubts of a seeker can be resolved through the logical presentation of the six fundamental truths. In the dialogue, a disciple puts forth his doubts regarding them and receives clarifications from a Sadguru. It portrays the firm eagerness of a seeker of truth and the sort of doubts that would arise in his mind while trying to understand the nature of the soul.

There are only two kinds of people who do not get doubts regarding the soul - the ignorant worldly ones and the enlightened ones. The former because they are not aware that there is something to be known and the latter because they have experienced the soul. However, a seeker will have doubts because he wants to know the soul. He presents his doubts to the Sadguru, who resolves them perfectly.

While the seeker can procure knowledge from the scriptures, there can be no substitute to a living Sadguru, who not only knows the scriptures but also knows the seeker. The Sadguru is fully capable of solving the seeker's doubts, answering dubious questions and opening a portal to a fresh perspective. He comes to the aid of the disciple whenever he is stuck in the rut of his own thinking. Through the Sadguru's actions, words, thoughts, silence and presence, a worthy disciple absorbs the fragrance of enlightenment. The Sadguru unravels deep secrets of the scriptures while resolving his doubts, thus fostering his spiritual growth.

Naming of the Six Fundamentals

Shrimadji has described the six fundamentals of the soul in experiential words to help one recognise the nature of the self. True understanding of these six aphorisms eliminates wrong vision and aligns one to the vision of the enlightened ones. Those who develop an unwavering faith in these truths will certainly be free from all misery.

To serve as an introduction to the main subject of the text, Shrimadji has composed the section, 'Naming of the six fundamentals'. It comprises two verses, which name the six fundamentals that Shrimadji has designed in the form of dialogue between a Guru and a disciple. These are framed in such a manner that they also impart a brief idea of the six schools of philosophy.

VERSE - 43

Naming six fundamental truths

In verse 42, Shrimadji had indicated that He would explain the six fundamentals for reflection upon the self. Naming these six fundamentals, Shrimadji says -

'આત્મા છે', 'તે નિત્ય છે', 'છે કર્તા નિજકર્મ';
'છે ભોક્તા', વળી 'મોક્ષ છે', 'મોક્ષ ઉપાય સુધર્મ'. ||૪૩||

'Ātmā chhe', 'te nitya chhe', 'chhe kartā nijkarma';
'Chhe bhoktā', vali 'moksh chhe', 'moksh upāy sudharma'. ||43||

Ātmā - soul; *chhe* - exists; *te* - it; *nitya* - eternal; *chhe* - is; *kartā* - doer; *nijkarma* - its karma; *chhe* - is; *bhoktā* - receiver of its fruits; *vali* - also; *moksh* - liberation; *chhe* - exists; *moksh* - liberation; *upāy* - path; *sudharma* - true religion

MEANING

The soul exists, it is eternal, it is the doer of its karma, it is the receiver (enjoyer or sufferer) of the fruits of karma, there is liberation and there is a path of liberation, which is true religion.

EXPLANATION

Is it truly necessary to be trapped in the ceaseless cycle of transmigration? Absolutely not. One can certainly disentangle if they wish from this continuous chain of birth and death by attaining liberation. However, one has to acquire knowledge of the truth first. Shri Ātmasiddhi Shāstra imparts the means and the method that every seeker can adopt and adapt to gain liberation. Since the soul is the epicentre of spirituality, one must know the six fundamentals regarding its nature.

Shrimadji has explained the six fundamentals in this scripture to enable the eager seeker of spiritual truth to discard all doubt, kindle right thinking and ensure that he understands the path of liberation. But before giving a detailed explanation with logic and reasoning, He has first introduced them to make it simple. The names of the six fundamentals have been mentioned in this verse to familiarise the readers with the subject of the text. They are: 'soul exists', 'it is eternal', 'it is the doer of karma', 'it is the receiver of the fruits of karma', 'there is liberation' and 'there is a path of liberation'. This path of liberation has been referred to as the true religion in this verse.

These six fundamentals form the very foundation of spiritual knowledge. They have been expounded in several Jain scriptures. The roots of these fundamentals can be traced all the way back to Lord *Mahāvir's* solutions to the doubts of the eleven *Brāhmin* scholars, who went on to become His principal disciples. This discussion, famously called *Gandharvād*, implicitly covers the six fundamentals, as all eleven doubts can be correlated to them. An explicit mention of the six fundamentals was first found in *Sanmatitark Prakaran* by *Āchāryashri Siddhasen Diwākarji* in the fourth-fifth century. They are also indicated in *Shāstravārtāsamucchay* by *Āchāryashri Haribhadrasuriji* in the eighth century. *Upādhyāyshri*

Yashovijayji Mahārāj composed a whole text depicting them, named *Samyaktva Shatsthān Chaupāi* in the seventeenth century. Shrimadji has also stressed their importance in numerous writings in the nineteenth century. It is important to note that the six fundamental truths are the basis for the path of liberation.

By introducing the names in this verse, Shrimadji inspires the reader to contemplate upon the six fundamentals. This narration gives the reader a feel so that he can imbibe the teachings of the fundamentals, which can bring about the dawn of self-realisation. Shrimadji possesses the unshakeable conviction regarding them through experience. He has expanded upon the six fundamentals purely out of compassion for the seekers and for their spiritual welfare. In the prologue of Shri Ātmasiddhi Shāstra, Shrimadji elucidated the necessity, importance and greatness of a Sadguru. He then portrayed the attributes of a *matārthi* and an *ātmārthi*. Now, He begins the main subject matter of this scripture - the six fundamental truths of the soul.

VERSE - 44

Purpose of explaining six fundamental truths

Shrimadji named the six fundamentals in verse 43. Prior to commencing with the dialogue of their detailed description, He composes another introductory verse, illustrating their universality amongst all philosophies as well as the purpose of explaining them. Shrimadji says -

ષટ્સ્થાનક સંક્ષેપમાં, ષટ્દર્શન પણ તેહ;
સમજાવા પરમાર્થને, કહ્યાં જ્ઞાનીએ એહ. ||૪૪||

Shatsthānak sankshepmā, shatdarshan pan teh;
Samjāvā   parmārthne,   kahyā   Jnānie   eh. ||44||

Shatsthānak - six aphorisms; *sankshepmā* - briefly; *shatdarshan* - six philosophies; *pan* - also; *teh* - that; *samjāvā* - to understand; *parmārthne* - supreme truth; *kahyā* - stated; *Jnānie* - enlightened ones; *eh* - them

MEANING

These six aphorisms are briefly stated here. They also constitute the six schools of philosophy. The enlightened ones have explained them to make us understand the supreme truth.

EXPLANATION

Propelled by ignorance, one races towards the non-self while moving away from the self. However, if he chooses to pause and listens to the enlightened ones, he will know where he is currently heading and where he should be actually heading. The enlightened ones reveal the right destination and the way to get there. It is necessary to know the six fundamental truths in order to attain liberation. Understanding them is essential to annihilate the false notion of 'I' and 'mine' in the non-self and develop faith in the pure self. Hence, they have been said to be the residence of *samyagdarshan* - right faith. The six fundamental truths have been briefly explained in Shri Ātmasiddhi Shāstra. A deep reflection upon them will reveal that they actually constitute the six main philosophies of Indian tradition.

The philosophical texts expounding the schools of thought in Indian tradition have classified them into two main categories, namely *āstik* - theist philosophies and *nāstik* - atheist philosophies. Those who believe in concepts of the soul, rebirth and karma are āstik while those who do not accept them are nāstik. Alternatively, those philosophies which believe that God created the universe are called theist and those which disbelieve are called atheist. Although these are the popular beliefs regarding āstik and nāstik, the premise for categorising the six Indian philosophies is slightly different. They have been categorised as āstik or nāstik by the followers of the *Vedas* - Hindu scriptures. While āstik philosophies are those which consider the Vedas to be authentic and interpret them in different ways, nāstik philosophies do not accept this, and were propounded independently. The first category includes (1-2) *Nyāy* and *Vaisheshik*, (3-4) *Sānkhya* and *Yog*, (5-6) *Purva Mimānsā* and *Uttar Mimānsā (Vedānt)*.

Each of these pairs are very similar in ideology and are hence grouped as one while categorising the philosophies. Therefore, there are three pairs of Vedic philosophies. The second category includes three non-Vedic philosophies - 1. *Chārvāk* 2. *Jainism* and 3. *Buddhism*. Thus, three Vedic and three non-Vedic philosophies comprise the '*shatdarshan*' - 1. Chārvāk 2. Jainism 3. Buddhism 4. Nyāy-Vaisheshik 5. Sānkhya-Yog 6. Purva Mimānsā-Uttar Mimānsā.

The six fundamentals are the very basis on which each philosophy builds its opinion. No matter which school of philosophy or spiritual knowledge, they do not revolve around any fundamental other than these six. Hence, by analysing the six fundamentals, one acquires the gist of the six philosophies too.

It is important to note that the enlightened ones have stated the fundamentals for the spiritually beneficial purpose of facilitating the right resolve and conviction about the soul. They have described them to elucidate the supreme truth. One interested in knowing the supreme truth should contemplate upon the six fundamentals.

Shrimadji's purpose in composing Shri Ātmasiddhi Shāstra is the explanation of the six fundamentals, not the six philosophies. However, in the spirit of integration, He has subtly woven them. He does not negate or appease any philosophy but appreciates all perspectives while presenting an unbiased understanding of the supreme truth. He expounds the truth from multiple viewpoints. Shrimadji's excellence lies in addressing each philosophy, without naming it and also without considering any of them to be wrong. This stems from His clarity of thought and purity of heart. His compassion runs so deep that He does not want the seeker to get lost in the maze of different ideologies, be confounded by a plethora of concepts or get caught in a cobweb of words. It is solely with the noble intent of enabling the aspirant to gain the right understanding of the ultimate reality, and drawing him towards the self that these fundamentals have been stated.

Hereafter, in the text, the worthy disciple will raise doubts regarding each fundamental, one after another, and the Guru will provide solutions with great love, in a tone steeped in the essence of the scriptures. The disciple will present his viewpoint and the Guru will reply appropriately from the right viewpoint. The disciple is a real seeker of truth and the Guru's replies put his doubts to rest. Thus, having established the background, Shrimadji now proceeds to unfold the six fundamentals.

First Fundamental
Soul exists

A true *ātmārthi* holds the firm resolve that 'Only the one who has attained self-realisation is a Sadguru. If I find such a Sadguru, I will align my mind, speech and body to His command, and certainly follow the path of liberation.' With such conviction, he reduces his passions, gives up all aspirations except that of liberation, becomes weary of the endless cycles of transmigration, cultivates compassion, and seeks a Sadguru for the upliftment of his soul. On meeting the Sadguru, he expresses the doubts resounding in his mind. The Sadguru gives him solutions, thus freeing his mind of these doubts. Since these solutions come from self-experience, they deeply penetrate the disciple's heart. By composing a dialogue between a Guru and a disciple regarding the six fundamentals, Shrimadji has made this difficult subject easier to comprehend.

The first among the six fundamentals is - 'soul exists'. To accept the existence of the soul is the very first step on the path to liberation. Logically, only if the soul exists can one even speak of liberating it. Therefore, it is most important to become fully devoid of doubt regarding the existence of the soul. For this fundamental, Shrimadji has composed fourteen verses 45-58. In the first four verses 45-48, of this section, He has presented the three well-known arguments of the *Chārvāks*, who do not believe in the existence of the soul. He has penned them without naming the philosophy itself, simply as the disciple's enquiry. Thereafter, in ten verses 49-58, Shrimadji gives the Guru's solutions to the doubts. He demonstrates the incorrectness of the disciple's doubt and establishes the existence of the soul, for his spiritual welfare.

VERSE - 45

Doubt 1 - Soul cannot be experienced by senses

The disciple's doubt regarding the first fundamental - existence of the soul, has arisen due to the influence of the *Chārvāk* philosophy. Presenting his first argument in favour of this doubt, the disciple says -

નથી દૃષ્ટિમાં આવતો, નથી જણાતું રૂપ;
બીજો પણ અનુભવ નહીં, તેથી ન જીવસ્વરૂપ. ||૪૫||

Nathi drashtimā āvto, nathi janātu roop;
Bijo pan anubhav nahi, tethi na jeevswaroop. ||45||

Nathi - not; *drashtimā* - in sight; *āvto* - comes; *nathi* - not; *janātu* - known; *roop* - form; *bijo* - other; *pan* - also; *anubhav* - experience; *nahi* - not; *tethi* - therefore; *na* - no; *jeevswaroop* - soul's existence

MEANING

Neither is the soul seen by the eyes, nor is its form known. As it is not even experienced by any of the other senses, it does not exist.

EXPLANATION

An aspirant is filled to the brim with the emptiness of sheer information parading as knowledge. He embarks on his journey for true knowledge by questioning everything. All through his life, he has believed in the authority of the senses. He finds relevance solely in things that can be experienced through sensory perception. He questions things that do not fall within the purview of his senses or logic. Everything else seems illusory and deceptive. Hence, it is only natural that any talk of the soul's existence seems baseless, false and even ridiculous to him.

The disciple aspires for true knowledge regarding the soul. He begins his quest by asking basic questions pertaining to its existence. He sets empirical tests for the soul. Expressing the doubt that plagues his mind, he says the soul cannot be seen by the eyes like all other objects in the world. The soul has no known form, colour or shape.

Even if the soul is formless, colourless, shapeless and hence, invisible, it should at least be experienced through other senses. There exist many substances in the world which cannot be seen but are still perceived through other senses. The wind cannot be seen by the eyes, but experienced when it touches the skin; taste, through the tongue; fragrance, through the nose and words, through the ears. Thus, the substances in the world which cannot be seen, are experienced by other senses, but the soul is not even known by other senses. The soul cannot be touched, tasted, smelt or heard. It does not come in the perception of any sense.

Thus, since the soul can neither be seen by the eyes, nor experienced by any other senses, the disciple doubts its existence. He feels that the soul has no special, unique, distinct nature like other substances and therefore, it is imaginary. It is not possible to believe in the soul as it cannot be identified by any senses. As the disciple does not find any proof regarding the existence of the soul, it seems to him there is no soul whatsoever. The disciple's first question is regarding the very existence of the soul.

— ⚬☙⚬ —

VERSE - 46

Doubt 2 - Soul is body, senses or breath

Having expressed the reason behind his doubt concerning the existence of the soul, presenting another argument, the disciple says -

અથવા દેહ જ આતમા, અથવા ઇન્દ્રિય પ્રાણ;
મિથ્યા જુદો માનવો, નહીં જુદું એંધાણ. ||૪૬||

Athvā deh ja ātamā, athvā indriy prān;
Mithyā judo mānvo, nahi judu endhān. ||46||

Athvā - or; *deh* - body; *ja* - itself; *ātamā* - soul; *athvā* - or; *indriy* - senses; *prān* - breath; *mithyā* - false; *judo* - separate; *mānvo* - believe; *nahi* - not; *judu* - separate; *endhān* - sign

MEANING
Or, the body itself is the soul, or the senses or the breath is the soul. It is false to believe that the soul is separate from them as it has no other distinct sign.

EXPLANATION
In the previous verse, the disciple presented the argument that since the soul cannot be seen by the eyes or experienced through any other senses, it is not possible that the soul exists. In connection to this logic, he now says that if one continues to insist that the soul is a real entity, he must accept that the body or the senses or the breath itself is the soul.

To believe the soul to be separate from these three is false, because apart from the body, senses or breath there is no other indication proving the soul's existence. This is discussed below:

Body - It is evident that a living body eats, drinks, walks and thinks. It is visibly apparent that it undertakes different activities. These are the signs of life. A living body knows and moves, hence it must be considered to be the soul. When we address insects, worms, flies, etc., as living beings, we are actually looking at their bodies. As all activities are performed by the body, it must be considered to be the soul.

Senses - If it is argued that knowingness is the attribute of the soul which proves its existence, then it can be said that it is the senses which perform this task of knowing. Knowledge is gained by sense organs. One touches through the skin, tastes with the tongue, smells with the nose, sees with the eyes and hears with the ears. Senses are the channels for knowledge. If any of these organs cease to function, the knowledge pertaining to that particular sense is blocked. If one loses his eyes, he is unable to see. If the ears stop functioning, he cannot gain the knowledge of sound. Therefore, if knowledge is the characteristic of the soul, the senses can be termed as the soul.

Breath - It can be said that the senses continue to function as long as the breath continues, and stop functioning once the breath ceases. Even if the senses stop functioning, one is said to be alive as long as he continues to breathe. Breathing is the infallible indication of life. Therefore, the breath should be accepted as the soul.

Thus, the soul can be equated with the body, senses or breath. Besides these three, there is no other visible sign of consciousness. There is no other known characteristic of the soul which distinguishes it from the body, senses and breath. Signs are very important to differentiate between two things. However, no special sign of the soul appears to the disciple. He cannot observe any difference between the soul and the body, senses or breath. Hence, he feels it is meaningless to talk about an entity which is separate from them. It feels only prudent to accept one of them as the soul. It is merely a synonym for any of these. The disciple accepts knowingness, but considers it to be an attribute of either the body, the senses or the breath. He does not accept the soul to be an independent substance.

VERSE - 47

Doubt 3 - Soul is not knowable like pot-cloth

As the disciple does not see a distinct sign of the soul, he is unwilling to accept its existence independent of the body, senses and breath. Putting forth another argument in this context, the disciple says -

વળી જો આત્મા હોય તો, જણાય તે નહિ કેમ?
જણાય જો તે હોય તો, ઘટ પટ આદિ જેમ. ॥૪૭॥

Vali jo ātmā hoi toh, janāy te nahi kem?
Janāy jo te hoi toh, ghat pat ādi jem. ॥47॥

Vali - moreover; *jo* - if; *ātmā* - soul; *hoi* - exists; *toh* - then; *janāy* - known; *te* - it; *nahi* - not; *kem* - why; *janāy* - known; *jo* - if; *te* - it; *hoi* - exists; *toh* - then; *ghat* - pot; *pat* - cloth; *ādi* - etc.; *jem* - as

MEANING

Moreover, if the soul exists, then why is it not known to us? If it exists, then it should be known just as the pot, cloth, etc., are known.

EXPLANATION

One has experienced the pangs of a hungry stomach, the hunger for wealth and prestige, but never for spirituality. To such people, life does not seem worthless without spiritual achievements, and their absence or deficiency is not regretted. The disciple of Shri Ātmasiddhi Shāstra has experienced the pangs of spiritual hunger and is yearning for self-realisation. However, his mind is plagued by doubt regarding the soul, which he presents to the Guru. He has delved deep into the subject, hence he has questions which need answering. Although people do use the word soul, they have not thought too deeply about it. They have not examined the truth with their intellect to affirm this belief. If one contemplates and gains conviction of the truth, right faith dawns on him.

The disciple expressed that the soul cannot be perceived by the senses, and there is an absence of any sign that it is separate from the body, senses and breath, therefore it does not exist. Further elaborating his argument regarding the existence of the soul, he says that all objects that exist in the world are certainly known to people. This is because they have some form of existence. They possess colour, smell, taste, etc., and so are certainly perceived by some sense or the other. If a substance like the soul does exist, why is it not perceivable? If the soul exists, then it should definitely be known through some sense.

The disciple says that just as all objects like a '*ghat*' - pot, or a '*pat*' - cloth, etc., exist and hence are known, the soul should also be known. Ancient scriptures of logic used the term 'ghat pat' to symbolise material objects of the world. They were used to represent inanimate substances. The authors probably used these terms because they observed a cloth being used to filter water in a pot or observed a pot covered by a cloth to keep the water cool. Another possibility is that rhyming words would perhaps make the concept easier to grasp. The disciple uses this metaphor and conveys that the soul is not known like the pot, cloth, etc., and therefore there is doubt regarding the existence of the soul.

Existence is normally associated with tangibility. One knows an object by virtue of its tangible nature. The disciple feels that if the existence of the soul is to be believed then it has to be a tangible substance, something which can be known. If it is intangible, then the question of believing in its existence does not arise. The disciple does not want to believe in the existence of the soul just because it is written in the scriptures. He seeks to know it himself by experience, the same way he knows and experiences other material objects.

VERSE - 48

Concluding his observations

Based on the arguments presented in verses 45-47, the disciple is inclined to believe there is no substance like the soul, which has an independent existence. Centred around this, the disciple concludes -

માટે છે નહિ આતમા, મિથ્યા મોક્ષ ઉપાય;
એ અંતર શંકા તણો, સમજાવો સદ્‌ઉપાય. ||૪૮||

Mātey chhe nahi ātamā, mithyā moksh upāy;
Ae antar shankā tano, samjāvo sadupāy. ||48||

Mātey - therefore; *chhe* - is; *nahi* - not; *ātamā* - soul; *mithyā* - useless; *moksh* - liberation; *upāy* - means; *ae* - that; *antar* - inner; *shankā* - doubt; *tano* - of; *samjāvo* - explain; *sadupāy* - satisfactory solution

MEANING

Therefore, the soul does not exist, so, the means of its liberation is futile. Please give me a satisfactory solution for the doubt I have in my mind.

EXPLANATION

In the previous three verses, the disciple put forth three arguments debating the existence of the soul: 1. The soul can neither be seen nor experienced by other senses. 2. The soul is not separate from the body, the senses or the breath. 3. The soul cannot be clearly known like objects such as pot, cloth, etc. Based on these arguments, the disciple definitely states that it is impossible for the soul to exist.

The disciple has arrived at the conclusion that there is no separate entity like the soul. Further, he wonders that if the soul itself does not exist, what is the sense in talking about its qualities and capacities? If there is no soul, then who is bound or liberated? What is the benefit derived from making the effort to attain liberation? If the soul exists, then the means of freeing it from bondage must be pursued. However, if it does not, then it proves futile to engage in the means to attain liberation.

Expressing his line of thought that it is meaningless to pursue the path of liberation because the soul itself does not exist, the disciple requests the Guru to resolve his doubt. Although he has concluded his arguments, he has not yet made a final judgement. It is admirable to note that he does not stubbornly believe what he thinks to be true. Some people pose questions but are not ready to accept the answers, as they feel they are right. They ask questions just for the sake of it, and are difficult to convince. However, the disciple is genuinely eager to know the truth. He has immense faith in the Guru's ability, believing that He will not let any doubt linger in him. He knows the Guru will give a satisfactory reply that will enable him to proceed on the path of liberation. Therefore, he places a request at the Guru's lotus feet for the clarification of his doubt. He humbly seeks the right remedy to eliminate the doubt he possesses regarding the existence of the soul.

Although the disciple expresses his doubt regarding the very existence of the soul, the attributes of an ideal disciple are clearly visible in him. Through his questions itself, it is evident he is a real seeker. He wants to attain self-realisation. He has respect for the Sadguru. He has no intention of testing the Guru by asking questions. He presents his arguments, concludes his observations but refrains from making a judgement. He wants to reach the right conclusion. So, when he requests the Guru and asks Him to dissolve all doubts, his qualities of humility and politeness come to light. Viewing his worthiness, the Guru will now resolve his doubt and establish the existence of the soul.

VERSE - 49

Root cause of doubt

The disciple presented his doubt regarding the existence of the soul to the Guru, in the previous four verses 45-48. Knowing that the disciple is worthy of knowledge, the Guru answers his doubt in ten verses 49-58.

Before sequentially answering the various arguments of the disciple, the Guru draws attention to the root cause of the doubt. In two verses, He strikes on the basic flaw, which is the reason for doubting the existence of the soul. In the first verse, the Guru says -

ભાસ્યો દેહાધ્યાસથી, આત્મા દેહ સમાન;
પણ તે બન્ને ભિન્ન છે, પ્રગટ લક્ષણે ભાન. ||૪૯||

Bhāsyo dehādhyāsthi, ātmā deh samān;
Pan te banne bhinna chhe, pragat lakshane bhān. ||49||

Bhāsyo - appears; *dehādhyāsthi* - because of identification with body; *ātmā* - soul; *deh* - body; *samān* - same; *pan* - but; *te* - they; *banne* - both; *bhinna* - separate; *chhe* - are; *pragat* - evident; *lakshane* - from characteristics; *bhān* - known

MEANING

The soul and the body appear to be the same due to the false identification of the soul with the body. However, both of them are separate entities and can be identified by their evidently distinct characteristics.

EXPLANATION

Possessed by a raging urge to know about the soul, the disciple had placed his doubt before the Guru. Pleased by the disciple's contemplation on the subject, the Guru commences with the solution. He demonstrates the flaws in the disciple's thinking, the incorrectness in his judgement, and establishes the truth. The disciple is doubtful of the existence of the soul as an independent substance. The Guru clarifies that in the first place, the method of identifying any substance must be appropriate. A substance can be recognised by its characteristics. Although the soul cannot be known through the senses, its independent existence can certainly be determined by contemplating its unique characteristics. Due to the absence of this knowledge, one commits the mistake of false identification with the body.

One has been repeating this mistake since time infinite and hence wanders in the world. Had this mistake been corrected earlier, transmigration would have certainly ended. This mistake is called '**dehādhyās**'. The word *adhyās* comprises two words - *adhi* and *ās*. Adhi means inside and ās means to sit. Along with *deh* - body, it means to sit inside the body. In totality, dehādhyās is the habit of identification with the body. It is so deep-rooted that one does not forget it even for a moment.

The reason for such strong identification is because the soul has been in close and constant contact with the body. Since time immemorial, the soul has continuously been associated with one body or another. Infinite births with infinite bodies. Although the multiple senses have varied across births, the soul has never been without a body. This constant contact coupled with ignorance results in identification with the body. Due to ignorance regarding the soul, the delusion, 'I am the body' prevails. Ignorantly, one believes the body to be himself and hence incessantly indulges in many false imaginations. Being acquainted with the body since countless lives, he gets attached to it and behaves as if he truly is the body.

Thus, due to being identified as the body, both the soul and the body appear as one entity. However, in reality, they are two separate beings, diametrically opposite in nature. The soul is different from the body, or rather, is the knower of the body. This difference and independence can be proved by their distinct characteristics. When granules of sugar and salt are mixed together, they appear to be a single substance, but they can be differentiated by their taste. Thus, they can be proved different by their independent characteristics. Similarly, the characteristic of the soul is consciousness and that of the body, inanimate. The soul constantly knows, whereas the body can never perform the act of knowing. The soul is formless, the body has a form. The soul is eternal and immortal, the body, transient and mortal. Although both exist in the same space, their characteristics can be clearly understood to be distinct. Hence, they are completely different from each other. If these characteristics are understood correctly, the soul and the body are clearly recognised as separate substances. By ascending the ladder of right thinking, a distinguishing dimension arises and one realises the self.

VERSE - 50

Root cause of doubt - analogy

Having demonstrated that the soul is a substance that has an independent existence, the Guru further strengthens this conviction. He clarifies that principle with an apt example. The Guru says -

ભાસ્યો દેહાધ્યાસથી, આત્મા દેહ સમાન;
પણ તે બન્ને ભિન્ન છે, જેમ અસિ ને મ્યાન. ||૫૦||

Bhāsyo   dehādhyāsthi,   ātmā   deh   samān;
Pan te banne bhinna chhe, jem asi ne myān. ||50||

Bhāsyo - appears; *dehādhyāsthi* - because of identification with body; *ātmā* - soul; *deh* - body; *samān* - same; *pan* - but; *te* - they; *banne* - both; *bhinna* - separate; *chhe* - are; *jem* - like; *asi* - sword; *ne* - and; *myān* - sheath

MEANING

The soul and the body appear to be the same due to the false identification of the soul with the body. However, both of them are separate entities, like the sword and the sheath.

EXPLANATION

The Sadguru continues to resolve the disciple's doubt by expounding the difference between the body and the soul. Reiterating what He explained in the previous verse, He states that the soul and body appear as one because of identification with the body. One does not realise the distinction between the two due to delusion but they are clearly separate. The soul and the body have independent identities.

By repeating the first three parts of the previous verse, the Guru draws the disciple's attention towards the severity of this flaw, which has incurred him much harm over infinite lifetimes. He emphasises this point so that the teaching properly penetrates into the heart of the disciple and all his efforts are focused on its destruction. The Guru sheds light on the subject by using the example of a sword and its sheath.

1. When the sword is inside the sheath, they both appear as one object although they are different. Similarly, when the soul is within the body, their separateness is not apparent, although they are completely different.

2. The sheath is visible and the sword, invisible. Similarly, the body is visible and the soul, invisible.

3. The sword takes up the entire space available in the sheath. Similarly, the soul pervades the entire body.

4. What the sword can do, the sheath cannot do. The sheath simply covers the sword. Similarly, the body, being inanimate, is devoid of knowingness and happiness. It is merely an external cover for the soul.

5. Although the sword might remain in the sheath for years before being drawn out, it does not become the sheath. Similarly, though the soul has been associated with one body or another since time immemorial, it has never become the

body and never will. The two remain separate in all three periods of time - past, present and future.

Thus, just as the sword and its sheath are different, so too are the soul and the body. All because of their distinct characteristics. The ignorant one falsely believes what he sees in the mirror, is his self. However, that is the body and he is the soul - the knower of the body and the universe. The body is merely a facade, it is the soul housed within, which is his true self. He needs to change his myopic belief and develop the right vision to see the truth.

VERSE - 51

Reply 1 - Soul is seer

After drawing the disciple's attention towards the basic flaw, which is the root cause of all doubts regarding the soul, the Guru systematically provides precise answers to all his arguments. In verses 51-52, the Guru addresses the doubt raised by the disciple in verse 45. His doubt is that since the soul is not seen with the eyes, its form and shape are unknown; even other experiences like touch, etc., do not reveal its existence, hence there is no independent substance like the soul. Resolving this doubt, the Guru says -

જે દ્રષ્ટા છે દ્રષ્ટિનો, જે જાણે છે રૂપ;
અબાધ્ય અનુભવ જે રહે, તે છે જીવસ્વરૂપ. ||૫૧||

Je drashtā chhe drashtino, je jāney chhe roop;
Abādhya anubhav je rahey, te chhe jeevswaroop. ||51||

Je - that; *drashtā* - seer; *chhe* - is; *drashtino* - of sight; *je* - that; *jāney* - knows; *chhe* - is; *roop* - form; *abādhya* - unobstructed; *anubhav* - experience; *je* - that; *rahey* - remains; *te* - it; *chhe* - is; *jeevswaroop* - soul's nature

MEANING

That which is the seer of sight and the knower of all forms, that very experience of consciousness, which is continuous and cannot be subtracted, is the nature of the soul.

EXPLANATION

The disciple had commenced his argument by stating that the soul is not visible to the eyes. He has accorded greater status to the eyes, compared to all the other senses. Eyes are vital organs which play a major role in life. Without them, life draws a dark blank and seems incomplete. They are integral in knowing things, and since the soul is imperceivable to the eyes and all other senses, the disciple doubts the existence of the soul.

The Guru explains that the soul cannot be seen by the eyes because it is the 'seer' itself. It is not visible through the eyes because that which sees through the eyes is the soul. The eyes are merely inanimate sense organs, an instrument to view external objects. Seeing and knowing are characteristics of the soul, whereas the eyes are just a medium. The soul guides and controls the eyes in order to fulfil the function of seeing objects. The eyes are powerless without the soul. Just as a person inside a house observes the view outside through a window, the soul within the body sees the external objects through the eyes. Windows are merely the medium, not the seer. It is the person who sees. Similarly, eyes are just the medium, not the seer. It is the soul which sees. Therefore, how could the eyes possibly see the soul. Thus, the soul cannot be seen because it is the seer of the sight and the knower of gross-subtle forms.

The nature of the soul is such that it cannot be perceived by the eyes or any other senses and therefore its very existence cannot be proven by any such experience of sight, touch, etc.

However, it definitely has an independent nature which can be experienced. The consciousness which is experienced continuously in an unobstructed manner is the nature of the soul. While excluding everything, that presence which cannot ever be excluded, that which is constantly existent, that experience of consciousness is the nature of the soul. The experience of 'I am' remains unbroken in every state. All are aware of this feeling. Even if any of the sense organs cease to function, the experience of 'I am' is ever-present. If the eyesight is lost, the feeling of 'I am' still remains. If the limbs are cut, the awareness of 'I am' still persists. That experience is without any hindrance and nothing can ever obstruct this feeling. The experience of consciousness which remains after eliminating everything else, is the nature of the soul.

Thus, the Guru proves the existence of the soul by stating that while it appears 'the eyes see', fundamentally and in actuality it is, 'the soul which sees'. The soul is beyond the senses and is formless. The truth is significantly more than what is in the purview of the senses. There is a lot more than meets the eyes or falls on the ears. The conscious nature of the soul is unique and that distinguishes it from all other substances. Its existence is devoid of dependence on anyone or anything.

VERSE - 52

Knower of all five senses

The Guru gave an accurate solution to the disciple's argument expressed in verse 45, by revealing that the nature of the soul is such, it cannot be perceived by the senses. It is of the nature of consciousness, beyond the senses. Elaborating upon this further and by kindling the conviction about the soul through the attribute of knowledge, the Guru states -

છે ઇન્દ્રિય પ્રત્યેકને, નિજ નિજ વિષયનું જ્ઞાન;
પાંચ ઇન્દ્રીના વિષયનું, પણ આત્માને ભાન. ||પર||

Chhe indriy pratyekne, nij nij vishaynu jnān;
Pānch indrinā vishaynu, pan ātmāne bhān. ||52||

Chhe - has; *indriy* - sense organ; *pratyekne* - each; *nij nij* - own; *vishaynu* - of subject matter; *jnān* - knowledge; *pānch* - five; *indrinā* - of sense organs; *vishaynu* - of subject matter; *pan* - but; *ātmāne* - soul has; *bhān* - knowledge

MEANING

Each sense organ has knowledge of its own subject matter, but the soul knows the subject matter of all five sense organs.

EXPLANATION

Drawing the disciple's attention to the knowing nature of the soul, the Guru says that each sense organ knows its respective subject matter, not that of the other sense organs.

Every sense organ has a different subject matter. The skin only feels the touch, the tongue only tastes, the nose only smells, the eyes only see and the ears only hear. They cannot know any subject matter besides their own. The eye which performs the function of seeing, cannot know the sound. The eye can see a distant bird but cannot hear the music of a nearby flute. If one loses his sight, he will not be able to see the form of the flute even when he holds it in his very hands, but will hear its music with his ears, even when it is played further away. Hence, it is apparent to all that the capacity of the five sensory organs is restricted to knowing their respective subject matter. One sensory organ cannot know two subject matters, and likewise, two sense organs cannot know the same subject matter.

Although each sensory organ has a limited capacity to know, it is experienced that we know the subject matter of all five senses. When a steaming hot dish is served, one can feel its touch, enjoy its taste, smell the aroma, see its form and hear a sizzling sound emanating. The subject matter perceived by all five sensory organs is known by a single entity. That entity is the soul, which is different from the five sensory organs of the body. The soul is the conductor of these five. They perform their respective activities with a limited ability to perceive, whereas the task of knowing all these activities, integrating them and remembering them is all orchestrated by the soul.

To say that each sensory organ perceives its own subject matter is actually a formality, as they are inert and therefore cannot know. They can only be the instruments of knowing. The sensory organs are inanimate - merely mediums for their respective subject matters. The knowing substance is the soul alone, without which the sensory organs cannot perform their activities. They are incapable of acquiring knowledge on their own. The soul perceives the subject matters through the senses, retains them and recollects them. Therefore, the substance which is the abode of the attribute of knowledge is the soul, not the sense organs.

The disciple claimed the primacy of the sensory organs in observing and understanding the world. However, the soul cannot be perceived by them, being beyond all material sensory organs. Shrimadji has logically proven that the soul, which presides over all sensory organs, is separate from them. The soul holds the reins of the sensory organs, orchestrates all bodily actions, and harmonises all thoughts in the mind. Yet, it is not praised or even perceived.

VERSE - 53

Reply 2 - Body, sense, breath function due to soul

After giving an apt solution to the argument presented by
the disciple in verse 45, the Guru now resolves the argument
put forth in verse 46. The disciple had said that either the
body, the senses or the breath should be considered to be
the soul. To believe that the soul is separate from them is
false, as there is no other apparent sign of its existence. The
first half of the argument is resolved in verse 53 and the
other half, in verse 54. Proving the independent existence of
the soul as separate from the body, senses and breath, the
Guru says -

દેહ ન જાણે તેહને, જાણે ન ઇન્દ્રી, પ્રાણ;
આત્માની સત્તા વડે, તેહ પ્રવર્તે જાણ. ||૫૩||

Deh na jāney tehne, jāney na indri, prān;
Ātmāni sattā vadey, teh pravarte jān. ||53||

Deh - body; *na* - not; *jāney* - knows; *tehne* - it; *jāney* - knows; *na* - not;
indri - senses; *prān* - breath; *ātmāni* - soul's; *sattā* - presence;
vadey - due to; *teh* - they; *pravarte* - function; *jān* - know

MEANING
Neither does the body know it, nor do the senses or the
breath. They all function only due to the presence of the soul.

EXPLANATION

The Guru explains the incorrect nature of the idea that the body, senses or breath are the soul. He says that neither of them is the soul as they do not have the nature of knowingness. As the body is merely a collection of atoms, it is inanimate. The five sensory organs which are a part of the body are also inanimate. Even the breath is inanimate, as atoms in the form of oxygen are absorbed and released during respiration. They do not know themselves, or each other. The senses and breath do not know in which part of the body they are functioning. As they do not have the capacity to know, they can never know the soul. Knowingness is the characteristic of the soul. Thus, it is established that the substance with the attribute of knowingness is different from the body, senses and breath. This knowing substance is the soul.

Moreover, the body, senses and breath carry out their functions through an association with the conscious entity, and when separated from it, they cease to function. All three are inactive on their own, engaging in their respective activities only as long as the soul resides in the body. If not, they lie inert. In the absence of the soul, the body ceases to have life, the activity of the senses ends, and the process of respiration stops. The soul alone is the propeller of them all.

Upon examining the phenomenon of death, one realises that since the propelling soul is absent in a corpse, the body is inactive. It does not have any sense of feeling, experiencing no pain even while being cremated. It simply burns like a log of wood along with the other logs in the funeral pyre and is soon reduced to ashes. A single gust of wind and the ashes are strewn all over. The body only remains active as long as the soul dwells in it. Therefore, the body cannot be the soul. The soul and the body can be compared to electricity and electrical appliances respectively. A television, refrigerator, fan, or tube light cannot work without electricity. In the same way, the body cannot function without the soul. Electrical appliances can be seen but electricity cannot be seen. In the same way, one can view the activities of the body, not the soul. Electricity is felt more in its absence, similarly the importance of the soul is felt more at death. The existence of electricity and the soul can be inferred and experienced.

At the time of death, the sensory organs remain in the body just as they were, but lose the capacity to experience anything. If food is placed on the tongue, it cannot taste. A flower near the nose, is not smelt. There is no sensation, as the soul itself is absent. Eyes are present in the dead body but they cannot see without the soul, which is the real seer. All the sense organs that used to function while the soul was present, are no longer able to perceive as soon as the soul leaves. Therefore, the senses cannot be the soul.

Respiration is an essential activity of a living body and it continues uninterrupted throughout the lifespan, so it is natural to regard the breath as life. It is commonly understood that the moment respiration ends, one is said to be dead.

However, the fact is that respiration stops because the soul leaves the body. As the departure of the soul and the cessation of respiration happen simultaneously, one does not realise it. Respiration is merely the indication of the soul's presence in the body, not the retention of the soul in the body. If this was possible, the longevity of life could be indefinitely extended with the help of oxygen cylinders. Although the respiratory system is undoubtedly essential for life to exist, it cannot be equated to life itself. Respiration is active as long as the soul remains in the body. Therefore, the breath cannot be the soul.

Thus, the body, senses and breath are active because of the presence of the soul. The brain too is non-living and works in conjunction with the soul. The soul is an independent conscious substance separate from all of them. The beauty of the body is due to the pulsation of the soul. A flower blooms because of its presence. Without the soul, it shrivels and dies, and is discarded as waste. It is the soul which propels the body, senses and breath. While the body is active and visible, the soul is silent and invisible, therefore ignored. The soul is like salt which gives taste to all but remains invisible. If one lets go of false identification, the soul shines through in all its immaculate, pristine glory.

VERSE - 54

Consciousness is sign of soul

The second part of the disciple's argument in verse 46 was that since there is no evident sign of the soul, it is wrong to believe it as separate from the body, senses or breath. Answering this, the Guru says -

સર્વ અવસ્થાને વિષે, ન્યારો સદા જણાય;
પ્રગટરૂપ ચૈતન્યમય, એ એંધાણ સદાય. ||૫૪||

Sarva avasthāne vishe, nyāro sadā janāy;
Pragatroop chaitanyamay, ae endhān sadāy. ||54||

Sarva - all; *avasthāne* - states; *vishe* - regarding; *nyāro* - separate; *sadā* - always; *janāy* - known; *pragatroop* - evident; *chaitanyamay* - consciousness; *ae* - that; *endhān* - sign; *sadāy* - always

MEANING
That, which is known to always remain separate during all states (like waking, dreaming, sleeping) and which also knows those states, such an evident consciousness is the ever-present sign of the soul.

EXPLANATION
The disciple has questioned the very existence of the soul in the absence of its distinct sign. In response, the Guru spells out the sign by which the soul can be recognised as separate from the body, in a beautiful style with the usage of very few

words. He explains that in the different states of the body, that which always remains separate from it and keeps knowing, such an evident, directly experiential conscious substance is the soul.

At birth, a state of infancy exists, followed by childhood, youth, adulthood and old age. All these states occur and are then destroyed. Infancy passes and childhood emerges. However, even though these states get destroyed, the experiences associated with them remain intact. The experiences of childhood are recollected even in old age. This proves that the knower of these states has been present throughout. It is a separate, independent substance which does not get destroyed with the various states that have passed. Throughout all these transitions, it remains constant. This substance is the soul.

The same phenomenon can be observed with respect to the three states of waking, dreaming and sleeping. Consciousness or knowingness is not only experienced while one is awake, but also while one dreams or sleeps. After waking up, one often remembers his dream and at times in abundant graphic detail. Even during sleep, one moves his hands to drive away mosquitoes. When he wakes up, he realises he has slept well, and feels fresh. This substantiates that some entity has experienced sound sleep which it remembers after waking up. The states have passed but the knower is the same. The knowing substance prevails in all states and remains different from them. This knowing substance is the soul.

That which is known to be separate from all the states, whose existence is known even after each state has passed and is the knower of each of these states, is the soul. Irrespective of which state one is in, the soul remains separate and conscious. This extremely evident consciousness is the indication of the soul's existence. The nature of constant knowingness is the sign by which the soul can be recognised. This sign is absolutely apparent and totally different from others. Consciousness is indisputably the permanent attribute of the soul.

An attribute can be defined as something which exists in all parts of a particular substance and in all its modifications too. Consciousness is the attribute of the soul which is present throughout the soul at all times. Although it passes through different states there is never any change in the nature of the soul. The soul always remains separate with its specific attribute of knowingness. The soul never loses its knowingness. This sign is never destroyed, remaining unchanged forever. Therefore, through this sign of consciousness, one can gain conviction regarding the soul.

Thus, in this verse, the Guru proves the existence of the soul through the ever-present sign of knowingness. It has been illustrated in such a simple, lucid manner that it can easily be understood even by a layperson. Everyone has gone through these different states and at the same time experienced that the knower is always separate from these states. By applying this evident experience, the presence of the soul in the body has been demonstrated, which can be grasped without much effort or practice. Faith in the existence of the soul is strengthened, although it is not apparent to the physical eye.

VERSE - 55

Reply 3 - Knowledge establishes knower

In verse 47, the disciple had presented the argument that if the soul exists, why is it not known the way a pot, cloth and other objects are known. If the soul truly exists it should be known in the same way as these objects. This argument has been resolved in verses 55-56. In His inimitable style, the Guru says -

ઘટ, પટ આદિ જાણ તું, તેથી તેને માન;
જાણનાર તે માન નહિ, કહીએ કેવું જ્ઞાન? ||૫૫||

Ghat, pat ādi jān tu, tethi tene mān;
Jānnār te mān nahi, kahiye kevu jnān? ||55||

Ghat - pot; *pat* - cloth; *ādi* - etc.; *jān* - know; *tu* - you; *tethi* - therefore; *tene* - them; *mān* - believe; *jānnār* - knower; *te* - that; *mān* - believe; *nahi* - not; *kahiye* - say; *kevu* - what kind of; *jnān* - knowledge

MEANING

You accept the existence of pot, cloth, etc., because you are able to know them. However, you do not accept the existence of the knower of those objects. What can one say about such knowledge?

EXPLANATION

The disciple believes that objects which can be perceived by the senses exist and those which cannot, do not. This logic, however, is flawed. There are many substances in the world which cannot be perceived directly by the senses. One needs the help of inference, testimony, etc., in order to know them.

There are various reasons why such objects cannot be perceived by the senses. An object could either be too far away, like the Eiffel Tower for someone in India, or too nearby, like collyrium applied to the eyes. It could either be miniscule, like an atom, or concealed like something on the other side of the wall. The object might be impossible to see like one's own back or might have existed in the past. The perception of objects could be hampered due to a disturbed mind or some defect in the senses. Thus, the existence of so many objects is accepted despite not being perceived directly by the senses due to certain reasons. Similarly, the soul is imperceivable to the senses because it is intangible, invisible, formless, devoid of touch, etc. Hence, it is erroneous to conclude or insist that the soul does not exist as it cannot be grasped by the senses.

Although the very premise of the disciple is invalid, he doubts the existence of the soul instead of realising that his knowledge is ill-founded. Making use of very simple logic, the Guru explains that there are many objects like pot-cloth, etc., in this world. Since they can all be perceived by the senses, you accept their existence, but why do you not accept the soul, which is the knower of those very objects? You know all these objects, so it is clear that there is a knower. The presence of a knower is made implicit by the knowledge of objects.

It is impossible to accept knowledge without a knower. If there was no knower then substances would not be known at all. However, substances are known and so the knower exists, which is the soul. Thus, the existence of the soul is established. The existence of the soul which knows is as true as the existence of the substances which are known.

Demonstrating the irony, the Guru tells the disciple that you believe that pot-cloth, etc., are objects of knowledge and do not believe the soul which is the knower of them all. What can such knowledge of yours be called? It is clear to even the rationally inclined that accepting the known and knowledge, but not accepting the knower is absurd! It is as surprising as a person who has seen the whole world but says he has no eyes. It is indeed strange that the soul who knows the objects of the world using its own knowledge, itself, declares that the soul does not exist!

Thus, if there is an object of knowledge, there is always a knower too. Therefore, just as objects of knowledge like pot-cloth exist, the soul also certainly exists. With this logic, the Guru proves the existence of the soul. As it is a formless substance, the soul cannot be perceived by the senses. However, being a conscious entity, it can be evidently experienced by its attribute of knowingness.

What the disciple has missed out on, is that a lot exists which is beyond the realm of tangibility. The problem is not in the 'object' but in the 'perceiving'. The disciple is only perceiving what his senses allow him to perceive. He looks through the glasses of senses and hence is unable to see anything which does not have a base in the empirical. While the senses are the means to acknowledge the existence of tangible objects, it is obvious there is a knower above and beyond all of them. The knower is the soul, which gives sense to the senses.

VERSE - 56

Body and soul are not one

In the previous verse, the existence of a knower who perceives objects like pot-cloth was established. Putting to rest even the slightest of doubt as to whether the body is that knower, the Guru says -

પરમ બુદ્ધિ કૃશ દેહમાં, સ્થૂળ દેહ મતિ અલ્પ;
દેહ હોય જો આતમા, ઘટે ન આમ વિકલ્પ. ||૫૬||

Param buddhi krush dehmā, sthool deh mati alp;
Deh hoi jo ātamā, ghatey na ām vikalp. ||56||

Param - supreme; *buddhi* - intelligence; *krush* - thin; *dehmā* - in body;
sthool - fat; *deh* - body; *mati* - intelligence; *alp* - little; *deh* - body;
hoi - is; *jo* - if; *ātamā* - soul; *ghatey* - arise; *na* - not; *ām* - such;
vikalp - contradiction

MEANING

Super intelligence is found in one who has a lean body, and lesser intelligence in one who has a large body. If the body is the soul, such a contradiction would not arise.

EXPLANATION

Knowledge of the objects substantiates the attribute of knowing. However, one might argue that establishing the attribute of knowing only proves there is a possessor of this attribute. It does not necessarily mean the soul possesses this attribute. Knowingness could be the nature of the body itself. In this verse, the Guru uproots this doubt and strengthens the conviction that the attribute of knowing is not the nature of the body, thus validating the separateness of the body and the soul. The Guru now takes this debate to another plane. He points out that if the theory about the body and soul being one is true, then the shape, size and volume of the body should be directly proportional to the knowledge it possesses. If knowledge is an attribute of the body, then a large body should have more knowledge. Likewise, a lean body should possess lesser knowledge. Knowledge should be in equal proportion to the body.

Upon observing, it is apparent that such a correlation between knowledge and the body does not exist. Even supreme intelligence in a frail body and little intelligence in a large body is witnessed. This fact proves that the amount of knowledge does not correspond to the size of the body. There is no connection between knowledge and the body. One should not measure or expect knowledge merely by observing the size of the body.

In the world, many examples that prove the contrary are found. It is observed that someone with a thin body possesses great intelligence. For instance, Shrimadji had a frail body but possessed extraordinary intelligence. Shri Ātmasiddhi Shāstra, His magnum opus, is testament to a supreme intellect. Several great sages had lean frames, yet immense knowledge flowed through them. The converse is also true, that a being with a large body could also have little intelligence. Elephants and rhinoceroses have large bodies but are much less intelligent than humans. This is precisely why humans are capable of controlling them.

Proving that knowledge is not an attribute of the body, there is some entity besides the body, which possesses the attribute of knowledge. This other entity is the soul. No other substance has the ability to know. The knower is within the body and yet separate from it. Therefore, the body is not the soul. Under no circumstance can knowingness be identified with the body. It is an attribute of the soul and can never be separated from it. Just as heat cannot be separated from fire or sweetness from sugar, knowingness cannot be kept apart from the soul.

VERSE - 57

Distinctness of both substances

The soul is a substance with the attribute of knowingness and is separate from inanimate substances like the body. After proving this line of thought with various potent arguments, to further strengthen this conviction, the Guru says -

જડ ચેતનનો ભિન્ન છે, કેવળ પ્રગટ સ્વભાવ;
એકપણું પામે નહીં, ત્રણે કાળ દ્વયભાવ. ||૫૭||

Jad chetanno bhinna chhe, keval pragat swabhāv;
Ekpanu pāmey nahi, trane kāl dvaybhāv. ||57||

Jad - inanimate; **chetanno** - of consciousness; **bhinna** - different; **chhe** - is; **keval** - absolutely; **pragat** - evident; **swabhāv** - nature; **ekpanu** - oneness; **pāmey** - attains; **nahi** - not; **trane** - all three; **kāl** - times; **dvaybhāv** - duality

MEANING

The nature of non-sentient and sentient substances is absolutely and evidently different. They can never become one, and this duality remains in all three times - past, present and future.

EXPLANATION

This verse highlights the independent nature of each category of substances. Each of these can be distinguished by specific attributes just as two football teams can be distinguished by different coloured jerseys. No substance can transform its nature. The states of a substance can change, but not their nature. Each substance is steadfast in its own nature and cannot become one with any other substance in the past, present or future.

The nature of the inanimate and that of the animate is completely different. That which can never have the nature of knowingness is inanimate, and that which is always of the nature of knowingness, is animate. It is evident that both have completely different natures. As their natures are clearly different, they are bound to be completely different as well. Just as fire can be identified by its heat and water by its coolness, the inanimate and animate can be identified by their varying natures.

Despite the inanimate and animate existing together, the inanimate never becomes animate and vice versa. It cannot be transformed into a substance of a completely different nature. They never attain oneness. If watermelons and oranges are placed together in a vessel for a long time, they do not become one. It is easy to separate them. Similarly, the animate soul has occupied the same space as the inanimate body for a long time, but they have never become one or the same. It is easy to identify them by their nature. This duality prevails in all three periods of time, and they certainly cannot attain oneness by either magic or logic.

Thus, this verse reaffirms the distinctiveness between the inanimate and animate, conveys that the attributes and functions of both are evidently different, and illustrates the independence of both substances. It also clearly states that the modification of each substance is independent. They never attain oneness by mutually transferring attributes. Such is the dual nature of substances. The absolute principle of duality of the inanimate and animate, which never changes, in all three periods of time, has been ascertained. In this way, the one-sided view that only matter exists, and the one-sided view that only consciousness exists have been simultaneously rebutted. The Guru draws a clear difference between the living consciousness and lifeless inanimate forms that occupy the world. To confuse the soul with something as dissimilar to itself as non-sentient matter is indeed perplexing.

VERSE - 58

Soul is doubter of itself!

Having satisfactorily resolved the disciple's doubts, from verses 49 to 57, finally expressing something astonishing that will lead the disciple into deep contemplation, the Guru says -

આત્માની શંકા કરે, આત્મા પોતે આપ;
શંકાનો કરનાર તે, અચરજ એહ અમાપ. ||૫૮||

Ātmāni shankā karey, ātmā potey āp;
Shankāno karnār te, achraj eh amāp. ||58||

Ātmāni - of soul; *shankā* - doubt; *karey* - does; *ātmā* - soul; *potey āp* - itself; *shankāno* - of doubt; *karnār* - doer; *te* - it; *achraj* - surprise; *eh* - that; *amāp* - beyond measure

MEANING

The one who doubts the existence of the soul is the soul itself. It is a matter of immeasurable surprise that the soul is the doubter of itself!

EXPLANATION

The Guru systematically resolved the arguments regarding the existence of the soul through proper foresight and meaningful replies, in a remarkably quick time. He has a knack of unravelling the deepest mysteries of philosophy in a simple way. He has a unique flair of explaining the most difficult principles in an easy, lucid manner. In this verse, in which the first fundamental truth culminates, the Guru classically establishes the existence of the soul through a logical proposition.

He says that the arising of doubt regarding the existence of the soul is in itself the proof of its existence. Who has the doubt whether the soul exists? Or rather, who has this doubting knowledge or in which substance does it arise? When one says 'I doubt', who is the 'I' that doubts? Contemplating on this will reveal that the 'I' who doubts is the soul itself. Only a substance with the attribute of knowingness can doubt and that substance is the soul. Inanimate substances do not possess the attribute of knowingness; hence they do not possess the capacity to doubt. The soul is evident through the existence of doubt and no other proof is required for its existence.

Doubting the soul is like accepting an image seen in the mirror, but not accepting the existence of the mirror itself. If the reflection is accepted, then it is only natural to accept that in which the reflection occurs. The reflection cannot occur simply in space, it needs a mirror. Similarly, while doubting the existence of the soul, it is obviously acceptable that there is a conscious entity which is the soul. Without the soul, there cannot be any doubt.

To ensure the disciple realises his folly, the Guru says that it is a wonder beyond measure that he doubts the soul's existence while being the very soul which creates this doubt. Can there be any greater surprise than to accept the doubt but not the doubter? It is like asking, 'Am I alive?' - as only a living person could ask such a question. It is indeed strange that one doubts his own existence.

Thus, expressing immense surprise at the disciple who harboured the doubt regarding the existence of the soul, the Guru sweetly taunts him. He makes the disciple doubt his very doubt and brings about a doubtless conviction in him regarding the soul, which is the doubter.

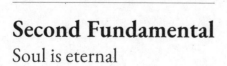

Second Fundamental
Soul is eternal

Having accepted the first fundamental, 'soul exists', the straightforward, humble disciple now expresses his confusion regarding the second of the six fundamentals - 'soul is eternal'.

Since the disciple is contemplative and has an eagerness to know the truth, his thoughts now flow in a sequential order. Although he has adopted the right conviction regarding the soul's existence, he is still not free of doubt regarding the eternal nature of the soul. Until now, the soul has not been thought of or known to be without a body, therefore the disciple is unable to get a clear understanding of how it can be eternal. To gain a satisfactory solution regarding the second fundamental, 'soul is eternal', and to establish a firm conviction in it, he presents his arguments and requests answers from the Guru.

Shrimadji has dedicated twelve verses 59-70, to the subject of the eternal nature of the soul. In two verses 60-61, the humble disciple puts forth two arguments supporting his doubt regarding the eternal nature of the soul. One is, under the influence of the *Chārvāk* philosophy, and the second, under the influence of the Buddhist philosophy. Shrimadji has presented well-known arguments of these two philosophies that do not accept the eternal nature of the soul. Without naming them, He has expressed their viewpoints as an enquiry from the disciple. Thereafter, He has given the Guru's solution to the doubt in nine verses 62-70. He shows the incorrectness in the disciple's doubt and establishes the eternal nature of the soul, for his spiritual welfare.

VERSE - 59

Disciple's conviction of soul's existence

Responding to the Guru's solution regarding the existence of the soul, the disciple says -

આત્માના અસ્તિત્વના, આપે કહ્યા પ્રકાર;
સંભવ તેનો થાય છે, અંતર કર્યે વિચાર. ||૫૯||

Ātmānā astitvanā, Āpe kahyā prakār;
Sambhav teno thāy chhe, antar karye vichār. ||59||

Ātmānā - soul's; *astitvanā* - regarding existence; *Āpe* - You; *kahyā* - explained; *prakār* - ways; *sambhav* - possible; *teno* - it; *thāy* - seems; *chhe* - is; *antar* - internally; *karye* - doing; *vichār* - contemplation

MEANING

By internally contemplating upon the clarification provided by You regarding the soul's existence, it seems possible to me.

EXPLANATION

The Guru compassionately showered His knowledge regarding the soul's existence upon the disciple, who imbibed the essence with a single-minded focus. To solve his doubt, the Guru utilised several methods by way of logic and appropriate examples, which made it simple and interesting to understand. As he reflected deeply upon the Guru's solution, it became more and more conclusive to him. Having contemplated upon the solution, the disciple has understood the flaw in his own reasoning and has now acquired the right conviction that the soul exists.

Such deep contemplation is absolutely necessary for spiritual progress. The impressions of attachment and aversion are so strong that the mind is constantly occupied by them. Contemplation is the unfailing antidote to this condition, as it aids the creation of indelible positive impressions. When one contemplates, the mind gets involved and influenced. So the impact is powerful. It affects one's thinking and behaviour, bringing about a transformation. With proper analysis, it does not take long for the understanding to turn into firm faith, which stays steadfast even when faced with extremely unfavourable circumstances. Therefore, an aspirant must contemplate deeply upon the truth so that it gets established as faith and is retained through the journey.

The disciple has reflected over the Guru's replies in great depth. He has contemplated upon the solutions imparted by the Guru and gained the conviction that the soul exists. Thereafter, he declares that through intense contemplation on the Guru's solution, his doubts regarding the soul's existence have been resolved, making the possibility of its existence a firm conviction. The disciple honestly uses the word '*sambhav*' - possible, or words to the effect, 'it seems possible'. This is because he has accepted the soul's existence through the process of thinking, not experience. He has become intellectually convinced, but has not yet attained self-realisation. This not only illustrates the humility, intelligence and eagerness of the disciple but also his honesty.

The word 'possible' by no means indicates that the disciple is uncertain about the soul's existence. He is convinced of it beyond all doubt, being satisfied with the Guru's replies after earnestly contemplating over them. He is absolutely clear about the difference between the body and the animate entity which is the soul. One is visible, perceptible to the senses and steeped in the material. The other is invisible, beyond the senses and completely spiritual. Such divine vision is awakening in the disciple through the Guru's invaluable words and immeasurable benevolence.

VERSE - 60

Doubt 1 - Soul is not eternal

In this verse, under the influence of the *Chārvāk* philosophy, from the perspective of gross modifications, expressing the impermanence of the soul, the disciple says -

બીજી શંકા થાય ત્યાં, આત્મા નહિ અવિનાશ;
દેહયોગથી ઉપજે, દેહવિયોગે નાશ. ||૬૦||

Biji shankā thāy tyā, ātmā nahi avināsh;
Dehyogthi upje, dehviyoge nāsh. ||60||

Biji - second; *shankā* - doubt; *thāy* - arises; *tyā* - now; *ātmā* - soul;
nahi - not; *avināsh* - indestructible; *dehyogthi* - association of body;
upje - created; *dehviyoge* - separation from body; *nāsh* - destroyed

MEANING

The second doubt arises that the soul is not indestructible. It is created with the association of the body and is destroyed on separation from the body.

EXPLANATION

Despite being free of doubt regarding the existence of the soul, another doubt arises in the disciple that this existence does not remain forever. The soul exists but it is not an indestructible eternal substance. The disciple comes up with a new doubt and wonders whether the soul is immortal. When a customer goes to a shop, he first asks whether a particular product is available.

If it is, he then enquires about its warranty period. In the same way, the disciple first questions the existence of the soul and after accepting that, he puts forth his doubt regarding the period of that existence. He presents his view that the soul is not an everlasting substance that exists in all three periods of time.

The disciple says there is no reason to believe the permanence of the soul as it is only recognised in a living body. It has no existence of its own apart from when it lives in the body. It exists only when the body is alive, and ceases to exist once the body perishes. The soul is an impermanent substance, destroyed along with the destruction of the body. Thus, the soul is created with the association of the body and is destroyed when separated from the body. When the body is born, the soul is born. When the body dies, so does the soul. Hence the period of existence of the body and the soul is the same.

This argument is influenced by the Chārvāk philosophy. The disciple has studied various philosophies and is aware of their principles. The Chārvāk believe that consciousness is created by the association of five elements - earth, water, fire, air and space. It expires at the disintegration of the five elements. Consciousness is formed with the birth of the body by the combination of these elements and when they get scattered, the body is destroyed, leading to its destruction too. They do not believe in the presence of consciousness in these individual elements but say that a knowing entity is created by the right mixture of these elements, which gets destroyed when they separate.

They support their belief with an example. The components used in making wine do not have any intoxicating quality. *Daturā* (a type of shrubby plant), jaggery, water, etc., are not intoxicants by nature. However, when they are mixed in the right proportion and through the right process, the intoxicating wine is produced. Similarly, the five elements do not possess consciousness, yet when they are mixed in the right proportion and right way, consciousness is generated. This intoxicating quality stays for a certain period and then dies out. Similarly, the nature of the soul is of creation and destruction. It is not an eternal substance whose existence remains the same in all three periods of time.

Thus, his doubt can be surmised as - the soul emerges with the formation of the body and gets destroyed when the body is decomposed. It is a substance that exists only as long as the body lives. It lasts for a limited period of time. Just as objects like pot, cloth, etc., last for a fixed amount of time, the soul remains only until the body does. The soul lives, dies and then just vanishes from the earth. There is nothing before and nothing after.

VERSE - 61

Doubt 2 - Soul is momentary

In this verse, the disciple, under the influence of the Buddhist philosophy, from the perspective of subtle modifications, expresses the impermanence of the soul. The disciple says -

અથવા વસ્તુ ક્ષણિક છે, ક્ષણે ક્ષણે પલટાય;
એ અનુભવથી પણ નહીં, આત્મા નિત્ય જણાય. ||૬૧||

Athvā vastu kshanik chhe, kshane kshane paltāy;
Ae anubhavthi pan nahi, ātmā nitya janāy. ||61||

Athvā - or; *vastu* - substance; *kshanik* - momentary; *chhe* - is; *kshane kshane* - every moment; *paltāy* - changes; *ae* - that; *anubhavthi* - from experience; *pan* - also; *nahi* - not; *ātmā* - soul; *nitya* - eternal; *janāy* - known

MEANING

Or else, the substance is momentary as it is observed that it changes every moment. From this experience as well, the soul does not seem to be eternal.

EXPLANATION

The disciple had previously expressed his argument regarding the indestructible nature of the soul, while under the influence of the *Chārvāk* philosophy. He now presents his argument about the eternal nature of the soul while under the influence of the Buddhist philosophy. In the previous verse, the disciple had said that the soul exists only for a limited amount of time. It is created due to the association with the body and destroyed on separation. Since its existence is limited by the lifespan of the body, it is impermanent. In this verse, he puts forth his argument to the Guru in a different way than that stated above, which is signified by the word '*athvā*' - or. He says that observing from the perspective of momentariness also, the soul is proven to be impermanent.

Providing another reason to prove the temporary nature of the soul, the disciple says it is an everyday experience that things change each moment. Change is the law of life. All things are clearly observed to be undergoing change. Things constantly evolve, grow, decay and decompose. With every passing moment, a new object becomes old. A new car deteriorates due to wear and tear, ultimately turning to scrap. Gross changes are most evident whereas subtle changes are not observed very easily.

There is nothing in the world that never changes. Objects like pot and cloth seem to undergo changes every moment. If they always stayed the same, they would never become old or get worn out. No substance can remain the same forever. As this is a universal experience, it should apply to the soul as well, as it is a substance too. The soul does not remain in the same form. It is found to be constantly changing. It is experienced that the auspicious and inauspicious feelings arising in the soul undergo continuous change. Feelings like calm, anger, repentance and forgiveness keep changing. Therefore, all substances, including the soul, must be transitory. Each substance in the world, whether psychical or physical is seen to be undergoing modifications every moment and hence cannot be eternal.

The argument of the disciple is due to the influence of the Buddhist philosophy. According to the Buddhist doctrine of momentariness, nothing is everlasting. All substances are momentary, including the soul. This theory of momentariness of all things is supported by elaborate arguments and examples. A lamp burns through the night, but the flame of each moment is dependent on its own conditions and different from the flame of another moment, which is dependent on other conditions. Yet there is an unbroken succession of different flames. Though these two flames are different, they are causally connected to each other. Similarly, there appears to be an unbroken stream of consciousness, but each soul lasts only for one moment. The soul is destroyed at one moment and another born at the next moment because of *vāsanā* - strong desires. Rebirth is not the migration of the same soul into another body, it is the causation of the next soul by the previous soul. The new soul inherits its characters from the previous one. This continuity of constant destruction and creation finally ends with complete annihilation of desires, like the lamp getting extinguished with the exhaustion of oil. The complete destruction of the soul is *nirvān* - liberation.

This theory of momentariness seems convincing enough to the disciple as it tallies with his experience. Viewing the changing nature of every object, he feels that the soul is momentary, impermanent and hence does not exist in all three periods of time. Thus, from the perspective of timespan of the body or the momentariness of all substances, the soul does not seem to be eternal. Either the soul is created and destroyed along with the body, or it exists only for a moment. It is far from immortal. The disciple humbly appeals to the Guru to resolve and eliminate this doubt.

VERSE - 62

Reply 1 - Who knows creation and destruction?

The Guru now provides a methodical, impactful, firm and wisdom-filled solution to the logical arguments arising out of the disciple's sequential thought process. As a result of this, the second fundamental 'soul is eternal' is proven to the disciple. Establishing this through different evidences like logic, experience and inference, the Guru completely uproots the doubt in the disciple's mind.

In verse 60, supporting his doubt that the soul is not eternal, the disciple had said, 'It is created with the association of the body, and is destroyed when separated from it.' The Guru answers this argument with three main points. To determine the creation and destruction of any substance, it is necessary to examine the three points listed below -

1. Is there a knower of this event of creation and destruction?
2. Does the substance that is created and destroyed have the same characteristics as the substance from which it is created or the substance which it dissolves into?
3. Is there any authentic evidence to prove that this substance is not created or destroyed?

The Guru has discussed these three points in six verses 62-67. The first point is discussed in verses 62-63, the second point in verses 64-66, and the third point has been discussed in verse 67. The Guru presents the deliberation regarding whether there is any knower of the event of the soul's creation and destruction in two verses 62-63. In the first verse the Guru says -

દેહ માત્ર સંયોગ છે, વળી જડ રૂપી દૃશ્ય;
ચેતનનાં ઉત્પત્તિ લય, કોના અનુભવ વશ્ય? ||૬૨||

Deh mātra sanyog chhe, vali jad roopi drashya;
Chetannā utpatti lay, konā anubhav vashya? ||62||

Deh - body; *mātra* - only; *sanyog* - association; *chhe* - is; *vali* - also; *jad* - inanimate; *roopi* - with form; *drashya* - visible; *chetannā* - soul's; *utpatti* - creation; *lay* - destruction; *konā* - whose; *anubhav* - experience; *vashya* - subject to

MEANING

The body is formed by the union of material particles and is only temporarily associated with the soul. Moreover, it is inanimate, possesses form and is visible. Then, who experiences, that is, who has the knowledge of the creation and destruction of the soul?

EXPLANATION

The disciple is extremely eager and possesses depth of thought. His urge to gain knowledge is evident from his questions. They are not haphazard but in a logical sequence. He has accepted the existence of the soul and then presented his doubt regarding its eternal nature. He feels that there is creation and destruction of the body as well as the soul. The soul is a substance that lasts only as long as the body. The

Guru commences the reply to his doubt by strengthening the disciple's foundation regarding the nature of the body.

The Guru elucidates that the body is only an association. It is made from the union of five elements - earth, water, fire, air and space which are known as *panchbhoot*. The elements disintegrate after a certain period of time. The body is only temporarily related to the soul, it is not a unification. There are two types of relationships -

1. *Tādātmya sambandh* - the relationship in which one cannot exist without the other. For example, sugar and sweetness.

2. *Sanyog sambandh* - the relationship in which substances can exist with and without each other. For example, hydrogen and oxygen.

The former is the relationship between the soul and consciousness and the latter, the relationship between the soul and the body. It is only a temporary association, which is subject to separation. Atoms of the body separate from the soul and new atoms come into association with it. Thus, the word '**sanyog**' has two meanings - the body is the union of five elements, and it is temporarily associated with the soul.

Moreover, the body is '**jad**' - inanimate. It is bereft of consciousness, without the attribute of knowingness, non-sentient and non-living. It is '**roopi**' - with a form. It has the nature of colour, shape, height and weight. It is '**drashya**' - visible, hence can be seen or perceived with the eyes. Thus, in the first line, the Guru explains the nature of the body with which the disciple imagines that the soul is created. In the second line, the Guru poses a question and inspires the disciple to deliberate over it.

Kindling the disciple's thinking, the Guru counters his argument by asking the following - Whose experience is it that the soul is created and destroyed? Who has known the soul being created through association with the body and being destroyed because of separation from it? The knower of the soul's creation and destruction can only be one of two substances, either the soul or the body, as only two types of substances exist in the universe - inanimate and animate. Thus, the knower of the creation and destruction of the soul can either be the body or the soul. The Guru encourages the disciple to contemplate on these two options, so that he himself realises the inappropriateness of his argument. Contemplating over both will reveal that the statement regarding the creation and destruction of the soul is not backed by actual experience, it is merely a figment of one's imagination.

The first option can be tackled by the first line of this verse itself. Since the nature of the body is inanimate, it cannot know anything. Neither can it know its own creation and destruction, nor that of the soul. How can a substance which itself is devoid of the attribute of knowingness, know that the soul is created and destroyed? That can only be known by a substance with consciousness. Thus, the body does not have the knowledge of the birth and death of the soul.

VERSE - 63

Knower has to be separate entity

In verse 62, the Guru negated the first option of the body knowing the creation and the destruction of the soul. In verse 63, He now shows how the second option, of the soul knowing this, is also impossible. The Guru says -

જેના અનુભવ વશ્ય એ, ઉત્પન્ન લયનું જ્ઞાન;
તે તેથી જુદા વિના, થાય ન કેમે ભાન. ||૬૩||

Jenā anubhav vashya ae, utpanna laynu jnān;
Te tethi judā vinā, thāy na keme bhān. ||63||

Jenā - whose; *anubhav* - experience; *vashya* - subject to; *ae* - that; *utpanna* - creation; *laynu* - of destruction; *jnān* - knowledge; *te* - that; *tethi* - from that; *judā* - separate; *vinā* - without; *thāy* - occurs; *na* - not; *keme* - in any way; *bhān* - know

MEANING

That which experiences the knowledge of the soul's creation and destruction, must be separate from it. Unless it is separate, it is not possible to know this, in any way.

EXPLANATION

The Guru prompts the disciple to think about who could be considered to have experienced the birth and death of the soul. From the explanation of the nature of the body, it is already crystal clear that it cannot know the emergence and extinction of the soul. Being inanimate, the body does not possess the property of knowingness. Hence, it cannot know anything about the soul, whether it is eternal or impermanent. If the body does not know, who could possibly be the knower? The other option is the soul itself. However, even the soul cannot know it. The concept seems illogical as it is not possible for an entity to know its own birth and death.

The soul does not exist before its own creation, hence cannot know its birth. If the soul which knows 'the soul has been created' is present, then how can it be said that the soul is created? If the soul which knows 'the soul has been destroyed' is present, then how can it be said that the soul is destroyed? Therefore, the statement is negated by its very utterance. To say that the soul knows its own creation and destruction is incorrect, because the creation and destruction of anything can be known only by one who is present before its creation as well as after its destruction. For the soul to know its own birth and death, it should have been present prior to its birth and survive its destruction. If the soul itself is deemed to be the knower of its own creation and destruction, then that itself proves the eternal nature of the soul. To believe that the soul knows its own creation and destruction is very strange and irrational.

Therefore, it can be concluded that some other substance apart from the soul can experience the creation and destruction of the soul. It is logical that the knower of the creation and destruction of a substance has to be separate from that substance. That which experiences the knowledge of the birth and death of the soul, can only know if it is separate from the soul. The knower must be independent of it. However, inanimate material substances that are different from the soul cannot know. The fact of the matter is that there is no conceivable agency that could ever know about it. Hence, those who say that consciousness is created and destroyed do not seem to be speaking based on evidence.

The disciple had presented the argument that the body and the soul are born together and die together. However, neither the body nor the soul can register the birth and death of the soul. Rather, the soul knows about the birth and death of the body. It is an unfounded belief that they are both born together and die together. The theory turns out to be merely a play of imagination, a hypothetical presentation, as there is no one who can know the soul's generation and destruction. The truth is the soul can neither be created nor destroyed, as it is eternal.

VERSE - 64

Soul not produced by association

In verses 62 and 63, the Guru proved that no one can know the creation and destruction of the soul. Therefore, the argument that the soul is created and destroyed through association with the body is not backed by experience. Now, through logical reasoning, in verses 64 to 66, the Guru will prove that the soul is uncreated and indestructible.

Resolving the disciple's probable doubt that the soul is also created by some association, the Guru says -

જે સંયોગો દેખિયે, તે તે અનુભવ દૃશ્ય;
ઉપજે નહિ સંયોગથી, આત્મા નિત્ય પ્રત્યક્ષ. ||૬૪||

Je sanyogo dekhiye, te te anubhav drashya;
Upje nahi sanyogthi, ātmā nitya pratyaksh. ||64||

Je - whatever; *sanyogo* - associations; *dekhiye* - seen; *te te* - those; *anubhav* - experiential; *drashya* - visible; *upje* - created; *nahi* - not; *sanyogthi* - through association; *ātmā* - soul; *nitya* - eternal; *pratyaksh* - evidently

MEANING

Whatever associations are visible, are known by the soul. Since the soul is not observed to have been created from any association, it is evidently eternal.

EXPLANATION

There are numerous objects in the world that are created from various associations. All those objects and associations are known to the soul. They can be observed by the soul, which sees and knows these associations. The body is a result of the combination of five elements. The soul knows its constituents and also the body's modifications. The soul is separate, the knower of the body and all other associations.

Contemplating upon the nature of those associations, not a single one of them is known from which the soul can be created. The soul is the knower of associations, not a substance created from associations. Regardless of the combinations of matter observed, the soul is not seen to be originating through any such one. It does not arise from a combination of atoms and molecules or a synthesis of material substances. No combination of inanimate substances can create a soul.

In a laboratory, a combination of chemicals forms a compound. However, it cannot generate life itself. Science has developed robots that resemble the structure of a human being, but has not been able to create life in them. It has built automobiles and computers, which work more efficiently than the humans, yet it cannot breathe life into them. Thus, all associations like the body, for example, are visible and the soul knows these associations. The soul cannot be created from any such association; hence it is a natural substance. It is self-existent, self-sustaining and self-contained.

Since the soul is not a product of association, it is logical that the soul is eternal. The body and other objects are created through associations and are therefore impermanent, whereas the soul is not created through any association and is therefore, permanent. In this way, the Guru has explained the impossibility of the creation and destruction of the soul through simple logic, establishing that the soul is evidently eternal.

VERSE - 65

Such experience cannot exist

The previous three verses 62-64, were the introduction to the solution of this argument. Now in this verse, addressing the argument directly, the Guru says -

જડથી ચેતન ઊપજે, ચેતનથી જડ થાય;
એવો અનુભવ કોઈને, ક્યારે કદી ન થાય. ||૬૫||

Jadthi   chetan   upje,   chetanthi   jad   thāy;
Evo   anubhav   koine,   kyāre   kadi   na   thāy. ||65||

Jadthi - from inanimate; *chetan* - consciousness; *upje* - created; *chetanthi* - from consciousness; *jad* - inanimate; *thāy* - arises; *evo* - such; *anubhav* - experience; *koine* - to anyone; *kyāre* - anytime; *kadi* - ever; *na* - not; *thāy* - occur

MEANING

No one can ever experience consciousness created from inanimate matter, or inanimate matter created from consciousness.

EXPLANATION

A well-accepted fact acknowledged by science is that the number of substances in the world can never be increased or decreased, added or subtracted. No original substance can ever be created. Not even a single atom. New objects are produced by the fusion of atoms. What is referred to as the production of objects, is in reality only a modification in the form of substances. No new substances are ever created. In the production of a shirt, there are various stages like the growing of the cotton plant, obtaining cotton fibres from its fruit, making the yarn and turning it into cloth. Although it feels like a new substance has been created, it is just the cotton that has changed form. Similarly, an animate substance is also eternal in nature, only undergoing transformations over time. However, no such transformation is possible in which an inanimate substance can ever be transformed into an animate soul. Matter and soul are independent natural substances.

It has never been, is not, and will never be anyone's experience ever, that an animate soul is created from inanimate substances like the body, or vice versa. This is because the qualities of the effect must be the same as those present in the cause. It can never happen that the cause has the qualities of the inanimate and the effect has the qualities of the animate. Also, if the cause has the qualities of the animate, the effect can never have the qualities of the inanimate. The inanimate and the soul are evidently distinct by nature. It is never possible for the characteristics of one to become that of the other or for both substances to become one. They cannot merge or create a substance with different attributes.

If the animate could be created from the inanimate, then the pot and cloth would also become conscious. And if the inanimate could arise from the animate, then one would be able to see the pot and cloth being produced by the soul. However, no one has ever experienced such phenomena. A table can never come to life and start speaking to people. The inanimate can never become the soul and the soul can never become the inanimate because both substances have very different attributes. It may seem that the soul becomes inanimate at the time of death because there is no movement of the body. However, it is erroneous to believe so because the body was always inanimate even when there was life. At death, the inanimate body and animate soul get separated. The soul leaves the body, hence, there is no movement.

One may question that isn't the soul produced by the fusion of the sperm and the ovum? The truth is, this fusion only brings about a favourable condition for the soul to enter and dwell. The soul enters the womb and a body begins to form around it. If the soul was created by the union of sperm and ovum, it would happen at every such union, but it does not. The soul arrives. It is not created. Even in the case of test tube babies, it is not that life is created. It is because life appears when the sperm and ovum are brought together. A test tube provides the same conducive situation like that in the womb, allowing the soul to enter.

The example of intoxicating wine being produced from non-intoxicating components had been furnished earlier to prove that consciousness can be produced even in a mixture of five elements which do not possess the attribute of consciousness. However, this example is flawed because the quality of intoxication is latent in the ingredients of wine, which manifests once they are mixed in the right manner. If they did not possess this latent quality of intoxication, then wine could have been produced with any mixture of ingredients. It raises the question why those particular ingredients were necessary to produce wine. Oil is obtained from mustard seeds because it is latent in them and not from sand or stones because it is not latent in them. Similarly, consciousness is not latent in the five elements, so it cannot be manifested or produced by their mixture. The soul cannot be created from the collection of material substances. The soul is the knower of associations, not a product of it.

Thus, the Guru speaks about the exclusive characteristics of the matter and the soul. The body is a conglomerate of atoms and can never become the animate soul. Similarly, the soul can never degenerate to lifeless matter. Consciousness cannot arise from the inanimate body. Therefore, the disciple's doubt that the soul is created by association with the inanimate body is incorrect. Through deductive logic, the Guru shows the fallacy of the belief that the soul is created.

VERSE - 66

Soul is definitely eternal

In verses 64 and 65, the Guru established that the soul is never created. Now, in this verse, He establishes the soul's indestructibility. The Guru says -

કોઈ સંયોગોથી નહિ, જેની ઉત્પત્તિ થાય;
નાશ ન તેનો કોઈમાં, તેથી નિત્ય સદાય. ||૬૬||

Koi   sanyogothi   nahi,   jeni   utpatti   thāy;
Nāsh   na   teno   koimā,   tethi   nitya   sadāy. ||66||

Koi - any; *sanyogothi* - from associations; *nahi* - not; *jeni* - that; *utpatti* - creation; *thāy* - occur; *nāsh* - destruction; *na* - not; *teno* - its; *koimā* - into anything; *tethi* - therefore; *nitya* - eternal; *sadāy* - always

MEANING

That which cannot be created from any association, cannot be destroyed into anything else; therefore the soul is definitely eternal.

EXPLANATION

The soul, which is of the nature of knowingness, cannot be created from inanimate substances. After contemplating upon every possible association, it becomes apparent that no such association from which the soul can be created, is known. No matter how many experiments scientists perform, or how passionately they endeavour, it is impossible to create the soul. The soul is not a product of association, it is a natural substance.

It is a universal law that whatever is created at some time is certainly destroyed at another. All objects created by association definitely disintegrate. Hence, objects like the pot and cloth surely disintegrate. No matter how strong a creation is, it certainly deteriorates and finally gets destroyed. Although a sturdy object might persist longer than others, it has a time limit. This holds true for all creation. Several magnificent palaces and mighty forts have turned into ruins. None can escape the principle that if it is created, it will be destroyed. The converse holds true as well. That which has not been created by any association, cannot be destroyed.

The soul is not a substance which has been created, therefore it cannot be destroyed either. There are no elements which create or destroy the soul. Since it is not created by atoms, the question of it being destroyed by their separation does not arise. There is no possibility of division as the soul is not a product of combination. The conscious entity cannot arise from the association of any substance, and hence can never be scattered or destroyed. Neither does it forego its independent nature and transform into another substance, nor does it merge into another substance.

The body is created from an association and is therefore destroyed, whereas the soul is not and therefore never destroyed. Thus, the Guru takes forward the discussion that not only is the soul separate from the body but also imperishable, immortal and permanent. In a simple and lucid manner, He invalidates the disciple's contention that the soul is liable to both creation and destruction. The soul by its very nature is uncreated and indestructible. It is an undying, unending, everlasting, eternal substance, which existed, exists and will exist in all three periods of time.

VERSE - 67

Tendencies confirm soul's eternity

In this verse, the Guru uses the inferential method to further strengthen the disciple's faith regarding the eternal nature of the soul. Here, the Guru says -

ક્રોધાદિ   તરતમ્યતા,   સર્પાદિકની   માંય;
પૂર્વજન્મ સંસ્કાર તે, જીવ નિત્યતા ત્યાંય. ||૬૭||

Krodhādi   tartamyatā,   sarpādikni   māy;
Poorvajanma sanskār te, jeev nityatā tyāy. ||67||

Krodhādi - anger etc.; *tartamyatā* - variation; *sarpādikni* - snakes etc.; *māy* - in; *poorvajanma* - past lives; *sanskār* - impressions; *te* - they; *jeev* - soul; *nityatā* - eternity; *tyāy* - there

MEANING

Variations of anger, etc., are found in snakes, etc., from their very birth. This is due to the impressions and tendencies of their past lives. This proves the eternity of the soul.

EXPLANATION

After deeply contemplating upon the Guru's solution regarding the eternal nature of the soul, the disciple feels his own argument pertaining to the soul's creation and destruction along with that of the body, is baseless. The roots of his false belief begin to weaken and right faith begins to emerge. To cement this conviction, the Guru now employs the technique of inference - a valid source of knowledge and a means by which things not evident through perception can be known. Inference is always based on what can be seen. For example, fire can be inferred on seeing smoke because wherever there is smoke, fire is inevitably present. Similarly, in this verse, based on the evident strangeness seen in the world, the previous births of the soul are inferred, thus proving its eternal nature.

There is enormous variety and diversity prevailing in the world. Tigers are cruel, leopards are violent, rabbits are fearful and cows are timid by nature. Despite them all being members of the animal kingdom, they are different. This disparity of nature also exists in humans. Even children born to the same mother have varied temperaments. Different species of living beings are seen to possess typical tendencies and behaviours. The tendency of anger and the instinct to bite is present to a great degree in snakes. This tendency of anger that propels them to strike and bite, is seen in them from birth. It is not based on any incident that occurs in their current life. It is inherent from the beginning.

The only possible reason for this is impressions from past births. The high intensity of anger seen in snakes, right from birth is the result of its practice in the past, because there has been no such activity in the present body. It can be inferred that these impressions have been carried forward from previous births. The natural traits seen in this birth are due to the retention of impressions from the past.

Science states that the physical variations are due to genes, but it cannot explain the differences in the tendencies of identical twins conceived at the same time and to the same parents. Despite the same environment and upbringing, one is greedy and the other is generous. One is naughty and the other is quiet. This proves the impressions of past lives. The soul must have indulged in that particular tendency and behaviour in previous lives, for it to be displayed in the present life without any training of the same. Thus, there is a deeper root for the traits he possesses. It is a result of past lives.

It is apparent that the variations in the tendencies and behaviours of living beings are due to the impressions of past lives. The present birth is certainly not the first birth. The soul has had to take several births before the present one. It carries impressions from one body to another. The body from the previous birth does not come along, only the impressions do. The body changes and the soul continues to exist as it always did. It can be determined that just as it existed in the past, it will also exist in the future. Therefore, it is established that creation and destruction are of the body, while the soul passing through different bodies is eternal, existing in all three periods of time. Thus, adding another dimension to the ongoing discussions, the Guru points out the cause of variation in tendencies and behaviours. The present traits are the fallout of previous births and with this proof of past life, the eternal nature of the soul is substantiated.

VERSE - 68

Reply 2 - Nature of soul

In verse 61, the disciple had presented the argument that the soul is momentary. The Guru resolves this argument in verses 68 to 70. In this verse, He gives a solution based on the principle of non-absolutism, supporting it with an apt example. The Guru says -

આત્મા દ્રવ્યે નિત્ય છે, પર્યાયે પલટાય;
બાળાદિ વય ત્રણયનું, જ્ઞાન એકને થાય. ||૬૮||

Ātmā   dravye   nitya   chhe,   paryāye   paltāy;
Bālādi   vay   tranyanu,   jnān   ekne   thāy. ||68||

Ātmā - soul; *dravye* - as a substance; *nitya* - eternal; *chhe* - is;
paryāye - states; *paltāy* - change; *bālādi* - childhood etc.; *vay* - age;
tranyanu - of three; *jnān* - knowledge; *ekne* - to one; *thāy* - occur

MEANING

The soul as a substance is eternal but its states change continuously. Childhood, adulthood and old age are different stages of life, but the eternal soul, which has the knowledge of all the three stages, remains the same throughout.

EXPLANATION

The disciple had expressed that since all objects are observed to undergo modifications every moment, they are momentary. From that experience too, the soul does not seem to be eternal. By observing the changes in objects, the disciple feels that an object's very nature is momentary. By noticing feelings like anger, which keep changing, the disciple feels that the soul is not eternal; it is a substance which remains only for a moment before being destroyed.

Replying to this argument, the Guru expounds the structure of a substance in the first line of this verse. Each substance by nature exists in all three periods of time. It abides eternally in its nature. It never changes into another substance, remaining the same throughout. However, there is a modification of various states in the substance. The state undergoes changes every moment. Therefore, the true characteristic of each substance is creation-destruction-constancy. Creation refers to the dawn of a new state, destruction is the elimination of the earlier state and constancy is remaining established in the eternal nature. Thus, the substance is permanent and its states keep changing.

Waves rise and fall in the ocean, but there is no change in the water. Similarly, a new state is created and the old one destroyed, but there is no change in the substance. When a golden pot is destroyed in order to make a crown, its shape and form change. Even then, the gold remains the same substance. Similarly, despite the continuous changing of states every moment, the substance remains constant as an entity.

Thus, a substance undergoes changes while maintaining its inherent essence. The soul too is always a constant substance and its state undergoes changes every moment. Observing through the eyes of *anekāntvād* - the theory of multiplicity of viewpoints; from the perspective of the substance, the soul is eternal. From the perspective of states, it is changing. The soul passes through different states of existence. It assumes the body of a human, animal, etc. However, with the changing forms its inherent properties do not change. The nature remains absolutely unaltered.

This conviction can easily arise from the example given in the second line of this verse. The embodied soul undergoes three states - childhood, youth and old age, however, the embodied one remains the same throughout. This is evident as the three states are known by the same person. One experiences that the events of childhood are retained by the memory even during youth, and those of childhood and youth, even in old age. If the soul was being destroyed every moment, it would not be possible for experiences of one state to be recalled in another. Although the states change, they are remembered. This proves that the soul as a substance does not change. Its state undergoes changes but the soul remains one, singular in identity. In this manner, using a beautiful example, the Guru proves the eternal and changing nature of the soul.

This analysis establishes that the soul is not momentary, but an eternal substance. The soul as a substance is permanent and as modifying states is impermanent. If the soul were momentary, it could not possess any knowledge other than the present modification. As this is not true, it is not momentary.

The mistake of the disciple is that he accepted the changing states but overlooked the unchanging substance. Although it is true that feelings like anger are constantly changing, the soul is not absolutely impermanent, it remains permanent as a substance. The soul enters the body, accompanies it on the long journey of life and then departs from the body at death. Throughout these modifications, as a substance it remains consistent, constant, continuous and changeless.

———— ⟨⟨◊⟩⟩ ————

VERSE - 69

Narrator is not momentary

Although every substance has both the qualities, permanence and impermanence, some believe the soul to be absolutely impermanent. They believe it is created and destroyed every moment. Logically proving that this belief is incorrect and explaining that it is impossible for the soul to have a momentary existence, the Guru says -

અથવા જ્ઞાન ક્ષણિકનું, જે જાણી વદનાર;
વદનારો તે ક્ષણિક નહિ, કર અનુભવ નિર્ધાર. ||૬૯||

Athvā jnān kshaniknu, je jāni vadnār;
Vadnāro te kshanik nahi, kar anubhav nirdhār. ||69||

Athvā - or; ***jnān*** - knowledge; ***kshaniknu*** - of momentariness; *je* - who; ***jāni*** - knows; ***vadnār*** - speaks; ***vadnāro*** - speaker; *te* - that; ***kshanik*** - momentary; ***nahi*** - not; ***kar*** - do; ***anubhav*** - experience; ***nirdhār*** - ascertain

MEANING

Or else, the speaker who knows and speaks about momentariness is not momentary himself. Ascertain this by your own experience.

EXPLANATION

In the previous verse, the Guru expounded that the soul is eternal as a substance and only changes its state. In this verse,

He proves that the soul is not momentary using a different argument altogether, signified by the word '***athvā***' - or. By referring to the subject of the narration of momentariness, the Guru points out the flaw in the theory of momentariness.

One experiences substances changing every moment, as all substances are subject to the law of change. Therefore, the disciple felt that each and every substance is momentary. However, this belief is not logical as the one propounding the principle of momentariness can never be momentary. The one who says that the substance is momentary cannot be momentary himself, because if it is known in one moment, its expression can only take place in the next moment. The first moment passes by only in experiencing that the substance is momentary. Even if he describes this experience immediately, it is already the second moment. If the one who experiences is momentary, he would be destroyed as soon as the second moment begins. In this case there would be no one to narrate the experience. If he himself is not present in the second moment, then how can that experience be described?

If every substance is momentary, then the soul too would get destroyed in the next moment, even before expressing its momentariness. It follows that the knower cannot exist to speak and the speaker cannot be the knower. If he is speaking without knowing then that is not authentic and if he is speaking after knowing then he is not momentary. Knowing and then speaking takes a minimum of two moments. Hence, if the knower is present to speak, he is not momentary, that is, he cannot exist only for a moment. Therefore, it is clear that the one propounding the principle of momentariness cannot be momentary.

It is an evident experience that one thinks before speaking. Thinking and speaking occur in different moments. If the thinker is destroyed in the next moment, he will not be able to speak. One can only say the weather is cold today if he does not have merely a momentary existence. Thus, the disciple's argument does not hold true. The Guru motivates the disciple to ascertain this by his own experience so he himself can conclude that the soul is not momentary.

VERSE - 70

No substance is completely destroyed

Of all the rational solutions given by the Guru regarding the eternal nature of the soul, this concluding verse is the pinnacle. He rebuts the false belief of momentariness and establishes the existence of the soul in all three periods of time. The Guru says -

ક્યારે કોઈ વસ્તુનો, કેવળ હોય ન નાશ;
ચેતન પામે નાશ તો, કેમાં ભળે તપાસ. ॥૭૦॥

Kyāre koi vastuno, keval hoi na nāsh;
Chetan pāmey nāsh toh, kemā bhaley tapās. ॥70॥

Kyāre - ever; *koi* - any; *vastuno* - substance; *keval* - completely; *hoi* - is; *na* - not; *nāsh* - destroyed; *chetan* - soul; *pāmey* - gets; *nāsh* - destroyed; *toh* - then; *kemā* - in what; *bhaley* - merges; *tapās* - examine

MEANING

No substance can ever be completely destroyed. Examine what the soul will merge into, if it is destroyed.

EXPLANATION

In this verse, the Guru very skilfully proves the eternal existence of the soul by drawing the disciple's attention to the universal law applicable to every substance. He expresses a timeless principle which is as scientific as it is spiritual. It is an undisputed truth that substance or matter can never be created or destroyed. It only changes forms. The creation and destruction that one sees are only of the various states, not of the substance.

It is observed that a pot breaks into shards, a cloth tears into pieces, a building collapses into rubble. However, no substance is ever completely destroyed. It only undergoes a transformation. When a clay pot breaks, its shape is destroyed. However, the clay itself is not destroyed. The particles of clay which were originally together in the form of a pot, remain the same even after they have been separated. Similarly, when any substance is destroyed, it changes its form. The substance itself is not completely destroyed. The original substance never disappears. A substance destroyed in one form certainly manifests in another form. It is never absolutely destroyed. It is present forever.

Just as an inanimate substance is not completely destroyed, the soul too is not destroyed. To emphasise this, the Guru asks the disciple to observe what form the soul merges into after its destruction. Contemplating upon this reveals that the soul does not merge into anything and is never completely destroyed. It changes states but remains constant in its own nature. Although it undergoes modifications, it does not get modified into something of another nature. Since the soul is not a product of association, it is a natural substance. It is never created or destroyed. It is without beginning or end. It is eternal.

Thus, the Guru imparted a logical understanding to the disciple from verse 62 until this concluding verse 70, of the second fundamental, and established the eternal nature of the soul. By reflecting upon the solutions given by the Guru, based on logic, experience and inference, the disciple realises the fallacy and inadequacy of his arguments. His doubt regarding the eternal nature of the soul stands uprooted. He now gains an understanding of the truth that the soul is uncreated and indestructible. The belief of an everlasting soul is now firmly lodged in his mind.

Third Fundamental
Soul is the doer of karma

Through the Guru's nectar-like words, the disciple's doubts are being eliminated and the right conviction regarding the soul is emerging. Now, he puts forward his confusion regarding the third of the six fundamentals - 'soul is the doer of karma'.

The eager disciple understands that the soul as a substance is eternal, and its state undergoes changes. As his chain of right thought evolves further, he wonders why all beings experience differences in circumstances, intensities, types of joy and sorrow. A huge degree of strangeness is witnessed in the world. What is the cause of all this? As all Eastern philosophies say, if karma is the cause, then who is the doer of karma?

The more the disciple contemplates on this question, the more he finds himself caught in a whirlpool of different options. He turns towards the Guru for the solution to his confusion. Shrimadji has composed eight verses 71-78, on the topic of the doership of the soul. In the first three verses 71-73, the humble disciple puts forward five arguments regarding the third fundamental. Here, the arguments that the disciple poses to show that the soul is not the doer of karma clearly reflect the influence of philosophies like *Sānkhya*, *Nyāy*, etc. Shrimadji has presented well-known arguments of philosophies that do not accept the doership of the soul, as the enquiry of the disciple, without naming them. Thereafter, He has given the Guru's solutions to these arguments in five verses 74-78. He has pointed out the inappropriateness of the disciple's doubt and proved the doership of the soul, for his spiritual welfare.

VERSE - 71

Doubt 1, 2, 3 - Soul is non-doer of karma

In the first verse of this section, the disciple presents arguments supporting his doubt regarding the third fundamental, 'the doership of the soul'. The disciple says -

કર્તા જીવ ન કર્મનો, કર્મ જ કર્તા કર્મ;
અથવા સહજ સ્વભાવ કાં, કર્મ જીવનો ધર્મ. ||૭૧||

Kartā jeev na karmano, karma ja kartā karma;
Athvā sahaj swabhāv kā, karma jeevno dharma. ||71||

Kartā - doer; *jeev* - soul; *na* - not; *karmano* - of karma;
karma - karma; *ja* - itself; *kartā* - doer; *karma* - karma; *athvā* - or;
sahaj - effortless; *swabhāv* - naturally; *kā* - or; *karma* - karma;
jeevno - soul's; *dharma* - nature

MEANING
The soul is not the doer of karma - karma itself is its own doer. Or, karma binds to the soul automatically, or binding karma is the nature of the soul.

EXPLANATION
The disciple reflects upon the question, 'Who is the doer of karma?' Pondering over this subject, he feels the soul cannot be the doer of karma. It does not appear to him that the soul is the acquirer of karma. Instead, he believes there are many other options that are more suitable. In this verse, the disciple presents three arguments -

1. The first option is that karma itself is the doer of karma. New karma is acquired through existing karma that was bound previously. Present karma is the result of past karma. There is a chain of karma in which the previous karma causes subsequent binding. New karma joins with the old. How can inanimate karma bind the animate soul? When a rope is tied around a cow's neck, the knot is in the rope and not in the cow's neck. Similarly, inanimate karma gets bound to inanimate karma but not to the animate soul.

2. Another option is that karma gets bound on its own - automatically and effortlessly. It is acquired without the soul making any effort. The flow of karma must be happening of its own accord without any attempt on the part of the soul. There seems no specific reason for karma to get bound. Karma binds to the soul accidentally. Hence, the soul cannot be held responsible for it.

3. If the above is not accepted and the soul itself is considered to be the doer of karma, then doing karma would become the soul's inherent quality, its very nature. Nature is that which can never be separated from a substance. If the nature of the soul is to do karma, then it would never become free from it. It would never be eliminated from the soul. The soul would constantly keep doing karma and if that were the case, no one would ever attain liberation. Therefore, it does not seem apt to believe that the soul is the doer of karma.

VERSE - 72

Doubt 4, 5 - Matter or God is doer

In this verse, the disciple presents two more arguments to support his view that the soul is not the doer of karma. It is clearly visible that both these arguments stem from the influence of *Vedic* philosophies. Despite being caught in a fierce whirlpool of confusion, he possesses an intense eagerness to know the true essence. The disciple says -

આત્મા સદા અસંગ ને, કરે પ્રકૃતિ બંધ;
અથવા ઈશ્વર પ્રેરણા, તેથી જીવ અબંધ. ||૭૨||

Ātmā sadā asang ne, karey prakruti bandh;
Athvā Ishwar prernā, tethi jeev abandh. ||72||

Ātmā - soul; *sadā* - always; *asang* - non-attached; *ne* - and; *karey* - does; *prakruti* - matter; *bandh* - binds; *athvā* - or; *Ishwar* - God; *prernā* - inspiration; *tethi* - therefore; *jeev* - soul; *abandh* - unbound

MEANING
The soul is always non-attached and it is *prakruti* (matter) that creates the bondage of karma. Or else, this happens through God's inspiration, therefore the soul is unbound.

EXPLANATION
Although the existence and eternal nature of the two substances - inanimate matter and animate soul, have been proven, the disciple's mind is unable to logically accept that

the soul is the doer of karma. Therefore, his thinking is bent towards proving that the soul is not the doer. He builds upon the previous arguments by presenting two more options in this verse.

4. The option presented in the first line of the verse is that the soul is always non-attached, and prakruti is the doer of karma. This argument is due to the influence of the *Sānkhya* philosophy. It accepts two ultimate realities, namely, *purush* - pure soul, and *prakruti* - primal matter. They are independent of each other with respect to their existence. Purush is the eternal consciousness which witnesses the changes and activities going on in the world, but remains totally inactive and changeless. Prakruti is an eternal inanimate principle and the ultimate cause of the world. The three constituents of prakruti are: *sattva* - goodness, *rajas* - activity and *tamas* - dullness. Prakruti holds them together in a state of equilibrium. The evolution of the world has its starting point in the association of the purush with prakruti, which disturbs the original equilibrium of prakruti and moves it into action. The history of the evolved universe is a play of twenty-four principles: prakruti, intellect, ego, mind, five sense organs (skin, tongue, nose, eyes and ears), five motor organs (mouth, hands, feet, anus and genitals), five subtle elements (sound, touch, colour, taste and smell), and five gross elements (space, air, fire, water and earth). These twenty-four along with purush make it a total of twenty-five principles in the Sānkhya philosophy. Purush is an uncaused, eternal, conscious reality which is pure and unaffected by all objects. While the king does not go to the

battlefield, and the soldiers fight the war, yet the victory or defeat is attributed to the king. Similarly, prakruti does everything, but it is attributed to the purush. The entire play is of prakruti.

In line with the above philosophy, the disciple says that the soul is always non-attached. It is always free of the association of karma - unbound, untouched, unblemished. Just as the non-attached sky cannot be entwined with a rope, the non-attached soul cannot be bound by karma. The soul which is forever non-attached from all associations, has no relation whatsoever with karma. It is not possible for the soul to be associated with karma. The soul is pure in nature and bereft of likes-dislikes. How can such a soul that is free from impurity create karma? The soul cannot indulge in anything that can lead to bondage. However, there can be no karma without a doer. Therefore, contemplating upon who is the doer of karma, it seems that prakruti does karma. The doership of karma is dependent upon prakruti. The soul has nothing to do with it. Therefore, it is appropriate to believe that the soul is not the doer of karma.

5. If this is not the case, then the disciple gives another option, in the second line of this verse. He says that one must believe that God inspires the soul to do karma. This belief is based on the *Nyāy* philosophy. It states that God is the creator of the universe. God is the Generator, Operator and Destroyer of the world. There are many ontological, teleological, metaphysical, moral arguments presented to establish the existence of God. Not only has God created the world, He

also prompts living beings to commit all actions. Although it seems the potter has made a pot, it is actually God who has prompted him to make the pot. He cannot do anything on his own. Whatever happens in the world happens by the wish of God.

Since this belief is registered in the disciple's mind, he puts forth the argument that the soul is not independent. Karma takes place due to the inspiration of God. If someone is possessed by a ghost, then he does not perform any actions as per his will, rather, the ghost that has possessed him causes him to act. In the same way, the soul does not do karma, rather, it is the will of God that makes it do karma. It does not act of its own accord; hence it is not responsible and not bound. If God Himself is the inspiration behind karma, then it is appropriate to believe that the soul is not the doer of karma.

Both the above options prove that it is not possible for the soul to be the doer of karma in any way, therefore the soul is unbound.

VERSE - 73

Concluding contention

Explaining the conclusion he has drawn based on the previous two verses, the disciple says -

માટે મોક્ષ ઉપાયનો, કોઈ ન હેતુ જણાય;
કર્મતણું કર્તાપણું, કાં નહિ, કાં નહિ જાય. ||૭૩||

Mātey moksh upāyno, koi na hetu janāy;
Karmatanu kartāpanu, kā nahi, kā nahi jāy. ||73||

Mātey - therefore; *moksh* - liberation; *upāyno* - of means; *koi* - any;
na - no; *hetu* - purpose; *janāy* - seems; *karmatanu* - of karma;
kartāpanu - doership; *kā* - either; *nahi* - not; *kā* - either; *nahi* - not;
jāy - go

MEANING

Hence, there seems to be no purpose in engaging in the means of liberation. Either the doership of karma is not there, or, if the soul is the doer, it cannot be free from this nature of doership.

EXPLANATION

Influenced by various beliefs prevailing in different philosophies, a doubt has arisen in the disciple with respect to the soul being the doer of karma. It is evident that the disciple is well-read and aware of several concepts regarding the non-doership of the soul. However, these contrasting opinions have confused his mind. Which is why, he put forth arguments in the previous two verses regarding the doership of karma. In this verse, he concludes his contention.

Contemplating upon these deep questions from various angles, the disciple now feels that the soul cannot be accepted as the doer of karma. He signifies this by the words, '*kā nahi*' - either the doership of karma is not possible in the soul. He presented four alternatives -

1. Karma itself is the doer of karma. New karma is bound because of past karma.

2. It happens automatically, completely on its own. Karma gets bound without any specific reason. The soul is a mere passive spectator.

3. *Prakruti* is the doer of karma. The soul is always pure and non-attached, all activities are performed by prakruti. Hence, prakruti should be held responsible.

4. God gives the inspiration to do karma. All acts are undertaken through the compelling inspiration of God. He directs the soul.

Thus, from all four standpoints, it appears that the soul is not the doer of karma.

If this is not believed and the soul is considered to be the doer of karma by its nature, then it can never be free from it. The disciple signifies this by the words, '*kā nahi jāy*' - or the doership of karma is such that it will never be eliminated. One's nature can never be given up. Nature is unchangeable.

Thus, either the soul is not the doer of karma or doing karma is the soul's nature. In both cases, there seems to be no purpose in engaging in the means of liberation. If the soul is not the doer of karma, then it is proved flawless and unbound. Therefore, speaking about its liberation is out of place. If the soul is the non-doer, the question of liberation does not arise. Neither is the soul responsible, nor is it in bondage. How can one, who is not bound, be freed? The concept of liberation is just a myth. Only one who is bound, needs to make efforts to attain liberation. If the soul does not do any karma, then it is certainly always free from it, hence there does not seem any need to undertake the means of liberation. The advice to undo should be given only to a doer. Preaching of the path to liberation should be imparted only to a doer. If the soul is the non-doer, then what is the point of religious preaching?

On the other hand, if the soul's nature is to do karma, then it will continue acquiring karma, it will not be able to stop and hence, liberation will be impossible. To think of liberation would be to divorce the soul from its very identity. So, it would be a waste of time to work for liberation, which proves to be simply an illusion. None of the above alternatives makes liberation possible, and hence there is no purpose in seeking it. It is futile to pursue the path of liberation.

The disciple puts forth his confusion to the Guru and humbly seeks a solution. He is incapable of coming to the right conclusion regarding the doership of the soul. He requests the Guru to unravel the mystery and free him from his doubt.

VERSE - 74

Reply 1 - Soul is inspirer of karma

In the previous three verses 71-73, the disciple put forth various alternatives to the Guru, regarding the soul not being the doer of karma, and instead some other entity being the doer of karma. In the next five verses 74-78, the Guru sequentially resolves each of the disciple's arguments.

In the first half of verse 71, the disciple expressed his belief that the soul is not the doer of karma, but karma itself is the doer of karma. Resolving this argument voiced by the disciple, the Guru explains -

હોય ન ચેતન પ્રેરણા, કોણ ગ્રહે તો કર્મ?
જડસ્વભાવ નહિ પ્રેરણા, જુઓ વિચારી ધર્મ. ||૭૪||

Hoi na chetan prernā, kaun grahe toh karma?
Jadswabhāv nahi prernā, juo vichāri dharma. ||74||

Hoi - if; *na* - not; *chetan* - soul; *prernā* - inspiration; *kaun* - who; *grahe* - acquires; *toh* - then; *karma* - karma; *jadswabhāv* - nature of inanimate; *nahi* - not; *prernā* - inspiration; *juo* - see; *vichāri* - contemplate; *dharma* - nature

MEANING

If there is no inspiration of the soul, who will acquire karma? It is not the nature of the inanimate to inspire. Reflect upon the nature of both the substances.

EXPLANATION

Karmic bondage can only take place if there is inspiration from a substance. The act of acquiring karma is impossible without some inspiration. Only the soul has the ability to inspire. Hence, only the soul is capable of acquiring karma. Without the inspiration of the soul, particles of *kārman varganā* - subtle material particles which become karma when attached to the soul, certainly cannot modify into karma. Through inspiration in the form of impure feelings, the soul acquires karma. Impure feelings generated by the soul lead to karmic bondage. Karma gets attracted to the soul due to feelings of attachment and aversion. It is at the behest of the soul itself that karma gets bound to the soul.

It is not in the nature of inanimate objects to inspire. They do not have the power to do so. A human can perform great tasks with his computer. However, the computer cannot inspire him to operate it. If he does not wish to use it, the computer cannot compel him to do so. A sword laying in its sheath on the waist of a soldier, cannot inspire him to employ it. Nor does it attack the enemy on its own. The soldier chooses when and how he wishes to wield it. It is merely an instrument to express his attacking intent. If the inanimate had the nature to inspire, then pot-cloth, would also modify into feelings of anger, pride, etc., and would acquire karma. However, this does not occur. Inanimate objects have never been observed to possess emotions. Since the inanimate does not have the ability to inspire in the form of feelings, it is incapable of acquiring karma.

Karma itself cannot be the doer of karma as it is inanimate, totally devoid of consciousness. It lacks the quality to inspire and hence is incapable of acquiring karma. If the cause in the form of inspiration is absent, karma cannot be acquired. The knot in the rope around a cow's neck is not tied by itself, there is definitely some conscious entity who has performed this action. Similarly, karmic bondage only occurs with the inspiration of the soul. Without a primary initiator, karma cannot bind the soul. Upon contemplating the inherent qualities of the inanimate and the soul, it will be clear that the inspiration to acquire karma arises in the soul, hence it is the doer of karma. When one reflects on the innate nature of both substances, as well as the insight into the principle of doership, it will be evident that the soul alone is the doer of karma.

Thus, the Guru takes the disciple to the root of the entire discussion and prompts him to consider who inspires karma - the soul or mundane matter? Matter cannot be held responsible as it has no consciousness, no ability to make a choice, and no capacity to make a decision. That leaves the soul alone to be the inspirer of acquiring karma. Since it possesses consciousness and has the ability to initiate karma, the soul itself is the doer of karma.

VERSE - 75

Reply 2, 3 - Soul's impure tendency is doer

In the latter half of verse 71, the disciple had said that karma automatically gets bound to the soul without any effort of the soul. Hence, it is appropriate to believe that the soul is not the doer. If this is not the case, and if the soul is the doer of karma, then to do karma becomes its inherent quality. Clarifying both these options in this verse, the Guru says -

જો ચેતન કરતું નથી, નથી થતાં તો કર્મ;
તેથી સહજ સ્વભાવ નહિ, તેમ જ નહિ જીવધર્મ. ||૭૫||

Jo chetan kartu nathi, nathi thatā toh karma;
Tethi sahaj swabhāv nahi, tem ja nahi jeevdharma. ||75||

Jo - if; *chetan* - soul; *kartu* - does; *nathi* - not; *thatā* - happen; *toh* - then; *karma* - karma; *tethi* - therefore; *sahaj* - effortless; *swabhāv* - naturally; *nahi* - not; *tem* - also; *ja* - certainly; *nahi* - not; *jeevdharma* - soul's nature

MEANING
If the soul does not do it, then karma is not accumulated. Therefore, neither is karma bound automatically, nor is it the nature of the soul to bind karma.

EXPLANATION
Karma is bound only when the soul engages in likes and dislikes. If the soul does not engage in these, then it refrains

from acquiring any karma. It is due to impure feelings that karmic bondage occurs. It stops once these feelings are eliminated. If the soul abstains from feelings of attachment and aversion then inanimate karma is not attracted. There is no influx of karma. Through the word '*jo*' - if, the Guru simultaneously answers two alternatives posed by the disciple. If the soul does not do, karma cannot occur. It neither happens automatically nor is it the soul's nature.

It is inappropriate to state that karma happens automatically and of its own accord, because if the soul does not harbour impure feelings, karma does not occur. It is illogical to adopt the view that karma happens without any effort of the soul because the act of binding occurs through the inspiration of the soul. If the soul inspires, karma is acquired. Likewise, if it does not, karma is not acquired. Therefore, it can be concluded that karma is not bound to the soul automatically, without a cause.

Moreover, it is also inappropriate to state that the acquisition of karma is the inherent quality of the soul because accumulation of karma ends once the soul ceases to harbour impure feelings. It is incorrect to say that doing karma is the soul's nature because karma does not occur unless the soul inspires. Even though karma is only acquired through the soul's inspiration, this is not the soul's inherent nature. The true nature of a substance can never be destroyed. The nature of fire is heat, and that never changes. However, the tendency of doing karma can be eliminated. If acquiring karma was the nature of the soul, it would keep getting bound and would never be free, at any point in time. However, the soul binds auspicious karma at times and inauspicious karma at times, intense karma on some occasions and mild karma on other occasions; whereas sometimes it does not bind any karma at all. This proves that binding karma is not the inherent nature of the soul. Rather, the tendency to do karma is an impure tendency of the soul, which can be destroyed. The soul has the freedom to stop acquiring karma. Therefore, acquiring karma is not the innate nature of the soul.

As a result of meritorious karma, one receives favourable situations, like tasty food. If he consumes it with detachment, he will not acquire new karma. If he devours it with attachment, he will acquire karmic bondage. Similarly, as a result of unmeritorious karma, one receives unfavourable circumstances, like a malicious neighbour who abuses him. If he bears it with equanimity, he will not bind karma. If he retaliates and combats him with anger, he will accumulate karma. Thus, it is the soul's choice to do or not to do karma. Neither is karma bound automatically nor is it the soul's inherent nature to acquire karma. Both alternatives have been proven incorrect. In this manner, the Guru clearly and succinctly puts to ease the disciple's confused mind.

VERSE - 76

Reply 4 - Soul is not absolutely unbound

The three arguments that the disciple put forth in verse 71, about the doership of the soul, were perfectly resolved by the Guru in verses 74 and 75. Now, the solution to the two alternatives presented in verse 72 of the doctrine of doership of *prakruti* and the doctrine of doership of God, will be provided in verses 76 and 77.

In the first half of verse 72, the disciple had said that the soul is always non-attached and prakruti binds karma. To state the soul as the doer of karma is inappropriate. Explaining the flaw in the disciple's thinking and bringing about the right conviction in him, regarding the doership of the soul, the Guru says -

કેવળ હોત અસંગ જો, ભાસત તને ન કેમ?
અસંગ છે પરમાર્થથી, પણ નિજભાને તેમ. ||૭૬||

Keval hot asang jo, bhāsat taney na kem?
Asang chhe parmārththi, pan nijbhāne tem. ||76||

Keval - absolutely; **hot** - was; **asang** - non-attached; **jo** - if; **bhāsat** - experienced; **taney** - by you; **na** - not; **kem** - why; **asang** - non-attached; **chhe** - is; **parmārththi** - from absolute viewpoint; **pan** - but; **nijbhāne** - experience of soul; **tem** - that way

MEANING

If the soul were absolutely non-attached, then why is this not experienced by you? It is non-attached from the absolute viewpoint, but from the relative viewpoint, it becomes non-attached only when it experiences its true nature, abides in it, and gets rid of all karmic bondage.

EXPLANATION

Influenced by the *Sānkhya* philosophy, the disciple had projected the doership of karma on prakruti and presented the soul as unbound. In his argument, he had described the soul as completely pure at all times. The disciple had expressed this by using the word '*sadā*' - always, along with '*asang*' - non-attached ('*Ātmā sadā asang ne, karey prakruti bandh*'). The soul is always non-attached, devoid of impurities, without the association of karma. The Guru does not totally refute this. He accepts as well as negates the disciple's contention. He accepts that the soul is non-attached, but only from a certain perspective. He negates that the soul is completely non-attached at all times, which He conveys through the word '*keval*' - absolutely, in this verse. He acknowledges the partial truth in the disciple's argument, but demonstrates his fallacy in believing it to be the full truth.

The Guru responds to the disciple's argument by asking him that if the soul was always non-attached, if it was never touched by the association of karma, then why are you unable to experience such a pure soul? If it was absolutely pure, then you should have been able to experience the completely non-attached soul right from the beginning itself. You should have had the experiential evidence of the non-attached, untainted, pure soul. However, such a non-attached soul is not experienced by you. You had doubted the very existence of the soul at the beginning of the discussion, so it is very clear that the soul certainly has the association of the veil of karma. Therefore, it cannot be said that the soul is completely non-attached.

The soul is certainly non-attached, from the absolute viewpoint. It is non-attached when one focuses on its true nature. However, from the relative viewpoint, it is saddled with the association of karma. It is impure when one focuses on its current state. There are two dimensions to the soul. Its true nature is non-attached, unalloyed, blissful, however, its current state is tainted, fettered and miserable. The former can never be involved in karma, whereas the latter, caught in the web of action and reaction, is involved in the doership of karma. From the relative viewpoint, the soul is in the embodied state. It is bound and full of impurities. It harbours feelings of likes and dislikes which cause the acquisition of karma.

Although the soul is pure by nature, this is not experienced because of its blemished state. The state becomes flawless only when the soul realises its pure nature. The non-attached nature manifests when one understands and focuses on it. By abiding in the non-attached nature, karmic bondage ceases and the completely non-attached state is attained. When the soul through its effort eliminates impure feelings, there is no further acquisition or accumulation of karma.

It becomes completely non-attached when it does not have the association of even a single particle of matter.

Thus, the enlightened ones have perceived the nature of the soul to be eternal, unblemished, and beyond the manifold variety of impure feelings. Despite this non-attached nature, the soul's present state is filled with frailties and flaws. Hence, purity is not experienced. This tainted state is responsible for acquiring karma. The impurity is instrumental in binding karma, and therefore it can be concluded that the soul is the doer of karma.

VERSE - 77

Reply 5 - God is not inspirer

In the latter half of verse 72, the disciple had said that God inspires the soul to do karma and therefore the soul is unbound. Resolving the disciple's argument, the Guru says -

કર્તા ઈશ્વર કોઈ નહિ, ઈશ્વર શુદ્ધ સ્વભાવ;
અથવા પ્રેરક તે ગણ્યે, ઈશ્વર દોષપ્રભાવ. ||૭૭||

Kartā Ishwar koi nahi, Ishwar shuddh swabhāv;
Athvā prerak Te ganye, Ishwar doshprabhāv. ||77||

Kartā - doer; *Ishwar* - God; *koi* - any; *nahi* - not; *Ishwar* - God;
shuddh - pure; *swabhāv* - nature; *athvā* - or; *prerak* - inspirer; *Te* - Him;
ganye - considered; *Ishwar* - God; *doshprabhāv* - influenced by flaws

MEANING

There is no God who is the doer of karma. God is the soul who has achieved the purest state. If He is considered to be the inspirer of the soul's karma, God will be associated with defects and contradictions.

EXPLANATION

The *Nyāy* philosophy advocates that God has created this movable and immovable world. All the activities of the world only take place as per God's will. Whatever karma is executed by worldly beings occurs only through His inspiration. The soul's karma is dependent on God's will. Influenced by this concept of God, the disciple stated that karma is due to God's inspiration, while presenting the case of the soul not being the doer of karma. The disciple believes the soul is not at fault when it comes to karma, it is unbound. However, this doctrine of God's doership is not logical, just like the doctrine of *prakruti's* doership.

It is essential to first understand who God really is. God is the purest, pristine, immaculate soul. God has manifested infinite knowledge, boundless perception, uninterrupted bliss and supreme power by abiding in His true nature. He is devoid of attachments and aversions. He has attained the state of dispassion, serenity and fulfilment. Godliness is a state that is divinely majestic and wholly holy.

If this is the true form of God, why would He give up the bliss of the self and become the doer of karma of worldly beings? Doing implies desires and desires imply imperfection, which lowers His purity. What is the reason for the arising of such an agitated desire? Is it boredom, tiredness or curiosity? Even a true seeker does not feel bored by his spiritual practices but continues his pursuit with unabated enthusiasm. Then why would a dispassionate, serene, fulfilled God need to indulge in such activities? Why would the all-accomplished God even wish to accomplish anything?

Why would God inspire some to perform good karma and others, bad karma? Even an ordinary ethical person is impartial. Then, why would God display such partiality? Why would He prompt someone to perform evil deeds and then make him suffer later? What joy could He derive from seeing someone miserable due to the harsh fruits of his sins? If He was compassionate, why would He make someone blind or engulf the world with cruel pandemics? Why would He create atheists who challenge His very authority?

It is a common argument to prove God to be the creator, as nothing can exist without a maker. Every design has a designer. In that case, the question arises - Who created God? From what was God created? If the answer is - God was created by a supreme God, then the question of who created this supreme God would arise too, leading to a never-ending chain of questions. If it is said that God always existed, He was never created; then why not accept that the world always existed and was never created. Many other questions would also arise - from what did God create the world? Did the raw materials already exist or did He create it from nothing? Where did He sit and create the world? When did He generate the world? What was the process? Did He actually perform the activity or did it come into existence simply by an intention to create?

God is not the creator or prompter of the world, He is only the knower of the world. There would be no end to His flaws if it is believed that the soul binds karma through the inspiration of God. If God gives the inspiration for karma, then He has to be considered to have worldly entanglements. If He possessed these, there would be no difference between Him and a worldly soul. He would not be God but an ordinary man. If God was the inspiration behind karma, then He would have to be influenced by flaws such as likes and dislikes. In that case, God would lose His Godliness.

Thus, the doership of God cannot be proved in any way. It has been established that neither prakruti nor God is the doer of karma - it is the soul. So, with hard-hitting words the Guru stresses that God can never have anything to do with the soul's karma. To assign the responsibility of karma to God is to associate Him with several defects. It is absurd to think that God could be involved as the creator and prompter. Such a perception only damages the majestic concept of God. It flaws the flawless and stains the spotless.

VERSE - 78

Soul is doer

In verses 74-77, the Guru perfectly explained how the soul
is the doer of karma by way of simple, fitting, heart-touching
and yet, logical arguments. Now, in this final verse of the
section on the third fundamental truth, He embellishes it
with the pinnacle. The Guru says -

ચેતન જો નિજ ભાનમાં, કર્તા આપ સ્વભાવ;
વર્તે નહિ નિજ ભાનમાં, કર્તા કર્મ-પ્રભાવ. ||૭૮||

Chetan jo nij bhānmā, kartā āp swabhāv;
Varte nahi nij bhānmā, kartā karma-prabhāv. ||78||

Chetan - soul; **jo** - if; **nij** - self; **bhānmā** - awareness; **kartā** - doer;
āp - its; **swabhāv** - nature; **varte** - abide; **nahi** - not; **nij** - self;
bhānmā - awareness; **kartā** - doer; **karma** - karma; **prabhāv** - influence

MEANING

If the soul abides in the awareness of its pure nature, then it
becomes the doer of its own nature, in the sense of its pure
manifestation. When it does not abide in the awareness of
its pure nature, then, it is the doer of impure feelings which
are instrumental in binding material karma.

EXPLANATION

After presenting various alternatives regarding the doership
of karma in verse 73, the disciple had expressed futility of

pursuing the path of liberation. Either the doership of karma is not possible in the soul and it is unbound, or if doing karma is the soul's nature then it cannot be eliminated, and freedom can never be attained. Deliberating upon both these options, it does not seem appropriate to him to make the required efforts for liberation. Through the solution in the previous four verses, the Guru cleared the disciple's confusion and explained how the soul was the doer of karma. The activity of acquiring karma does not happen because it is the soul's nature, but it happens through the soul's inspiration in the form of impure feelings such as likes-dislikes. Out of selfless compassion, the Guru steered the disciple's flow of thoughts which had been blemished by one-sidedness, in the right direction. Concluding this subject, He now expounds the eternal principle. He encapsulates the concept of doership by throwing light on the two states of the soul.

If the soul abides in the awareness of its pure nature, then it becomes the doer of its own nature, in the sense of its manifestation. When it is engrossed in its own flawless, non-attached, conscious nature, it is the doer of its own natural disposition. Remaining steadfast in its nature, the soul does not harbour impure feelings and hence does not incur karmic bondage. In the absence of feelings such as likes-dislikes, karmic particles do not get bound to the soul. If it stays in soul-consciousness, it is the doer of pure feelings and the non-doer of karma. The soul dwells in peace, in stillness and in inner silence. There are no desires, it is content in the here and now. It does not get affected by the vagaries of the world.

If the soul does not abide in the awareness of its true nature, it becomes the doer of impure feelings, which are instrumental in acquiring material karma. During the manifestation of previously bound karma, if the soul loses awareness of itself and modifies in the form of likes-dislikes, then it becomes the doer of karma. The soul has the ability to modify as impure feelings like delusion, and bind karma. When it ventures out of its inherent nature, it indulges in impure feelings that lead to karmic bondage. Unaware of its true nature, it gets caught up in defiling tendencies, becoming involved in endless cycles of action and reaction, activity and result.

Summing up the discussion about the doership of karma, the Guru illuminates the difference between the two states of the soul. If the soul remains in the awareness of its true nature, it becomes the doer of pure feelings. If it does not, it becomes the doer of impure feelings, which are instrumental in the binding of material karma. The soul's doership is always present, either of pure feelings or of karma. Thus, showing the soul's pure and impure modifications, the Guru gives the disciple a complete perspective and opens the door to the right conviction regarding the doership of the soul.

Fourth Fundamental
Soul is the receiver of the fruits of karma

By deeply reflecting upon the Guru's logical solutions regarding the soul being the doer of karma, the disciple finds himself free of the relentless thorn-like doubts pricking his mind. With the uprooting of all doubts concerning the doership of the soul, a strong belief develops within him. The disciple now expresses his confusion regarding the fourth fundamental, 'soul is the receiver (enjoyer or sufferer) of the fruits of karma'.

The thoughtful disciple contemplates that if the karma bound by the soul was exhausted without it receiving the fruits, how can there be a system of bondage and liberation? Although he feels it is absolutely necessary to receive the fruits of karma, he is still not logically convinced about this fundamental. Being influenced by the beliefs of various philosophies, his mind is confused and many questions about the soul being the receiver of the fruits of karma emerge. To gain a firm conviction, he puts forth his arguments to the Guru and humbly requests for a satisfactory solution.

Shrimadji has composed eight verses 79-86, on the subject of the soul being the receiver of the fruits of karma. In the first three verses 79-81, the humble disciple expresses two arguments regarding the soul as the receiver. Thereafter, the Guru solves these arguments in five verses 82-86. He explains the incorrect nature of the disciple's doubt and establishes the soul as the receiver of the fruits of karma, for his spiritual welfare.

VERSE - 79

Doubt 1 - Karma devoid of knowingness

To show that it is impossible for the soul to be the receiver of the fruits of karma, in this first argument, the disciple says -

જીવ કર્મ કર્તા કહો, પણ ભોક્તા નહિ સોય;
શું સમજે જડ કર્મ કે, ફળ પરિણામી હોય? ||૭૯||

Jeev karma kartā kaho, pan bhoktā nahi soi;
Shu samje jad karma ke, fal parināmi hoi? ||79||

Jeev - soul; *karma* - karma; *kartā* - doer; *kaho* - say; *pan* - but; *bhoktā* - receiver of fruits of karma; *nahi* - not; *soi* - be; *shu* - what; *samje* - understands; *jad* - inanimate; *karma* - karma; *ke* - that; *fal* - fruit; *parināmi* - resulting; *hoi* - becomes

MEANING

The soul can be accepted as the doer of karma, but not the receiver of the fruits of karma. How can inanimate karma possess the understanding to give fruits to the doer?

EXPLANATION

The Guru established the doership of the soul through logical arguments. Accepting this, the disciple says he can now rationally understand that the soul is the doer of karma. If the soul remains in the awareness of its nature, then it becomes the doer of pure modifications. If it does not remain in the awareness of its nature, then it undergoes impure modifications of feelings such as likes-dislikes, and becomes the doer of karma. This is the firm conviction held by the disciple. However, he does not feel it is true that the soul is the receiver of the fruits of karma.

Presenting his first argument, the disciple says that it is not logically possible for the soul to be the receiver of the fruits of karma in any way. According to him, an entity which gives fruits should possess knowledge. However, karma being an inanimate substance, is totally devoid of knowledge, and therefore cannot give fruits. Karma does not have any capacity to understand. It does not even know it has been acquired by a particular soul. Karma is unaware whether it is meritorious or unmeritorious. Then how can it judge whether the soul should receive the fruits of particular auspicious or inauspicious feelings? How can lifeless karma assign a reward or a punishment to the soul? How can inanimate karma possess the understanding to give the animate soul a specific fruit for a specific action? How can karma plan what, where, when and how much is to be given to the soul? How does karma know that the time is ripe to produce results?

Everyday observations display that no inanimate object can produce results by itself. When one sits down to eat lunch, he needs to put food in his mouth to eat. Food does not have the capacity to reach the mouth on its own and offer the result of satiating hunger. Likewise, inanimate karma cannot offer any result to the soul. Pot-cloth lack the ability of possessing knowledge, hence they cannot think of giving joy or sorrow to the soul. Similarly, karma also does not possess the ability of knowledge, hence it cannot think of giving joy or sorrow to the soul.

Thus, for the soul to be the receiver of the fruits of karma, there needs to be a giver. If karma itself gives fruits, then it must possess knowledge. However, it has no such capacity. Therefore, it does not seem logical that karma gives fruits. If inanimate karma cannot extend results, then how can the soul be called the receiver of the fruits of karma? Hence, it does not seem appropriate to the disciple to consider the soul to be the receiver of the fruits of karma.

———— ⟨∼৹⟩ ————

VERSE - 80

Doubt 2 - God bestows fruits of karma

In the previous verse, the disciple reasoned that since karma is devoid of the ability to know, it cannot be the giver of fruits on its own. He now presents another argument in two verses. Exploring a different option regarding the giver of the fruits of karma, the disciple says -

ફળદાતા ઈશ્વર ગણ્યે, ભોક્તાપણું સધાય;
એમ કહ્યે ઈશ્વરતણું, ઈશ્વરપણું જ જાય. ||૮૦||

Faldātā Ishwar ganye, bhoktāpanu sadhāy;
Em kahye Ishwartanu, Ishwarpanu ja jāy. ||80||

Faldātā - fruit giver; *Ishwar* - God; *ganye* - considered; *bhoktāpanu* - receiving; *sadhāy* - established; *em* - by this; *kahye* - stating; *Ishwartanu* - God's; *Ishwarpanu* - Godliness; *ja* - itself; *jāy* - goes away

MEANING

If God is considered the bestower of the fruits of karma, then it can be established that the soul is the receiver of karma. However, by stating this, God loses His Godliness.

EXPLANATION

The disciple feels that since inanimate karma cannot possess the inclination to give fruits, the soul cannot be proved to be their receiver. As the thinking of the eager disciple progresses, he adds another angle to the discussion. He reckons that unless one accepts the existence of some other conscious entity which gives joy or sorrow as per karma, it cannot in any way be established that the soul is the receiver of karma. There definitely has to be some special conscious entity which gives the fruits of karma. A thief who commits robbery does not get the fruits of his actions on his own. A judge determines the severity of his crime and accordingly awards an appropriate punishment. Similarly, there has to be someone who gives the fruits of auspicious-inauspicious karma.

The proposition of the soul being the receiver of the fruits of its karma can be valid only if some other conscious entity is also involved in the process. The disciple feels that this supreme conscious entity can be none other than God Himself. That proposition holds true only on the condition that God is the giver of the fruits of karma. If one accepts the existence of a God who gives the fruits of auspicious and inauspicious karma, then it can easily be proven that the soul is the receiver of the fruits of karma. Hence, one must be compelled to believe that God makes the soul receive the fruits of karma. He is the dispenser of justice.

Although the belief that God is the giver of fruits solves the issue of inanimate karma, it gives rise to several other problems. It is like a conundrum which mimics jumping from the frying pan into the fire. Harbouring this belief reduces God to the position of a mere judge. Like the ruler of a court, He would simply pronounce sentences according to the karma that souls have acquired. He would keep extending one's consequences in the form of rewards and punishments.

Giving the fruits would make God no more than an accountant who keeps a tab of the deeds of living beings. Just as an accountant pays wages to employees according to the pay scale decided by the employer, God gives rewards or punishments according to the karma of the soul. Moreover, since each soul has to receive the fruit of karma every moment, God has to extend the fruit of karma every moment too. If God was to get involved in giving the fruits, He would have to remain continuously engaged in this activity. Why would God, who is abiding in the pure self, interfere in the functions of infinite souls? Why would a dispassionate, non-attached, liberated, supreme being get entangled with the management of innumerable beings? Thus, accepting God as the manager between the soul and karma seems illogical. Bestowing results is definitely an uncalled for, intermedial botheration.

If God was to engage in the act of giving joy and sorrow to others, His pure state would not last. If He was to indulge in these activities, His purity would surely be damaged. Therefore, in the act of accepting Him as the bestower of the fruits, God's Godliness itself is lost. If God is considered the giver of the fruits of karma, His Godliness cannot remain. If He is considered Godly, then His position as the giver of the fruits of karma cannot remain. This gives rise to a mutually nullifying contradiction. If God is not the bestower of the fruits of karma, then how could the soul receive the fruits of its actions? Neither does God do it, nor the inanimate karma, thus it cannot at all be proven that the soul is the receiver of the fruits of karma.

VERSE - 81

Fallacious conclusion

While deeply contemplating whether the soul could be considered the receiver of the fruits of karma or not, the thoughtful disciple has understood that God cannot be proved as the bestower of the fruits of karma in any manner. However, if it is not God, then many other difficulties arise. Expressing his confusion, the disciple says -

ઈશ્વર સિદ્ધ થયા વિના, જગત નિયમ નહિ હોય;
પછી શુભાશુભ કર્મનાં, ભોગ્યસ્થાન નહિ કોય. ||૮૧||

Ishwar siddh thayā vinā, jagat niyam nahi hoi;
Pachhi shubhāshubh karmanā, bhogyasthān nahi koi. ||81||

Ishwar - God; *siddh* - established; *thayā* - been; *vinā* - without; *jagat* - world; *niyam* - law; *nahi* - not; *hoi* - be; *pachhi* - then; *shubhāshubh* - auspicious and inauspicious; *karmanā* - of karma; *bhogyasthān* - places to receive fruits; *nahi* - not; *koi* - any

MEANING

Without establishing the existence of God, there would be no order and system in the world. There would also be no designated places to receive the fruits of auspicious and inauspicious karma.

EXPLANATION

Eager to know the supreme truth, the disciple does not think it logical to consider God as the bestower of the fruits of karma.

This is because of the belief that if God makes the soul receive joy and sorrow, then God's purity ceases and Godliness itself cannot be established within Him. The consideration that God is the giver of the fruits of karma would only prove He is involved in mundane activities and engaged in worldly entanglements. This certainly cannot be accepted.

However, if God is absolutely non-attached, if He does not indulge in worldly activities, then this vast world would have no governing entity. If God's existence is not proved, then no law could prevail in the world. It is observed that the mechanism of the world runs ever so smoothly. The rising and setting of the sun, days and nights, climatic cycles, movement of the planets, growing of trees, flowing of streams - such perpetual phenomena occur regularly and systematically. If God does not exist, who runs the affairs of the world? The disciple jumps to the conclusion that by rejecting the existence of God, the order and system in the world are also rejected.

The disciple is deeply influenced by the concept that the scheme of the universe cannot operate without God. The accrual of the fruits of karma in designated places can occur only if some mediatory power is instrumental to the process, and not otherwise. In the same way as there are designated places like jails to serve sentences and hospitals for medical treatment, there need to be places like heaven and hell to bear the consequences of auspicious and inauspicious karma. Who would create and maintain such places without God? If places like heaven and hell are not proven to exist, the soul too cannot be proven to be the receiver of the fruits of karma.

Thus, the disciple examined two hypotheses regarding the soul being the receiver of the fruits of karma. He denies them both because inanimate karma has no understanding of how to give fruits to the soul, and if God was the bestower of fruits then it would compromise His Godliness. Neither can it be believed that karma itself gives the fruits nor can it be accepted that God makes the soul receive the fruits. Since both karma or God cannot be proven to be the giver of the fruits, the law of receiving joy and sorrow cannot be established in any way. If there is no receipt of joy and sorrow, then how could there be places like heaven or hell to receive them. This leads to the conclusion that the soul is not the receiver of the fruits of karma. Expressing his mental churning to the Guru, the disciple displays his earnest desire to completely understand the essence of the truth.

VERSE - 82

Reply 1 - Process of bondage

The Guru now sequentially answers the disciple's logical arguments with heart-touching solutions. In verse 79, the disciple had wondered how inanimate karma could possess the understanding to give fruits. Pondering over this statement, he felt that the soul could not possibly be the receiver of the fruits of karma. The Guru resolves this argument in three verses 82-84. To explain how the soul is the receiver of the fruits of karma, He first illustrates how and why the association with karma takes place. The Guru says -

ભાવકર્મ નિજ કલ્પના, માટે ચેતનરૂપ;
જીવવીર્યની સ્ફુરણા, ગ્રહણ કરે જડધૂપ. ||૮૨||

Bhāvkarma nij kalpanā, mātey chetanroop;
Jeevviryani sfurnā, grahan karey jaddhoop. ||82||

Bhāvkarma - impure feelings; **nij** - own; **kalpanā** - illusion; **mātey** - therefore; **chetanroop** - conscious; **jeevviryani** - soul's energy; **sfurnā** - activates; **grahan** - acquire; **karey** - does; **jaddhoop** - karmic matter

MEANING

Impure feelings arise within the soul. Therefore, they are a form of consciousness. This activates the soul's energy. Due to the vibration of the soul, karmic particles are acquired, resulting in bondage with the soul.

EXPLANATION

Karmic particles exist everywhere in the universe. If the soul abides in its true nature, they would simply pass by without impacting it. When the soul indulges in impure feelings, it attracts and binds karmic particles. This is not the soul's inherent nature, but its capacity to indulge in impure feelings. This behaviour attracts karmic particles from the atmosphere and converts them into karma. It is akin to a person smeared with oil being prone to attracting dust particles. Karma stays bound to the soul until it matures and extends consequences. At that time, if the soul reacts to the situation generated as the consequence of karma, it binds new karma. However, if it remains equanimous, it does not acquire new karma, and existing karmic bondage is stripped off in due course.

The Guru points out this karmic philosophy to eliminate the disciple's doubt. The disciple had only spoken of material karma in his argument. He had contended that inanimate karma is incapable of giving fruits. How can lifeless karma understand that a particular soul should be given a particular type of fruit? Karma cannot extend the right consequences because it lacks consciousness. In response, the Guru explains that from one perspective, karma is conscious too. He elucidates that there are two types of karma - *bhāvkarma* and *dravyakarma*. **'Bhāvkarma'** are the soul's impure feelings of likes-dislikes. These bhāvkarma are instrumental in attracting material karmic particles which get bound to the soul, known as dravyakarma. In this verse, dravyakarma has been signified by the word **'jaddhoop'**.

Dravyakarma are inanimate in nature. However, bhāvkarma, such as likes-dislikes are the soul's illusion and therefore are a form of consciousness. Bhāvkarma are the soul's own modifications which arise out of ignorance. When the soul is unaware of its true nature, it creates several defilements like attachment and aversion. These are generated in the soul itself. Since these are feelings of a conscious substance, they are animate. In accordance with these bhāvkarma, the soul's energy is activated and inanimate karmic particles are acquired.

By nature, the soul is only the knower, an inherently blissful and peaceful substance. It neither does anything in the non-self nor does it indulge in the non-self. However, when it gets involved in the manifestation of past karma and strays from its true nature, its energy is activated, destabilising the energies of mind-speech-body. The destabilisation of these energies becomes instrumental in attracting the karmic particles existing in the same space as the soul. They get bound to the soul as dravyakarma. At the appropriate time, when this karma manifests, once again, under the influence of ignorance, the soul generates bhāvkarma. The vicious cycle of bhāvkarma leading to dravyakarma and dravyakarma leading to bhāvkarma has been continuing ceaselessly on the axis of delusion since time immemorial.

Animate bhāvkarma is instrumental in the formation of inanimate dravyakarma. Based on the bhāvkarma, four things are determined at the time of binding dravyakarma -

1. *Prakrutibandh* - the nature of karma.
2. *Sthitibandh* - the duration for which the karma will stay with the soul.
3. *Anubhāgbandh* (*Rasbandh*) - the intensity of the fruit of karma.
4. *Pradeshbandh* - the amount of karmic particles.

This can easily be understood with the four aspects of a pastry -

1. The type of pastry.
2. The duration of the pastry.
3. The sweetness of the pastry.
4. The volume of the pastry.

These four aspects of dravyakarma are determined according to the bhāvkarma and when the time is ripe, the dravyakarma gives the appropriate fruit, which the soul definitely has to receive.

Thus, the Guru develops a background to demonstrate how inanimate karma can affect the animate soul. Despite being inanimate, it derives the power of giving fruits from the soul's impure feelings. At the right time, it manifests and impacts the soul. Just as an alarm clock rings as per the time set by a person, a time bomb explodes as per the specifications set by the programmer, karma gives fruit as per the impure feelings harboured by the soul. The purpose of this verse is to indicate that it is the soul's activity that results in karmic bondage, and it is the bhāvkarma which empowers the dravyakarma to give fruits to the soul. How else can the inanimate karma ride the infinitely strong animate soul. The soul itself becomes the doer of karma and therefore becomes the receiver of the consequences. Every action, emotion and thought carries with it the burden of bondage. Each will bear fruit in this life or another.

VERSE - 83

Non-sentient matter shows effects

From verse 82, the Guru explains how material karma bound to the soul gives fruits and how the soul receives them. Using an example that will make it easy to understand how inanimate karma gives fruits, the Guru says -

ઝેર સુધા સમજે નહીં, જીવ ખાય ફળ થાય;
એમ શુભાશુભ કર્મનું, ભોક્તાપણું જણાય. ||૮૩||

Jher sudhā samje nahi, jeev khāy fal thāy;
Em shubhāshubh karmanu, bhoktāpanu janāy. ||83||

Jher - poison; *sudhā* - nectar; *samje* - understands; *nahi* - not; *jeev* - person; *khāy* - consumes; *fal* - results; *thāy* - occur; *em* - similarly; *shubhāshubh* - auspicious and inauspicious; *karmanu* - of karma; *bhoktāpanu* - receiving; *janāy* - understood

MEANING

Poison and nectar do not know their qualities or effects but the person who consumes them experiences the results. Similarly, experiencing the fruits of auspicious and inauspicious karma by the soul can be understood.

EXPLANATION

The disciple had claimed that since karma is devoid of consciousness, it is incapable of giving fruits. Invalidating this view, the Guru asserts in this verse that it is not necessary for a substance to possess consciousness to affect another substance. An inert substance has no knowledge, intention or plan to impact another substance, yet it does. Non-sentient matter cannot know its own qualities or effects and can still produce an effect in line with its qualities. Inanimate substances do not have the capacity to know whether they are beneficial or harmful, they do not know the entity to whom they will cause benefit or harm, and yet they can bring about one of these results.

Several such instances can be observed in everyday life. Food items are inanimate. They do not know how they help sustain the body, yet they provide nutrition. Even though alcohol is devoid of consciousness, it affects even an intelligent person to behave weirdly due to its capacity to intoxicate. A thorn causes pain despite being lifeless. Once anaesthesia is administered to a patient, he feels no pain even when his body is cut open. All these substances are inanimate and yet their effect on the body and the mind is experienced. They do not know what they are, what their own capacity is, what results they can produce, and yet extend their consequences due to an inherent ability. Similarly, even karma is devoid of knowledge but it can give its fruits to the soul.

Absence of consciousness is not an obstruction to giving results. To enable the disciple to quickly grasp this fact, the Guru gives a simple example of poison and nectar. They are both inanimate substances. They do not know their own nature, but whoever consumes them receives the corresponding effects. They do not know what fruit the person should be given, yet, if one consumes poison, it results in death and if one consumes nectar, it results in rejuvenation. Poison and nectar affect the one who consumes them in accordance with their nature. The same also holds true for karma. The soul's auspicious and inauspicious feelings are instrumental in creating the power of the auspicious and inauspicious karma. This power results in auspicious and inauspicious consequences being given, on its own, at the appropriate time. The inanimate auspicious and inauspicious karmic particles themselves do not know anything, yet they give auspicious and inauspicious fruits to the soul. They do not know what type of fruits they will give, yet they give results that correspond to whatever karma the soul has done. The soul enjoys or suffers when karma yields consequences.

Despite being inanimate, karma can inflict results on its doer. It should be borne in mind that the soul is instrumental in generating this power in karmic particles. The soul receives the fruit of karma in a certain form, on a certain scale, at a certain place, for a certain period, however, the impure feelings of the soul are responsible for it. The soul that does auspicious karma receives favourable outcomes and the soul that does inauspicious karma receives unfavourable outcomes. Karma provides its fruit the moment it ripens, and after extending the result, gets stripped from the soul. Karma gives results but the animate soul plays a crucial part in the process. Ultimately, it is the animate soul which masters the inanimate karma.

—— ⟨⦾⟩ ——

VERSE - 84

Nothing happens without reason

In verses 82-83, the Guru explained the process of karmic bondage and proved that accumulated karma gives fruits on its own, at the appropriate time. It is only due to the results of karma, that the soul attains different states. Proving that the soul is the receiver of the consequences of auspicious and inauspicious karma with a familiar example, the Guru says -

એક રાંક ને એક નૃપ, એ આદિ જે ભેદ;
કારણ વિના ન કાર્ય તે, તે જ શુભાશુભ વેધ. ||૮૪||

Ek rānk ne ek nrup, ae ādi je bhed;
Kāran vinā na kārya te, te ja shubhāshubh vedya. ||84||

Ek - one; *rānk* - poor; *ne* - and; *ek* - one; *nrup* - king; *ae* - that; *ādi* - etc.; *je* - such; *bhed* - differences; *kāran* - cause; *vinā* - without; *na* - not; *kārya* - effect; *te* - that; *ja* - itself; *shubhāshubh* - auspicious and inauspicious; *vedya* - experienced

MEANING

One is a pauper, another a prince - this and other such differences are observed in the world. Such differences prove the experience of the fruits of auspicious and inauspicious karma as there is never an effect without a cause.

EXPLANATION

The world consists of differences, diversities and disparities. The difference between a prince and a pauper is clearly visible.

One is born with a silver spoon, while the other is burdened, frustrated and struggles his entire life. While one is unaware of the extent of his wealth, the other cannot even afford one square meal a day.

Intelligent-foolish, beautiful-ugly, healthy-sick, mighty-weak, are some of the many differences that are observed in the world. Even in the case of identical twins, there are differences. Although their facial features are the same, their fingerprints are different and so are their emotions and tendencies. Animals, birds and insects seem identical but are all different. When they are viewed as a group, the differences are not observable but each one has separate distinguishing features. There are other strange occurrences as well, for example, some pets like dogs live in mansions, rest on cosy beds, eat the food of their choice and even roam around in super luxury cars. However, their owners are busy in offices and do not have the luxury of time to rest, have meals, or even indulge in a casual jaunt.

These disparities cannot exist without a cause. According to the law of causation, there is never an effect without a cause. These differences are an effect for which there definitely has to be a cause. If some are said to be rich because they are smart or hard working, then why are others not wealthy despite being immensely intelligent and assiduous? Moreover, how does one explain the distinction of some children being born rich and others, poor? In the absence of a visible reason, it is said that they are lucky or fortunate. It is destiny. Before saying this, one must understand why and what destiny really is. It is not a horoscope drafted by some invisible maker, but the meritorious and unmeritorious karma which the soul has accumulated in previous births and brought along with it in this lifetime.

Contemplating these differences must lead to the conclusion that there can be no other cause that can create such an effect other than the manifestation of auspicious and inauspicious karma. As a fruit of the auspicious and inauspicious feelings harboured in the past by the soul, it receives corresponding consequences. Despite being inanimate, karma extends different results as per the soul's impure feelings which were instrumental in binding them. As long as karmic particles are not transformed into karma, they are neutral, identical, without any difference. Due to the variety of feelings of attachment and aversion, the soul brings about a variety in the karmic particles. Whatever auspicious and inauspicious karma the soul does, it receives the fruits accordingly.

Thus, through the simple concept of cause and effect, the Guru states that the differences prevailing in the world prove that the soul is definitely the receiver of the fruits of auspicious and inauspicious karma. The results of auspicious and inauspicious karma are unmistakably experienced by every living being in the world. All souls do not have similar karma. The accumulated karma is of different types on account of the various feelings harboured. As an effect they get varied results and hence the differences, diversities and disparities in the world.

— ∽◦∾ —

VERSE - 85

Reply 2 - Karma fructify by their own nature

In verse 80, the disciple had said that if God is considered the bestower of the fruits of karma, then it can be established that the soul is the receiver of the fruits of karma. However, if this holds true, then His Godliness itself will not remain. To eliminate the confusion of the disciple, in this verse the Guru says -

ફળદાતા ઈશ્વરતણી, એમાં નથી જરૂર;
કર્મ સ્વભાવે પરિણમે, થાય ભોગથી દૂર. ॥૮૫॥

Faldātā   Ishwartani,   emā   nathi   jarur;
Karma swabhāve pariname, thāy bhogthi dur. ॥85॥

Faldātā - fruit giver; *Ishwartani* - God; *emā* - in that; *nathi* - not; *jarur* - necessary; *karma* - karma; *swabhāve* - by its nature; *pariname* - bears fruits; *thāy* - happens; *bhogthi* - having experienced; *dur* - shed

MEANING

It is not necessary to consider God as the giver of the fruits of karma. Karma bears fruits by its own nature, and is shed as soon as its effects have been experienced.

EXPLANATION

The consequence of each action is inescapable. The movement linking cause and effect is inexorable, unstoppable and irrevocable. It has its own momentum and mechanics.

The effect of consuming poison is death, whereas the effect of consuming sugar is the taste of sweetness and a surge in energy levels. Getting burnt is the result of putting one's hand in fire, whereas feeling cool is the result of touching snow. Similarly, the karma acquired by the soul has the potency to yield definite results. Although inanimate karma is incapable of knowing its ability to give fruit, this very ability is its nature. This amazing ability to give appropriate fruit is inherent in karma and the soul's feelings are instrumental in its manifestation. Despite being inanimate, karma provides fruits to the soul. Hence, there is no necessity to believe God to be the dispenser of consequences. Just as a seed becomes a fruit when the time is ripe, karma gives fruit to the soul at the appropriate time. Hence, there is no need for a God to give the fruits of karma to prove that the soul is the receiver of karma.

Reaffirming the point elucidated in previous verses, the Guru stresses that even though karma is inanimate, it has the power to extend the consequences. When the soul's impure feelings become instrumental in transforming karmic particles into karma, the entire system is precisely set with respect to type, place, time and intensity, which enables it to give the fruits. Just as a man-made engine carries along tons and tons of cargo; due to the soul's inspiration, karma develops the ability to provide results in a certain form, in a certain quantum, with a certain intensity and at a certain time.

Thus, there is no need to believe that God gives joy and sorrow to the soul. The auspicious and inauspicious karma bound by the soul themselves modify as the givers of joy and sorrow, as per their nature. Karma is shed having made the soul receive its fruits. It is released from the soul after extending the consequences. The soul becomes free from that karma after experiencing its fruits. A snake whose venom has been extracted is no longer dangerous, it is merely like a harmless giant caterpillar. Similarly, karma yields appropriate results at the right time and thereafter becomes ineffective. It gets stripped from the soul and transforms back into neutral karmic particles.

Hence, it can be concluded that karma has the natural power to give definite results. The soul is that which experiences the consequences. In this equation, God is not needed as the provider of rewards and punishments, to prove that the soul is the receiver of the fruits of karma. God is a soul in its purest form, possessing infinite knowledge; thus, He can only be the knower of the soul's bondage. He does not get entangled in any occurrences of the world. He plays no part in it.

VERSE - 86

Deep subject explained briefly

In verse 81, the disciple had stated that without establishing the existence of God, no law could prevail in the world and there would be no designated place to receive the fruits of auspicious and inauspicious karma. Solving this confusion of the disciple, the Guru says -

તે તે ભોગ્ય વિશેષનાં, સ્થાનક દ્રવ્ય સ્વભાવ;
ગહન વાત છે શિષ્ય આ, કહી સંક્ષેપે સાવ. ||૮૬||

Te te bhogya visheshnā, sthānak dravya swabhāv;
Gahan vāt chhe shishya ā, kahi sankshepe sāv. ||86||

Te te - those; *bhogya* - to experience; *visheshnā* - special; *sthānak* - places; *dravya* - substance; *swabhāv* - nature; *gahan* - deep; *vāt* - subject; *chhe* - is; *shishya* - disciple; *ā* - this; *kahi* - stated; *sankshepe* - briefly; *sāv* - very

MEANING

In order that the soul experiences the fruits of karma, there are designated places, through their inherent nature. O disciple! This is a deep subject, which has been stated here very briefly.

EXPLANATION

The disciple had claimed that if God was to be accepted as the bestower of the fruits of karma and the creator of the world, it would hamper His Godliness. If such a God is not proven, then neither order in the world, nor designated places where the fruits of karma are received, can be proven to exist. The Guru proceeded to explain in a beautiful manner how auspicious and inauspicious karma give fruits to the soul. All acts certainly have their aftermath. All intentions carry within them the seeds of merit or demerit. Karma or its fruits cannot be denied. Now, in this verse, the Guru explains about the designated places to receive the fruits of karma.

There are four states of existence - heaven, hell, human and animal. Corresponding to the feelings the soul has engaged in, it gets the association of an appropriate place where it receives the fruits. One goes to heaven due to extremely auspicious feelings, hell due to extremely inauspicious feelings, and human-animal forms due to mixed feelings. The arrangement is such that one who harbours intense feelings goes very high or very low with a long lifespan, and one who harbours mild feelings is born in the middle world, with a medium lifespan. Auspicious karma takes the soul higher, inauspicious karma takes it lower, and mixed karma takes it to the middle level.

It is not that the soul receives a certain fruit because it is in a particular realm. Rather, it has certain karma which has taken it to that realm, to receive the fruits. If a person is convicted for murder and sentenced to death, he is jailed and hanged. The act of hanging takes place in the jail, not at his residence. However, it is not true that he is hanged just because he was in the jail. If that were the case, then the superintendent and guards who work in the jail too would be hanged. Only those who have committed a crime are punished in the jail. Similarly, the soul goes to the corresponding realm due to its karma and receives the results.

Thus, the soul has to go to the appropriate places to receive the fruits of karma. This occurs according to the feelings in which it has engaged. Heaven and hell are the places where one receives the fruits of greater amounts of auspicious or inauspicious karma. This arrangement has existed in the world since time immemorial. No God has created these places. Such places exist in the universe on their own. Moreover, the soul with karmic bondage goes to these places on its own to receive the fruits. There is no need of God to send the soul to these places. Therefore, it is not true that the soul can be proved to be the receiver of the fruits of karma, only if God is proved to be the bestower of the results and the creator of the world. The designated places to receive the fruits of karma exist naturally, and such is the nature of a soul which is under the influence of karma, to go to those places.

This profound truth has been very briefly explained here. The philosophy of heaven and hell is a deep subject. It has been elaborately explained in the scriptures, and is difficult to grasp. Moreover, the main purpose here is to prove that the soul is the receiver of the fruits of karma. Hence, it has been mentioned very concisely in this verse. Only a brief idea about the subject has been given. Thus, the Guru winds up His explanation by pointing out that this subject is vast, and He has given the disciple only a glimpse of the immense territory it encompasses.

Fifth Fundamental
There is liberation

The pious association with the Guru has led to the dispelling of the disciple's doubts, giving rise to the right knowledge. From among the six fundamentals, the disciple now expresses his confusion regarding the fifth fundamental, 'there is liberation'.

Until this point, the Guru had explained that the soul exists, it is eternal, it binds karma, and receives the fruits of karma; using fitting logic and examples to prove them. As the disciple's thinking evolves, yet another doubt arises in his mind. He feels that just as the world is beginningless and endless, the relationship between the soul and karma must also be beginningless and endless. The disciple is unable to accept with certainty the fact that it is possible for the soul to be completely free from karma and attain the state of liberation. He puts forth these doubts to the Guru, and yet again, humbly requests for a solution.

In order to establish the existence of liberation, Shrimadji has composed five verses, 87-91. In the first two verses, 87 and 88, the humble disciple presents two arguments regarding the fifth fundamental truth - 'there is liberation'. Here, the influence of the *Purva Mimānsā* philosophy can be clearly seen in the arguments put forth by the disciple. Shrimadji has woven the well-known argument of this philosophy which does not accept liberation, without naming it, as the disciple's enquiry. He then resolves these arguments through the Guru's reply, in three verses, 89-91. He illustrates the incorrectness of the disciple's doubt and establishes that there is liberation, for his spiritual welfare.

VERSE - 87

Doubt 1 - There cannot be liberation

In the first verse, presenting an argument in support of his doubt regarding the fifth fundamental, 'there is liberation', the disciple says -

કર્તા ભોક્તા જીવ હો, પણ તેનો નહિ મોક્ષ;
વીત્યો કાળ અનંત પણ, વર્તમાન છે દોષ. ||૮૭||

Kartā bhoktā jeev ho, pan teno nahi moksh;
Vityo kāl anant pan, vartmān chhe dosh. ||87||

Kartā - doer; *bhoktā* - receiver; *jeev* - soul; *ho* - is; *pan* - but; *teno* - its; *nahi* - not; *moksh* - liberation; *vityo* - passed; *kāl* - time; *anant* - infinite; *pan* - but; *vartmān* - present; *chhe* - is; *dosh* - flaw

MEANING

Although the soul is the doer of karma and the receiver of the fruits of karma, it cannot attain liberation from karma, as infinite time has passed by and the flaw of impurity yet remains.

EXPLANATION

From the above discussion, the disciple has properly understood that the soul is the doer of karma and the receiver of its fruits. By reflecting deeply upon the Guru's pearls of wisdom, he is firmly convinced about the doership of the soul and it being the receiver of the fruits of karma. The disciple now turns his attention to another aspect of spirituality. He points out that while the soul is the doer and the receiver, it can never be free from karma. He does not accept that karma can completely stop getting bound to the soul, and it can be liberated from it forever.

It does not seem logical to the disciple that the soul can become absolutely free from karmic bondage as infinite time has passed and yet flaws such as likes and dislikes, which cause bondage, have not been eliminated. They still persist in the soul. The flaw of doing karma has been present since time immemorial, it has not been destroyed. Therefore, the disciple feels that it is impossible for this flaw to be completely annihilated. Consequently, it appears to him that the soul cannot attain liberation, which is freedom from the bondage of karma. Since the flaw still exists, he does not see the possibility of liberation.

The cycle of binding karma and receiving its fruits has been operating continuously since infinite time. While receiving the fruits, the soul reacts to situations and accumulates new karma. Hence, the cycle of doing and receiving karma has always persisted. Even in the present, this cycle goes on and the soul has not attained liberation. If the soul can get liberated, then why has it not been liberated until now, despite the passage of infinite time? If it were to attain liberation, it should have happened by now. The relation between the soul and karma that has existed since infinite time is the same even today. Hence, there is no liberation.

The soul has been in bondage since the infinite past and is in bondage even today. That which could not be removed in the past or in the present, can easily be assumed to be irremovable in the future as well. Thus, the cycle of birth and death which was ongoing in the past, is ongoing in the present, and will continue in the future, forever. The soul will be eternally linked both to the action and its aftermath. Neither the passage of time nor change in circumstances can alter this state. The bondage is endless and the very notion of liberation is baseless. Hence, it is futile to work towards a mere chimera, something no more than an illusion.

VERSE - 88

Doubt 2 - Soul is nowhere without karma

Observing the transmigration of worldly souls in the four states of existence, another logical argument supporting his doubt regarding liberation arises within the disciple. This argument has been influenced by the *Purva Mimānsā* philosophy. The disciple says -

શુભ કરે ફળ ભોગવે, દેવાદિ ગતિ માંય;
અશુભ કરે નરકાદિ ફળ, કર્મ રહિત ન ક્યાંય. ||૮૮||

Shubh karey fal bhogve, devādi gati māy;
Ashubh karey narakādi fal, karma rahit na kyāy. ||88||

Shubh - auspicious; **karey** - does; **fal** - fruits; **bhogve** - receives; **devādi** - heaven etc.; **gati** - states of existence; **māy** - in; **ashubh** - inauspicious; **karey** - does; **narakādi** - hell etc.; **fal** - fruits; **karma** - karma; **rahit** - without; **na** - not; **kyāy** - anywhere

MEANING

If the soul does auspicious karma, it enjoys the fruits in states of existence like heavenly beings, etc.; if it does inauspicious karma, it bears the fruits in states of existence like hellish beings, etc. However, the soul is not observed to be without karma anywhere.

EXPLANATION

The soul has been harbouring auspicious and inauspicious feelings since time infinite. Therefore, it keeps binding the corresponding karma. The soul is constantly doing karma and receiving its fruits. If it does auspicious karma, then it receives meritorious outcomes in the states of heavenly beings, etc. If it does inauspicious karma, then it receives unmeritorious outcomes in the states of hellish beings, etc. Due to auspicious karma, it enjoys material pleasures in heaven or human life. Due to inauspicious karma, it suffers adversities in hell or animal life. The soul certainly receives the corresponding fruits of whatever type of karma it does.

In order to receive the fruits of both types of karma, it takes birth in those respective states of existence. While receiving the fruits of this karma, it harbours impure feelings and binds new karma. Hence, it is not observed to be devoid of karma in any of the four states of existence. The soul can choose to do auspicious karma leading to heaven, etc., or inauspicious karma leading to hell, etc., but is never karmaless in any state of existence. It is never without auspicious or inauspicious karma. The soul is not noticed to be without karma anywhere, while liberation is a karmaless state. Therefore, it does not seem possible that the soul can attain liberation and gain total freedom from karmic association. The soul was never free and will never become free.

The disciple bemoans the fate of the soul. He says that it does not matter whether there is auspicious or inauspicious karma, as the soul is bound by both. The soul is never free of bondage. Hence, liberation is only hypothetical, there is no such state. If this is the case then the disciple feels he has a right to be cynical, lose hope and find no reason to rejoice. He requests the Guru with humility to clarify his doubt.

Although the disciple doubts the existence of liberation, it is noteworthy that he has a clear concept of what liberation ought to be. There is a myth prevalent in religious communities that liberation is attained by doing auspicious deeds. They mistakenly believe that auspicious deeds have the capacity to lead them to liberation. If they are undertaken to a lesser extent, one gets comforts and luxuries. If they are undertaken to a greater extent, one attains liberation. Hence, they believe in the power of auspicious deeds and feel fulfilled by doing them. However, this is sheer ignorance. Auspicious deeds lead to the acquisition of karma and there cannot be liberation as long as there is karma. Liberation can only be attained by elimination of both auspicious and inauspicious karma. Auspicious karma leads to bondage, so it cannot be the cause of liberation. Thus, both auspicious and inauspicious karma cause the continuation of worldly life and as an effect of this, liberation is not possible.

VERSE - 89

Reply 1 - Cessation of karma is liberation

In verse 87, the disciple had expressed his doubt regarding the existence of liberation. He wondered that if liberation of the soul was truly possible, then despite infinite time having passed by, why has this state not yet been attained? The Guru gives the solution to this doubt in two verses. In this verse, He proves the existence of liberation. The Guru says -

જેમ શુભાશુભ કર્મપદ, જાણ્યાં સફળ પ્રમાણ;
તેમ નિવૃત્તિ સફળતા, માટે મોક્ષ સુજાણ. ||૮૯||

Jem shubhāshubh karmapad, jānyā safal pramān;
Tem nivrutti safaltā, mātey moksh sujān. ||89||

Jem - just as; *shubhāshubh* - auspicious and inauspicious; *karmapad* - karma; *jānyā* - known; *safal* - fruitful; *pramān* - evidence; *tem* - similarly; *nivrutti* - cessation; *safaltā* - fruitfulness; *mātey* - therefore; *moksh* - liberation; *sujān* - knowledgeable

MEANING
Just as you understood through evidence that auspicious and inauspicious karma are fruitful, similarly, retreating from karma is also fruitful. O wise one, therefore, there is liberation.

EXPLANATION
Feelings such as likes and dislikes are the causes of karmic bondage. As the soul engages in these causes, it binds new

karma. The karma manifests when the time is ripe and gives its appropriate fruit, which the soul certainly has to receive. Auspicious and inauspicious karma lead to heaven and hell respectively, to bear the consequences. The soul must definitely receive the fruits of the auspicious and inauspicious karma bound by it on account of its flaws. This principle has been established with sufficient proof. Now, convincing him regarding the state of liberation, the Guru conveys that the disciple has evidentially understood that the soul is the doer of karma and the receiver of its fruits. Similarly, it is also necessary to properly understand about retreating from karma and its fruit.

Every action certainly has some outcome. No action is without a result. Just as doing auspicious and inauspicious karma certainly leads to receiving their fruits, the soul also certainly receives the fruit of retreating from auspicious and inauspicious karma. The effort of a soul engaged in auspicious and inauspicious karma is not without fruit, similarly, the soul's effort to eliminate auspicious and inauspicious karma is also not without fruit. The activity of withdrawal is also fruitful the way the activity of indulging is fruitful.

The withdrawal from auspicious and inauspicious karma bears consequences and that fruit is liberation. The soul involved in auspicious or inauspicious feelings attains a good or bad state of existence, where it certainly experiences the fruits as joy or sorrow. Likewise, when it retreats from both auspicious and inauspicious feelings, it certainly attains the fruit of liberation. As the soul withdraws from both types of feelings, it begins to eliminate the causes of karmic bondage. It does not incur new bondage and gradually destroys existing bondage. When all karma is destroyed, the soul is liberated. Thus, the Guru assures the disciple regarding the attainment of liberation. He employs the simple logic that auspicious and inauspicious karma are not without fruit, they certainly give the result of transmigration. Similarly, refraining from auspicious and inauspicious karma too is not without fruit, it certainly confers the result of liberation.

The Guru plumbs the depths of spiritual science and explains that every deed certainly carries with it the burden of karma. This is true for both good and bad deeds, which result in reward and punishment respectively. Both bind the soul to the world, condemning it to the cycles of birth and rebirth. It is possible to refrain from indulging in the causes of bondage and consequently, liberation as its result is also possible.

The Guru lovingly addresses the disciple as '*sujān*' - wise, since he is thoughtful and capable of comprehending the truth. The Guru says, 'O, intelligent one! Understand this well and accept that the soul can become completely free of karma. Reflect upon this correctly and determine that there is liberation.'

VERSE - 90

Elimination of impure feelings

Explaining the cause of the soul's transmigration and how to bring about its end, the Guru says -

વીત્યો કાળ અનંત તે, કર્મ શુભાશુભ ભાવ;
તેહ શુભાશુભ છેદતાં, ઉપજે મોક્ષ સ્વભાવ. ||૯૦||

Vityo kāl anant te, karma shubhāshubh bhāv;
Teh shubhāshubh chhedtā, upje moksh swabhāv. ||90||

Vityo - passed; *kāl* - time; *anant* - infinite; *te* - that; *karma* - karma; *shubhāshubh* - auspicious and inauspicious; *bhāv* - feelings; *teh* - those; *shubhāshubh* - auspicious and inauspicious; *chhedtā* - destroying; *upje* - manifests; *moksh* - liberation; *swabhāv* - nature

MEANING

Since infinite time, the soul is engaged in auspicious and inauspicious feelings. When these auspicious and inauspicious feelings are destroyed, the soul attains liberation, which is its true nature.

EXPLANATION

The Guru made it clear in the previous verse that when the soul indulges in feelings, it receives the corresponding fruits. If it engages in auspicious and inauspicious feelings, it receives the fruit of transmigration. If it engages in pure feelings by eliminating auspicious and inauspicious feelings, it receives the fruit of liberation. However, this state has not been attained even after the passage of infinite time, as the soul has only engaged in harbouring auspicious and inauspicious feelings. It has never attempted to overcome them. It has made no effort at all to withdraw from them. It is not even aware that it is possible to refrain from them. So far, it has not eliminated impure feelings and hence has been wandering in all four states of existence, without attaining liberation.

Although auspicious and inauspicious feelings have persisted since time infinite and appear permanent, they can be eliminated. Despite the doership of impure feelings and the receipt of their fruits since time immemorial, they can be eradicated. This is possible because auspicious and inauspicious feelings are not the soul's nature, although it has the ability to modify into them. Rather, auspicious and inauspicious feelings are contrary to its pure nature. Hence, they can be destroyed. When the soul eliminates both these feelings, modifications in the form of pure, natural feelings emerge within. Retiring from impure feelings gives rise to pure feelings which are diametrically opposite to the auspicious and inauspicious ones. The soul remains engrossed in pure feelings, thus stabilising its natural disposition. The impure state of the soul goes on waning and the pure state goes on waxing. Ultimately the soul becomes completely devoid of impure feelings, stays steady in the pure feelings, and attains liberation.

If the soul stops engaging in auspicious and inauspicious feelings, its nature of liberation manifests. The soul's pure nature has been latent since time infinite and its complete manifestation itself is liberation. The nature of water is cool, however, when placed over a stove it acquires the state of boiling. If it is taken away from the stove, it cools down to its natural state. Similarly, the nature of the soul is pure, but its state gets impure once it attaches to the fruits of karma. If it detaches itself from the fruits of karma, its state becomes pure, which is the manifestation of its true nature. The manifestation of the inherent, pure and unbound nature is liberation.

Thus, the Guru informs the disciple that from time immemorial, the soul has been caught in a web of cause and effect, reward and punishment. Every action only enmeshes it further, strangling its freedom. If the soul does not develop awareness of the self, it will continue to remain in bondage. In order to avoid such dire consequences, the key is freedom from ego and selfish desires. Then it will need nothing, want nothing and remain content. Vanquishing attachment and aversion, it will be completely liberated. The soul which eliminates auspicious and inauspicious feelings and manifests its true nature attains the state of liberation.

VERSE - 91

Reply 2 - Concept of liberation

In verse 88, the disciple had expressed that he is unable to find the soul devoid of karma in any state of existence. Resolving this doubt and describing the nature of liberation, the Guru says -

દેહાદિક સંયોગનો, આત્યંતિક વિયોગ;
સિદ્ધ મોક્ષ શાશ્વત પદે, નિજ અનંત સુખભોગ. ||૯૧||

Dehādik sanyogno, ātyantik viyog;
Siddh moksh shāshvat padey, nij anant sukhbhog. ||91||

Dehādik - body etc.; **sanyogno** - of associations; **ātyantik** - ultimate; **viyog** - dissociation; **siddh** - accomplished; **moksh** - liberation; **shāshvat** - permanent; **padey** - state; **nij** - own; **anant** - infinite; **sukhbhog** - enjoys bliss

MEANING

With the ultimate dissociation from the body and other associations, the soul attains the permanent state of liberation, where it revels in its own infinite bliss.

EXPLANATION

The disciple had conveyed that the soul engrossed in auspicious and inauspicious feelings procures the results of wandering in heaven, hell, etc. It is not without karma anywhere. The beginning of transmigration is untraceable and the end seems inconceivable. Hence, liberation must not be possible. In response to this argument, the Guru portrays liberation as a completely karmaless, bodiless state.

The soul has been separated from the body at death, infinite times in the past. However, this dissociation was always temporary. It merely left one body to enter another, as karma compelled it to associate with a body. When the soul separates from the body in such a manner that no such association is required again, it is called liberation. In other words, the occurrence of dissociation without reassociation is liberation. Temporary separation from the body is death, whereas permanent, total, absolute, ultimate dissociation from the body is liberation, which is signified by '*ātyantik viyog*'.

The soul's association with the body, etc., is caused by material karma, which in turn is created due to karma-binding feelings such as likes and dislikes. When the soul abides in its true nature, karma-binding feelings are eliminated. As a result, the incurrence of material karma also stops. Moreover, through the strength of abiding in its inherent nature, past karma is annihilated. The prevention of new karma being bound and the shedding of old karma ultimately causes the manifestation of a state totally bereft of karma. This is the purest state of any being, completely devoid of material associations like karma and body. There is no bondage or embodiment. Through a powerful effort, the soul has accomplished everything. Such a liberated being is called '*Siddh*'.

The state of liberation is eternal and unwavering. Once attained, it can never be lost. The liberated soul never has to undergo the worldly cycles of birth and death again, as there remains no reason or need to take birth. It is the end of becoming. The liberated state is permanent which is denoted by the word *'shāshvat'*.

The liberated one revels in pure, uninterrupted, complete bliss for time infinite. Worldly miseries are destroyed forever and the everlasting bliss of the soul is experienced. The bliss is endless as it has been attained by totally destroying the karma, which was obstructing its true nature. Now with the manifestation of its pure nature, the liberated soul enjoys its own boundless bliss. This is indicated by *'nij anant sukhbhog'*.

In the previous verse, the Guru had propounded non-physical liberation in the form of freedom from auspicious and inauspicious feelings. In this verse, He has expounded physical liberation, in the form of freedom from associations like the body, etc. This verse also clarifies the definition of a liberated soul from both the outer and inner viewpoints. From the external perspective, the liberated soul is permanently dissociated from the body and karma. From the internal perspective, it eternally revels in its own infinite bliss.

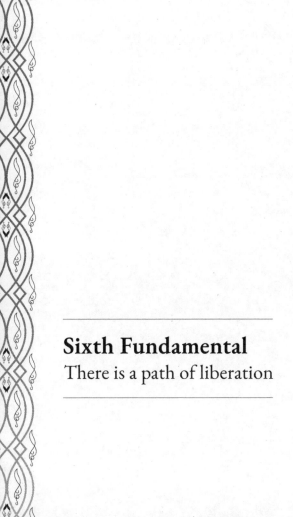

Sixth Fundamental
There is a path of liberation

A fter contemplating the solution given by the Guru regarding the existence of liberation, the disciple no longer has any doubt, instead he gains a firm conviction about it. Now, he puts forward his doubt regarding the last of the six fundamentals, 'there is a path of liberation'.

The correct understanding of the nature of liberation and the benefits bestowed by its attainment kindles a strong desire in him to reach the ultimate state. The disciple is an *ātmārthi*, longing for freedom, yearning to break free from the endless chain of transmigration. He now sincerely wishes to be free from the misery he has endured over infinite lifetimes across various states of existence; to cross the ocean of birth and death and attain the infinite, independent, blissful state of liberation. So, with indomitable enthusiasm and eagerness, the disciple aspires to understand the correct method to attain liberation.

Shrimadji has composed a total of 27 verses 92-118, in order to explain the sixth fundamental. In the first five verses 92-96, the humble disciple conveys three arguments regarding this fundamental. He presents well-known arguments of those who are not convinced about the undisputed path of liberation, as the disciple's queries, and solves all doubts through the Guru's replies in 22 verses 97-118. He proves the invalidity of the disciple's doubt and establishes the pathway to liberation, for his spiritual welfare.

VERSE - 92

Doubt 1 - Annihilating karma in one lifetime

Presenting his confusion regarding the path of liberation, the disciple says -

હોય કદાપિ મોક્ષપદ, નહિ અવિરોધ ઉપાય;
કર્મો કાળ અનંતનાં, શાથી છેદ્યાં જાય? ||૯૨||

Hoi kadāpi mokshpad, nahi avirodh upāy;
Karmo kāl anantnā, shāthi chhedyā jāy? ||92||

Hoi - there; *kadāpi* - even if; *mokshpad* - state of liberation; *nahi* - no; *avirodh* - undisputed; *upāy* - way; *karmo* - karma; *kāl* - time; *anantnā* - of infinite; *shāthi* - how; *chhedyā* - destroyed; *jāy* - can be

MEANING

Even if a state of liberation exists, there appears to be no undisputed path towards attaining it. How can karma accumulated over an infinite period of time possibly be annihilated?

EXPLANATION

The Guru proved the existence of liberation, and after some deliberation, the disciple is convinced of it. Now, since his doubt concerning the liberation of the soul has been cleared, he asks another seminal question regarding the means of liberation. He states that even if it is possible to attain the completely pure state of the soul, there seems to be no undisputed and universally accepted path towards it.

Without a definite path, how could an infinite amount of karma accumulated over an infinite period of time possibly be annihilated?

The soul is constantly being bound by karma - in fact, heaps and heaps of it every moment. This is true especially for the worldly-minded soul who is conditioned to react to every situation that arises, therefore perpetuating endless bondage. Karma can be destroyed in two ways - by fruition or its release through the right effort of the soul. Liberation can be attained only by total destruction of all karma.

Based on this knowledge, the disciple questions how an infinite amount of karma can be eliminated in this present human birth, having a relatively short lifespan. This possibility seems too far-fetched and he cannot even begin to comprehend it. He feels the soul must require an endless amount of time to destroy all karma of countless past lives. Its complete extinction in the short span of the current lifetime appears almost impossible.

Thus, although the disciple has shown progress by accepting the existence of liberation, he remains unaware of an unfailing path through which karma can be annihilated in a short period of time. He seeks clarity regarding this undisputed path to liberation. Hence, the eager disciple puts forth his confusion to the Guru, pleading for a solution. He politely requests the Guru to show the flawless and unopposed path of liberation.

— ∽⚬∾ —

VERSE - 93

Doubt 2 - No undisputed means to liberation

In the previous verse, the disciple, riddled with doubt, presented the argument that there is no unfailing path towards attaining liberation. Putting forth a second argument supporting his premise, the disciple says -

અથવા મત દર્શન ઘણાં, કહે ઉપાય અનેક;
તેમાં મત સાચો કયો, બને ન એહ વિવેક. ||૯૩||

Athvā mat darshan ghanā, kahey upāy anek;
Temā mat sācho kayo, baney na eh vivek. ||93||

Athvā - or; *mat* - creeds; *darshan* - schools of thought; *ghanā* - many; *kahey* - stipulate; *upāy* - path; *anek* - numerous; *temā* - of them; *mat* - opinion; *sācho* - true; *kayo* - which; *baney* - happens; *na* - not; *eh* - that; *vivek* - discrimination

MEANING

Or, there are many beliefs and philosophies which show innumerable ways for liberation. It is difficult to decide which of the proposed paths is correct.

EXPLANATION

Presenting the difficulty which arises while attempting to determine a path of liberation acceptable to all, the disciple claims the human birth is too short to annihilate infinite karma bound in the past. By this, he implies that it cannot be destroyed in such a short span of time. Well, even if one has to drop this argument, the differences in each of the paths proposed are many, rendering it extremely difficult for one to decide the right, spiritually beneficial path.

There are several philosophies, faiths, sects prevalent in the world. Each holds a different view regarding the nature of the soul, liberation, etc. This implies that their ideologies regarding the path of liberation also differ. They describe the method to attain liberation in diverse ways. One philosophy propounds a set of means to achieve liberation, while the other offers a totally different approach. Some insist on true knowledge, while others on pure devotion; some focus only on harsh austerities, while others adhere to selfless service as the only way to the goal. Each philosophy and religion formulates its own path of liberation, professing its superiority over all others.

Expectedly, these varying approaches leave the disciple indecisive and he is unable to commit to a particular path, entrapped in the midst of a maze with no means to exit victorious. This vast plethora of opinions surrounding liberation and the means towards it has baffled the disciple, leaving him in a state of confusion. There is a great upheaval in his mind over the path of liberation. Stuck in this scenario of multiple paths to liberation, he remains perplexed, not knowing which one to follow.

The disciple feels that there are as many schools of thought as there are thinkers. As many roads to salvation, as seekers. Filled with verbal promises, they offer lots of dreams, but do little to genuinely guide the aspirants. Viewing the diverse opinions laid before him, the disciple stands tangled in a state of confusion.

In this moment of confusion, the worthy disciple admits his incapability to recognise the correct path. He is unable to distinguish the right path from the wrong one. He knows that liberation would be impossible if he followed the wrong path. He cannot decide which path to accept. He therefore states that it is beyond his ability to decide which one is true and worthy of adoption. Accepting his lack of discernment, he harbours an earnest desire to be shown the undisputed path of liberation by the Guru; or else he would spend all his life trying to find the truth and be none the wiser. He thus surrenders to the Guru's judgement.

———❧———

VERSE - 94

Doubt 3 - Multiplicity of views regarding caste and clothing

The thoughtful disciple has studied several religions and philosophies. He is aware of their ideologies, and various differences of opinion. He is confused by the differences in the path of liberation advocated by them and therefore feels that there is no undisputed path of liberation. Putting forth the third argument in support of his doubt, the disciple says -

કઈ જાતિમાં મોક્ષ છે, કયા વેષમાં મોક્ષ;
એનો નિશ્ચય ના બને, ઘણા ભેદ એ દોષ. ||૯૪||

Kai jātimā moksh chhe, kayā veshmā moksh;
Eno nishchay nā baney, ghanā bhed ae dosh. ||94||

Kai - which; *jātimā* - in caste or gender; *moksh* - liberation; *chhe* - is; *kayā* - which; *veshmā* - in garb; *moksh* - liberation; *eno* - that; *nishchay* - decision; *nā* - not; *baney* - happens; *ghanā* - many; *bhed* - differences; *ae* - that; *dosh* - fault, problem

MEANING

Which caste or gender, and external attire is required to attain liberation? It is extremely difficult to determine this because of the diverse opinions.

EXPLANATION

The diversity of views is the main cause of confusion for the disciple. Many differences of opinion pertaining to caste and religious attire prevail in the world, making it extremely difficult to determine which of these could contribute to attaining liberation. The disciple questions which caste and clothing are required to attain liberation, because until he is certain, he cannot tread the path.

The word *'jāti'* means caste. The four major castes are *Brāhmin* - priests, *Kshatriya* - warriors, *Vaishya* - businessmen and *Shudra* - labourers. This arrangement has been prevailing in India since ancient times. Society was divided into four castes for it to function smoothly and efficiently. Brāhmins managed religious matters, Kshatriyas ensured the protection of people, Vaishyas handled commerce and finance whereas Shudras looked after the necessities of societal life. There was harmony and unity among the castes. However, with changing times, values stood eroded and the balance between the four was lost. The caste system began to decay and Shudras were despised. They were not given the right to follow religion, enter temples or even read scriptures. They were punished if they did so. Based on this, some denounce Shudras, branding them as absolutely unworthy of attaining liberation. Some believe that only Brāhmins are worthy of attaining liberation, while others believe that the rest are also capable of it.

The word *'jāti'* can also be interpreted in terms of gender - with some believing that only males can achieve liberation, not accepting the ability of females and neuter genders to attain it. They hold a strong belief that only males are eligible for liberation, whereas some say that other genders can also attain it.

Just as there are various opinions regarding the caste or gender that is worthy of attaining liberation, there are also many differences regarding the *'vesh'* - attire. Some accept that liberation can be attained even as a householder, without donning the attire of a monk; whereas some believe that in all three periods of time, it is impossible to attain liberation without embracing the attire of a monk. Adding another layer of chaos are the differences regarding a monk's attire. Some insist on red robes, others advocate yellow robes. White robes alone are accepted by certain people, while others claim that remaining unclad is the only way to liberation. They believe that only those who perform the religious activities propounded by them and don the external attire accepted by them, are worthy of attaining liberation. They have become like advertising hoardings, marketing the commodity of the means of liberation. Each strives to establish their opinion alone as the final truth. They say that unless one is loyal to their sect, one cannot attain liberation. They even resort to ridicule, and scorn upon other religions which embrace different attires and rituals.

Thus, various doctrines, creeds and sects expound different paths to attain liberation. If the path of liberation does exist, then everyone should expound the same path. However, different opinions are expressed regarding caste, gender and attire. These diverse beliefs are the very reason the disciple is confused. His confusion is justifiable. The disciple remains indecisive in the face of mutually contradictory views. Caught in the outer facets of different faiths, he is entangled in a sticky web of mere external norms and therefore  feels that there is certainly no undisputed and universally approved path of liberation.

VERSE - 95

Conclusion drawn from discussion

The disciple presented three arguments in verses 92-94 supporting his doubt regarding the last fundamental truth. Expressing the conclusion he has drawn regarding the path of liberation on account of his doubt, the disciple says -

તેથી એમ જણાય છે, મળે ન મોક્ષ ઉપાય;
જીવાદિ જાણ્યા તણો, શો ઉપકાર જ થાય? ||૯૫||

Tethi em janāy chhe, maley na moksh upāy;
Jeevādi jānyā tano, sho upkār ja thāy? ||95||

Tethi - therefore; *em* - it; *janāy* - appears; *chhe* - is; *maley* - attain; *na* - not; *moksh* - liberation; *upāy* - means; *jeevādi* - soul etc.; *jānyā* - knowing; *tano* - of; *sho* - what; *upkār* - benefit; *ja* - indeed; *thāy* - happens

MEANING

Therefore it seems that the path of liberation is unobtainable. In that case, what benefit can be gained by knowing about the soul, etc.?

EXPLANATION

The disciple's confusion is multi-layered. It seems far-fetched to think that karma accumulated over infinite lifetimes can be eliminated in a single lifetime. Furthermore, numerous religious doctrines, creeds and sects propound diverse and varied means to realise the soul. Unsurprisingly, there is a plethora of opinions regarding which caste, gender and attire are required for liberation. From these three arguments, he concludes that there is no undisputed path of liberation.

If there is no well-ascertained, spiritually beneficial, effective path of liberation, then the knowledge of the five fundamental truths - the existence of the soul, etc., is meaningless. There is no benefit of knowing the five fundamental truths if the sixth is not known.

The purpose of knowing the nature of the soul is attaining liberation. This knowledge is only worthwhile if it is used to advance towards liberation. If liberation cannot be attained due to the absence of an unfailing path, then the discussion regarding the soul is futile. If the path of liberation is a sheer impossibility, then all attempts are a waste of time, all exercises are worthless.

The disciple is interested in achieving liberation. The aim of his discussions is not to incite arguments, but to attain the ultimate state. Therefore, he firmly believes that if there is no path to attain the completely pure state of the soul, then there is no use of gaining knowledge regarding the five fundamental truths. Although he has presented his doubts regarding the soul to the Guru, and received clarifications, the absence of a path leads him to believe there is no practical benefit to it. He seems a little pessimistic and depressed, however, he has not yet given up. He still believes the Guru will show him the way. Hence, the disciple expresses his bewilderment to the Guru, and humbly seeks a solution.

VERSE - 96

Intense longing for path

In the concluding verse of his doubt regarding the sixth fundamental truth, expressing an intense longing to understand the path of liberation, the disciple says -

પાંચે ઉત્તરથી થયું, સમાધાન સર્વાંગ;
સમજું મોક્ષ ઉપાય તો, ઉદય ઉદય સદ્‍ભાગ્ય. ||૯૬||

Pānche uttarthi thayu, samādhān sarvāng;
Samju moksh upāy toh, uday uday sadbhāgya. ||96||

Pānche - all five; *uttarthi* - by replies; *thayu* - happened; *samādhān* - solution; *sarvāng* - completely; *samju* - understand; *moksh* - liberation; *upāy* - means; *toh* - then; *uday uday* - arising; *sadbhāgya* - good fortune

MEANING

Upon receiving the five earlier answers, I am entirely satisfied as all my doubts have been resolved. I will consider myself most fortunate if I could now obtain similar satisfaction with regards to the path of liberation.

EXPLANATION

The disciple accepts that he has understood the first five fundamental truths and now expresses his desire to understand the path of liberation. He says that he did possess several doubts regarding the nature of the soul. However, these vanished once he resorted to deep contemplation upon the Guru's solutions to the first five fundamental truths of the soul - its existence, eternal nature, doership of karma, receiving the fruits of karma and liberation. He has now understood all five fundamentals completely and holds a firm conviction of their truth.

Owing to the Guru's logical solutions regarding all five fundamental truths, the disciple is now confident that his doubt regarding the path of liberation will also certainly be resolved. He feels he will definitely receive the undisputed path of liberation and elatedly expresses full satisfaction with the Guru's replies to his five doubts. If he can understand the path of liberation, it will be the dawn of his good fortune. The word '*uday*' - dawn, has been used twice in the verse, indicating the intensity of enthusiasm and eagerness within the worthy disciple to know the truth.

The word *bhāgya* denotes material objects such as good health, wealth, family, luxuries, etc. In contrast, the word '*sadbhāgya*' refers to the circumstances conducive to the attainment of the supreme truth. Hence, the disciple zealously uses this word as he is convinced that he can appropriately utilise the present lifetime to realise the truth.

The word '*sadbhāgya*' also implies *Shri Saubhāgyabhāi,* whose request was instrumental in the composition of Shri Ātmasiddhi Shāstra. Shrimadji has mentioned his name thrice in the text - verse 20, this verse, and a verse which was written after verse 127 but later deleted. Thus, He has remembered Shri Saubhāgyabhāi in this verse.

So, the disciple conveys that with the Guru's clarifications regarding the five fundamental truths, not an iota of doubt remains in him. If he gets the clarification regarding the sixth fundamental truth, it will be the dawn of his great fortune. Though the disciple seemed pessimistic, depressed and anxious at the beginning due to the multiple opinions, he has regained his optimism and positivity. This indicates his faith in the Guru's compassion and capacity to dispel his doubt, resolve his crisis, and unravel the undisputed path of liberation. The disciple commits that if he receives the true path, then he will dive headlong into it and spare no effort to achieve liberation.

VERSE - 97

Assurance to disciple

The sixth fundamental truth is extremely important because without knowing the path of liberation, all other knowledge is useless. Therefore, a detailed solution regarding the same has been given in the next 22 verses. These verses can be divided into three groups - verses 97-107 are the solutions to the disciple's arguments, verses 108-113 map the sequential progress on the path to liberation, and verses 114-118 are inspirational to attain perfect purity. When the Guru notices the disciple's sincerity, He feels pleased and explains the path of liberation at length with utmost clarity. Before beginning to resolve the disciple's arguments sequentially, comforting him, the Guru says -

પાંચે ઉત્તરની થઈ, આત્મા વિષે પ્રતીત;
થાશે મોક્ષોપાયની, સહજ પ્રતીત એ રીત. ॥૯૭॥

Pānche uttarni thai, ātmā vishe pratit;
Thāshe mokshopāyni, sahaj pratit ae reet. ॥97॥

Pānche - all five; **uttarni** - of answers; **thai** - happened; **ātmā** - soul; **vishe** - in; **pratit** - belief; **thāshe** - will happen; **mokshopāyni** - regarding path of liberation; **sahaj** - easily; **pratit** - belief; **ae** - that; **reet** - manner

MEANING
Just as you are convinced of the existence, etc., of the soul through the five replies; similarly, you will also be easily convinced about the means of liberation.

EXPLANATION

It is imperative to cultivate worthiness. The disciple is thoughtful, humble and eager to absorb the truth. Therefore, the Guru's knowledge is naturally flowing towards him. The disciple has expressed a deep yearning for the path of liberation, prompting the Guru to respond with a sentiment matching his depth.

Accepting the disciple's humble request, the Guru states that the solutions regarding the five fundamental truths of the soul dispelled his doubts. He determined that they are correct and logical. The disciple gained a firm conviction regarding the five fundamentals, namely 'soul exists', 'it is eternal', 'it is the doer of karma', 'it is the receiver of the fruits of karma', and 'there is liberation'. The Guru uses the word *'pratit'* - belief, indicating that the conviction of the five fundamental truths has reached deep within, due to the disciple's profound and lengthy contemplation. The knowledge is not mere information for him, but has turned into faith, having received it well and accepted it.

The Guru assures the worthy disciple that just as he has gained conviction regarding the five fundamentals, he will easily gain conviction regarding the sixth fundamental truth, 'there is a path of liberation'. Here by using the word *'sahaj'* - easily, the Guru indicates the ease with which the disciple will obtain right conviction of the sixth fundamental truth of the soul. His doubt about the means of liberation will be easily dispelled as in the case of the earlier five doubts. It would be very simple for such an intelligent and worthy disciple to understand the path of liberation. Grasping the true means of liberation will not require much effort. Then there will be no more questions, no further doubts will arise.

With the word *'thāshe'* - will happen, the Guru certifies that the disciple will be convinced regarding the path of liberation, fuelling his enthusiasm. With this certainty and confirmation, the Guru gives him a solid ground to stand on. He comes forward with an assurance that the disciple will cross the final frontier. The Guru benevolently bestows blessings upon him that he will understand and attain spiritual welfare.

VERSE - 98

Reply 1 - Knowledge dispels ignorance

In verse 92, the disciple had posed the argument that even if the state of liberation existed, no undisputed path to attain it is apparent. Moreover, how could karma accumulated over an infinite period of time be annihilated in such a short lifespan. The Guru provides a complete solution to this argument in verses 98-104. The verses 98-101 briefly describe the absolute path of liberation, thus resolving the doubt expressed in the first line of verse 92. The verses 102-104 explain the means to annihilate karma, thus resolving the doubt expressed in the second line of verse 92.

In the opening verse of the solution to the doubt regarding the undisputed means of liberation, showing the complete path of liberation, the Guru says -

કર્મભાવ અજ્ઞાન છે, મોક્ષભાવ નિજવાસ;
અંધકાર અજ્ઞાન સમ, નાશે જ્ઞાનપ્રકાશ. ||૯૮||

Karmabhāv   ajnān   chhe,   mokshbhāv   nijvās;
Andhkār   ajnān   sam,   nāshe   jnānprakāsh. ||98||

Karmabhāv - soul's identification with karmic manifestations; *ajnān* - ignorance; *chhe* - is; *mokshbhāv* - liberation; *nijvās* - abiding in self; *andhkār* - darkness; *ajnān* - ignorance; *sam* - like; *nāshe* - destroyed by; *jnānprakāsh* - light of knowledge

MEANING

Identification with karmic manifestations is ignorance of the self, whereas abiding in the self is liberation. Just as darkness is destroyed by light, ignorance is destroyed by the light of knowledge of the self.

EXPLANATION

Although the inherent nature of water is cool, it is found in two states - cool or warm. Similarly, the inherent nature of the soul is pure, but it modifies as pure or impure states. Explaining these two states, Shrimadji reveals the undisputed path to attain liberation. Since time immemorial, the soul has been in the impure state, as it is deluded regarding its true nature. It has forgotten its own pure, blissful, untainted inherent nature and has identified itself with the karma-created personality. This state is termed as '*karmabhāv*'. To harbour the delusion of 'I-ness' and 'my-ness' towards the karmic manifestations is ignorance. To abide in one's own nature, which is constant, eternal and pure is liberation. This state is termed as '*mokshbhāv*'.

The impure state must be transformed by identifying with the pure nature of the self. The awareness that 'I am separate from associations like the body, etc., and impurities such as likes, dislikes, etc.', leads to liberation and is true knowledge. Thus, one who remains engrossed in the manifestations of karma, acquires karmic bondage and wanders in the cycles of transmigration, whereas one who shifts his focus from the karmic identity towards his pure eternal nature is able to attain the state of liberation. Karmabhāv is the path of bondage and the pursuit of mokshbhāv is the path of liberation.

If someone asks, who are you? One would reply: 'I am a human, I am a male or I am Bhavin.' This answer is fine from the practical viewpoint, but from the spiritual dimension, it is ignorance to believe that I am human, male, Bhavin. This personality is the result of karma, whereas the true nature is that he is a pure soul. To believe the state that has arisen due to karma as one's real self is ignorance. Once true knowledge is gained, there is no false identification or attachment, in spite of the association.

Ignorance which causes karmic bondage is compared with darkness. In darkness one thing is seen as another, illusions are created, mistakes occur and fear is experienced. Extending the analogy, in ignorance, one wrongly understands the innate nature of substances and identifies with the non-self, likes-dislikes arise, and the fear of undesirable association and separation is experienced. Just as light immediately dispels darkness, allowing objects to be viewed as they really are, eliminating illusions, and vanquishing fear; with the dawn of knowledge, ignorance is dispelled, the identification with the body and passions is severed as one realises his innate nature.

Darkness cannot be driven away by a stick, but by lighting a lamp. Similarly, the darkness of ignorance cannot be removed by mere external rituals, but by igniting the lamp of enlightenment. In summary, the pursuit of abiding in the self by differentiating oneself from the karma-created states is the path of liberation. Uninterrupted abidance in the self is liberation.

VERSE - 99

Path of bondage and liberation

Expanding on the truth stated earlier, the Guru throws light on the subtleties of the path of liberation. In verse 99, indicating the path that leads to bondage and the path that leads to liberation, the Guru says -

જે જે કારણ બંધનાં, તેહ બંધનો પંથ;
તે કારણ છેદક દશા, મોક્ષપંથ ભવઅંત. ||૯૯||

Je je kāran bandhnā, teh bandhno panth;
Te kāran chhedak dashā, mokshpanth bhavant. ||99||

Je je - whichever; *kāran* - causes; *bandhnā* - of bondage; *teh* - that; *bandhno* - of bondage; *panth* - path; *te* - those; *kāran* - causes; *chhedak* - destroys; *dashā* - state; *mokshpanth* - path of liberation; *bhavant* - end of embodiment

MEANING

Whatever causes bondage is the path of bondage. The state that eliminates the causes is the path of liberation - the end of the cycles of birth and death.

EXPLANATION

A general rule of logic is that if a particular cause is known to create a particular effect, engaging in that cause will give rise to that effect. An extension of this logic proves that engaging in a contrary cause will generate a contrary effect.

Using the same rhetoric, this verse explains that the causes of karmic bondage constitute the path of bondage, resulting in entrapment in the endless cycles of birth and death. This also clarifies that the state of the soul which annihilates those causes of bondage constitutes the path of liberation. That is the remedy to transmigration, bringing about an end to rebirth. Therefore, feelings which lead to bondage will not lead to liberation. And likewise, embracing feelings that are contrary to them will bring about liberation.

There are five main factors that lead to bondage - wrong belief, lack of restraint, indolence, passions and activities of mind-speech-body. The more one indulges in these causes, the more karma he generates, termed as *āshrav*. This is the path of bondage. As one proceeds to annihilate these five causes, the end of transmigration draws closer. The state which stops the causes of bondage is called *samvar*, mentioned here as **'chhedak dashā'**. The corresponding states which annihilate the five causes are - right faith, restraint, consistent constant awareness, dispassion and withdrawal from mental-verbal-physical activities. Thus, the prevention of karmic influx is the path of liberation, and treading it puts a stop to the endless cycles of birth and death.

The Guru directs the disciple to track down the causes which have resulted in the imprisonment of his soul since time immemorial. There is no sense in hacking at the branches of a tree, whose roots have turned rotten. By introspecting and detecting the causes of his shackles, he will find that the mind is ceaselessly caught between regrets and desires of the past and the future. In trying to work out a balance between the opposing pulls and pressures, the mind loses peace and stillness. The soul is gripped in bondage. The presence of the causes holds it back on the path to liberation. However, when the state which can break through these causes appears in the soul, it progresses on the path of liberation, and results in ending of the impure feelings. If one severs the causes of bondage, liberation is certain.

VERSE - 100

Path of liberation - negative assertion

Presenting the causes resorting to which one advances on the path of bondage, and the causes retiring from which one advances on the path of liberation, the Guru now says -

રાગ, દ્વેષ, અજ્ઞાન એ, મુખ્ય કર્મની ગ્રંથ;
થાય નિવૃત્તિ જેહથી, તે જ મોક્ષનો પંથ. ||૧૦૦||

Rāg, dwesh, ajnān ae, mukhya karmani granth;
Thāy nivrutti jehthi, te ja mokshno panth. ||100||

Rāg - likes; *dwesh* - dislikes; *ajnān* - ignorance; *ae* - that; *mukhya* - principal; *karmani* - of karma; *granth* - knots; *thāy* - happens; *nivrutti* - withdrawing; *jehthi* - by which; *te* - that; *ja* - alone; *mokshno* - of liberation; *panth* - path

MEANING
Attachment, aversion and ignorance are the main knots of karma. The means by which one recedes from them constitutes the path of liberation.

EXPLANATION
In this verse, the Guru enumerates the reasons of bondage. The entire world is trapped in a vicious cycle of attachment, aversion and ignorance. All three are impure modifications of the soul. Each one of these is potent poison for they bring

along with them desires, expectations, disappointments, as well as the added baggage of uncertainty and fear. The soul is sucked in this whirlpool deeply and immediately. Therefore, attachment, aversion and ignorance are the fundamental knots of bondage.

The process of stitching clothes with a needle and thread is successful only when the thread is straight and effortlessly pierces the cloth. However, it fails when knots are present, and hence, removing the knots is absolutely essential for further progress. Where there is a knot, a tangle, even relationships get stuck. They become sour and take a turn for the worse. The relationship between people is smooth if there is no knot of misunderstanding. Similarly, the knots of likes, dislikes and ignorance, come in the way of spiritual progress. One has to undo them in order to escape transmigration and achieve the goal of liberation. If he puts in the right efforts, the knots gradually loosen and once unshackled, he becomes completely free.

The knot of ignorance is the root of transmigration. Ignorance implies 'wrong' knowledge, not 'without' knowledge. Every living being possesses knowledge, either less or more, but is never completely devoid of it. The soul would have to be an inanimate substance if it possessed no knowledge at all. Thus, this meaning is not relevant here. A person might be very intelligent, well-versed in scriptures but he can be deluded. Due to the misleading knowledge he forgets the true nature of the self and falsely identifies with the non-self.

This long-standing practice of identifying with the non-self is the primary cause of the generation of likes and dislikes. From the sense of 'I-ness' in the body, a sense of 'my-ness' arises towards family, house, etc. In order to fulfil worldly desires like comfort, security, etc., attachment and aversion arise, and a gush of karma is channelled through mind-speech-body, drowning the soul in the ocean of transmigration. Owing to the basic mistake of identification with the body, a series of mistakes occur, preventing the manifestation of the continual bliss of the self. Thus, the deluded false knowledge that, 'I can do something in the non-self', 'I can enjoy the non-self'; likes stemming from the belief that one can benefit from the non-self; and dislikes stemming from the belief that one can be harmed by the non-self are the main knots of karma.

The attainment of self-realisation gives one a glimpse of his own unobstructed, blissful consciousness, separate from the body. This unprecedented experience brings about an inconceivable transformation in his outlook of the world and himself. Thereafter, he no longer harbours intense likes or dislikes that he earlier possessed. Once the knot of ignorance, that is, the identification with the body is severed, it leads to the basis of likes-dislikes being uprooted - prompting an end to likes and dislikes forever. With the complete elimination of the causes, bondage is destroyed and liberation can be attained. To summarise, the freedom from likes, dislikes and ignorance is the path of liberation and the means that bring about this disentanglement are the means of liberation.

VERSE - 101

Path of liberation - positive assertion

In verse 100, the Guru explained the path of liberation through the method of negative assertion. Now in verse 101, He explains the path through a method of positive assertion. The Guru says -

આત્મા સત્ ચૈતન્યમય, સર્વાભાસ રહિત;
જેથી કેવળ પામિયે, મોક્ષપંથ તે રીત. ॥૧૦૧॥

Ātmā sat chaitanyamay, sarvābhās rahit;
Jethi keval pāmiye, mokshpanth te reet. ॥101॥

Ātmā - soul; *sat* - everlasting existence; *chaitanyamay* - consciousness; *sarvābhās* - all illusions; *rahit* - free of; *jethi* - by which; *keval* - pure soul; *pāmiye* - attained; *mokshpanth* - path of liberation; *te* - that; *reet* - method

MEANING

The nature of the soul is eternal existence, consciousness and devoid of all illusions. The means through which one experiences and abides in the pure self is the path of liberation.

EXPLANATION

The Guru explained the impure modifications of the soul. Now, He describes the pure nature of the soul to abandon the impurity and attain the pure state. In this verse, He establishes the true nature of the soul and explains that the way by which it can be attained is the path of liberation. That is, one should consider only those means by which the pure soul can be experienced and abided in, as the right means to attain liberation. The Guru explains the nature of the soul through three characteristics:

'*Sat*' - denotes the soul is an eternal existence. It is not created by a combination of elements but is an independent original substance. While wandering in the different states of existence, the body gets destroyed, but the soul does not get destroyed. The soul is an indestructible, imperishable substance which always continues to exist.

'*Chaitanyamay*' - denotes consciousness. The inherent nature of the soul is knowingness. This property stays with it forever because no substance can be devoid of its inherent property. This is its distinguishing quality, which is not present in inanimate substances. The soul shines with its own light and illuminates all objects. As the soul is of the nature of knowingness, no other activity apart from knowing is its natural activity.

'*Sarvābhās rahit*' - denotes it is devoid of illusions. From the external perspective, the soul appears as the body or as impure feelings, which is only an illusion and not its true nature. If a red flower is placed behind a transparent crystal, it appears red. However, it is only an appearance, an illusion created by the colour of the red flower. The soul and the crystal are parallels. In both cases, they appear to be something else due to the association of an external substance, but the truth is their real nature is masked. The soul is inherently pure, bereft of all types of associations and impure feelings. It is a mistake to consider the karma-created personality as its true nature.

One must get awakened, stay continuously aware, and abide in the soul with the properties of eternal existence, constant knowingness and separateness from karma-created states. The way by which the pure soul is attained, is the path of liberation. The soul is glowing, effulgent, radiant with peace and joy. To experience it, one needs calmness, stillness and awareness. Without realising it, one remains entangled in the external and continues transmigration. Thus, this verse expounds that the means by which one turns towards the pure nature of the soul and abides in it, is the only path of liberation.

VERSE - 102

Chief karma is deluding karma

Until now, the Guru has explained the path of liberation, primarily from the perspective of eliminating impure feelings. Now, in three verses 102-104, He answers the argument expressed by the disciple in the latter half of verse 92 regarding how one can annihilate karma that has accumulated over an infinite period of time. This explanation is primarily based on the perspective of annihilating material karma. The Guru says -

કર્મ અનંત પ્રકારનાં, તેમાં મુખ્યે આઠ;
તેમાં મુખ્યે મોહનીય, હણાય તે કહું પાઠ. ||૧૦૨||

Karma anant prakārnā, temā mukhye āth;
Temā mukhye mohaniy, hanāy te kahu pāth. ||102||

Karma - karma; *anant* - infinite; *prakārnā* - kinds of; *temā* - among them; *mukhye* - chief; *āth* - eight; *temā* - among them; *mukhye* - chief; *mohaniy* - deluding karma; *hanāy* - destruction; *te* - that; *kahu* - state; *pāth* - lesson

MEANING
There are infinite types of karma. Of these, there are mainly eight broad categories. Amongst these eight, deluding karma is the most prominent. I will explain the way to destroy it.

EXPLANATION
This verse addresses the disciple's question regarding the annihilation of infinite amounts of material karma acquired

over an infinite period of time. The Guru delves deep into the concept of karma, keeping in line with Jain philosophy, which has spoken so specifically about it. Since time immemorial, every worldly soul is bound by infinite material particles of karma. Every moment, some of these particles get detached while some new ones get bound. When the soul does not know its true nature and modifies to impure feelings, karmic particles get bound to it. Since the varieties of impure feelings are infinite, and karmic bondage occurs due to these feelings, it follows that the types of karma are also infinite.

There are eight main categories of these infinite types of karma - *jnānāvarniya, darshanāvarniya, vedniya, mohaniya, āyushya, nāma, gotra* and *antrāya*. Jnānāvarniya karma obscures one's knowledge. Darshanāvarniya karma obscures one's perception. Vedniya karma leads to pleasant-unpleasant circumstances. Mohaniya karma leads to wrong belief and conduct. Āyushya karma makes the soul remain in the body. Nāma karma gives the soul different types of bodies, shapes, physical features, etc. Gotra karma is accountable for one being born in a family with high or low status. Antrāya karma creates obstacles.

These eight categories are grouped into two divisions, namely, *ghāti* - destructive karma, which obscure the true nature of the soul, and *aghāti* - non-destructive karma, which do not obscure the true nature of the soul, but affect the body in which the soul resides. Ghāti karma include jnānāvarniya darshanāvarniya, mohaniya and antrāya. Aghāti karma include vedniya, āyushya, nāma and gotra.

The main category of karma among the eight is mohaniya - the deluding karma. Jnānāvarniya and the other ghāti - destructive karma, obscure the virtues of the soul, or obstruct the strength of these virtues, whereas mohaniya karma distorts the virtues. Much like an octopus, it entraps one in the firm grip of its tentacles. One has lured himself into such a helpless state that he is no longer capable of discriminating the true from the false. Under the influence of delusion, the soul forgets its true nature and tends to harbour several falsities regarding identification, doership, enjoyership, dependency, happiness, etc., in relation to the non-self. Due to this delusion, it acts with passions and accrues new karmic particles.

Thus, mohaniya karma being the cause of binding new karma, is the very basis of the eight main categories of karma. Being the most powerful of all karma, it is termed as the king of karma. The strength of other karma is dependent on its strength. Hence, if mohaniya karma's strength diminishes, the strength of other karma also diminishes. Just as by vanquishing a king, his army, kingdom and power are won over; if mohaniya karma is annihilated, all other karma can be conquered. So, it is absolutely essential to completely destroy this king of karma. Therefore, the Guru will state the method for its destruction in the next verse. He emphatically promises to explain the means to annihilate mohaniya karma, the most prominent of all eight karma.

VERSE - 103

Unfailing remedy to destroy deluding karma

The deluding karma is instrumental in the creation of all other karma. Therefore, it is vital for an aspirant seeking liberation to know the means to destroy the deluding karma. Revealing the unfailing means to destroy deluding karma, in this verse, the Guru says -

કર્મ મોહનીય ભેદ બે, દર્શન ચારિત્ર નામ;
હણે બોધ વીતરાગતા, અચૂક ઉપાય આમ. ॥૧૦૩॥

Karma mohaniy bhed bey, darshan chāritra nām;
Haney   bodh   vitrāgtā,   achuk   upāy   ām. ॥103॥

Karma - karma; *mohaniy* - deluding; *bhed* - kinds; *bey* - two;
darshan - faith; *chāritra* - conduct; *nām* - name; *haney* - destroys;
bodh - enlightenment; *vitrāgtā* - dispassion; *achuk* - infallible, unfailing;
upāy - means; *ām* - this

MEANING

The deluding karma are of two kinds, pertaining to belief and behaviour - faith deluding karma and conduct deluding karma. Enlightenment and dispassion are the unfailing remedies that destroy them.

EXPLANATION

The function of *mohaniya* - the king of karma, is to create delusion. The deluding karma are of two types - *darshanmoh* - faith delusion, and *chāritramoh* - conduct delusion. Darshanmoh does not allow one to perceive correctly by clouding judgement and creating confusion. He cannot discriminate between the transient and the eternal. He remains enmeshed in wrong beliefs considering the non-self as the self. Chāritramoh does not allow abidance in the true nature of the soul by creating passions. Likes, dislikes, prejudices, conditioning and other strong habits prevent the soul from achieving a state of complete dispassion, hence hindering spiritual progress.

Wrong belief is the root of transmigration as it leads to wrong conduct. Due to ignorance, the soul is crushed in the grindstone of likes and dislikes. Attachment-aversion towards objects keep the wheel of transmigration in a state of perpetual motion. To mobilise the wheel of religion, it becomes imperative for one to understand the unfailing means to annihilate darshanmoh and chāritramoh.

Light dispels darkness, that is, light is the infallible means to destroy darkness. Similarly, **'bodh'** - enlightenment, is the infallible means to annihilate darshanmoh, which is in the form of ignorance; and **'vitrāgtā'** - dispassion, is the infallible means to destroy chāritramoh, which is in the form of likes and dislikes. A spiritual aspirant must seek a Sadguru and listen to Him with utmost reverence to understand the truth of all substances. Upon deeper contemplation of a Sadguru's ignorance-dispelling teachings, an aspirant understands that his beliefs concerning the 'I', 'my', happiness, etc., are wrong. This awakens him from a deep slumber, prompting the development of a discerning ability. A constant practice of awareness helps him to experience the self. With self-realisation, darshanmoh is destroyed. *Samyagdarshan* - right faith, dawns and false belief is eliminated.

Once darshanmoh is annihilated, the root is destroyed and so chāritramoh does not last for long. With awareness and abidance in the self, the spirit of dispassion increases and likes-dislikes keep decreasing. Gradually, chāritramoh gets eliminated and ultimately, dispassion reaches a level where he effortlessly stays in a state free of all attachments. Therefore, enlightenment and dispassion is the unfailing, sure, definite method to destroy both types of mohaniya karma. As a result, the soul dwells in the state of liberation, experiencing infinite bliss.

VERSE - 104

Evident experience of all

In the earlier verses, the Guru made it crystal clear that the path of destroying deluding karma is the path of liberation. He now explains the practical aspect of achieving this goal, so that even a layman may understand it.

Ensuring a doubtless conviction for an aspirant regarding the path of liberation, the Guru says -

કર્મબંધ ક્રોધાદિથી, હણે ક્ષમાદિક તેહ;
પ્રત્યક્ષ અનુભવ સર્વને, એમાં શો સંદેહ? ||૧૦૪||

Karmabandh krodhādithi, haney kshamādik teh;
Pratyaksh anubhav sarvane, emā sho sandeh? ||104||

Karmabandh - karmic bondage; *krodhādithi* - due to anger etc.; *haney* - destroys; *kshamādik* - forgiveness etc.; *teh* - that; *pratyaksh* - evident; *anubhav* - experience; *sarvane* - to all; *emā* - in that; *sho* - what; *sandeh* - doubt

MEANING
The karmic bondage caused by anger, etc., can be destroyed by forgiveness, etc. This experience is evident to everyone. How can there be any doubt about it?

EXPLANATION
In order to annihilate karmic bondage, one must first understand the causes of karmic bondage. It is undisputable

that bondage can be destroyed by engaging in the causes which are contrary to those that create it. The Guru points out through a practical approach, how the bondage of conduct deluding karma, mentioned in the previous verse, can be destroyed. The impact of *chāritramoh* is experienced in the form of defilements called *kashāy*. The Jain tradition classifies them in four categories - anger, pride, deceit and greed.

Anger is an impure feeling, and leads to bondage, whereas the exact opposite is true for forgiveness - it stops bondage. Hence, by cultivating pure feelings like forgiveness, it is universally evident that impure feelings like anger are destroyed. In other words, everyone can experience the agitation caused by anger, and the calm experienced by forgiveness. With the arrival of anger, there is a disturbance on the physical, mental and spiritual level. Happiness and peace are shattered. However, through forgiveness, compassion, love, acceptance, understanding; the feelings of anger, hatred, enmity, hostility, rejection vanish.

Just as fire can be extinguished by water; anger can be stopped by cultivating forgiveness; pride can be countered by practising humility; deceit can be arrested by nurturing straightforwardness; and greed can be restrained by developing contentment. Harbouring feelings contrary to the soul's true nature is *adharma*. In contrast, retreating from impure feelings and generating pure feelings through self-awareness is dharma. Impure feelings which cause karmic bondage, can be stopped by harbouring pure feelings.

This is experienced or can be experienced by all. It can be experienced here and now. Therefore, there is no ground for uncertainty for the means of liberation. It is inappropriate to doubt the path of liberation. It can be experientially proven that forgiveness nullifies anger. There is no doubt at all regarding this fact. The disciple must be absolutely doubt-free about the path of liberation and must engage in the right pursuit. In other words, he must understand the true path and expend the effort necessary to tread on it. Thus, the Guru briefly and simply explains the key to annihilating impurity.

VERSE - 105

Reply 2 - Impartial perspective leads to liberation

In verse 93, the disciple had said that there are many beliefs and philosophies prevalent in the world, which expound different paths to attain liberation, making it impossible to determine the correct one. Putting an end to his confusion, the Guru says -

છોડી મત દર્શન તણો, આગ્રહ તેમ વિકલ્પ;
કહ્યો માર્ગ આ સાધશે, જન્મ તેહના અલ્પ. ||૧૦૫||

Chhodi mat darshan tano, āgrah tem vikalp;
Kahyo mārg ā sādhshe, janma tehnā alp. ||105||

Chhodi - giving up; *mat* - creeds; *darshan* - schools of thought; *tano* - of; *āgrah* - insistence; *tem* - and; *vikalp* - choices; *kahyo* - indicated; *mārg* - path; *ā* - this; *sādhshe* - follows; *janma* - birth; *tehnā* - his; *alp* - few

MEANING
Giving up insistence of opinions and choice of viewpoints regarding his beliefs and philosophy, one who pursues the path mentioned above, attains liberation in only a few births.

EXPLANATION
The only true path of liberation is that which annihilates the causes of karmic bondage such as likes, dislikes, ignorance and leads to the attainment of the self, which is of the nature

of eternal existence, consciousness and devoid of all illusions. One who follows the absolute path of liberation as stated in verses 98-104, certainly attains liberation. The practice or the means which lead to this absolute path of liberation are worth adopting.

As different religions, faiths, sects and philosophies advocate different practices, several contrasting external methods of achieving liberation exist. The ignorant soul loses sight of the absolute path and gets enmeshed in the rituals and methods shown by his sect. Furthermore, he strives relentlessly to prove the superiority of his own practice over others, wrongly believing that liberation is only possible through the means of his sect. Clinging to the sectarian views of his faith, he builds strong opinions and insists upon their accuracy. He holds the choice of his viewpoint as the only one worth adopting. Insistence and choices keep him away from the truth. Thus, his transmigration increases instead of decreasing. Dharma cannot begin without letting go of one's insistence and choices as they involve a lot of attachments and aversions.

When one leaves his insistence and choices, and strives to attain the pure self, *samyagdarshan* - right faith manifests. With the dawn of samyagdarshan, likes and dislikes are gradually eliminated. On their complete destruction, one attains liberation. After attaining samyagdarshan, if one puts in the best effort, he completely annihilates impurities such as likes-dislikes and attains liberation in that very birth. However, if his efforts are weak, he attains liberation in very few births. Setting aside obstinacy and preferences, pride and prejudices, likes and dislikes, one following the path indicated in the earlier verses will be liberated in a short time. Putting in the right effort with an impartial perspective, he will be free from the cycles of birth and death in the near future. Jainism is a universal religion with a broad vision. It does not discriminate between seekers of different sects. Whoever pursues the absolute path in his own way will attain liberation soon, in this life or the next few lives.

Thus, in this verse, the Guru advises the disciple to pursue the absolute path of liberation and not get entangled in the gamut of external rituals, methods, norms or practices. One needs to be a lover of truth and not remain in the narrow limits of sects, as stubborn attitude and prejudices are hurdles in the spiritual pursuit. One should honour the differences and respect the diversity. In fact, it is this diversity which makes spirituality a carnival.

VERSE - 106

Complete understanding of six aphorisms

Having asked questions out of a genuine desire to know the truth, the worthy disciple receives apt solutions from the Guru. Strengthening the disciple's conviction in the path of liberation, the Guru says -

ષટ્પદનાં ષટ્પ્રશ્ન તેં, પૂછ્યાં કરી વિચાર;
તે પદની સર્વાંગતા, મોક્ષમાર્ગ નિર્ધાર. ||૧૦૬||

Shatpadnā shatprashna te, puchhyā kari vichār;
Te padni sarvāngtā, mokshmārg nirdhār. ||106||

Shatpadnā - of six aphorisms; **shatprashna** - six questions; *te* - you; *puchhyā* - raised; *kari* - doing; *vichār* - ponder; *te* - that; *padni* - of aphorisms; *sarvāngtā* - in totality; *mokshmārg* - path of liberation; *nirdhār* - determine

MEANING
You have very thoughtfully asked six questions regarding the six fundamental truths. Determine with certainty that an understanding of these fundamental truths in totality is the sure path of liberation.

EXPLANATION
After thoroughly pondering the fundamental truths, the disciple who has a strong desire to attain the pure self, humbly expresses his doubts to the Guru. Observing his worthiness, the Guru

proceeds to resolve them. Having fittingly answered all the disciple's questions, the Guru states that accepting these six fundamental truths in totality constitutes the path of liberation.

All six fundamental truths are strongly interconnected, possessing an inseparable relation to one another. In fact, to such an extent that harbouring doubt for even one or completely negating it, obscures the path of liberation. Hence it becomes imperative to give up one-sided beliefs and understand them from multiple viewpoints. Let go of all doubts and establish true faith in all six fundamental truths. The deeper one delves, the more one realises about the truths.

To achieve liberation, one needs to understand each truth individually, weave them together to perceive one's own nature, and personalise them as - 'I exist', 'I am eternal', 'I am the doer', 'I am the receiver of the fruits of karma', 'I can attain liberation', 'the path shown by the Guru is the path of my liberation'.

Thus, addressing a worthy disciple, who considers understanding the path of liberation as the dawn of great good fortune; the Guru puts the onus of attaining enlightenment onto him. The disciple must now diligently and decisively practise the guidance prescribed by the Guru. He needs to carry out every step that has been laid out for his spiritual welfare with persistence and patience to receive the highest reward of liberation.

VERSE - 107

Reply 3 - Caste or clothing have no role

The Guru has previously illuminated the right path of liberation to the disciple who has an intense longing to attain liberation. He now resolves the last question regarding the path of liberation stated in verse 94 pertaining to caste or gender, and attire required to attain liberation. The Guru says -

જાતિ, વેષનો ભેદ નહિ, કહ્યો માર્ગ જો હોય;
સાધે તે મુક્તિ લહે, એમાં ભેદ ન કોય. ||૧૦૭||

Jāti, veshno bhed nahi, kahyo mārg jo hoi;
Sādhe te mukti lahey, emā bhed na koi. ||107||

Jāti - caste or gender; *veshno* - of garb; *bhed* - discrimination; *nahi* - no; *kahyo* - stated; *mārg* - path; *jo* - if; *hoi* - there; *sādhe* - follows; *te* - he; *mukti* - liberation; *lahey* - attains; *emā* - in that; *bhed* - difference of opinion; *na* - no; *koi* - any

MEANING
There is no discrimination based on caste or gender, and external attire on the prescribed path of liberation. Whoever pursues it, attains liberation. There are no doubts regarding this fact.

EXPLANATION
The way by which the impure state of the soul is eliminated and the pure state is manifested, is the path of liberation,

which remains the same in all three periods of time. The oneness of right faith-knowledge-conduct alone is the path of liberation. The understanding of the pure self is right knowledge, conviction in it is the right faith and abidance in it is the right conduct. One who pursues the path in the form of these three jewels will certainly attain liberation, irrespective of caste, gender or attire.

In pursuit of the path of liberation described in verses 98-104, there exists no discrimination based on caste (*Brāhmin, Vaishya, Kshatriya, Shudra*), gender (male, female, neuter) or any specific external attire. There is no such law which states that only a particular caste or gender or adoption of a particular attire can lead to liberation. Hence, on the absolute path, there is no place for caste, gender or sectarian attire, which are dependent on the body. On this path only the feeling of dispassion is the prime requisite. The pursuit which leads one to steadfastly remain in the conscious, blissful self, without indulging in likes and dislikes, is the path of dispassion. Liberation can only be attained by those who have achieved this state of dispassion and who manifest pure feelings irrespective of caste, gender or attire.

Caste is immaterial on the path of liberation. One may be born in a noble dynasty or lower caste, the soul has to be awakened to its true nature for liberation. One can be of any caste, following the true path is of supreme importance. In Jain scriptures, there are examples of those who have attained liberation from all four castes: *Brāhmin - Shri Gautamswāmi, Kshatriya - Shri Prasannchandra Rājarshri, Vaishya - Shri Jambuswāmi* and *Shudra - Shri Harikeshi*. The label of caste applies to the body, not to the soul. The caste system was only an arrangement that facilitated the organisation and functioning of society, it has never been a hindrance in the pursuit of liberation.

Similarly, the path of liberation is not related to a person's gender. Males like *Shri Bāhubali*, females like *Shri Chandanbāla* and people of neuter gender like *Shri Gāngey* have attained liberation. No matter what gender one belongs to, if the prescribed path is followed, then liberation is achieved without fail. Gender makes no difference.

Amongst the 15 ways of attaining liberation enumerated in *Shwetāmber* Jain Canons, there are examples of Jain monks like *Shri Sudharmāswāmi*, ascetics of other religions like *Shri Valkalchiri*, and householders like *Shri Bharat Chakravarti*. So it is evident that there is no discrimination of attire on the path to liberation. Attire is merely an external custom, an arrangement to provide an identity. The attire of a monk can help in cultivating detachment, but just adopting a particular clothing in itself does not bring about a transformation. When a policeman is in his uniform, people follow his instructions. It is helpful for identification, but the uniform itself does not give him physical or mental strength. Similarly, the body may be clothed in any attire, what is required is inner purity. Merely adopting external attire has no bearing on the attainment of liberation.

Insisting upon a particular caste, gender or external attire to be the right way demonstrates a lack of correct understanding of the path of liberation. In fact a proper understanding leads to the insignificance of these subjects, dissolving prejudice. Thus, in this verse, the Guru advocates giving up blind attachment towards caste, gender and external attire, and striving to attain the state of complete dispassion. For liberation, one needs to focus on the pure nature of the soul and not on body related matters like caste, gender and attire.

VERSE - 108

Four virtues of aspirant

Having established the path of liberation in the previous verses, the Guru now proceeds towards the second group of verses 108-113. He provides a stepwise course for the pursuit of liberation in six verses. The ascending sequence of the *gunasthānak* - stages of spiritual development, has also been subtly woven into the steps. In this verse, demonstrating who is worthy of attaining the path of liberation, the Guru says -

કષાયની ઉપશાંતતા, માત્ર મોક્ષઅભિલાષ;
ભવે ખેદ અંતર દયા, તે કહીએ જિજ્ઞાસ. ||૧૦૮||

Kashāyni upshāntatā, mātra mokshabhilāsh;
Bhavey khed antar dayā, te kahiye jignās. ||108||

Kashāyni - of passions; *upshāntatā* - subsidence; *mātra* - only; *mokshabhilāsh* - desire for liberation; *bhavey* - transmigration; *khed* - grief; *antar* - inner; *dayā* - compassion; *te* - that; *kahiye* - called; *jignās* - aspirant

MEANING

One whose passions have subsided, whose only desire is for liberation, who possesses grief for the cycles of birth and death, who holds compassion from within, is called a spiritual aspirant.

EXPLANATION

A thoughtful person desires everlasting happiness and to achieve that he wants life to be peaceful. Peace cannot be achieved without purity, and those filled with impure feelings remain in a disturbed state despite possessing comfort and luxury. Hence, a pure life is imperative for peace; and one must cultivate virtues to achieve purity. Only when one kindles virtues, can he embark on the path of liberation. Explaining the necessary worthiness that must be developed to pursue the path of liberation, Shrimadji spells out four qualities of an aspirant -

1. *Kashāyni upshāntatā* - Subsidence of passions
The first attribute is pacification of passions like anger, etc., with firmness and understanding. Only he who reduces the strength of his passions is eligible for the path of liberation.

2. *Mātra mokshabhilāsh* - Liberation being the only desire
The second attribute is to harbour a burning passion to attain liberation. He who has no other aspiration except to attain inner purity is eligible for the path of liberation.

3. *Bhavey khed* - Grief for the cycles of birth and death
The third attribute is the feeling of dread towards transmigration which has been caused by attachment towards worldly objects. He who wishes to become detached from sensual indulgence is eligible for the path of liberation.

4. *Antar dayā* - Inner compassion
The fourth attribute is the inner feeling to be free from suffering. He who holds compassion within is eligible for the path of liberation.

It should be noticed that the first three virtues are the same as those mentioned in verse 38. This is mainly to reinforce their importance in the spiritual pursuit. The fourth virtue is presented a little differently. The word used in verse 38 is *'prānidayā'*, while the word used here is *'antar dayā'*. While both words specify compassion, the former was compassion for all living beings while the latter emphasises on compassion for oneself. Upon introspection, the aspirant realises the suffering he has undergone in innumerable births due to impure feelings. It is paramount to have compassion for oneself and decide to undertake the path that averts further pain of transmigration. For this to occur, the tendency to defile should not be present within, nor sinful acts without - on the external. One who has compassion for himself is bound to extend the same to others, proving that prānidayā and antar dayā are not contradictory at all. The meaning of these can be better understood as compassion from within - for oneself and all.

Shrimadji has stressed the importance of these virtues by explaining them twice, in verse 38 and in this verse of Shri Ātmasiddhi Shāstra. Further, He has encouraged those desirous of attaining the path of liberation to make an effort to develop them. In verse 38, they are described as the attributes of an *ātmārthi* - a soul seeking spiritual welfare for itself, and in verse 108 as the attributes of a *jignāsu* - a true aspirant of liberation. Although there appears to be a difference between the two, they convey the same meaning. Both are terms used for the seekers of truth.

The aspirant eligible to enter the path of liberation is recognised by these attributes. In other words, these four virtues will always be present in an aspirant seeking liberation. The absence of these virtues implies the impossibility of embarking on the path. The attainment of these  virtues marks the auspicious beginning for an aspirant on the path of liberation.

VERSE - 109

Guru's guidance triggers inner quest

The Guru perfectly expressed the attributes by which an aspirant on the path of liberation is accurately recognised. Now, He describes how one possessing such a state advances sequentially on the path after gaining the Sadguru's association. The Guru says -

તે જિજ્ઞાસુ જીવને, થાય સદ્‌ગુરુબોધ;
તો પામે સમકિતને, વર્તે અંતરશોધ. ॥૧૦૯॥

Te   jignāsu   jeevne,   thāy   Sadgurubodh;
Toh   pāmey   samkitne,   varte   antarshodh. ||109||

Te - that; *jignāsu* - aspirant; *jeevne* - to soul; *thāy* - gets; *Sadgurubodh* - advice from enlightened Mentor; *toh* - then; *pāmey* - attains; *samkitne* - right faith; *varte* - acts; *antarshodh* - internal purification

MEANING
If such a spiritual aspirant receives guidance from a true Guru, he attains unwavering faith in Him and His teachings. The aspirant then engages in an inner quest, embarking on a journey of self-purification.

EXPLANATION
The aspiration to know the truth has awakened in a seeker endowed with the four attributes. Hence, there is a constant churning within him, regarding the answers to questions

like: 'Who am I?', 'What is the purpose of my existence?', 'Where does complete happiness lie?', 'How can I attain it?' A deep contemplation upon these and other fundamental questions keep arising in him prompting an intense yearning for solutions. His eagerness to satisfy his need to know the truth is so great that he embarks on an extensive quest to understand it.

As his search progresses, he realises the limitations of scriptural study. So he considers adopting the guidance of self-realised beings in his spiritual pursuit. He has understood that the scriptures are many and the intellect is petty, hence he chooses to honour and contemplate upon the Sadguru's teachings. He is clear about the importance of the Sadguru who initiates, inspires, instructs and inspects the disciple, leading by precept and practice.

The aspirant now has an intense longing to gain that supremely beneficial association of an enlightened one, for the attainment of self-realisation. Due to the manifestation of previously acquired, spiritually meritorious karma, at a blessed moment he meets who he seeks. He recognises the enlightened one by His characteristic virtues and surrenders at His pious lotus feet. Observing the worthiness and intensity of longing in the disciple for the truth, the Guru imparts the knowledge of the truth out of selfless compassion. He reveals the right methods of spiritual pursuit to the disciple, whose worthiness enables receptivity of the essence of the teachings.

Through the Guru's teachings, the disciple acquires a firm conviction in the veracity of the supreme truths, thus attaining *vyavhār samkit* - right faith based on the Sadguru's teachings. This is the first phase of right faith. When someone who has been to Switzerland advises and inspires another to visit, the other person is convinced and ready to follow. Similarly, the aspirant is convinced about the Guru's teachings, free of doubt, and ready to undertake the journey towards self-realisation.

Having understood the truth with the sole purpose of spiritual welfare, the aspirant puts his understanding into practice, engaging in an inner quest. This includes three steps - introspection, contemplation and meditation. Through introspection, he detects, negates and substitutes his faults; purifying himself and developing higher virtues. Through contemplation on the teachings, he employs his energies into reasoning, analysing, recalling and chanting. Through meditation, he steadily remains in awareness of the pure nature of the self.

Engaged in the inner quest, the aspirant's interest in external associations keeps on reducing, and interest in the self keeps on rising. On every occasion and in every activity as he contemplates upon the Sadguru's teachings, the intensity of delusion and disturbance decreases, and the intensity of interest in the pursuit of the self increases. He develops the worthiness to attain self-realisation, *nishchay samkit* - right faith based on the experience of the self.

VERSE - 110

Achieves pure experiential faith

In the previous verse, the worthy soul attains faith in the fundamental truths and the one discoursing those truths, which is called *vyavhār samkit*. This verse explains how the disciple attains that pure faith which emerges from the experience of the self, called *nishchay samkit*. The Guru says -

મત દર્શન આગ્રહ તજી, વર્તે સદ્‍ગુરુલક્ષ;
લહે શુદ્ધ સમકિત તે, જેમાં ભેદ ન પક્ષ. ||૧૧૦||

Mat darshan āgrah taji, varte Sadgurulaksh;
Lahey shuddh samkit te, jemā bhed na paksh. ||110||

Mat - opinions; *darshan* - philosophies; *āgrah* - insistence; *taji* - giving up; *varte* - acts; *Sadgurulaksh* - guidance of enlightened Mentor; *lahey* - attains; *shuddh* - pure, experiential; *samkit* - right faith; *te* - he; *jemā* - in that; *bhed* - differences; *na* - no; *paksh* - divisions

MEANING

The one who follows the path laid forth by a true Guru, giving up insistence regarding his opinions and beliefs, attains pure experiential faith. Irrespective of any religion, sect, caste, method or means, through which it is attained, the experience of the true nature of the self is the same for all aspirants. There are no differences or divisions in it.

EXPLANATION

Since time immemorial, the worldly soul has been acting under the influence of ignorance. He has been living with different beliefs and ideologies which he has inherited from his family or gained from an *asadguru*. He has formed opinions regarding the spiritual pursuit and concepts regarding the conduct of enlightened souls. He believes that only a specific external attire or ritual leads to liberation, and that enlightened ones only behave in a certain way, so on and so forth. These beliefs pose a major obstruction to his goal.

A continued insistence on the validity of his sect and philosophy obscures the truth from him. An unhealthy attachment to such ideas stifles his progress and unless his mind is open to new ideas, no real discovery can take place. One needs to open the windows of the mind to attain self-realisation. It must be freed from conditioned beliefs, preconceived notions, prejudices, and biases held in the past.

The true seeker forgoes insistence and transforms completely, aligning his understanding of everything with the Sadguru's teachings. He wholeheartedly pursues whatever path the Sadguru lays forth, accepting and following all His pious commands and engaging in spiritual pursuits as per His guidance. Furthermore, he contemplates deeply upon the Sadguru's teachings regarding the nature of the self. Assigning an unparalleled importance to the self, the worthy disciple remains absorbed in it.

The more he reflects on the self, the more he gets engrossed in his true nature, with all thoughts dissipating and the steady awareness of reality dawning. Thus, when one makes the effort to turn towards his self, under the Sadguru's guidance, at a supremely blessed moment, he experiences the unblemished, calm, limitlessly blissful self. He attains *nishchay samyagdarshan* - experiential faith. This is the second phase of right faith called **'shuddh samkit'**. Although the glimpse of the pure conscious self might be a momentary experience, the aspirant never forgets its taste, transforming his vision forever.

No matter through which religion, sect or community; in which place or period of time; through which Sadguru or spiritual practice, this nishchay samyagdarshan or shuddh samkit is attained, the experience of the self universally remains the same. It is identical for all spiritual aspirants. There are no differences or divisions in it. It is beyond all theoretical distinctions and disputes.

VERSE - 111

State of enlightened self

The aspirant embarked on the journey towards self-realisation, taking refuge in the Sadguru. He connected to the eternal, conscious self. Having focused single-mindedly on the nature of the pure self, He experienced it. Describing the state of the one who has tasted the sweet nectar of self-realisation, the Guru says -

વર્તે નિજસ્વભાવનો, અનુભવ લક્ષ પ્રતીત;
વૃત્તિ વહે નિજભાવમાં, પરમાર્થે સમકિત. ||૧૧૧||

Varte   nijswabhāvno,   anubhav   laksh   pratit;
Vrutti   vahey   nijbhāvmā,   parmārthe   samkit. ||111||

Varte - prevails; *nijswabhāvno* - of own nature; *anubhav* - experience; *laksh* - awareness; *pratit* - conviction; *vrutti* - tendency; *vahey* - flows; *nijbhāvmā* - within; *parmārthe* - supreme; *samkit* - right faith

MEANING
Where there exists direct experience, constant awareness, firm conviction of one's own nature, and the tendency flows inwards; such a state is termed as the highest form of right faith.

EXPLANATION
In verse 110, Shrimadji stated how *shuddh samkit* could be attained. In that state, the aspirant experiences the pure self but it is a momentary glimpse, like a flash. In this verse,

He describes the state of an enlightened one, constantly and consistently drenched in the bliss of the soul. Though His state is splashed with the colour of experience, He continues to live in the material world, forced to adhere to worldly responsibilities due to the manifestation of past karma. A glimpse of His state is extraordinarily presented in an unparalleled manner in just three words.

1. *Anubhav* - Experience
As the aspirant progresses on the spiritual path, He increasingly experiences the consciousness flowing within. This direct experience provides bliss beyond the senses, peace, relaxation, calm, steadiness, contentment and equanimity. And to such an extent that one would never wish it to end. An enlightened soul has experienced such immense joy that He wants to remain immersed in it. Therefore, when He is withdrawn or disengaged from all activity, His attention is entirely focused on experiencing the soul. His meditative state deepens and lengthens as He endeavours to retain and prolong this absorption. Thus, in *nivrutti dashā* - during the state of retirement, He flows in *anubhavdhārā* - direct experience of the self.

2. *Laksh* - Awareness
Due to the limitations that embodiment poses, an enlightened one's attention is drawn towards the physical needs of the body and other duties. However, the glory of the experience of the self is such that it cannot be forgotten. It remains permanently etched in the memory, prompting a continual tendency to remain engrossed in it. The taste

of its nectar cannot be ignored, to such an extent that even while performing routine activities like eating, walking and talking, the inclination towards the experience remains strong. The requirement to fulfil worldly responsibilities due to karma, prevents one from continually residing in the self. However, this does not dissuade Him from maintaining awareness of the self. Despite engaging in other activities, He is inclined to steadfastly remain in the self. No matter what His karmic manifestations are, even that of a wedding or a war, nothing can come between Him and the goal. He never loses focus on the self, even while living in the world. He discharges His worldly duties with the awareness that, 'this is not my goal, it is just my role, I am the pure soul'. This constant awareness of the true nature keeps Him detached from objects, persons, situations and passions. Thus, in *pravrutti dashā* - during the state of involvement in activities, He is in *lakshdhārā* - awareness of the true nature and inclination of the pure state.

3. *Pratit* - Conviction

An embodied soul requires sleep as it is necessary for survival. When the enlightened one is in the sleep state, the experience and the awareness of the self are not present. However, the conviction of His true nature never disappears. We remember our names even when we are asleep. If someone calls out our name, we wake up and respond to the call. This is because the identification with the name continues even during sleep. Similarly, the firm conviction of the true nature continues even when the enlightened one sleeps. This does not mean that He is always awake but it signifies that He is ever alert of the truth even while asleep. The belief in the pure self is so deep-rooted through first-hand experience, that it remains even during sleep. Thus, in *sushupt dashā* - during the state of sleep, He is in *pratitidhārā* - conviction of the pure consciousness.

In this way, a self-realised one has experience, awareness and conviction regarding His true nature. The flow of His tendencies are only inclined towards steadfastly remaining in the self. He maintains His spiritual height by remaining attuned to the pure self, having no interest in anything other than His own true nature. This state is termed as **'parmārth samkit'**. It is the supreme right belief. This is the third and highest phase of right faith. In this state, the absorption in the soul is like the steady beat of the heart. Every thought and action of the enlightened one propels Him only towards the pure self.

— 〜◦〜 —

VERSE - 112

State of complete dispassion

In verses 109-111, the Guru described the nature of *vyavhār samkit* and *nishchay samkit*, providing a glimpse into the inner state of a self-realised soul. Now in this verse, explaining how the fruit of self-realisation - the state of dispassion is attained, the Guru says -

વર્ધમાન સમકિત થઈ, ટાળે મિથ્યાભાસ;
ઉદય થાય ચારિત્રનો, વીતરાગપદ વાસ. ॥૧૧૨॥

Vardhmān   samkit   thai,   tāley   mithyābhās;
Uday   thāy   chāritrano,   vitrāgpad   vās. ॥112॥

Vardhmān - increase; **samkit** - right faith; **thai** - happens; **tāley** - removes; **mithyābhās** - conduct delusion; **uday** - rise; **thāy** - happens; **chāritrano** - of right conduct; **vitrāgpad** - state of dispassion; **vās** - dwells

MEANING
As the state of right faith gets intensified, all feelings arising under the influence of the deluding karma get gradually destroyed. Through the advent of right conduct, one abides in a state of complete dispassion.

EXPLANATION
When one experiences the true nature of the self, purity of belief occurs instantly. However, purity of conduct occurs gradually. The total purity of conduct is attained at the

twelfth *gunasthānak* - stage of spiritual development. The earlier verses 110 and 111 described the state of one possessing right faith at the fourth gunasthānak. This verse describes the state of the soul from the fifth to the twelfth gunasthānak, where passions are destroyed gradually, and then completely annihilated at the twelfth.

From the moment one gains right faith, He begins to lose interest in worldly activities, moving away from defiling instincts. Especially after the dawn of self-realisation, He firmly resolves that, 'I do not want anything from this world, I only want to abide in my true nature.' This awareness of the self reduces His karmic bondage, and the impact of conduct deluding karma decreases.

Based on the intensity of the impact of conduct deluding karma, passions are divided into four categories - grossest, less gross, lesser gross and subtle. Or also called *anantānubandhi*, *apratyākhyāni*, *pratyākhyāni* and *sanjvalan*, respectively. The most intense of these is anantānubandhi, passions that infinitely binds one in cycles of birth and death. This category has already been overcome with the advent of self-realisation.

As samkit intensifies, the enlightened one progressively advances towards liberation, with self-abidance increasing and other categories of passions decreasing. As the soul's purity rises, the less gross forms of passions are overcome. Apratyākhyāni - passions that hinder partial vows, and pratyākhyāni - passions that hinder complete vows, are annihilated.

With the destruction of these passions, right conduct appears. As the steadiness in the self increases, the state of monkhood manifests. He revels in the awareness of the pure nature of the self, going into deep meditative states several times even within a span of 48 minutes. He even gains effective control over the last remaining category, sanjvalan - subtle passions. Abidance in the self reduces passions and increases dispassion continuously. Passions can be overcome in two ways - the pacifying ladder called *upsham shreni,* and the destructing ladder called *kshapak shreni*. In upsham shreni, the passions arise again, whereas in kshapak shreni, they are totally annihilated. With the right efforts, the monk ascends the kshapak shreni and destroys all conduct deluding karma steadily, swiftly and rapidly.

Eventually, all defiling instincts are overcome and the monk reaches the twelfth gunasthānak known as *kshinmoh* - state devoid of delusion and distraction. He now attains the state of total dispassion, termed as **'vitrāgpad'**. Thus, due to the increasingly uninterrupted flow of samkit, the enlightened one eliminates conduct deluding feelings from the soul. Right conduct in the form of abidance in the self manifests, and advancing sequentially, He attains the state of complete dispassion.

VERSE - 113

Attainment of omniscience

The state of dispassion results in the unblemished, pure, constant, complete state of omniscience. Demystifying the extraordinary essence of the nature of omniscience, the Guru says -

કેવળ નિજસ્વભાવનું, અખંડ વર્તે જ્ઞાન;
કહીએ કેવળજ્ઞાન તે, દેહ છતાં નિર્વાણ. ||૧૧૩||

Keval nijswabhāvnu, akhand varte jnān;
Kahiye kevaljnān te, deh chhatā nirvān. ||113||

Keval - exclusively; ***nijswabhāvnu*** - of own nature; ***akhand*** - constant; ***varte*** - prevails; ***jnān*** - knowledge; ***kahiye*** - called; ***kevaljnān*** - omniscience; ***te*** - that; ***deh*** - body; ***chhatā*** - in spite of; ***nirvān*** - liberation

MEANING

When there is uninterrupted constant absorption in one's nature only, it is known as omniscience. In spite of the association of the body, it is known as a liberated state.

EXPLANATION

This verse describes the thirteenth *gunasthānak* in the soul's journey of spiritual evolution. It is a state of constant absorption in the self, of complete bliss and peace. One is filled with ecstatic, effervescent joy which lasts forever.

The shackles of the world are broken, and the soul stands liberated.

The state of total dispassion specified in the previous verse enables one to stay absorbed in His true nature. When such awareness becomes exclusive and remains uninterrupted, it is termed as '*kevaljnān*' - omniscience. An omniscient one constantly experiences His soul. Whether one eats just a piece of chocolate or an entire bar, the taste and quality remain the same. Similarly, the experience of the true nature remains the same in self-realisation and omniscience, the only difference being that it is interrupted in the former and is continuous in the latter.

Although the omniscient one possesses absolute knowledge of the self, as well as that of the entire universe, He remains engrossed in the self only. People equate kevaljnān to possessing complete knowledge of the three worlds and three periods of time. Thereby, knowing the past, present and future of every substance in the universe. This meaning, however, is intended for the layman. It is true that the omniscient one knows all substances, but it is equally true that He does not aspire to know them because of dispassion. Remarkably, though the universe is reflected in His pure and complete knowledge, He is not concerned by it at all, solely being engrossed in the true nature of the self. When one switches on the light in a room to find something, several other objects are illuminated as well. Likewise, the aspirant's effort is only for the complete abidance in the self. On attaining omniscience, the three worlds and the three periods of time also become visible. He possesses absolutely no desire for these. They come to be known only because the all-illumining capacity of the soul has manifested.

When omniscience manifests, the soul is still in association with the body. Despite this, it is in a liberated state, because the omniscient one revels in a state beyond the body. Until the soul reaches the twelfth gunasthānak, the spiritual journey experiences a lot of rising and falling. However, these highs and lows vanish once omniscience is attained at the thirteenth gunasthānak, because the aspirant achieves an unfluctuating, irreducible, indestructible state. Hence, this state is termed as liberation.

Omniscience is attained due to the annihilation of the four *ghāti* - destructive karma. Yet, the body exists due to the four *aghāti* - non-destructive karma, being present. When these too are annihilated, the state of *siddhahood* - accomplishment, is attained at the end of that very life. Thus, in this verse, Shrimadji defines omniscience from the spiritual perspective, and calls it liberation despite embodiment because the potential of the soul has fully blossomed.

VERSE - 114

Delusion of infinity vanishes on awakening

After explaining the stages of spiritual progress, the Guru begins the third group of verses 114-118, which are inspirational and relate to the attainment of perfect purity.

The soul has been engaging in feelings contrary to its pure nature since time immemorial. Citing a simple example to briefly answer how impure feelings of the infinite past could be eliminated, and how long it would take, the Guru says -

કોટિ વર્ષનું સ્વપ્ન પણ, જાગ્રત થતાં શમાય;
તેમ વિભાવ અનાદિનો, જ્ઞાન થતાં દૂર થાય. ||૧૧૪||

Koti varshnu swapna pan, jāgrat thatā shamāy;
Tem vibhāv anādino, jnān thatā dur thāy. ||114||

Koti - million; **varshnu** - of years; **swapna** - dream; **pan** - even; **jāgrat** - awake; **thatā** - becoming; **shamāy** - disappears; **tem** - similarly; **vibhāv** - impurity; **anādino** - of beginningless time; **jnān** - knowledge; **thatā** - attaining; **dur** - disappeared; **thāy** - gets

MEANING

Just as a dream of millions of years vanishes as soon as one awakens, delusion prevailing since infinity vanishes as one attains enlightenment.

EXPLANATION

Although the impure state of the soul has prevailed for an infinite period of time, the elimination of this state does not require the same amount of time. The soul has spent an infinite past being impure but does not require an infinite future to destroy this impurity. Just as a dream persisting for millions of years disappears immediately upon waking, impurities present since eternity are also annihilated upon attaining self-realisation.

When a person is neither awake nor in deep sleep, his subconscious mind is most likely working, leading to a dream state. The dream might make sense or none at all, might be short or long. They might have many fantasies playing out, which all appear real to the observer, as though the events have actually occurred. However, the dream vanishes as soon as he wakes up, regardless of whether his eyes remain open or shut - proving it was only an illusion, not reality. No matter how long, alluring or real a dream seems, it ends the moment wakefulness dawns. In the exact same manner, when one awakens to his true nature, the state of impurity present since time immemorial is vanquished in totality.

Since time infinite, one has remained enslaved in a state of delusion. Only because he is blinded by the obscurity and the firm grip of ignorance. Forgetting his true blissful nature, he falls prey to this ignorance, which descends upon his mind, clouding his intelligence and masking his awareness. He is trapped in the illusion of what is seen. Looking at the non-self, he forgets the self. Therefore, he harbours impure feelings such as likes-dislikes, binds karma, and undergoes suffering. Freedom from the throes of impurity can be attained only by awakening, that is, by attaining self-realisation.

The dream-like impurity of the soul in the slumber of ignorance, prevalent since infinity, disappears with the awakening of self-realisation. Just as a dream ends in a single moment on waking, the advent of self-realisation severs the identification with the karma-created personality. Once the truth strikes, it tears apart the veil of ignorance and one sees himself as he really is. He is no more than an actor, playing different roles, having entrances and exits on the stage of the world, none capable of affecting the soul.

VERSE - 115

Essence of true religion

Having perfectly demonstrated that one does not require an infinite amount of time to annihilate the delusion of infinity, the Guru presents three mystical verses 115-117, which can be considered the 'pinnacle of verses'. Illuminating the essence of dharma, in the first of these three verses, the Guru says -

છૂટે દેહાધ્યાસ તો, નહિ કર્તા તું કર્મ;
નહિ ભોક્તા તું તેહનો, એ જ ધર્મનો મર્મ. ॥૧૧૫॥

Chhoote dehādhyās toh, nahi kartā tu karma;
Nahi bhoktā tu tehno, ae ja dharmano marma. ||115||

Chhoote - ceases; ***dehādhyās*** - identification with body; ***toh*** - then; ***nahi*** - not; ***kartā*** - doer; ***tu*** - you; ***karma*** - karma; ***nahi*** - not; ***bhoktā*** - receiver; ***tu*** - you; ***tehno*** - of its fruits; ***ae*** - that; ***ja*** - alone; ***dharmano*** - of religion; ***marma*** - essence

MEANING

On renouncing the false identification with the body, you no longer remain the doer of karma, nor the receiver of its fruits. This is the essence of religion.

EXPLANATION

In this spiritually profound verse, the very essence of religion has been revealed, for the spiritual welfare of worthy souls. The essence refers to the hidden secret, not apparent to laymen, which is the ultimate key that unlocks all the treasures of the soul. In society's current structure, several beliefs, rituals, practices and methods prevail in the name of religion. Some people believe that performing duties translates to religion whereas others undertake auspicious activities in the name of religion. The ignorant and indiscreet ones do not know what religion really is, and so in spite of engaging in several means, they do not escape transmigration. The Guru presents the right understanding of religion in a simple way to ensure that true religion manifests in the disciple.

Explaining the true nature of religion, the Guru proclaims that if identification with the body ceases to exist, the soul's 'doership' and 'receivership' of karma are eliminated, and it gradually becomes free of karmic bondage. Due to falsely identifying with the body, one generates 'I-ness' and 'my-ness' in the non-self, which leads to the acquisition of karma. Through the strength of discrimination between the non-self and the self, false identification gets annihilated, replaced by identification with the pure, eternal and perpetual self.

One whose false identification stands destroyed, remains nothing but an indifferent observer, no matter what happens in life. He no longer possesses a craving or aversion for any situation or outcome that arises. He recognises everything else to be distinct from the self, and remains only as its knower. Since His stream of focus is constantly flowing towards the self and nothing else, He becomes the 'doer' and 'enjoyer' of pure feelings. Therefore, He ceases to be the doer of karma and does not bear its consequences. As the discerning ability appears, 'doership' and 'receivership' of karma begin to dissolve and the witnessing attitude evolves.

Thus, He does not acquire new karma, hence the possibility of receiving the fruit of karma does not arise either. However, past karma remain bound to the soul, raising a pertinent question: Is He still liable to bear its fruits? Or does the law of karma cease to operate upon Him? The answer is, the law continues to operate for Him but as He has rid Himself of false identity, nothing that happens to the body or its associations affects Him. He remains free from both pain and pleasure, a mere spectator, and hence it is said that He does not bear the consequences of karma. When one is not influenced by karmic dispositions, remaining solely as a knower, karma is annihilated. This is the path of liberation, the true religion, through which a mass-scale destruction of karma is prompted. Just as a huge bale of cotton is burnt to ash with a tiny spark of fire, a mass of karma is extinguished with the spark of enlightenment. Hence, the gist of spiritual pursuit is getting free from false identification. It is therefore rightly termed here as the essence of religion. This verse, composed from the spiritual perspective is a highly mystical verse.

VERSE - 116

Only this religion leads to liberation

The effort to retreat from impure feelings and remain established in the true nature of the self alone is dharma. Thus, implicitly stating that dharma is dependent on the self, describing the nature of the self in the next two verses, the Guru says -

એ જ ધર્મથી મોક્ષ છે, તું છો મોક્ષ સ્વરૂપ;
અનંત દર્શન જ્ઞાન તું, અવ્યાબાધ સ્વરૂપ. ||૧૧૬||

Ae ja dharmathi moksh chhe, tu chho moksh swaroop;
Anant darshan jnān tu, avyābādh swaroop. ||116||

Ae - that; *ja* - only; *dharmathi* - through religion; *moksh* - liberation; *chhe* - is; *tu* - you; *chho* - are; *moksh* - liberation; *swaroop* - nature; *anant* - infinite; *darshan* - perception; *jnān* - knowledge; *tu* - you; *avyābādh* - unobstructed; *swaroop* - nature

MEANING
Only that religion mentioned in the previous verse, leads to liberation. As the pure self, you are liberation itself. You are infinite perception and knowledge. You are of an unobstructed nature.

EXPLANATION
Liberation is not an award originating outside. As it is a complete manifestation of the soul's inherent eternal nature,

it cannot possibly be sought externally. It is only attained through abidance in the true nature within. The state of liberation is the result of self-realisation. Since the latter is gained by renouncing false identification, it is stated here that liberation is attained by practising 'that religion'.

Thus, in tandem with the previous verse, the Guru says, only that religion leads to liberation. This occurs once false identification is annihilated and one awakens to the self. He keeps on retreating from impure feelings and abiding abundantly in the true nature. To retreat from impure feelings and become established in the true nature alone, is dharma. To identify with other objects and feelings is adharma. Whoever establishes faith in the nature of the self, understands and abides in it, will attain liberation.

Describing that true nature, the Guru says that the soul is inherently free. Eternally unbound, its nature is devoid of all mental-physical-circumstantial afflictions. Now, one may wonder if the soul were really unbound, then why is it said that it attains liberation through religion? If one correctly understands the viewpoints from which these statements are made, he will realise that they are non-contradictory. To make it simpler, 'You are liberated right now' indicates the eternal nature. Whereas, 'You will be liberated' indicates the manifestation of the purest state. Although the nature is always unbound, the state of the soul also becomes unbound through the practice of true religion.

The soul is an abode of infinite perception, infinite knowledge, and is of unobstructed nature. Here, the word unobstructed implies infinite bliss and infinite energy. Thus, *anant chatushtay* - the four infinite virtues namely, *anant jnān, anant darshan, anant sukh* and *anant virya*, are woven into the second line of this verse. The Guru tells the disciple that these qualities are not separate from you, rather they are inherent in you but presently not manifested.

To develop faith in such nature and become engrossed in it, is religion. And this religion alone, leads to liberation. In this verse, encouraging the pursuit of the self, the Guru addresses the disciple with affection, revealed through the word *'tu'* - you, establishing an intimate relation with him. The Guru points out more qualities of the soul in the next verse.

— ⌒⟋⟍ᵒ —

VERSE - 117

Splendour of soul

In this verse, the Guru describes some more qualities of the soul. He defines its nature through five wondrous attributes. The Guru says -

શુદ્ધ બુદ્ધ ચૈતન્યઘન, સ્વયંજ્યોતિ સુખધામ;
બીજું કહીએ કેટલું? કર વિચાર તો પામ. ॥૧૧૭॥

Shuddh buddh chaitanyaghan, swayamjyoti sukhdhām;
Biju kahiye ketlu? Kar vichār toh pām. ॥117॥

Shuddh - pure; *buddh* - knowledgeable; *chaitanyaghan* - compact consciousness; *swayamjyoti* - self-illuminating flame; *sukhdhām* - abode of bliss; *biju* - more; *kahiye* - say; *ketlu* - how much; *kar* - do; *vichār* - think; *toh* - then; *pām* - attain

MEANING

You are pure, knowledgeable, full of consciousness, self-luminous and the abode of bliss. What more should I say to you? Contemplate this deeply and realise your self.

EXPLANATION

This verse describes the true nature of the soul which the enlightened ones experience during self-realisation. The attributes of the soul are infinite and cannot be expressed entirely. This can be gauged from the following fact. Heavenly beings of the highest heaven, called *Sarvārthsiddh devas*, are self-realised and discuss the attributes of the soul for countless years. Even without repeating a single attribute, they cannot list them all during their entire lifespan. In this verse, Shrimadji has mentioned five attributes of the soul -

1. *Shuddh* - Pure
The nature of the soul is completely pure, bereft of all other objects and feelings. Although it seems stained by karma, possessing an impure state since time infinite, nothing can change its inherent purity. This purity remains latent in the worldly state and gets manifested in the liberated state.

2. *Buddh* - Knowledgeable
Infinite knowledge is the property of the soul, which has the inherent capacity to know everything. All objects are reflected in its knowing capacity. In its current state, the soul requires the medium of the senses to know them, as the capacity to know is obscured by *jnānāvarniya* karma. When this capacity manifests, no dependency on any external medium remains. Since the soul possesses this capacity, it is called knowledgeable.

3. *Chaitanyaghan* - Full of consciousness
The soul is an indivisible mass of consciousness and not even a single unit can fall apart. Consciousness pervades every part of the soul. It is a complete, compact and dense entity. Although the soul is closely associated with the body, neither does consciousness transfer to the body, nor does the soul change into inanimate matter. The conscious soul expands or

contracts as per the size of the body, be it an elephant or an ant, but never breaks apart or separates.

4. *Swayamjyoti* - Self-luminous

The soul is a self-illuminating flame, lighting up the self and the non-self. The light of knowledge is eternal, existing on its own independently. Fire depends on fuel for its existence, but not the light of knowledge. It shines by itself, it is self-radiant. Just like no lamp is required to see the sun, no other substance is required to know the soul.

5. *Sukhdhām* - Abode of bliss

Since the soul is full of infinite happiness, it is called the abode of eternal, indestructible bliss. No other substance besides the soul has this attribute of bliss, proving to be an important characteristic. Since one has not experienced this inherent nature, he seeks happiness outside. However, such happiness is dependent on the senses, not objective, temporary and disappears quickly. The bliss of the soul is transcendental, beyond the senses. It can be experienced by withdrawing from the world and abiding within.

Such is the inconceivable glory of the soul whose attributes are infinite. It is impossible to completely describe them in words. The glory of the soul is a subject of experience, this description providing only an idea of its magnificence. It truly does not matter how mighty or miniscule, fantastic or fragile each of us are, as within us all lies the pure eternal nature. Therefore, Shrimadji inspires us to climb unscaled heights and plunge into immeasurable depths. He pushes aside the veil of ignorance and shows us who we really are. It is time to reclaim our identity.

One must understand the nature of the soul from an enlightened one. By focusing on the self and by immersing in it, infinite virtues like knowledge and bliss completely manifest. Contemplation upon the latent nature and abiding in it, leads to the attainment of the absolute supreme state.

Thus, the path to attain liberation begins with contemplating the self. Without deep contemplation upon the nature of the self, it is impossible to attain self-realisation. Therefore, at the end of this verse, the Guru asks what more should He possibly say than what is already said above? Stating that if the disciple contemplated the true nature of the self, he would attain it.

In this verse, the very embodiment of wisdom, Shrimadji, has propounded the profound subject of the path to liberation, briefly and in simple language, serving as a guiding light to seekers. The last quarter of this verse, *'Kar vichār toh pām'* - 'If you think, then you will attain' - has become a maxim amongst aspirants.

VERSE - 118

Universal message of all enlightened ones

In 21 verses, Shrimadji conveyed the fundamental nature of the path to liberation through the Guru. It incorporated a comprehensive, continuous sequence of attaining the path and three highly mystical 'pinnacle verses'. Now, in this verse, He concludes the dialogue between the Guru and the disciple that had commenced in verse 45. In this last verse addressed to the disciple, the Guru says -

નિશ્ચય સર્વે જ્ઞાનીનો, આવી અત્ર સમાય;
ધરી મૌનતા એમ કહી, સહજસમાધિ માંય. ||૧૧૮||

Nishchay sarve Jnānino, āvi atra samāy;
Dhari mauntā em kahi, sahajsamādhi māy. ||118||

Nishchay - conclusion; *sarve* - all; *Jnānino* - of enlightened ones; *āvi* - comes; *atra* - here; *samāy* - included; *dhari* - becomes; *mauntā* - silent; *em* - this; *kahi* - saying; *sahajsamādhi* - effortless and deep meditative state; *māy* - into

MEANING
The conclusion of all the enlightened ones has been encompassed here. Having said this, the Guru assumes silence and enters into effortless self-absorption.

EXPLANATION
Having imparted an understanding of the important aspects about the path of liberation to the disciple, the Guru does

not feel the need to say anything more. This is because the entire essence of the path of liberation has been included here. Moreover, the Guru says that everything explained in these verses is acceptable to all the enlightened ones. The purport of all the enlightened ones is encompassed here and the conclusion of all their teachings converge at this point.

As a matter of fact, there is only one absolute path of liberation. All the enlightened ones have only one opinion regarding the way to attain liberation. The Guru declares that all the enlightened ones have arrived at the same conclusion expounded here. Whatever has been stated here is their universal message and infinite souls have attained liberation this way.

Having stated that He has propounded the message acceptable to all the enlightened ones, the Guru ends His speech and immerses into self-absorption. The enlightened ones are primarily immersed in the state beyond thought, revelling in the self. This is their core activity. However, compassion arises when they come across a worthy soul and they impart religious teachings to him. The Guru lovingly provided perfect solutions to all the doubts faced by the worthy disciple and established a firm conviction in him. He propounded the path of liberation in a simple and concise manner. Encouraging the disciple to deeply contemplate and pursue it, the Guru ends His explanation and abides effortlessly in the self.

The Guru resorted to speech only for the disciple's benefit, in order to resolve his doubts. Since that purpose is served,

He withdraws from the activity of speech. With this withdrawal, the Guru becomes silent, immersed in the self, entering a deep meditative state. A state of innate ecstasy completely independent of external factors. A state that occurs of its own accord. Thus, the third group of this section, from verses 114-118, comes to a close.

Expression of the Disciple's Enlightenment

Following the Guru's command mentioned in verse 117, stating that if you think, you will attain, the worthy disciple deeply contemplates each solution provided by the Guru and thereby develops a doubtless conviction in the six fundamental truths. Imbibing the wondrous teachings, his heart is full of inexplicable emotion and his joy knows no bounds.

When the disciple ruminates upon these teachings, the divine essence embedded in the words begins to touch him and the belief 'I am the body' gradually fades. As the awareness of the self becomes steady, the worthy disciple goes completely beyond the senses, and transcending the thoughts, he experiences the self, distinctly separate from the body. When such a direct experience is gained, it is called the attainment of enlightenment.

This section, 'Expression of the disciple's enlightenment' consists of nine verses 119-127. Through the disciple's words, Shrimadji gives an amazing heart-touching account of the disciple's state after attaining self-realisation as well as his feeling of devotion towards the benevolent Guru. From verses 119-123, the worthy disciple recounts his experience of the self to the Guru. From verses 124-127, he expresses his indebtedness towards the Guru, who has been instrumental in that experience. In these verses, Shrimadji has portrayed the disciple's feelings of surrender. This section is a thanksgiving for the guidance given and destination reached.

VERSE - 119

Disciple's attainment of enlightenment

Immersed in the feelings of gratitude, expressing his attainment of enlightenment, the worthy disciple says -

સદ્ગુરુના ઉપદેશથી, આવ્યું અપૂર્વ ભાન;
નિજપદ નિજમાંહી લહ્યું, દૂર થયું અજ્ઞાન. ||૧૧૯||

Sadgurunā updeshthi, āvyu apurva bhān;
Nijpad nijmāhi lahyu, dur thayu ajnān. ||119||

Sadgurunā - of enlightened Mentor; *updeshthi* - by teachings; *āvyu* - attained; *apurva* - unprecedented; *bhān* - realisation; *nijpad* - own self; *nijmāhi* - within me; *lahyu* - obtained; *dur* - away; *thayu* - went; *ajnān* - ignorance

MEANING

By the teachings of the true Guru, I realised my true self within, which I had never experienced before, and my self-delusive ignorance was destroyed.

EXPLANATION

The Guru has ignited the spark of knowledge in the disciple. The ignorance which had blinded him thus far has been conquered and his 'seeing eye' has opened. Now with the attainment of self-realisation, the disciple's attention is diverted towards the soul but his devotion to the Guru remains the same. Or rather, it increases. He knows that the Guru was the instrumental cause behind attaining self-realisation. This verse describes the respect given to the Guru by the self-realised disciple.

The Guru had gotten absorbed in a trance, immersed in His self. Upon observing the transcendental state of the Guru abiding in the self, the disciple got inspired and was motivated to achieve it too. The process was activated within him. He realised the self at the experiential level, which earlier he had understood only at the intellectual level. He realised the soul in the light of his own experience.

Emanating from the depths of his soul, the disciple expresses that the self has awakened and that realisation has occurred. The soul is now not just a concept based on information but an experience gained by undergoing transformation. This realisation is unprecedented. It had never been gained or attained earlier. Until now, the disciple had been groping in the dark, wandering in ignorance. Now, he has realised the self and the energy of joy has been released.

Recounting this experience, the disciple conveys that he has discovered his self within. He realised his true nature as it is. Until now, he had established the 'I' in the body, senses, intellect, etc. He had been wallowing in the belief that the body is the self. Now, the 'I' is established in the soul, the eternal conscious substance. He is aware that 'I am only knowingness'. With the experiential conviction of the soul, his self-delusive ignorance has been eliminated. Identification with the self has been attained and ignorance of identification with the body that was prevalent since time immemorial, has been dispelled.

The disciple declares that this unique realisation regarding the self and the annihilation of ignorance has been attained due to the Sadguru's supreme teachings. It is only due to His teachings and blessings that the disciple has awakened. It would not have been possible otherwise. He would not have turned towards the self without the Sadguru's teachings. Although he has attained the self through himself, within himself, the disciple gives the entire credit to the benevolence of the Sadguru. He believes to the core that had the Sadguru not motivated him, he would not have experienced the self. The unlimited benefaction and association of the Sadguru have proved responsible for his enlightenment. He acknowledges the Sadguru's debt, feels obliged, and expresses his heartfelt devotion towards Him.

—⟨✣⟩—

VERSE - 120

Experienced himself as pure consciousness

Expressing his right knowledge of the first fundamental truth, 'soul exists' and the second fundamental truth, 'soul is eternal', the worthy disciple says -

ભાસ્યું નિજસ્વરૂપ તે, શુદ્ધ ચેતનારૂપ;
અજર, અમર, અવિનાશી ને, દેહાતીત સ્વરૂપ. ||૧૨૦||

Bhāsyu nijswaroop te, shuddh chetnāroop;
Ajar, amar, avināshi ne, dehātit swaroop. ||120||

Bhāsyu - experienced; *nijswaroop* - own nature; *te* - that; *shuddh* - pure; *chetnāroop* - consciousness; *ajar* - unchanging; *amar* - immortal; *avināshi* - imperishable; *ne* - and; *dehātit* - separate from body; *swaroop* - nature

MEANING

I now experience my self as pure consciousness, which is ageless, immortal, indestructible and distinct from the body.

EXPLANATION

For the very first time, the disciple has risen above the barrier of his body and broken the chain of his limited understanding. He has awakened from the slumber that made him believe in the world of illusion. A firm conviction has emerged in him that this ageing, decaying, perishable bag of bones called the body, which has no guarantee and comes with the label 'anytime expiry', certainly cannot be his true self. He has discovered his real nature on the attainment of self-realisation.

This verse describes the nature of the soul which was experienced by the disciple. When he achieved self-realisation, all illusions were broken and he experienced his true self. This is indicated by the word *'bhāsyu'* - experienced. In this verse, he describes his experiential conviction regarding the first two fundamental truths in the words - 'pure consciousness', 'ageless', 'immortal', 'indestructible' and 'separate from the body'.

When the self was attained within, the worthy disciple experienced his nature as *'shuddh chetnāroop'* - pure consciousness. He realised that his nature is only that of a knower and an observer. Just as a burning lamp exudes light and smoke, the soul emanates knowledge and impure feelings, but they are not one. The disciple's illusion regarding the self has been wiped off. He has realised his self in the original form, independent of all inanimate objects and impure modifications. His nature is devoid of any coating of the body or contamination of impurities such as attachments or aversions. It is pure knowingness.

The disciple's experiential conviction regarding the first fundamental truth is expressed in the first line of the verse, and that of the second fundamental truth in the next line. Experiencing his own self as pure consciousness, he realises that he exists in all three periods of time. This truth had not been understood earlier because of his ignorance but has been clearly understood and experienced with the dawn of enlightenment. Stating his experience regarding the eternal nature of the soul, he says -

1. *Ajar* - Ageless

Birth, old age, etc., are modifications of the material body. The soul is neither born nor does it age. The nature of the body is that it grows, undergoes wear and tear, and becomes old with the passage of time. However, the soul is an original substance. It is not produced from any association, therefore there is no question of dissociation or disintegration. It never loses its vigour. The body shows symptoms of wearing out - grey hair, wrinkles, etc., and enhancers like dyes and cosmetics are used to cover up the ageing process. However, the soul is free from old age, it is unchanging. The body grows old but not the soul.

2. *Amar* - Immortal

Death occurs to the body, not to the soul. The soul is endless, free from death. The soul remains in the body as determined by karma. After that, it separates from the body, goes elsewhere and occupies another body. The soul never dies, it only changes bodies. The ignorant one is attached to the body and hence is fearful of death. He experiences anxiety and sorrow. The enlightened ones have no fear of death, and not even of the present or future birth.

3. *Avināshi* - Indestructible

While the body is destructible and perishable, the soul cannot be destroyed - it does not perish. It is unbreakable and indivisible. During infinite wandering in transmigration, the soul has adopted various bodies. Regardless of that it has never been damaged. It has not been divided into parts and no parts have fallen apart. No external substance can afflict the soul. Weapons cannot shred it, fire cannot burn it, water cannot wet it, wind cannot dry it.

4. *Dehātit* - Distinct from the body

The soul is transcendental, different from the body. It is diametrically opposite to the body. Both are separate entities. The soul is in the body, but is distinct from the body. It is the knower of the body. The disciple has now experienced the self as separate from the body. He is aware of his true self, which is beyond the body.

The body is made up of matter. Old age, death, destruction are the modifications of the material body and never of the self. The pure conscious self is completely distinct from the body. The soul neither ages, nor dies, nor gets destroyed. Since the soul is not material, it is touchless, tasteless, odourless, colourless and speechless. It is a union of infinite attributes. However, it is experienced as a single entity. Just like a chocolate is made up of many different ingredients, but when one takes a bite, it is experienced as a unified chunk; the soul has infinite qualities, but during self-realisation, it is experienced as one entity.

VERSE - 121

Experiences himself as non-doer of karma

The disciple stated that he was convinced regarding the first two fundamental truths - the soul's existence and eternal nature. Now, in verses 121 and 122, he conveys the right conviction he has gained with respect to the third and fourth fundamental truths. That is, the soul being the doer and enjoyer of karma.

Describing how the soul's doership and enjoyership modifies after the advent of self-realisation, the worthy disciple says -

કર્તા ભોક્તા કર્મનો, વિભાવ વર્તે જ્યાંય;
વૃત્તિ વહી નિજભાવમાં, થયો અકર્તા ત્યાંય. ||૧૨૧||

Kartā bhoktā karmano, vibhāv varte jyāy;
Vrutti vahi nijbhāvmā, thayo akartā tyāy. ||*121*||

Kartā - doer; *bhoktā* - enjoyer; *karmano* - of karma; *vibhāv* - delusion; *varte* - prevails; *jyāy* - where; *vrutti* - tendency; *vahi* - flowed; *nijbhāvmā* - within; *thayo* - became; *akartā* - non-doer; *tyāy* - there

MEANING

The soul is the doer and enjoyer of karma as long as delusion exists. When the attentiveness flowed towards my own self, I became the non-doer of karma. (Also the non-enjoyer of its fruits.)

EXPLANATION

In this verse, the disciple expresses the invaluable insights he has gained regarding the doership and enjoyership of the soul. When true understanding awakens, all false beliefs change and truth percolates into faith. The disciple is awakened and expresses to the Guru all that he has been experiencing. This enunciation will enhance the continuity of that experience. He states, 'O Sadguru! By Your blessings I have rightly understood the doership and enjoyership of the soul.'

Since time immemorial, the disciple was harbouring impure feelings by forgetting his pure, peaceful, blissful and conscious nature. He was becoming the doer-enjoyer of impure feelings such as likes or dislikes. These impure feelings were instrumental in attracting material karmic particles which modified as karma. After giving the appropriate fruits at the right time, they were shed. Thus, because of ignorance he experienced himself as the doer-enjoyer of material karma.

The disciple says that he was the doer-enjoyer of karma due to *'vibhāv'*. The meaning of this word needs to be understood correctly. The word literally means opposite of its nature. Therefore, it would denote unnatural. However, this would imply that the nature of the soul becomes inanimate, which is impossible. So, it does not mean going against the nature, it indicates going beyond the nature. The soul cannot become inanimate, but it is capable of going beyond its pure nature. It has the capacity of indulging in impure feelings.

Under the effect of self-delusive ignorance, the soul does karma and enjoys its fruits. However, once the attention turns inwards, it experiences itself as neither the doer nor the enjoyer of karma. He remains aloof during the manifestation of karma. He does not get involved in karma and becomes a spectator. The disciple was the doer and enjoyer of karma only when he was in the state of ignorance. Now, with the transformation that has occurred due to self-realisation, he is no more a doer of impure feelings and consequently material karma which they were instrumental in binding.

With the emergence of enlightenment, the doership and enjoyership of karma ends, and stability in the self is experienced. The disciple developed right conviction through the Sadguru's teachings, practised differentiation between the self and the non-self and increased self-awareness. He channelised his attention towards the soul from the body and other associations. Single-pointedly focusing on the true nature, he attained self-realisation. With the dawn of self-realisation, his ignorance was dispelled and illusion was shattered. Engrossed in the pure nature, he does not remain the doer and enjoyer of karma. This personal experience is indicated by the word '*vahi*' - flowed. In verse 111, the word '*vahey*' - flows, was used in third person whereas in this verse, the word vahi is used in first person, signifying that the disciple's tendency flowed towards his own nature and he became the non-doer of karma.

VERSE - 122

Doer and enjoyer of pure state

When the tendencies flow towards one's own pure nature, the soul becomes the non-doer and non-enjoyer of impure feelings and material karma. Explaining the transformation in his doership and enjoyership, the worthy disciple says -

અથવા નિજપરિણામ જે, શુદ્ધ ચેતનારૂપ;
કર્તા ભોક્તા તેહનો, નિર્વિકલ્પ સ્વરૂપ. ||૧૨૨||

Athvā nijparinām je, shuddh chetnāroop;
Kartā bhoktā tehno, nirvikalp swaroop. ||122||

Athvā - or; *nijparinām* - own modifications; *je* - which; **shuddh** - pure; **chetnāroop** - consciousness; *kartā* - doer; **bhoktā** - enjoyer; *tehno* - of that; **nirvikalp** - beyond thoughts; **swaroop** - nature

MEANING

Alternatively, it may be said that I became the doer and enjoyer of my own modifications, which are of the nature of pure consciousness without any thought activity.

EXPLANATION

By using the word '*athvā*' - or, the disciple expresses what he had stated in the previous verse, but in another way. In other words, he says he became the doer and enjoyer of the soul's pure manifestations. One whose impure feelings have been eliminated, whose tendency has flowed within, has become the doer of pure modifications and enjoyer of inner bliss. The worthy disciple says, 'O Sadguru! I turned within and became a spectator of the manifestations of karma. I am now only an observer, unaffected by it. I experienced pure consciousness and swayed in its bliss. Immersed in that marvellous state, my ego and desires vanished. I am no longer a doer or enjoyer of karma. I am now a doer and enjoyer of my natural disposition.'

The soul is never the doer or enjoyer of changes in other substances. It is only the doer and enjoyer of its own feelings. Upon the attainment of self-realisation, these feelings are transformed from impure to pure. Therefore, it becomes the doer and enjoyer of pure feelings. The soul always remains active as doership is its nature. It cannot be a complete non-doer at any point in time. If the doership ceases, the soul would leave its very nature. The doership is present even in the liberated state. Here, it is no longer a doer of impure feelings. It is the doer of pure manifestations. Similarly, it is not the enjoyer of impure feelings. It only enjoys boundless bliss. There is abidance in the pure conscious nature, therefore it becomes the doer and enjoyer of pure conscious feelings. So, the doership and enjoyership are constant, the only choice is between pure and impure feelings. As the tendency flows within, the doership and enjoyership of karma is replaced by that of pure feelings.

The moment one becomes enlightened, he becomes the doer and enjoyer of the pure state. The tendency remains steady in the pure nature and he attains a peaceful state. In the impure state, thoughts arise leading to instability. The pure state is devoid of thoughts and hence is stable. In the state of experience there are no thoughts like, 'I am doing it', 'I am enjoying it', 'I did it', 'I enjoyed it', 'I wish to do it'. It is a state beyond thoughts. Not a single thought arises, he just experiences immaculate feelings and manifestations of purity.

Thus, when oneness with the pure, unblemished nature is attained, he becomes the non-doer and non-enjoyer of karma, as well as the doer and enjoyer of pure modifications. He revels in the novel bliss of his true nature, which is beyond the senses. The Guru had explained in verse 78, that if the soul abides in the awareness of its nature, then it is the doer of its pure nature in the sense of its manifestation. In accordance with that, the worthy disciple says that because of the Sadguru's teachings, his awareness is immersed in the true nature. In the state beyond thoughts, he became the doer and enjoyer of feelings of pure consciousness. This verse declares that the worthy disciple has gained experiential conviction of the Guru's teachings regarding the third and fourth fundamental truths.

⁓ ∿⁓

VERSE - 123

Liberation and its path

Now, the disciple narrates how the Guru had explained and how well he understood the last two fundamental truths of the soul - 'there is liberation' and 'there is a path of liberation'. The worthy disciple says -

મોક્ષ કહ્યો નિજશુદ્ધતા, તે પામે તે પંથ;
સમજાવ્યો સંક્ષેપમાં, સકળ માર્ગ નિર્ગ્રંથ. ||૧૨૩||

Moksh kahyo nijshuddhtā, te pāmey te panth;
Samjāvyo sankshepmā, sakal mārg Nirgranth. ||123||

Moksh - liberation; *kahyo* - said; *nijshuddhtā* - purity of soul; *te* - this state; *pāmey* - attains; *te* - that; *panth* - path; *samjāvyo* - explained; *sankshepmā* - concisely; *sakal* - complete; *mārg* - path; *Nirgranth* - without knots

MEANING

Liberation is the pure state of one's own self. The way it is attained is the path. The entire path of the disentangled Lord has been explained in brief.

EXPLANATION

The state devoid of desires, expectations and passions is liberation. That which leads to this state is the path of liberation. The path is one of relentless toil and repeated effort. It demands the deepest dedication, highest devotion and selfless determination. The worthy disciple has yet to attain liberation, but has tasted a drop of it. The path of liberation is taking shape for him. He says, 'O Sadguru! I have understood liberation and the path of liberation that You had explained earlier. The completely pure state of the soul is liberation. The effort made to attain that state is the path of liberation.'

Purity is the inherent nature of the soul. At present, the soul modifies into an impure state. Indulging in impure feelings, it acquires the impurity of karma which leads to impure states of existence like hell, animals, etc. If the soul becomes an observer and brings an end to impure feelings, it leads to dissociation from the body, karma, etc., and the attainment of liberation. Thus, liberation is the absolute purity of the soul. It is the name given to the purest, indestructible state of the soul. A commonly-held belief, particularly amongst Jains, is that liberation is a place situated at the topmost part of the universe. According to the Jain cosmology, the abode of the liberated souls is at the end of the fourteenth *rājlok* - realm. However, if liberation was solely associated with a place, then all beings present there would have to be pure and blissful. However, that is not the case. At the same place, along with infinite liberated souls, there are also infinite beings of *nigod* - the lowest form of life, which are impure and suffering. Therefore, from the spiritual viewpoint, liberation is not a place, but the attainment of the pure state of the soul.

Through the Guru's teachings, the disciple has properly absorbed that attaining absolute purity by constantly abiding in the self is liberation. It is apparent that the means by which this purity is attained is the path of liberation. The way through which the supremely pure, indestructible, blissful state, which is free of karma and impure feelings is attained, is the true path of liberation. Through complete stability and unperturbed abidance in the soul, liberation is attained.

In the second line of the present verse, the disciple expresses gratitude towards the Guru, who has perfectly explained the path of liberation as expounded by the omniscient dispassionate ones. To annihilate the impure state which has continued due to the series of auspicious and inauspicious feelings, the Guru has concisely yet completely explained the path of liberation. It is like a locket size picture of a large portrait which is small but yet full. To elucidate something in brief without missing out on any important aspect is an art. The Sadguru has such mastery.

The path of liberation has been propounded by the *'Nirgranth'* - disentangled ones, liberated Lords. They are without any external knots like associations, relations; and internal knots like attachments, aversions, ignorance. Such knots signify bondage, but the omniscient ones have severed all knots. They have annihilated the knots and displayed the path to be free from them.

VERSE - 124

Disciple's gratitude towards Guru

In verses 119-123, Shrimadji had imparted the essence of the understanding of the six fundamental truths in the form of the disciple narrating his own experience. Now, from verses 124-127, the immensely exhilarated disciple expresses gratitude to the Guru for His compassion, for showing him the path to liberation. These four verses clearly depict the incessant flow of reverence and devotion, gushing with full force towards the benevolent Guru. In the first of these verses, the worthy disciple says -

અહો! અહો! શ્રી સદ્‌ગુરુ, કરુણાસિંધુ અપાર;
આ પામર પર પ્રભુ કર્યો, અહો! અહો! ઉપકાર. ॥૧૨૪॥

Aho! Aho! Shri Sadguru, karunāsindhu apār;
Ā pāmar par Prabhu karyo, Aho! Aho! Upkār. ॥124॥

Aho! Aho! - O! O!; *Shri Sadguru* - enlightened Mentor; *karunāsindhu* - ocean of compassion; *apār* - boundless; *ā* - this; *pāmar* - wretched; *par* - on; *Prabhu* - God; *karyo* - done; *Aho! Aho!* - O! O!; *upkār* - favour

MEANING

O! O! The great enlightened Guru, unfathomable ocean of compassion; on this worthless being, O Lord, You have bestowed immense benevolence.

EXPLANATION

With overflowing excitement, the disciple lies submerged in the bliss of discovering the soul. There is another emotion longing to be expressed - sincere gratitude. However, the disciple finds that he has little means to express the boundless joy bursting from his heart on being shown the path of liberation. All he longs for is to profess how the Guru has transformed and redeemed his life forever. He venerates the Guru in such a manner that the Guru becomes his very soul.

The worthy disciple met the enlightened Guru who explained the six fundamental truths to him. The disciple was awakened. The proximity, vibrations, teachings of the Guru threw open the doors within him. He has realised both - the pure nature of the soul and the benevolence of the Guru. However, he struggles to put this benevolence into words. Words cannot do justice to his feelings. Although he has experienced it, he cannot express it, and so the exclamation Aho! - O!, slips out from him. When one sees some extraordinary form, quality, knowledge or greatness, he gets exceedingly impressed by it. He is unable to describe the phenomenon and only utters such exclamations. The disciple finds the divinity and benevolence of the Guru unparalleled. Nothing can match His greatness. So, with a feeling of awe, he exclaims the pair of '**Aho! Aho!**' twice in this verse.

The disciple uses several adjectives to describe the Guru - '**Shrī**' to emphasise His wealth of knowledge, '**karunāsindhu**' to extol the ocean of compassion, and '**apār**' to indicate that His grace is boundless, limitless, immense. The disciple recounts the benefaction and states that the Guru is an embodiment of the ocean of compassion. Just as the depth and vastness of the ocean cannot be measured, the Guru's compassion too cannot be measured. He is the very personification of selfless compassion.

Such is the humility of the disciple that he states that the Guru showered compassion on a *'pāmar'* - wretched person, like me. The disciple calls himself lowly, unworthy, bereft of any capacity. Such words are only possible if the ego has departed. The disciple narrates that the Guru handheld a worthless and undeserving soul like himself. He imparted spiritual teachings and illuminated the right path. The Guru raised his enthusiasm for right efforts and made him reach the high state of self-realisation. Due to His benevolence, infinite transmigration and the subsequent infinite suffering come to an end, paving the beginning of abidance in the independent, unobstructed bliss of the soul.

The worthy disciple realises the greatness of this divine benevolence, therefore instead of saying the Guru bestowed benevolence, he says, *'Prabhu karyo upkār'* - God bestowed benevolence. He can no longer see any difference between the Guru and God. A disciple who has tasted the nectar of the Guru's grace, will certainly say that the Guru and God are not separate entities, but one. The Guru Himself is God. With such realisation, the disciple immerses in utmost devotion towards Him.

The disciple has seen the Guru's magnificent state and experienced His enormous grace. He humbly expresses, 'O Sadguru! Despite me being worthless, You were ever-willing to guide me without a single selfish motive. You led me on the path of liberation to end my ceaseless wandering. You took the trouble to elevate me only for my liberation. I was on the lowest rung of the ladder, full of flaws, shortcomings, and worldly attachments. You uplifted me from the worldly mire to new peaks of enlightenment. I was suffering in the cycles of birth and death. You saved me from endless transmigration. You removed my self-delusion and directed all my energies towards the soul. When I think of what I was, and what I am, I realise Your boundless compassion. I experience Your immense obligation done to me.'

Thus, the disciple holds great reverence in his heart for the limitless benevolence of the Sadguru, the unfathomable ocean of compassion, who has brought him on the true path of freedom from all ties. Singing the glory of the Guru's benevolence he says, 'O Lord, the ocean of compassion, by Your boundless grace, this ignorant one has so easily attained the path of self-realisation, which he had never known, never believed and never practised before. Since time immemorial, I had wandered in the forest of transmigration because of my own self-will. By harbouring impure feelings, I had burdened every part of my radiant soul with the unbearable weight of karma. As a result, I had become extremely pitiable, foolish and wretched. Due to my good fortune, I was blessed to meet You. The strength of Your wisdom and dispassion inspired me to take refuge in You. You gave a new direction to my thinking, adding speed to my steps. Having received Your benefaction, my effort gained unimaginable momentum. Your infinite grace has burnt down the blinding veil of my ignorance. It has shattered the shell of my indolence and freed me. Divinity has manifested in this wretched one by the power of Your supreme grace. In every moment, I experience Your great benevolence. Since infinite time, my knowledge was the cause of transmigration. You have categorically changed that very knowledge, making it the cause of freedom from transmigration. O embodiment of divinity! O embodiment of auspiciousness! O Lord! The benevolence that You have bestowed upon me is boundless.'

VERSE - 125

Offers himself at Guru's feet

As the disciple wishes to reciprocate the supreme benevolence bestowed upon him by the Guru, he ponders how he could possibly do so. In a humble expression of offering at the holy feet of the Guru, the worthy disciple says -

શું પ્રભુચરણ કને ધરું, આત્માથી સૌ હીન;
તે તો પ્રભુએ આપિયો, વર્તું ચરણાધીન. ||૧૨૫||

Shu Prabhucharan kaney dharu, ātmāthi sau heen;
Te toh Prabhue āpiyo, vartu charanādheen. ||*125*||

Shu - what; *Prabhucharan* - God's feet; *kaney* - at; *dharu* - offer; *ātmāthi* - than soul; *sau* - everything; *heen* - lower; *te* - that; *toh* - indeed; *Prabhue* - by God; *āpiyo* - given; *vartu* - act; *charanādheen* - under Your directions

MEANING

O Lord! What can I offer at Your lotus feet in return for Your immense benefaction? Everything in this world is inferior to the soul. The soul itself has been bestowed upon me by You. Since it is impossible for me to offer anything, I firmly decide to live by Your command for the rest of my life.

EXPLANATION

As the disciple reflects on his journey so far, he is overwhelmed with gratitude for the Guru. When he was lost, the Guru held his hand and guided his steps. When he was lonely, the Guru befriended him. When he was deluded and confused, the Guru cleared his vision. The more he reminisces about the Guru's majestic state and limitless compassion, the more he feels obliged to Him. The desire to reciprocate His immense benevolence emerges in his heart.

During ancient times, according to Indian tradition, after completing his training, a disciple would offer something to the Guru as a symbol of gratitude for His benevolence. It is called *Gurudakshinā*. From an ethical viewpoint too, it is considered one's duty to repay someone's favour. One should never forget to repay his debts. Even the favour received from a person who helped remove a thorn from one's foot, should not be forgotten. A gentleman never forgets even the smallest of favours afforded to him. Instead, he wishes to repay it to the best of his ability, and eagerly looks for opportunities to do so. Here, the disciple is humble and worthy. So, it is impossible that he could forget the immense obligation of the Guru, who helped him attain enlightenment. Rather, he naturally wishes to reciprocate the boundless benevolence bestowed upon him by the Guru.

Although the debt of the Guru can never be repaid, the urgency to reciprocate has inevitably arisen in the worthy disciple. He thinks, 'Out of selfless compassion, the Guru has bestowed infinite grace upon me. He has fulfilled me by blessing me with the gift of self-realisation. My transmigration had no limit, He has brought it to an end. What can I offer my supremely beneficial Guru that will reciprocate His benevolence? What can I lay at my Guru's lotus feet?'

In worldly interactions, if someone wants to give something to another, it is given in the hands. However, as the disciple looks upon the Guru to be God, this devotion prompts him to offer something at the Guru's lotus feet. This feeling shows his respect and reverence for the Guru.

While pondering what he can offer at the lotus feet of the Guru, the disciple realises that *'ātmāthi sau heen'* - all substances in the world are inferior to the soul. All objects are petty in comparison to the soul. Through the Guru's teachings, the disciple has evidently experienced that the most supreme substance in all three worlds and across all three periods of time, is the soul. Everything else is less precious and lower than the soul.

There is nothing other than the soul, worthy of being offered at the Guru's lotus feet, but now the disciple realises that it is the Guru who has given him this soul. The Guru revealed to him the nature of the soul. The disciple was not even aware of its existence. While he was trapped in the consciousness of the body, the Guru unveiled to him the splendour of the soul. He would not have realised the soul without the Guru's help. In that sense, the Guru has given him the soul. The wonder that has manifested in his life is due to His blessing alone. How can he return what he has received from the Guru? It is not appropriate to give back to someone the same thing that was given by him.

The disciple totally dedicates his life at the Guru's lotus feet. He firmly resolves to live in obedience to His guidance and stay in accordance with His commands completely. The disciple's sole wish is that all his actions be as per the Guru's wish. He accepts the servitude of the Guru. Thus, instead of reciprocating by offering an object, the disciple surrenders himself at the pious feet of the supremely benevolent Guru, which is indicated by the words *'vartu charanādheen'*.

This verse emphasises the devotion of the ideal disciple towards the ideal Guru. The Guru is selfless, expecting nothing in return while the disciple offers everything at His feet. The disciple wants to reciprocate but nothing can equal the most unique gift bestowed upon him - the discovery of his soul. Hence, despite knowing that it is insignificant, he offers himself at the lotus feet of the Guru.

VERSE - 126

Sense of servitude

The humble disciple harboured the wish to offer his all at the Guru's lotus feet and lead a life of surrender. In this verse, strengthening the desire to live as per His will, the worthy disciple says -

આ દેહાદિ આજથી, વર્તો પ્રભુ આધીન;
દાસ, દાસ હું દાસ છું, તેહ પ્રભુનો દીન. ||૧૨૬||

Ā dehādi ājthi, varto Prabhu ādheen;
Dās, dās hu dās chhu, teh Prabhuno deen. ||126||

Ā - this; *dehādi* - body etc.; *ājthi* - from today; *varto* - act; *Prabhu* - God; *ādheen* - as commanded; *dās* - servant; *hu* - I; *chhu* - am; *teh* - that; *Prabhuno* - of God; *deen* - humble

MEANING
From now onwards, let this body, etc., be employed in the service of the Lord. Let me be a servant, a humble servant, the humblest servant of the Lord.

EXPLANATION
By the grace of the Guru's teachings, the disciple attained the unprecedented realisation of the self. He experienced his pure nature. Without understanding this true nature, he underwent infinite suffering in the past. Understanding the self brought him closer to the shore from the ocean of

worldly existence. This is solely the result of the Guru's infinite grace. For the disciple, the Guru is the supreme power. This power may be called *Brahmā, Vishnu, Mahesh* or supreme soul, they are all encompassed within the Guru. To value the Guru any less than this, is to delude oneself. The disciple has realised His value. Even if offered the entire world in exchange for his Guru, he would decline, considering it dirt in comparison. Not even the pleasures of heaven can compare to the Guru. His devotion is to such an extent that he does not even want the joy of liberation in exchange for his Guru. He will always remain indebted to Him. In this verse, the disciple commits everything in service of his Guru.

Experiencing the Guru's boundless benevolence, inspired by the feeling of surrender, the disciple declares, 'From today, from this moment, I offer this body, etc., to You.' The mind-speech-body and all other possessions in the world, that are deemed his, will be utilised as per the Guru's commands. Until now, he employed his body, senses and mind towards material enjoyment. Now, he promises that he will employ them to follow His commands. The usage of body, mind and wealth has been transformed. The disciple vows to dwell at the lotus feet dedicating everything that is called his own, in the service of the Guru. His readiness is indicated by the word '*ājthī*' - from today. So eager is he to do it right away, without the delay of even a single moment. He is filled with intense yearning. Not even allowing a moment to be wasted, he resolves to act as per the Guru's commands from now itself. His body and breath will engage in following the Guru's instructions.

The disciple commits to remain a humble servant, obeying the Guru's commands. The word '*dās*' - servant, has been used three times in the second line of this verse. The purpose behind doing so can be interpreted in two ways. The first meaning is that the disciple is accepting servitude in three ways, through mind, speech and body. He will harbour thoughts, speak words and use the body in accordance with the Guru's commands. His behaviour will be completely aligned to Him. He is prepared to single-pointedly follow His guidance. All three energies will act as the Guru's servants. The second meaning is that of the many servants of the Guru, I am the lowliest servant - that is, 'I am a servant of the servant of Your servant. This lowly soul has nothing more than this to offer at Your lotus feet.'

In this manner, the disciple accepts his lowliness and gives up his ego. The feeling of lowliness expressed here is not one of helplessness or compulsion, rather it is the humility that has arisen from the realisation of the Guru's greatness and his own insignificance. It has not been conveyed as a norm or custom but as the natural outcome of the disciple's humility and modesty. It indicates the departure of his ego. His pride has totally melted and his vanity has worn out. The utmost devotion flows from his inner self.

Thus, the entire life of the disciple has been transformed. Everything about him has taken on a new appearance. Like a caterpillar emerging from the cocoon, the disciple emerges, spreading his wings, knowing he is finally a butterfly, and can fly. Central to this transformation, crucial to this process has been the Guru. He is aware of the immense role the Guru has played in his metamorphosis. The disciple is swift to render gratitude emanating from the very core of his being. He dedicates his life and all his endeavours to his benevolent Guru.

———⌇———

VERSE - 127

Guru's benevolence is immeasurable

Again and again, reminiscing the boundless, wondrous, divine grace of the Guru, his heart overflows with reverence. Expressing the nature of the Guru's benevolence, in the concluding verse of this section, the worthy disciple says -

ષટ્ સ્થાનક સમજાવીને, ભિન્ન બતાવ્યો આપ;
મ્યાન થકી તરવારવત્, એ ઉપકાર અમાપ. ||૧૨૭||

Shat sthānak samjāvine, bhinna batāvyo Āp;
Myān thaki tarvārvat, ae upkār amāp. ||127||

Shat - six; **sthānak** - aphorisms; **samjāvine** - explaining; **bhinna** - separate; **batāvyo** - shown; **Āp** - You; **myān** - sheath; **thaki** - from; **tarvārvat** - like sword; **ae** - that; **upkār** - benevolence; **amāp** - immeasurable

MEANING
By Your convincing teachings regarding the six fundamental truths, You have revealed to me the nature of my self, as distinct and different from the body as the sword from the sheath. This is Your immeasurable favour to me.

EXPLANATION
The disciple expressed his unwavering faith, devotion, respect and dedicated his all at the lotus feet of the benevolent Guru. Experiencing the benefaction bestowed upon him, the disciple is overwhelmed. His ecstasy is at its peak, the flow of

thought incessant as he recounts the showers of grace he has experienced. The most crucial has been the transformation in his attitude. An attitude that influences all activities, whose fragrance permeates all areas of life. An attitude of self-awareness. In this verse, the disciple narrates how grateful he is to the Guru for making him understand and experience the soul, which is separate from the body.

The disciple says that the six fundamental truths of the soul were explained by the Guru - 'soul exists', 'soul is eternal', 'soul is the doer of karma', 'soul is the receiver of the fruits of karma', 'there is liberation' and 'there is a path of liberation'. The Guru dispelled all doubts regarding these six fundamentals and elucidated them appropriately. He expounded them clearly from different viewpoints and showed the nature, sign, etc., of the animate and the inanimate. He ensured that right conviction was established regarding the soul, which is worthy of embracing.

The Guru bestowed supreme benevolence upon the worthy disciple by describing the soul to be different from the body. He enabled the disciple to experience his soul separate from the body just like the sword is separate from the sheath. A sheath, hanging from the waist of a king, even if made of gold and studded with jewels, is of no value in a war. It is merely a decorative piece. The sharp-edged blade of the sword, even though made of steel, is most important and useful in a war. The sheath is visible but the sword inside is not. Similarly, the body is visible and can be perceived by the eyes. The soul is not visible and cannot be perceived by the eyes. It does not matter whether the body is fat or thin, tall or short, beautiful or ugly, male or female - ultimately it is reduced to ashes. The soul is pure, peaceful, blissful consciousness and is immortal. The Guru not only clearly explained the distinctness, with His grace, the disciple also had a direct experience of the soul.

Until now, the disciple struggled with illusory beliefs, being entrapped in a state of ignorance. The Guru opened his eyes, cleared his vision, dispelled all ignorance and thus, kindled enlightenment in him. Due to the unprecedented teachings of the Guru, the disciple, who was steeped in the darkness of ignorance since time immemorial, stepped into the radiant realm of consciousness. The luminous sun of self-realisation dawned and the conviction of his own independent, blissful nature was established. Through the right guidance and inspiration, the Guru enabled the disciple to enter the pious path of the supreme truth, gave him the strength to manifest the unparalleled virtues and made him the master of eternal bliss.

Indeed, the Guru's benefaction is immeasurable. The Guru is the bestower of self-realisation, which is like the wish-fulfilling tree, nectar-like, supremely beneficial, and a definite annihilator of all suffering. Therefore, His benevolence is truly immense and limitless. The disciple is forever indebted to the Guru for this immeasurable obligation. Thus, concludes the disciple's joyful expression of his enlightenment and the heart-touching acknowledgement of the Guru's benevolence.

Conclusion

Having bestowed the gift of the most outstanding verses, which illustrate an unparalleled devotion towards the Guru, the supreme benefactor of the soul, Shrimadji now proceeds towards the end of Shri Ātmasiddhi Shāstra. He completes this extraordinary scripture with a grand 15-verse *Upsamhār* - Conclusion. Just as each section of this scripture is uniquely special, so is the conclusion.

It contains such divine depth that it can serve as an independent scripture by itself. Every sentence, every word of an enlightened one is filled with infinite scriptures - the truth of this statement is evidently understood here. A seeker, eager to pursue his own spiritual welfare, can determine what is beneficial and harmful to him based on this concluding section.

Deep insights pertaining to spiritual principles and practices are skilfully woven into this section and have been simply explained in a style that is comprehendible to all. As the text progresses, the fabric and style of its exposition proves more and more profound. Weighty subjects have been elucidated in such an accessible manner that they effortlessly penetrate within.

This section can be divided into two main parts. Verses 128-136 chart out the pitfalls on the spiritual path, thus cautioning the seeker of their peril and the need to steer clear of them. Verses 137-142 depict the state of the enlightened ones and worthy aspirants. Shrimadji culminates the scripture with heartfelt obeisance to the enlightened one.

VERSE - 128

Doubtless conviction on contemplation

In verse 42, Shrimadji had said that He would state the six fundamentals of the soul in the form of a dialogue between a Guru and a disciple, so that the path of liberation could be understood. Furthermore, in verse 44, He had stated that the purposeful spiritual discussion of the six schools of philosophy is encompassed within these six fundamentals. In accordance with that, through the dialogue between the Guru and the disciple, Shrimadji expounded the six fundamental truths which pervade the six schools of philosophy. Now concluding this subject, Shrimadji says -

દર્શન ષટે સમાય છે, આ ષટ્ સ્થાનક માંહી;
વિચારતાં વિસ્તારથી, સંશય રહે ન કાંઈ. ||૧૨૮||

Darshan shatey samāy chhe, ā shat sthānak māhi;
Vichārtā vistārthi, sanshay rahey na kāi. ||128||

Darshan - philosophy; **shatey** - all six; **samāy** - included; **chhe** - are; **ā** - this; **shat** - six; **sthānak** - aphorisms; **māhi** - in; **vichārtā** - on contemplation; **vistārthi** - at length; **sanshay** - doubt; **rahey** - remains; **na** - not; **kāi** - any

MEANING
All the six schools of philosophy are encompassed in these six fundamental truths. No doubt can remain if one contemplates them in detail.

EXPLANATION

In order to eliminate ignorance regarding the self, various means have been propounded by many philosophers in different places and at varied times. Based on these, six main philosophies came into existence in India - *Chārvāk, Jainism, Buddhism, Nyāy-Vaisheshik, Sānkhya-Yog* and *Purva Mimānsā-Uttar Mimānsā*. All the thoughts expounded in these six philosophies regarding the soul are encompassed within the six fundamental truths. The teachings of the six schools of thought are covered by the six fundamentals of the soul, which have been enumerated, established and explained in this scripture. One who deeply studies these six aphorisms will not fail to find the principles of all six embedded in them. To the discerning eye, it seems that the six tenets actually embody the six major Indian philosophies.

Those who hold on to a one-sided view become stuck in their beliefs. This results in flaws in their expositions, which had been skilfully presented by Shrimadji as the disciple's doubts. Based on the opinions of various philosophies on subjects like the soul's existence, eternal nature, etc., several doubts were raised by the disciple. Using a conciliatory approach and giving appropriate solutions, the Guru clarified them.

Shrimadji has simply stated the truth without condemning any philosophy. In advertisements, it is sometimes seen that the positive aspects of their own products are shown and other products are criticised. Shrimadji has discussed the six fundamental truths without criticising any philosophy, not even naming them while stating their beliefs. He has explained how the concepts of various philosophies can be accepted through different perspectives. He has thus demonstrated that all philosophies are correct from a certain viewpoint.

Such is the amazing, distinctive style in which Shrimadji has propounded the six fundamentals. He has succinctly put together the diverse and often extremely complex thoughts that govern Indian philosophies. He has elucidated the truth using the method of non-absolutism. The principle of non-absolutism minutely examines and depicts reality from various viewpoints. The doctrine of multiplicity of viewpoints is accommodative. Just as an ocean has the capacity to absorb water emptied into it by several rivers, the theory of multiplicity of viewpoints absorbs all one-sided viewpoints within itself. This is its immense magnitude.

Using this approach, Shrimadji has conveyed a clear understanding of the six fundamentals in Shri Ātmasiddhi Shāstra. The more one thinks about them, the easier it becomes to discard doubts regarding them. If these six fundamentals are contemplated at length, it is a certainty that no doubt will remain regarding the nature of the soul. To be doubtless regarding the six fundamental truths itself is *samkit* - right faith, as one believes the nature of the soul as it truly is. Thus, through these six fundamental truths, Shrimadji has imparted the technique required to swim across the ocean of birth and death to the eternal shore of liberation.

VERSE - 129

Remedy of spiritual ailment

In this verse, Shrimadji describes the disease of self-delusion and its remedy. He has beautifully portrayed this through the analogy of treating a disease. Shrimadji says -

આત્મભ્રાંતિ સમ રોગ નહિ, સદ્ગુરુ વૈદ્ય સુજાણ;
ગુરુ આજ્ઞા સમ પથ્ય નહિ, ઔષધ વિચાર ધ્યાન. ||૧૨૯||

Ātmabhrānti sam rog nahi, Sadguru vaidya sujān;
Guru ājnā sam pathya nahi, aushadh vichār dhyān. ||*129*||

Ātmabhrānti - self-delusion; *sam* - like; *rog* - illness; *nahi* - no; *Sadguru* - enlightened Mentor; *vaidya* - physician; *sujān* - expert; *Guru* - Mentor; *ājnā* - commands; *sam* - like; *pathya* - dietary restrictions; *nahi* - no; *aushadh* - medicine; *vichār* - contemplation; *dhyān* - meditation

MEANING

There is no disease like self-delusion. An enlightened Mentor is an expert physician capable of curing this disease. There is no regimen like the instructions of the Guru. The only medicine is contemplation and meditation upon the true self.

EXPLANATION

When the body is fraught with illness, it becomes weak, and one experiences pain and frailty. Similarly, the soul is also plagued with disease which renders it weak and distressed. It is obvious that one wishes good health for himself and not malady, hence the disease needs to be diagnosed and cured. This process of treatment has been wonderfully explained in this verse through four aspects.

'*Ātmabhrānti sam rog nahi*' - The first aspect is the identification of the disease. The biggest disease of the soul is self-delusion. To forget one's own nature and identify with the non-self is self-delusion. It is characterised by the behaviour in which one cannot distinguish between the self and the non-self, and believes himself to be the body. False belief of the self is the worst disease one can endure. There is absolutely no greater disease than this. It is the root of all types of suffering. The soul has been affected by this disease since time immemorial. It is because of self-delusion that the soul has to undergo the cycles of birth and death in the world.

'*Sadguru vaidya sujān*' - Although the disease of self-delusion is grave, it can be eradicated by the right remedy. The only physician capable of curing this disease is the Sadguru. Just as a proficient physician is needed to cure a bodily ailment, a Sadguru is needed to cure a spiritual ailment. If one takes refuge in an inexperienced, untrue Guru, this extremely deadly disease is likely to go out of control. Therefore, one must search for a Sadguru who can accurately cure the disease of wrong belief and bestow spiritual health. The Sadguru is well acquainted with the dreadful disease of self-delusion and its cure. This expertise has not been obtained just from books, but by diving deep within. He has not learnt merely by reading scriptures, but has experimented and experienced the truth

Himself. Therefore, there is no shortcoming in His advice and instructions. He is the most reliable physician for the disease. Only such an experienced proficient Sadguru can free souls from this grave disease.

'*Guru ājnā sam pathya nahi*' - Despite being aware of the illness and finding a physician who can cure it, the disease does not stop increasing unless the patient follows the necessary restrictions. The treatment of a disease requires a wholesome diet as well as proper medication. Both have to be administered in a balanced way. Following the prescribed dietary restrictions prevents the disease from worsening and taking the medicine eliminates the disease from its root. If one takes the medicine but does not control the diet, his illness will not be cured. If one only regulates his diet but does not take the medicine, his illness will not be uprooted. Thus, it is necessary for one who wishes to cure the disease of self-delusion, to follow the prescribed regimen - the Guru's commands. Completely accepting everything that has been approved by the Guru, refraining from whatever He has negated, and acting as per His guidance is the regimen. There should be faithful obedience to the instructions of the Guru. One must have the firm resolve to follow His directions. If one is not willing to act according to the commands of the Guru and behaves of his own volition, the disease cannot be eliminated. Hence, it is said that there is no other regimen equivalent to following the Guru's commands. By practising this, the disease of self-delusion comes under control and by taking the medicine it is wholly eradicated.

'**Aushadh vichār dhyān**' - Shrimadji has stated that the medicine for this disease is contemplation and meditation. Contemplation is effortful right thinking, whereas meditation is the effortless state of witnessing. Contemplation detaches one from the world, whereas meditation attaches him to the pure self. Contemplation is engaging in thought, whereas meditation is advancing towards the state beyond thought. Shrimadji's prescription is clear - intense inner contemplation and meditation through which one can discover the truth of his self, by himself, through silence and stillness. Only then can one, who is lost in the turmoil and trauma of the material world, find himself. Once he has found himself, he is the master of his soul and consequently, his fate. Thus, one who hears about the nature of the soul from the Guru, contemplates on it and delves into meditation, finds his disease of self-delusion eliminated.

To summarise, no disease is as deadly as self-delusion. The living Sadguru is the only expert physician who can cure this disease. The regimen to observe is the wholehearted acceptance and execution of the Guru's commands. The medicine is contemplation and meditation. Through the analogy of treating a disease, Shrimadji has explained the remedy to eradicate the ailment of the soul.

VERSE - 130

Strive hard for supreme goal

In this concluding section, Shrimadji has composed several profound verses to iterate the grave flaws one commits, that render him incapable of curing the disease of self-delusion. So that a worthy soul can reflect upon them and make the necessary effort to eradicate them.

In the first counsel among a series of beneficial teachings given in this concluding section, inspiring one to put in the right effort, Shrimadji says -

જો ઇચ્છો પરમાર્થ તો, કરો સત્ય પુરુષાર્થ;
ભવસ્થિતિ આદિ નામ લઈ, છેદો નહિ આત્માર્થ. ॥૧૩૦॥

Jo iccho parmārth toh, karo satya purushārth;
Bhavsthiti ādi nām lai, chhedo nahi ātmārth. ||130||

Jo - if; *iccho* - wish; *parmārth* - supreme truth; *toh* - then; *karo* - do; *satya* - true; *purushārth* - effort; *bhavsthiti* - destiny; *ādi* - etc.; *nām* - name; *lai* - taking; *chhedo* - destroy; *nahi* - not; *ātmārth* - spiritual welfare

MEANING

If you desire to attain the supreme goal of liberation, then put in the right effort. Do not block your spiritual progress by using excuses such as time, fate, destiny, etc.

EXPLANATION

Using motivational words of wisdom, Shrimadji makes it clear that if there is a true desire to attain the supreme truth, then there has to be a proper effort to achieve it. The soul has infinite power and one is capable of freeing himself from bondage. He himself has to awaken and ensure spiritual welfare through effort. No one else's effort is responsible for accomplishing this goal. One certainly needs to take inspiration and guidance from the Sadguru, but ultimately has to put in the effort himself. If he sincerely aspires for spiritual welfare, he must engage in the right effort.

One needs to have a correct understanding of the right effort. Mere physical rituals and scriptural study do not comprise true effort. Cultivating awareness of the self is true effort. One who possesses a strong yearning for spiritual welfare must comprehend the nature of the soul from an enlightened one, realise its unfathomable glory, and repeatedly focus all his energy towards it through practice. When the awareness becomes steady in the conscious nature, it experiences bliss beyond thoughts and senses.

Those who do not wish to put in the effort, produce a variety of excuses. The main among these is '*bhavsthiti*'. It means the number of births one is destined to take to attain liberation. When the time is ripe, he will be liberated. If this is not interpreted properly, one abandons effort, and there remains no possibility of attaining the supreme truth. Every effect has five *samvāy kāran* - causal factors:

1. *Kāl* - The time period taken for the effect to materialise. E.g. time between conception and delivery of a baby.

2. *Swabhāv* - The nature of the substance to produce the effect. E.g. only a male body grows a moustache.

3. *Bhavitavyatā* - The effect will happen according to destiny. E.g. in a mango tree, some flowers perish, whereas some grow into mango fruits.

4. *Karma* - The effect is generated according to past efforts. E.g. a dim-witted person becoming a billionaire.

5. *Purushārth* - Effort needs to be undertaken to obtain the desired effect. E.g. effort of crushing sesame seeds to extract oil.

The combination of these five causal factors brings about the effect. Therefore, one should not disregard or negate any cause. In fact, effort is of prime importance, because it is the only cause which one has control over. One should not forsake effort by overglorifying other causes.

One who is not truly desirous of attaining the supreme truth, misinterprets the principles, does not put in any effort, and remains bereft of spiritual benefit. He brings to the forefront reasons like the impossibility of attaining liberation in the fifth era, the absence of *Tirthankars*, the rarity of enlightened ones, unavailability of conducive atmosphere, the power of karma, etc., and thus prevents his spiritual welfare.

Behind all these excuses lies the absence of a strong desire for liberation. If an intense desire to be liberated existed, there would be no room for excuses and one would enthusiastically engage in the right effort. As the well-known maxim goes, 'Where there is a will, there is a way'. No effort is wasted, all endeavours are rewarded on the spiritual path. Therefore, in this verse, Shrimadji encourages one to make the right effort. A firm determination is all one needs to strive for liberation. This invaluable human birth should not go in vain by giving excuses and discarding effort.

VERSE - 131

Attain goal with right balance

Having given clear guidance to those who are bereft of right effort in verse 130, now in verses 131-134, Shrimadji points out the flaw in harbouring one-sided beliefs. He states that only an outlook which integrates the absolute and relative viewpoints will be beneficial on the path of liberation.

This verse is addressed to those who one-sidedly adopt the absolute viewpoint and have turned away from the path of liberation. The guidance to steer them towards the path has been given here. Shrimadji says -

નિશ્ચયવાણી સાંભળી, સાધન તજવાં નો'ય;
નિશ્ચય રાખી લક્ષમાં, સાધન કરવાં સોય. ||૧૩૧||

Nishchayvāni sāmbhli, sādhan tajvā no'i;
Nishchay rākhi lakshmā, sādhan karvā soi. ||131||

Nishchayvāni - speech from absolute viewpoint; *sāmbhli* - listening; *sādhan* - means; *tajvā* - leave; *no'i* - not; *nishchay* - absolute viewpoint; *rākhi* - keeping; *lakshmā* - in focus; *sādhan* - means; *karvā* - do; *soi* - that

MEANING
Upon listening to the statements regarding the self from the absolute viewpoint, one should not give up the means of attaining it. The means should be pursued, keeping the absolute viewpoint in mind.

EXPLANATION

It is necessary to understand the truth from multiple viewpoints in order to not misinterpret the scriptures. Without the correct understanding of the absolute and relative viewpoints, one holds on to only one of them and goes astray from the path, moving further and further away from the destination. Therefore, one treading the path of liberation should exercise utmost caution that he does not lose his direction.

In this verse, striking a beautiful balance, Shrimadji says that listening to statements made from the absolute viewpoint such as, 'the soul is unbound, it is completely pure' should not make one give up the practices which aid the attainment of the supreme truth. It is by focusing on the pure nature of the self and engaging in spiritual practices that this goal is accomplished. Awareness of the true self, and appropriate conduct together are capable of yielding liberation. One practised without the other cannot destroy delusion. Both are essential.

Dry intellectualists adopt the absolute viewpoint only in words. They speak of the absolute truth but fail to imbibe its essence. Moreover, they negate practices which are helpful in attaining the supreme truth, such as lifelong vows, short-term disciplines, restraint, renunciation, detachment, devotion, etc. They insist that the soul is pure, without even an iota of blemish, and so there is no need for any of these practices. They believe these practices generate auspicious feelings, which lead to bondage. Due to a lack of discernment, they are devoid of proper conduct and nurture self-will. They act in an unrestrained manner under the influence of delusion. By believing that the soul cannot be defiled through their actions, they indulge in the non-self and become irreligious, even immoral at times. Disregarding right conduct, they deprive themselves of the right effort required to manifest the inherent purity of the soul, and thus increase their transmigration.

Impractical theorists believe themselves to be pure and unbound. Though this is true from the absolute viewpoint, it is equally true that from the relative viewpoint, their present state is impure with bondage. The soul is in an embodied state, with karma, engaging in impure feelings. It is yet to manifest its pure nature. The state needs to be purified by the right means. In order to eliminate impurity, spiritual practices must be undertaken with the aim of the absolute. Just as one aims to reach a particular town and then drives in that direction, so also with the aim of attaining the absolute, one must engage in the right practices. One can leave the vehicle once the destination has arrived, not before that. Similarly, one can let go of the means once the goal has been accomplished. However, he cannot afford to discard spiritual practices before this, as abandonment will definitely prove detrimental.

Earlier in Shri Ātmasiddhi Shāstra, while describing the traits of dry intellectualists, Shrimadji had shown the flaws in their belief and behaviour. In this verse, He has compassionately explained how one can eliminate these flaws and put in the right effort to attain liberation. He advocates adopting spiritual practices propounded by the omniscient ones, instead of forsaking them by simply hearing the statements of absolute viewpoint. The absolute truth that has been revealed must be recognised and respected. It is like the pole star, a constant reminder of the goal. However, merely being attracted to the destination is not enough. Persistent, painstaking effort is required. It is only with ceaseless action, consistent practice and steadfast adherence that one reaches the ultimate goal. In this way, integration of the absolute viewpoint  and spiritual practices leads to the attainment of liberation.

VERSE - 132

Integrating both viewpoints

The path of liberation is the combination of the awareness of the pure self and right conduct. However, it is often observed that seekers are unable to maintain a balance of both and hence, cannot progress on the path of liberation. In order to emphasise that the goal of liberation cannot be accomplished by pursuing it with a one-sided approach, in this verse Shrimadji says -

નય નિશ્ચય એકાંતથી, આમાં નથી કહેલ;
એકાંતે વ્યવહાર નહિ, બન્ને સાથ રહેલ. ||૧૩૨||

Nay nishchay ekāntthi, āmā nathi kahel;
Ekānte vyavhār nahi, banne sāth rahel. ||132||

Nay - viewpoint; *nishchay* - absolute; *ekāntthi* - one-sidedly; *āmā* - here; *nathi* - not; *kahel* - stated; *ekānte* - one-sidedly; *vyavhār* - relative viewpoint; *nahi* - not; *banne* - both; *sāth* - together; *rahel* - present

MEANING
Here, in this scripture, the account has not been given from the one-sided view of the absolute standpoint or the one-sided view of the relative standpoint. The harmony of both the standpoints has been kept in view.

EXPLANATION
The nature of an object can be known by *naya* and *pramān*. Naya means viewpoint and pramān means the whole truth.

Naya is a part of the pramān, therefore both the absolute and relative viewpoints are two parts of the whole truth. Although both are completely powerful in their own place, they are only partial truths themselves and not the entire truth. Therefore, the complete nature of a substance cannot be understood without considering both views.

In practical life, it is said that this is a pot of water. However, the pot is of clay, containing water. Similarly, it is said that he is human. From the absolute viewpoint, he is a pure, free, unblemished soul. From the relative viewpoint, he is impure, embodied and bound by karma. He is the doer of karma and the receiver of its fruits. Thus, the nature of the soul needs to be understood from both viewpoints.

Since it is impossible to explain the nature of the soul from both viewpoints simultaneously, the enlightened ones use one viewpoint at a time. However, the other viewpoint is not negated, it is silent at that time. When one churns buttermilk in a pot to make butter, he uses a rope which goes back and forth. The two ends of the rope are like the two viewpoints. Although both are needed to understand the truth, but any one viewpoint can be used at a time. One is emphasised, the other is subordinated as per the purpose and requirement.

The nature of the soul is pure, non-attached, consciousness, knowingness - this is the subject matter of the absolute viewpoint. To attain purity, spiritual practices like scriptural study, devotion, vows, austerities, etc., are required - this is the subject matter of the relative viewpoint. Just as the two tracks of a railway line never meet, yet the train only moves with the support of both, the train of spiritual pursuit too advances with the help of both tracks, the absolute and the relative viewpoints.

A true seeker must understand the soul from both viewpoints and make an effort to manifest the pure nature, because one-sidedly adopting one of the two viewpoints only causes one to stray from the path. As both viewpoints are equally beneficial in their rightful place, one must not insist on any one viewpoint. Only one viewpoint will not be of any help. If either viewpoint is ignored, it proves harmful to the seeker on his spiritual journey.

To clearly show the importance of integrating the absolute and relative viewpoints, Shrimadji says that Shri Ātmasiddhi Shāstra does not one-sidedly state either of them. This scripture propounds both views appropriately. Neither does it speak solely of the viewpoint which indicates the eternal pure nature, nor does it speak solely of the viewpoint which indicates the present impure state. Each has been presented in the appropriate manner as needed, without contradicting the other. Shrimadji's heart overflowed with compassion on seeing the sorry state of those insisting on one-sided views. Therefore, He has tied up concepts from both the viewpoints so that an aspirant can understand the truth.

A true seeker will be able to appreciate the wonderful balance that Shrimadji has maintained between the ideal and the practical. He has painted a vivid picture of the ultimate reality, holding up an idyllic image of the perfect nature and giving the seeker succinct and simple steps to achieve it. Shrimadji strides both viewpoints,  illustrating how fluidly the movement can be made from one to the other.

VERSE - 133

Essence of spiritual pursuit

Describing those who wrongly adopt the relative viewpoint and those who are deluded regarding the absolute viewpoint, Shrimadji says -

ગચ્છમતની જે કલ્પના, તે નહિ સદ્વ્યવહાર;
ભાન નહીં નિજરૂપનું, તે નિશ્ચય નહિ સાર. ॥૧૩૩॥

Gacchmatni je kalpanā, te nahi sadvyavhār;
Bhān nahi nijroopnu, te nishchay nahi sār. ॥133॥

Gacchmatni - of sect and creed; **je** - those; **kalpanā** - imagined distinctions; **te** - that; **nahi** - not; **sadvyavhār** - right conduct; **bhān** - focus; **nahi** - not; **nijroopnu** - of own self; **te** - that; **nishchay** - absolute viewpoint; **nahi** - not; **sār** - beneficial

MEANING

Sectarian views and imaginary opinions of religious orders do not constitute the right practice. In the same way, where there is no awareness of one's pure self, the knowledge from the absolute standpoint is futile.

EXPLANATION

The deluded ones fail to understand that the path of liberation is a combination of the absolute and relative viewpoints. Some cling to the relative viewpoint and get stuck in the outer acts prescribed by their sect. While others cling to the absolute viewpoint without awareness of the true self. The verse depicts how both are mistaken.

The desire to divide, differentiate and distinguish drives humanity towards conflict. This desire has not even spared the religious realm, with so many divisions observed amongst religious people. Such separation and segregation weakens people. Feelings of competition and superiority build barriers instead of bonds. Only when the unity in diversity is perceived, can the mind anchor itself. When the truth is perceived with clarity and lucidity, all differences merge, all distinctions harmonise, all diversities collapse.

In the absence of a unifying approach, one tends to believe that only the concepts and customs of his sect and creed are the right conduct. He harbours attachment and insistence in the name of religion. He develops bitterness towards others due to the difference of opinions between various sects and creeds. He criticises and condemns them, creating animosity. These imaginary beliefs regarding one's sect and creed can never lead to even the slightest benefit to the soul. Stubbornly sticking to ideas does not help one move even an inch closer to liberation. Therefore, it cannot be considered right conduct. In contrast, any practice which helps overcome attachment and aversion is right conduct.

Similarly, developing awareness of the true self is the right adoption of the absolute viewpoint. Mere verbal statements or discussions about the absolute truth without a focus on the true self are meaningless. Simply speaking about the absolute viewpoint amounts to hollow words, and is a barren endeavour. It cannot bear fruit on the path of liberation. Parroting the metaphysical truths of the soul cannot help.

The ultimate goal of resorting to the absolute viewpoint is experiencing the true self. However, even after reading many scriptures, if one cannot focus within, he has not achieved the true result of his studies. His identification with the body, strong attachment to sensual pleasures and self-willed behaviour remain intact. He speaks of the soul being pure, but indulges in impure feelings. He does not even cultivate virtues like compassion, reduction of passions, etc. He may not even be moral or ethical, let alone spiritual. Therefore, the practice of renunciation, detachment, devotion, etc., is also necessary to get rid of impurities, enabling a steady focus on the self.

Thus, the first line of this verse describes what cannot be considered right conduct. The second line iterates that barren knowledge of the absolute viewpoint is also not beneficial. Through this, Shrimadji has emphasised that practising right conduct with the aim of attaining the absolute truth, is the path of liberation. Contemplating upon the self, based on the Sadguru's teachings, and engaging in rituals to cultivate virtues is the right pursuit of liberation.

VERSE - 134

The path in all times

Shedding light on the path of supreme truth, Shrimadji says -

આગળ જ્ઞાની થઈ ગયા, વર્તમાનમાં હોય;
થાશે કાળ ભવિષ્યમાં, માર્ગભેદ નહિ કોય. ||૧૩૪||

Āgal Jnāni thai gayā, vartmānmā hoi;
Thāshe kāl bhavishyamā, mārgbhed nahi koi. ||134||

Āgal - in past; *Jnāni* - enlightened ones; *thai gayā* - have been;
vartmānmā - in present; *hoi* - are; *thāshe* - will be; *kāl* - times;
bhavishyamā - in future; *mārgbhed* - difference in path; *nahi* - not;
koi - any

MEANING

All the enlightened ones of the past, present and future
have attained, do attain and will attain liberation in the same
way; there is no difference in the path. It is definite and
undisputable in all three periods of time.

EXPLANATION

The self is of the nature of pure consciousness, separate
from the body. Until this belief is firmly established within,
there is always a possibility of ego and attachment arising,
even in one's religious activities. Such religious activities do
not result in the annihilation of transmigration. The seeker
can only attain the inner treasures if he directs his focus from

the karma-created personality towards the pure nature of the self. Remaining fastened to external religious activities and refraining from turning towards the self will not accomplish the goal.

Similarly, without the awareness of separateness between the self and the non-self, and without engaging in practices which aid this awareness, simply uttering lofty statements of the absolute viewpoint will also not accomplish the goal. It can only be accomplished by focusing on the pure nature of the self, and by practising the means that have been prescribed to attain it. Thus, it is only by pursuing the path of liberation through the right integration of both the absolute and relative viewpoints that infinite souls have attained enlightenment in the past, are attaining it in the present, and will attain it in the future.

In this verse, it is said that the enlightened ones are present in every period of time. The enlightened Masters were there in the past, are here in the present, and will be there in the future as well. These souls attain liberation in the same way, regardless of the time period. It is unchangeable in the past, present and future. The enlightened ones prescribe different remedies based on seekers' flaws, time period, place, etc. However, they all lead to the same outcome. In spirit, there is no difference regarding the path of liberation. It is one, definite and undisputable at all times.

There are many wrong paths, but only one right path, in all periods of time. This is the path of realising the true self and abiding in it. All the enlightened ones have attained the supreme truth only in this way, and have indicated the same path for everyone. The path of liberation is not changeable, it is eternally constant over all eras.

As one turns the pages of history, he will realise that every civilisation has stood on the shoulders of great souls. They have founded schools of thought, established methods of thinking, and created unique ways to attain the truth. Despite this, the absolute path to liberation has been the same at all times and in all places. They felt compassion and concern for deluded souls and led them towards spiritual growth with clarity and simplicity. Their lives were a testament to their teachings. They are not torchbearers, but the light itself. To even live in their shadow is to be truly blessed.

———— ∽০৯০ ————

VERSE - 135

Two causes of liberation

From verses 131-134, Shrimadji demonstrated that the path of supreme truth is the integration of the absolute and relative viewpoints. He pointed out a significant fact that there is no spiritual benefit in holding on to one-sided beliefs. Now, in verses 135-136, He states that the path of liberation is the acceptance of both the principal and instrumental causes. Shrimadji says -

સર્વ જીવ છે સિદ્ધ સમ, જે સમજે તે થાય;
સદ્ગુરુઆજ્ઞા જિનદશા, નિમિત્ત કારણ માંય. ||૧૩૫||

Sarva jeev chhe Siddh sam, je samje te thāy;
Sadguruājnā Jindashā, nimit kāran māy. ||135||

Sarva - all; *jeev* - souls; *chhe* - are; *Siddh* - liberated; *sam* - like; *je* - who; *samje* - understands; *te* - he; *thāy* - attains; *Sadguruājnā* - commands of enlightened Mentor; *Jindashā* - state of omniscient one; *nimit* - instrumental; *kāran* - causes; *māy* - are

MEANING
All souls by nature are like the liberated ones. The one who realises this fact becomes liberated. The commands of a true Guru and the pure state of the omniscient ones are the instrumental causes of this.

EXPLANATION
It is a universally accepted truth that every effect has a cause. No effect can occur without its corresponding cause.

These causes are of two kinds - a principal cause called *upādān* and instrumental cause called *nimit*. The substance which undergoes a modification to produce the effect is the principal cause. The means which aid this modification is the instrumental cause. For instance, in the creation of a pot, clay is the principal cause because clay itself modifies as the pot. It is the material cause. The potter, wheel, stick, etc., are the instrumental causes because they aid the process of modification of the clay into the pot. A pot can neither be created without clay, nor without the potter or wheel. This proves the necessity of both causes. It applies to the attainment of liberation as well. This verse indicates the principal and instrumental causes for liberation.

Elucidating the principal cause, Shrimadji says that all beings in the world are the same as the liberated Lords, in terms of potential. The liberated ones possess infinite knowledge, infinite perception, infinite bliss and infinite vigour in the manifested form. Whereas other souls have them in the form of potential, although unmanifested. One who experiences his pure self and makes the effort to abide in it, attains the state of liberation. The understanding that 'my true nature is the same as that of the liberated ones' and remaining steadfast in this awareness leads to the manifestation of the potential, which is liberation itself.

To achieve such a lofty pursuit, powerful instrumental causes are necessary. Although the unblemished, unbound nature is within, it needs to be awakened, requiring the support of instrumental causes. Adherence to the Sadguru's *ājnā* and contemplation upon the state of the omniscient ones are helpful in manifesting one's pure nature. Both factors are strong instrumental causes in making the right effort.

One needs to surrender at the lotus feet of the Sadguru and follow His commands. The Sadguru is the guide who steers the seeker in the right direction and warns him of the pitfalls along the way. The seeker should learn to place his faith in Him. Abandoning attachment to worldly objects and pursuits, he should conduct himself according to the Sadguru's ājñā. Adhering to His commands by giving up self-willed behaviour and indolence, the seeker accomplishes his goal. Likewise, contemplating upon the state of the omniscient Lords with inner zeal is helpful in realising the self. Although all souls are like the liberated ones, the seeker does not worship all souls. He worships the *Jinas*, and not other souls as they have not yet manifested their true nature. Their modifications are impure whereas the modifications of the Jinas are pure. They are reservoirs of infinite bliss and peace. Reflecting on the flawless state, the seeker cultivates awareness of his own self and abides in it.

Thus, the first line of this verse illustrates the potential of the principal cause of liberation and how this infinite power can be manifested. The second line highlights two strong instrumental causes to manifest this potential and inspires one to take their support.

VERSE - 136

Forsaking one cause is fatal

Explaining what fate awaits those who adopt only the principal cause and disregard the contribution of the instrumental causes, Shrimadji says -

ઉપાદાનનું નામ લઈ, એ જે તજે નિમિત્ત;
પામે નહિ સિદ્ધત્વને, રહે ભ્રાંતિમાં સ્થિત. ||૧૩૬||

Upādānnu nām lai, ae je taje nimit;
Pāmey nahi siddhatvane, rahey bhrāntimā sthit. ||*136*||

Upādānnu - principal cause; *nām* - name; *lai* - taking; *ae* - he; *je* - who; *taje* - forsakes; *nimit* - instrumental cause; *pāmey* - attains; *nahi* - not; *siddhatvane* - liberation; *rahey* - remains; *bhrāntimā* - in delusion; *sthit* - established

MEANING

Putting forward the principal cause, one who abandons the instrumental cause does not attain liberation, remaining entangled in delusion.

EXPLANATION

The potential of a substance to change from one form to another is called *'upādān'*. The instrumental cause which activates this potential is called *'nimit'*. For liberation, the soul itself is the upādān. The soul possesses the capacity to become absolutely free from bondage. It is the principal cause of liberation. The precepts of a Sadguru and the state of the *Jinas* are the nimit for liberation. The principal and instrumental causes are both essential for liberation. Clay turns into a pot only when someone puts it on a wheel, otherwise it could be lying for thousands of years. Also, a pot cannot be made with sand or water even by an expert potter, as these substances do not have the potential to be turned into a pot. Likewise, it is not possible to attain liberation through any single cause alone. Therefore, Shrimadji shows that to insist on only one of the two causes is to go against the pious principles of the Jinas.

The absolute viewpoint states that no substance can make any modification in another substance. The soul becomes free of bondage through its own effort. Only the principal cause is important, and it will manifest its nature by itself. There is no contribution of the instrumental cause. However, the relative viewpoint states that the soul becomes free of bondage due to the instrumental cause. If the principal cause is important then why has it not happened until now? Neither can the defiled modification nor the pure modification of the soul occur without the instrumental cause. It is the instrumental cause that does everything. The importance of the instrumental cause is inevitable.

The absolute and relative viewpoints are analogous to the two eyes of a person. Even though a person can see with only one eye, he does not destroy the other one. In fact, sometimes, to observe an object minutely he concentrates using only one eye and closes the other. Yet, he does not destroy the other. Similarly, to understand a particular aspect, one viewpoint is emphasised, while the other remains subservient at the time. However, this other viewpoint must not be negated, as a one-sided approach cannot lead to liberation.

Therefore, Shrimadji cautions those who think that the goal is accomplished by the principal cause alone and that there is no need for an instrumental cause. Influenced by this belief, if one gives up the support of the Sadguru and spiritual practices, his disease of delusion cannot be eradicated. By forsaking these evidently beneficial instrumental causes, like devotion towards the Sadguru and following His commands, he remains bereft of liberation despite having the same innate nature as the liberated ones. He is unable to revel in the bliss of the self and merely keeps on blabbering statements like 'I am pure.' He causes limitless harm to himself as he gives up spiritual practices without attaining the state of enlightenment.

The importance of the principal cause highlighted in the scriptures is not to disregard the instrumental causes. Rather, its purpose is for one to realise that he will not attain spiritual welfare even though he is associated with instrumental causes, unless he awakens. Despite having innumerable associations of instrumental causes in the past, they have fallen by the wayside due to lack of right effort. Therefore, in the association of instrumental causes, one must take their wholehearted support and focus on the principal cause. This is the intent behind such statements of the scriptures.

One who merely talks about the principal cause and neglects the instrumental cause does not accomplish the goal. Just as both legs are necessary for a man to walk, both causes are necessary to tread the path of liberation. Those who do not understand this truth are unable to gain liberation, and keep wandering in the cycles of birth and death. Therefore, this verse is extremely beneficial as it acts as a guide to prevent one from depriving himself of the right pursuit of liberation.

Thus, there are two aspects of the spiritual pursuit - the priceless potential of every soul and the ceaseless guidance of the Sadguru. One is soil, the other, fertiliser. The seeker must anchor himself in his own potential and trust the immense reservoir he possesses. However, it is important to note that this alone will not get him anywhere. The facilitator is the Sadguru. An aspiring singer needs to learn how to convert his voice to a tune from a music teacher. Similarly, when the seeker is aligned to the Sadguru, it creates a symphony.

VERSE - 137

Hypocrites betray enlightened ones

In verse 136, Shrimadji illustrated the state of the dry intellectualist, who one-sidedly holds the absolute viewpoint. Now, clearly depicting the offence of the dry intellectualist, Shrimadji says -

મુખથી જ્ઞાન કથે અને, અંતર્ છૂટ્યો ન મોહ;
તે પામર પ્રાણી કરે, માત્ર જ્ઞાનીનો દ્રોહ. ||૧૩૭||

Mukhthi jnān kathe ane, antar chhootyo na moh;
Te pāmar prāni karey, mātra Jnānino droh. ||137||

Mukhthi - verbally; *jnān* - knowledge; *kathe* - preaches; *ane* - and; *antar* - inside; *chhootyo* - left; *na* - not; *moh* - delusion; *te* - that; *pāmar* - wretched; *prāni* - being; *karey* - does; *mātra* - only; *Jnānino* - towards enlightened ones; *droh* - betrayal

MEANING

One who engages in lofty discussions of knowledge, despite internally possessing strong delusion, is a hypocrite. Such a wretched one only betrays the enlightened ones.

EXPLANATION

In this verse, Shrimadji vividly portrays the behaviour of one who speaks honeyed words of wisdom but conceals within himself a hypocritic heart. He possesses only superficial knowledge and preaches philosophy to gain the profit of pride. One should possess the ability to understand such people, to distinguish yellow metal from gold. In the world, where everything shines and glitters, it is a great boon to be able to discern the false from the true. To enable such identification, this verse discusses one who has superficial knowledge but no self-knowledge, who speaks of the scriptures but does not follow them.

A dry intellectualist is neither steadfast in his pure nature, nor respectful of the auspicious means that help achieve steadfastness. He has scriptural knowledge, having learnt some catchwords by heart, which he goes on dropping everywhere to display he is madly in love with the soul. Although he speaks of the soul being pure, eternal, unbound, and unattached, his actions are inconsistent with these statements. He remains bereft of the touch of experience within, despite engaging in lofty discussions about the soul. He is able to have such discussions because of his vast study of the scriptures. However, his inner beliefs have not yet changed. Participating in discussions about the soul, without making any effort to abide in it does not lead to any spiritual welfare whatsoever.

Such a hypocrite speaks of the soul but is internally attached to the body and worldly pleasures. Full of ignorance and infatuation, he is dependent on, and seeks happiness from the world. If examined internally, he is observed to be filled with attachments and aversions, neck deep in passions, desirous of comforts, reactive to adverse situations and fearful of death. His ego has not melted, in fact is even stronger than other ignorant ones because of his scriptural knowledge and oratory expertise. He yearns for fame and status. For importance and admiration from society. This longing is so strong that he projects himself as an enlightened being. To be considered enlightened, he gives in to treacherous tendencies and remains engrossed in lowly activities.

Even if he meets an enlightened one, he is unable to express reverence and devotion for Him. On the contrary, he harbours feelings of comparison, jealousy and animosity towards Him. He tries to find fault in the words and behaviour to prove Him wrong and speaks ill of Him too. Instead of respecting Him, he commits the sin of insulting Him. In this manner, indulging in a series of flaws, he shows irreverence for the enlightened ones. Behaving in such an undignified manner, he remains unworthy of self-realisation. Instead, he becomes a culprit by betraying infinite enlightened ones and thereby causes immense harm to himself.

Pitiable is his state for he remains deprived of spiritual benefit despite possessing scriptural knowledge. Even more pitiable is his desire to be considered enlightened as it leads him to misjudge and underrate the real enlightened ones. Such lowly souls are worthy of compassion and this verse acts as a siren to save them.

VERSE - 138

Seven cardinal virtues of seeker

One who engages in lofty speeches of knowledge despite possessing strong delusion within, is certainly not an enlightened one. He is not even worthy of being called a true seeker. Portraying the virtues that adorn a true seeker, that is, the qualities which have blossomed in one desirous of liberation, Shrimadji says -

દયા, શાંતિ, સમતા, ક્ષમા, સત્ય, ત્યાગ, વૈરાગ્ય;
હોય મુમુક્ષુ ઘટ વિષે, એહ સદાય સુજાગ્ય. ||૧૩૮||

Dayā, shānti, samtā, kshamā, satya, tyāg, vairāgya;
Hoi mumukshu ghat vishe, eh sadāy sujāgya. ||138||

Dayā - sympathy; *shānti* - peace; *samtā* - equipoise; *kshamā* - forgiveness; *satya* - truth; *tyāg* - renouncement; *vairāgya* - non-attachment; *hoi* - are; *mumukshu* - desirous of liberation; *ghat* - heart; *vishe* - in; *eh* - these; *sadāy* - constantly; *sujāgya* - vigilant

MEANING
Compassion, tranquillity, equanimity, forgiveness, truthfulness, renunciation, detachment are qualities that are constantly awake in the heart of an aspirant of liberation.

EXPLANATION
After describing the speech and behaviour of a dry intellectualist, Shrimadji has discussed the virtues of a '*mumukshu*' - one desirous of liberation. True yearning for

liberation cannot exist without the manifestation of these virtues. Where the state of yearning for liberation itself has not manifested, how can the state beyond that - the state of enlightenment, possibly exist? With the aim of expounding this truth, the essential virtues that exist in the stage of mumukshu have been portrayed here. This verse describes seven cardinal virtues which a mumukshu possesses. The attributes are -

1. *Dayā* - Compassion
A mumukshu wishes to free himself and others from suffering. He does not indulge in harming or hurting others by mind, speech or body. He endeavours to contribute towards others' happiness.

2. *Shānti* - Tranquillity
A mumukshu subsides, reduces and weakens passions to experience peace. Peace is not attained by changing situations, but by purifying one's internal state. Due to the purification of his mind, he becomes calm and steady.

3. *Samtā* - Equanimity
A mumukshu remains equanimous in both, favourable and unfavourable circumstances. He does not generate likes and dislikes towards happiness and sorrow. He maintains a neutral attitude without any imbalance of feelings.

4. *Kshamā* - Forgiveness
A mumukshu knows the destructive consequences of anger. As a result, he remains unperturbed despite encountering

the triggers of anger. He nurtures the feelings of forgiveness and love, not enmity and hatred.

5. *Satya* - Truthfulness
A mumukshu knows and describes substances exactly as they are. There is integrity in his thought, speech and conduct. He does not have the need to engage in lies or deceit for personal gain.

6. *Tyāg* - Renunciation
A mumukshu renounces objects that hinder his spiritual progress. He gives up worldly pursuits and entanglements. He not only reduces his possessions, but also diminishes his possessiveness.

7. *Vairāgya* - Detachment
A mumukshu has a proper understanding of the nature of substances. Hence, he sheds attachment towards the world, the sensual pleasures and the body. He remains indifferent to mundane occurrences.

Thus, this verse enumerates the characteristics of a true seeker of liberation in very simple language. The seven virtues can be compared to the seven colours of a rainbow. Just as the seven colours make the rainbow an attractive and captivating sight, the seven virtues render the mumukshu pleasant and endearing. These seven virtues are always alert and active in the heart of the mumukshu, enabling him to combat all inner enemies. Neither is he driven by passions, nor does he crave for anything. He is not buffeted by life's currents.

He does not bow to sorrow or get bowled over by joy. The virtues of compassion, peace, etc., are certainly seen in a genuine aspirant of liberation. In the absence of these virtues, one cannot be considered a vigilant aspirant of liberation. It is not possible to have a sincere longing for liberation without these virtues. One has to examine himself in the light of these virtues. This verse serves as a thermometer to measure one's inner state. It is a guide for all seekers on the path of liberation and is therefore very important.

⁓

VERSE - 139

Enlightened one and verbal intellectualist

In the previous verse, describing the virtues of a true seeker in seven words, Shrimadji portrayed a *mumukshu*. Now in verses 139 and 140, He describes the attributes of an enlightened one. In this verse Shrimadji says -

મોહભાવ ક્ષય હોય જ્યાં, અથવા હોય પ્રશાંત;
તે કહીએ જ્ઞાનીદશા, બાકી કહીએ ભ્રાંત. ||૧૩૯||

Mohbhāv kshay hoi jyā, athvā hoi prashānt;
Te kahiye Jnānidashā, bāki kahiye bhrānt. ||139||

Mohbhāv - delusion; *kshay* - destroyed; *hoi* - is; *jyā* - where; *athvā* - or; *hoi* - is; *prashānt* - calmed down; *te* - that; *kahiye* - is called; *Jnānidashā* - enlightened state; *bāki* - all else; *kahiye* - is called; *bhrānt* - illusion

MEANING
Where delusion has been destroyed or has subsided, that is the state of an enlightened one. All others are in illusion.

EXPLANATION
All impurities of the soul are caused by delusion. The two kinds of delusion are faith delusion and conduct delusion. The former is identification with the non-self, such as the body, whereas the latter is harbouring likes and dislikes. Indulging in passions leads to the continuation of transmigration. Delusion

hinders abidance in the self. The pure state of the soul cannot emerge until delusion is removed.

Delusion can be removed in two ways - destruction and subsidence. Dust particles in a glass of water render it impure. The water can be purified by filtration, that is, eliminating the dust particles permanently. Alternatively, the dust particles can be allowed to settle down, which is temporary subsidence. Similarly, delusion can be annihilated or subsided. In both cases, there is purity in the state of the soul.

One who has annihilated or subsided delusion is an enlightened being. One whose delusion has been uprooted or pacified, awareness has turned towards the self and has become steadfast in it, is said to have manifested the state of enlightenment. Such an enlightened one considers gold as mud, a royal throne as low status, attachment to someone as death, feelings of greatness to be cow dung, grandeur like supernatural powers as sickness, ambition to be worshipped in the world as meaningless, material body as ashes, worldly pleasures as a web of entanglements, the wish to increase popularity as saliva of the mouth, desire for fame as nasal filth and the manifestation of meritorious karma as excreta.

Such is the splendid state of the enlightened one, which has awakened due to the annihilation or subsidence of delusion. In stark contrast to this is one who has memorised several scriptures but whose delusion has neither been destroyed nor pacified. His focus has not become steady on the self, and yet he considers himself enlightened. However, one cannot proclaim to be enlightened until delusion has been eliminated or has subsided. Only one who has experienced the pure nature of the self is truly enlightened. One who has not removed delusion, and believes that he has attained the state of enlightenment is in fact truly ignorant. Scriptural knowledge has created the illusion of enlightenment in him. Experiential knowledge of the soul removes delusion, but mere knowledge of the scriptures does not do the same. He may feel that he is enlightened because he has read a lot of scriptures, but he is in fact blinded by delusion. Worldly desires still erupt in him. He nourishes his ego and expects respect. The true enlightened one has no such deluded feelings.

The verification of enlightenment is the absence of delusion. One may have read fewer scriptures than the dry intellectualist, but is considered enlightened if He has removed delusion. Equally true is the scenario in which one considers himself enlightened without removing delusion, although he may have read numerous scriptures. Shrimadji dispels the illusion of such people who believe themselves to be enlightened without having attained enlightenment. The purpose of this verse is to shatter such hypocrisy.

VERSE - 140

How world appears to enlightened ones

The difference between an enlightened one and a verbal intellectualist became clearly visible in the previous verse. Describing two analogies regarding how the world appears to an enlightened one, Shrimadji says -

સકળ જગત તે એઠવત્, અથવા સ્વપ્ન સમાન;
તે કહીએ જ્ઞાનીદશા, બાકી વાચાજ્ઞાન. ॥૧૪૦॥

Sakal jagat te ethvat, athvā swapna samān;
Te kahiye Jnānidashā, bāki vāchājnān. ॥140॥

Sakal - whole; *jagat* - universe; *te* - that; *ethvat* - like leftover food; *athvā* - or; *swapna* - dream; *samān* - like; *te* - that; *kahiye* - is called; *Jnānidashā* - enlightened state; *bāki* - all else; *vāchājnān* - verbal knowledge

MEANING

When the whole world appears like leftover food or like a dream, that is considered the enlightened state. Otherwise it is mere verbal knowledge.

EXPLANATION

The enlightened one has attained that which is most worthwhile, the self, so He lives with a sense of fulfilment. The world appears worthless and transient to the one who has attained self-realisation. Therefore, He remains completely detached from it. Shrimadji has employed perfect analogies to describe the worthlessness and transitoriness of the world as it appears to the enlightened one. The whole world seems unattractive as leftover food and fleeting as a dream to the enlightened one.

1. *Sakal jagat te ethvat* - Leftover food

If someone leaves behind half-eaten food, another person would not want to consume it. Even though it might be his favourite food or an expensive dish, but leftover food is considered trash. He would rather stay hungry than eat leftovers. One does not dribble and drool at the sight of such food, rather it makes one nauseous to the extent that one may even throw up. Leftover food is worth discarding and is universally despised. People do not want to touch it or even see it. An enlightened one considers the entire world to be like leftover food and hence has no desire to touch, see or enjoy it.

All objects of the world are actually transactions of atoms. Whether it is the body, clothes, ornaments or a mansion, everything involves adoption and discarding of atoms. So even the most precious possession is actually the atoms one has adopted which have been discarded by someone else. Hence, it proves to be like leftover food. In this case, how can the enlightened one possibly have a sense of gratification or pride in worldly objects?

People usually do not like second-hand things. The enlightened one knows that all worldly objects are second-hand and have been used multiple times. In effect, what one thinks is new has actually been used by someone before in one form or the other. The only genuine, original and important substance is one's soul, which has never been possessed or enjoyed by anyone else. The enlightened one views the world as completely meaningless and therefore remains unattached to it.

2. **Swapna samān** - Dream

One may get fascinated by the objects or the occurrences of dreams. He may not even possess a two-wheeler but will be driving around in a flashy sports car in his dream. However, the dream is temporary. Everything vanishes upon awakening. It does not last. It has no capacity to disburse satisfaction. Similarly, the entire world is transitory. It does not have the power to give satisfaction. One who knows the transient nature of the dream does not get affected by the happenings in the dream. The enlightened one knows the whole world is a dream, and so remains untouched by it. He observes the series of events in His life as a witness. It is effortless for Him to remain equanimous in the dualities of life.

Thus, the enlightened one considers all objects of the world to be as worthless as leftover food and as ephemeral as a dream. Only the one who is detached from the world is truly an enlightened one. Unless there is disinterest in the world, it cannot be called an enlightened state. Those who have not lost interest in the world are pseudo-enlightened, even if they speak about the soul. It is mere meaningless talk if the spirit of detachment is absent. A dry intellectualist is not indifferent towards the world, therefore what he speaks amounts to hollow words. Using lofty words of knowledge which are hollow is merely a verbal exercise. He may be an expert orator but finds the world wonderful and attractive. He is desirous of worldly objects, gets thrilled on obtaining them, and remains possessive of them. He knows the art of conversation but remains immersed in delusion. Such scholars and orators have not attained self-realisation, but yet believe and prompt others to believe they are enlightened. However, the fact is that they are immersed in delusion and are certainly ignorant. Their knowledge is merely theoretical, not put into practice. It is like a sword without the sharpness, so it cannot help in vanquishing inner enemies.

VERSE - 141

Result of studying this scripture

Describing the nature of the enlightened one, which can clearly be differentiated from the verbal intellectualist, Shrimadji brought this subject to a close. Before completing Shri Ātmasiddhi Shāstra, He shows what one should do after studying this scripture. Shrimadji says -

સ્થાનક પાંચ વિચારીને, છઠ્ઠે વર્તે જેહ;
પામે સ્થાનક પાંચમું, એમાં નહિ સંદેહ. ॥૧૪૧॥

Sthānak pānch vichārine, chhatthe varte jeh;
Pāmey sthānak pānchmu, emā nahi sandeh. ॥141॥

Sthānak - aphorisms; *pānch* - five; *vichārine* - pondering; *chhatthe* - sixth; *varte* - acts; *jeh* - who; *pāmey* - attains; *sthānak* - abode; *pānchmu* - fifth; *emā* - in that; *nahi* - no; *sandeh* - doubt

MEANING

Contemplating over the five aphorisms, if one acts according to the sixth, which is the path of liberation; he will attain the fifth, which is liberation. There is no doubt about it.

EXPLANATION

In Shri Ātmasiddhi Shāstra, Shrimadji has established the six fundamental truths through logical arguments which have been expressed as a dialogue between a Guru and disciple. He has expounded them for the benefit of seekers. In this verse, He proposes a final recommendation on what one needs to do after correctly grasping these teachings. He states that out of the six fundamental truths, five have to be thought over and one has to be acted upon.

Through the power of contemplation, one must properly understand the first five fundamental truths. Namely, 'soul exists', 'it is eternal', 'it is the doer of karma', 'it is the receiver of the fruits of karma', and 'there is liberation'. If they are deeply contemplated upon, he will achieve cogent clarity, and the mysteries of the soul will begin to unravel. In other words, with the right deliberation of the first five aphorisms, he will gain a firm conviction about them. Hence, it is very important to reflect upon them.

After developing right thinking of the first five fundamentals, one should act according to the sixth, 'there is a path of liberation'. A proper analysis of the five aphorisms helps in following the sixth. The thought process that began with questions regarding the truths, transforms into efforts on the path of liberation. Through questioning, a quest awakens and one becomes eager to experience the self. Treading the path of liberation, his attachments-aversions begin to reduce, and he progresses towards complete abidance in the self.

Whoever contemplates over the five fundamentals and acts as per the sixth, certainly attains the fifth fundamental - the state of liberation. As he ascends the ladder of right thinking, his inner effort increases and he achieves liberation. It is not the time spent but the earnestness which matters in the effort for liberation. There have been instances where liberation has been attained in a very short time due to tremendous effort. In contrast, there have been instances where liberation has not been attained due to a lack of right effort. If one puts in the necessary effort according to the sixth fundamental, he undoubtedly secures liberation. Shrimadji unhesitatingly promises that if the soul is devoted towards the path of liberation, then the accomplishment of the goal is definite.

Thus, in the penultimate verse of Shri Ātmasiddhi Shāstra, in His inimitable style, through a beautiful play of words, Shrimadji assures the reader that one who contemplates the five and follows the sixth, definitely attains the fifth. He has encompassed the result of this scripture in a wonderful manner. Shrimadji has indicated the way, it is the reader who must now walk. He has unveiled the staircase, it is the reader who must now climb. He has pointed to the water, it is the reader who must now drink. Once the goal is in front of him and the path is clear, once the heart is set and the journey has begun, the attainment of liberation is certain.

VERSE - 142

Innumerable salutations to enlightened one

Just as authors commence a scripture in an auspicious manner by offering obeisance to their revered deity, they also conclude the scripture by bowing to their venerable Lord. This stems from the satisfaction of completing the text without any hindrance. It is an expression of gratitude. In keeping with this ancient tradition, with a heart full of devotion, Shrimadji concludes -

દેહ છતાં જેની દશા, વર્તે દેહાતીત;
તે જ્ઞાનીના ચરણમાં, હો વંદન અગણિત. ||૧૪૨||

Deh chhatā jeni dashā, varte dehātit;
Te Jnāninā charanmā, ho vandan aganit. ||142||

Deh - body; *chhatā* - despite; *jeni* - whose; *dashā* - state; *varte* - prevails; *dehātit* - beyond body; *te* - that; *Jnāninā* - of enlightened one; *charanmā* - at feet; *ho* - be; *vandan* - obeisance; *aganit* - innumerable

MEANING

My innumerable salutations at the lotus feet of that enlightened one, whose state of existence is beyond the body, though in an embodied condition.

EXPLANATION

The verses of the supremely benevolent Shri Ātmasiddhi Shāstra now draw to a close. The six fundamental truths of the soul have been enumerated in totality. The confusion of the seeker has been resolved. The path of liberation, defined. The pitfalls, depicted. Gracious guidelines, invaluable instructions, precious pointers - elucidated. The only thing left is to put them into practice. All that remains is to assimilate, integrate and internalise the teachings.

This final auspicious verse encompasses the essence of the philosophy espoused by the dispassionate ones. Shrimadji says that despite having the association of the body, one whose delusion regarding the body has been annihilated, who has transcended the body, is an enlightened being. One whose delusional identification with the body, whose thoughts of 'I am the body', 'the body is mine', 'I am the doer of bodily activities' have been destroyed, He alone is a truly enlightened being. When the water in the coconut dries up, the kernel separates from the shell. Similarly, once the water of identification with the body dries up, a state beyond the body is attained. His identification has turned away from the body and is established in the self.

The existence of the body is one thing and the existence of attachment for the body is another. Association with the body is due to the past karma whereas attachment for the body is caused by delusion. An enlightened one's life is a closing ceremony. He lives only to repay karmic debt, without any interest in it. If a piece of iron is placed near a horseshoe magnet, it gets influenced. However, there is no such influence on a piece of wood. If the pieces of iron and wood are joined together, the magnet draws the combined piece towards it. Despite appearing to influence both, the magnet only influences the iron piece. The wooden piece remains unaffected, drawn only because of the association. Similarly, karma can only influence the body of an enlightened one, but has no effect on His inner state whatsoever, despite the association.

Although the enlightened one is in an embodied state, He does not have any attachment to the body. He lives in the awareness of being separate from the body. He has annihilated body identification, attained oneness with His own pure nature, and revels in the boundless bliss that is beyond the senses. He remains indifferent - whether the body is sick or hurt, eating or resting. He experiences neither joy nor sorrow on account of physical comfort or discomfort. He is steady in the pure self. He is in the body, yet has transcended it, and hence has attained the unparalleled state of being liberated while living.

The enlightened one is a treasure trove of virtues. From these magnificent virtues, Shrimadji has highlighted non-attachment with the body in this concluding verse because it is the purpose of this scripture. The objective of Shri Ātmasiddhi Shāstra is to realise the soul - the most supreme and worthwhile of all substances. However, the soul is not even registered due to the identification with the body. Even if there is knowledge of the soul, it is only at a superficial level. There is no awareness of the self. Only if one breaks the identification with the body can he experience the self. Therefore, to reinforce the necessity of breaking body identification, the state beyond the body has been portrayed here.

The body itself is not the cause of transmigration, identification with the body is the main cause. The enlightened one exists within the body and yet does not get attached to it. He lives in the world and yet is not of it. The feeling of humbly and reverentially offering salutations to such an enlightened one comes naturally to a true seeker, as he himself is desirous of that state. The only aim of a seeker is to attain the pure blissful state of the soul. To gain impetus in that direction the seeker pays obeisance to the enlightened one. The seeker unreservedly falls at His feet for guidance and spiritual upliftment. He bows to Him, praises Him, acts according to His instructions with complete harmony of mind-speech-body, and thereby abides in the self. Such salutations are unfailing.

Shrimadji has offered innumerable salutations at the lotus feet of the enlightened one. He does not offer a hundred, a thousand, or even a million salutations, but pays obeisance countless times to the enlightened one, who is the very embodiment of liberation. Such a feeling can arise only in a heart filled with amazing devotion. So, with this heart-touching expression of devotion, Shrimadji auspiciously concludes the scripture by offering obeisance to the enlightened one - not once, but innumerable times - *'ho vandan aganit'*.

About the Mission

Shrimad Rajchandra Mission Dharampur is a global manifestation of Pujya Gurudevshri's vision and efforts dedicated to the holistic well-being of humanity. A spiritual movement for inner transformation through wisdom, meditation and selfless service, the organisation encompasses 108 centres in five continents. The Mission Statement is:
Realise one's True Self and serve others selflessly

INTERNATIONAL HEADQUARTERS

Nestled on a quiet hillock in the outskirts of Dharampur in Southern Gujarat, India, is Shrimad Rajchandra Ashram, the Mission's International Headquarters. Spread over 223 acres, this lush spiritual sanctuary is dedicated to the pursuit of a higher existence. Located around the spiritual valley, a spectrum of housing options for ashramites include courtyard villas, sky villas, stepped terraces, and crescent blocks.

Jinmandir
Adorning the highest point of the Ashram, the magnificent and divinely ornate 108-pillar temple stands testimony to the timeless tenets of Jainism for generations to come.

World's Tallest Statue of Shrimad Rajchandraji
The Ashram's spirit converges in the amphitheatre where the majestic 34-foot idol - the world's tallest statue of Shrimad Rajchandraji, towers over the spiritual valley.

Satsang and Meditation Complex
The iconic satsang and meditation complex is a powerful site to uncover the hidden depths of spirituality and get elevated. It is in the shape of a lantern with a capacity of over 10,000 seekers.

SPIRITUAL ACTIVITIES

Pujya Gurudevshri has revitalised the path to self-realisation. Each spiritual activity taps into a deeper dimension, allowing one to bloom into an awakened existence.

Wisdom

Satsangs are empowering discourses by Pujya Gurudevshri for clarity of mind, purity of heart, and discovery of the self. Shibirs, udghosh, mahotsavs, and the paryushan mahaparva bring this ocean of wisdom to every seeker.

Meditation

Pujya Gurudevshri has crafted a unique blend of sadhana bhattis or meditation retreats for seekers of all levels. Explore the inner universe and unveil its vastness.

SRMD Yoga

Asana, pranayama and mudra, underscore SRMD Yoga, a multi-level journey augmenting holistic well-being from experimental to experiential levels of yoga.

Shrimad Rajchandra Global Youth

Fondly known as the leader of youth, Pujya Gurudevshri steers them to higher goals through the 5-S programme of satsang, sadhana, seva, sanskruti and sports, across 90 youth centres.

Shrimad Rajchandra Divinetouch

A global chain of value-education classes for children aged 4-16, spread across 250 centres, Magictouch, Arhat Touch, and Spiritualtouch, enable the blossoming of their fullest potential.

SOCIAL INITIATIVES

Shrimad Rajchandra Love and Care is a unique 10-fold benevolent programme with over 50 high-quality projects powered by motivated volunteers. Enjoying special consultative status with the United Nations Economic and Social Council, this international initiative has touched millions globally.

1. Health Care	6. Community Care
2. Educational Care	7. Humanitarian Care
3. Child Care	8. Animal Care
4. Woman Care	9. Environmental Care
5. Tribal Care	10. Emergency Relief Care

Shrimad Rajchandra Hospital
A state-of-the-art 250-bed multi-specialty charitable hospital in Dharampur with the latest technology and leading doctors.

Shrimad Rajchandra Vidyapeeth
A modern science college, a centre of educational excellence, is the first and only one across 238 villages in South Gujarat.

Shrimad Rajchandra Jivamaitridham
A secure shelter for hundreds of animals, and a one-of-its-kind 100-bed animal hospital for medical care.

Raj Uphaar
Empowering underprivileged women towards self-reliance by producing snacks, fragrances and utility products.

PUBLICATIONS AND PRODUCTS
Books in English

- **Benevolent Principles of Bhagwan Mahavira**
Elucidating the precepts of non-violence, non-possessiveness, non-absolutism, and awareness

- **Shrimad Rajchandra - Saga of Spirituality ***
Life of Shrimad Rajchandraji

- **A Life Worth Living *B**
Inspiring seekers to lead a meaningful life

- **Embark on the Inner Journey *B**
Transformation through introspection

- **Shrimadji Spake**
English translation of 100 letters

- **Sadguru Insights**
50 Enlightening lessons from the Master

- **Sadguru Alerts**
50 insightful questions from the Master

- **Sadguru Communion**
50 prayers to the Master

- **Sadguru Encourages**
50 experiments for inner growth from the Master

- **Sadguru Nuggets**
100 quips from the Master

- **Sadguru Capsules**
Weekly profound contemplations from the Master

- **Seek Thy Eternal Self**
Inspiring the search for self-realisation

- **The Path Enlightened**
Discovering the essence of religion

- **Bliss Within**
Shattering the illusion of false happiness to attain true joy

- **Time to Awaken**
Ending transmigration and accelerating the journey to liberation

- **Invitation to the Infinite**
A call to enter the inner world

- **A Divine Union**
Courageously tread the path of renunciation

- **Dhyanmulam Gurumurti**
His form I will meditate

- **Pujamulam Gurupadam**
His lotus feet I will worship

- **Mantramulam Guruvakyam**
His word I will follow

- **Mokshmulam Gurukrupa**
His grace I will seek

• Asato Ma Sadgamaya
Lead me from untruth to truth

• Mrutyorma Amrutam Gamaya
Lead me from death to eternity

• Rajgeeta
English translation of Shri
Atmasiddhi Shastra

• Reflections
Impact of Shri Atmasiddhi Shastra
on the worthy disciples

• Impressions
Impact of Shri Atmasiddhi Shastra
on great personalities

• Expressions
Influence of Shri Atmasiddhi
Shastra in proceeding towards
the supreme

• Ajnabhakti
Daily prayers in the morning
and evening

• Jinpuja
Understanding importance and
meaning of puja

**• SRMD Yoga - Daily
Workout Book**
Unique yoga sequences for
each day of the week

Monthly Magazines

• Sadguru Echoes (Multilingual
- English, Gujarati and Hindi)

• Divinetouch Champs
(English)

Books and Products for Children

**• Yugpurush -
Shrimad Rajchandraji**
His Life and His Mission

• Nourish Your Heart
Heart-warming stories
for children

• What Would Bapaji Say?
Magical mantras from
the Sadguru

**• Amazinga Adventures
Book**
Timeless values through a
journey across the world

**• Amazinga Adventures
Board Game**
A value-based game for the family

• iDeal Card Game
Ideals and values through a fun
card game

* These books are available in 10 languages including - Spanish,
German, French, Mandarin, Marathi, Bengali and Tamil.
ᴮ- These books are available in Braille, in both English and Hindi.

Books in Gujarati

• **શ્રીમદ્ રાજચંદ્ર - જીવન અને કવન**
શ્રીમદ્ રાજચંદ્રજીનું જીવન અને સાહિત્ય

• **'શ્રી આત્મસિદ્ધિ શાસ્ત્ર' વિવેચન ગ્રંથ (ભાગ ૧ થી ૪)**
શ્રીમદ્ રાજચંદ્રજીની અમૃત કૃતિ ઉપર વિસ્તૃત ભાષ્ય

• **શ્રી આત્મસિદ્ધિ શાસ્ત્ર સંક્ષિપ્ત અર્થ**
શ્રીમદ્ રાજચંદ્રજીની અમૃત કૃતિનું સારરૂપ અર્થઘટન

• **ભગવાન મહાવીરના મંગલમય સિદ્ધાંત**
અહિંસા, અપરિગ્રહ, અનેકાંત અને અપ્રમાદના સિદ્ધાંતોની સમજણ

• **આરંભ કરીએ આજથી અંતર્યાત્રા**
આત્મનિરીક્ષણ થકી રૂપાંતરણ સાધવાની પ્રેરણા

• **શુભ દેહ માનવનો મળ્યો**
અર્થપૂર્ણ જીવન અર્થે સાધકને પ્રેરણા

• **સ્વરૂપ સંવેદન**
આત્માનુભૂતિ તરફ આગેકૂચનો અનુબોધ

• **વીતરાગનો ધર્મ**
પરમના પંથે પ્રોત્સાહન આપતો બોધ

• **સુખનું સરનામું**
સુખાભાસની ભ્રાંતિ તોડી સાચા સુખની પ્રાપ્તિનો બોધ

• **અવસર આત્મકલ્યાણનો**
ભવયાત્રાનો અંત લાવી કલ્યાણયાત્રાને વેગીલી બનાવવાનું માર્ગદર્શન

• **અંતર્મુખતાનું આમંત્રણ**
નિજ સ્વરૂપ પ્રવેશાર્થે દ્વાર ઉદ્ઘાટન

• **વિરાટ સાથે વિવાહ**
સંયમના સન્માર્ગે સાહસ પ્રેરતો બોધ

• **ધ્યાનમૂલં ગુરુમૂર્તિ**
સદ્ગુરુની મંગળવર્ષિણી મુદ્રાનો મહિમા

• **પૂજામૂલં ગુરુપદં**
સદ્ગુરુચરણની ઉપાસનાથી પરાભક્તિની પ્રાપ્તિ

• **મંત્રમૂલં ગુરુવાક્યં**
સદ્ગુરુની આત્મકલ્યાણકારી વાણીનો મહિમા

• **મોક્ષમૂલં ગુરુકૃપા**
ભક્તહૃદય માટે ગુરુકૃપા એ જ મોક્ષ

• **અસતો મા સદ્ગમય**
અસત્યથી સત્ય તરફની યાત્રા

• **મૃત્યોર્મા અમૃતં ગમય**
મૃત્યુના અભિશાપમાંથી અમૃતની અનુપ્રાપ્તિની ઉડાન

• **મળ્યો બોધ સુખસાજ**
શ્રી આત્મસિદ્ધિ શાસ્ત્રનો પ્રભાવ ભક્તરત્નો ઉપર

• **સદ્ગુરુ બોધ સુહાય**
શ્રી આત્મસિદ્ધિ શાસ્ત્રનો પ્રભાવ મહાનુભાવો ઉપર

• **આવ્યું અપૂર્વ ભાન**
શ્રી આત્મસિદ્ધિ શાસ્ત્રના પ્રભાવથી અપૂર્વ પ્રતિ પ્રયાણ

• **આજ્ઞાભક્તિ**
પ્રાતઃકાળ અને સાયંકાળનો ભક્તિક્રમ

• **જિન સ્તવના**
જિનેશ્વર ભગવાનને સમર્પિત સ્તવનો

• **રાજ ભજના**
શ્રીગુરુને સમર્પિત ભજનો

• **આત્મનિવેદન - અંતરમંથન**
પ્રાર્થનાસંગ્રહ

• **પ્રવચન પુસ્તિકા**
૨૦૦૧ થી ૨૦૨૦ (દરેક વર્ષની ૧૨ પ્રવચન પુસ્તિકા)
શ્રીમદ્ રાજચંદ્રજીનાં અમૃત વચનો ઉપર પૂજ્ય ગુરુદેવશ્રી દ્વારા થયેલ પ્રવચનની પુસ્તિકા

Books in Hindi

• **श्रीमद् राजचंद्र - जीवन और साहित्य**
श्रीमद् राजचंद्रजी का जीवन और साहित्य

• **भगवान महावीर के मंगलमय सिद्धांत**
अहिंसा, अपरिग्रह, अनेकांत तथा अप्रमाद के
सिद्धांतों की समझ

• **आरंभ करें आज से अंतर्यात्रा**
आत्मनिरीक्षण द्वारा रूपांतरण की प्रेरणा

• **शुभ देह मानव का मिला**
अर्थपूर्ण जीवन हेतु साधक को प्रेरणा

• **स्वरूप संवेदन**
आत्मानुभूति की ओर अग्रसर होने हेतु अनुबोध

• **वीतराग धर्म**
परमपुरुषों के पंथ पर प्रयाण की प्रेरणा

• **स्वयं सुखधाम**
सुखाभास की भ्रांति को तोड़कर सच्चे सुख की
प्राप्ति का बोध

• **अवसर आत्मकल्याण का**
भवयात्रा का अंत लाकर कल्याणयात्रा को तेज़
करने का मार्गदर्शन

• **अंतर्मुखता का निमंत्रण**
निजस्वरूप में प्रवेश हेतु द्वार उद्घाटन

• **विराट के साथ विवाह**
संन्यास के सन्मार्ग पर प्रेरित करता
हुआ बोध

• **ध्यानमूलं गुरुमूर्ति**
सद्गुरु की मंगलवर्षिणी मुद्रा की महिमा

• **पूजामूलं गुरुपदं**
सद्गुरु के चरणों की उपासना से पराभक्ति
की प्राप्ति

• **मंत्रमूलं गुरुवाक्यं**
श्रीगुरु के आत्मप्रभावक बोध
का माहात्म्य

• **मोक्षमूलं गुरुकृपा**
भक्तहृदय के लिये गुरुकृपा ही मोक्ष

• **असतो मा सद्गमय**
असत्य से सत्य की यात्रा

• **मृत्योर्मा अमृतं गमय**
मृत्यु के अभिशाप से अमृत की अनुप्राप्ति
की उड़ान

• **मिला बोध सुखसाज**
श्री आत्मसिद्धि शास्त्र का प्रभाव भक्तरत्नों पर

• **सद्गुरु बोध सुहाय**
श्री आत्मसिद्धि शास्त्र का प्रभाव महानुभावों पर

• **हुआ अपूर्व भान**
श्री आत्मसिद्धि शास्त्र के प्रभाव से अपूर्व
की ओर प्रयाण

• **शरणागति**
प्रार्थनासंग्रह

Discourses in Gujarati and Hindi

શ્રીમદ્ રાજચંદ્ર વચનામૃતજી પર પ્રવચનો

- વર્ષ ૨૦૦૧ થી વર્ષ ૨૦૨૦
  (દરેક વર્ષનાં ૧૮ પ્રવચન)
- સર્વસમ્મત ધર્મ (પત્રાંક-૩૭)
- પરિભ્રમણનાં પ્રત્યાખ્યાન (પત્રાંક-૧૨૮)
- સમ્યગ્દર્શનનાં લક્ષણો (પત્રાંક-૧૩૫)
- મોક્ષનાં સર્વોત્તમ કારણરૂપ
  વચનામૃત (પત્રાંક-૧૬૬)
- મુમુક્ષુતા (પત્રાંક-૨૫૪)

- સત્સંગની સાર્થકતા (પત્રાંક-૪૫૪)
- છ પદનો પત્ર - સમ્યગ્દર્શનના નિવાસનાં
  સર્વોત્કૃષ્ટ સ્થાનક (પત્રાંક-૪૯૩)
- જ્ઞાનીનો સમાગમ સર્જે કલ્યાણ (પત્રાંક-૫૨૨)
- આત્મજ્ઞાનનો યથાર્થ પુરુષાર્થ (પત્રાંક-૫૬૮)
- સત્સંગના યોગે અસંગપણું (પત્રાંક-૬૦૯)
- સમાધિદશાના ઉપાય (પત્રાંક-૬૫૬)
- શ્રીમદ્ રાજચંદ્ર વચનામૃતજી પર પ્રવચન (હિંદી)

અન્ય ધર્મગ્રંથો પર પ્રવચન

- શ્રી ઉત્તરાધ્યયન સૂત્ર
- શ્રી ભક્તામર સ્તોત્ર
- યોગદૃષ્ટિસમુચ્ચય
- ગણધરવાદ
- શાંત સુધારસ
- જ્ઞાનસાર
- શ્રી આનંદઘન ચોવીસી
- શ્રીમદ્ દેવચંદ્રજીકૃત ચોવીસી
- યોગસાર
- સમાધિતંત્ર
- અનુભવપ્રકાશ
- ઇષ્ટોપદેશ
- શ્રી અધ્યાત્મ કલ્પદ્રુમ
- આત્માનુશાસન

- તત્ત્વજ્ઞાન તરંગિણી
- સમ્યગ્જ્ઞાનદીપિકા
- સામ્યશતક
- હૃદયપ્રદીપ
- શ્રી સીમંધરસ્વામીને વિનંતીરૂપ
  ૧૨૫ ગાથાનું સ્તવન
- શ્રી નવપદ મહિમા
- શ્રીમદ્ ભગવદ્ગીતા
- શ્રી યોગવાસિષ્ઠ મહારામાયણ
- અષ્ટાવક્ર ગીતા
- વિવેકચૂડામણિ
- મોહમુદ્ગર (ભજ ગોવિંદમ્)
- નારદ ભક્તિ સૂત્ર
- ગંગાસતી એમ બોલિયાં રે

All content is available as digital downloads in audio-video formats on the Mission's website, mobile application and on YouTube.

Discourses in English

- Shri Atmasiddhi Shastra Jnan Yajna 2021
- Dealing with Anger Effectively
- Introspection
- Taking Charge of Yourself
- The Happiness Sensex
- Mastering Meditation
- Karma Café
- 6 Ways to Deal with Stress
- Overcoming Depression Skilfully
- Emotional Fitness
- Sadguru Serving Desserts
- Sadguru Prasad

Bhajans

- આજ્ઞાભક્તિ
- બીજમંત્ર - સહજાત્મસ્વરૂપ પરમગુરુ
- અંતિમ આરાધના
- સ્મરણમ્
- યુગપુરુષ યશોગાન
- અદ્ભૂત અસ્તિત્વ

- ઓવારણાં
- કૃપાનિધાન
- નૈવેદ્યમ્
- પ્રભુતા
- નમામિ રાજચંદ્રમ્
- વંદે જિનેન્દ્રમ્
- પરમના પંથે

- मेरे गुरुदेव
- मेरे सितारे
- मेरे राज
- निजानंद
- बैरागी
- नैवेद्यम्
- प्रभुता
- धम्मो मंगलम्
- गुरवे नमः

SRMD Bhakti is a soulful blend of bhajans, chants, prayers, original compositions and curated-playlists available on 50+ online streaming platforms, including Spotify, Apple Music and Amazon Music.

Meditations & Prayers

- Sakshi (English, Gujarati)
- Sadgurum Tam Namami - Melting in meditation (English, Gujarati)
- Kshama - Meditations on forgiveness (English, Gujarati, Hindi)
- Divine Love - I am yours
- Hey Dev and a series of connecting prayers

Digital Connect

Sadguru Whispers
Get connected with a daily message straight from Pujya Gurudevshri's desk, fuelling your spiritual pursuit every morning.

Sadguru Enlightens App
View and download discourses, elevating events and articles from your phone. Available on Android and iOS.

TV Channels
Pujya Gurudevshri's blissful discourses are telecast regularly on the SRMD channel on JioTV, Aastha, Arihant, Soham and more.

Social Media
Stay in touch with the Mission's activities anytime, anywhere, through the social media handles.

Shrimad Rajchandra Mission Dharampur	SRMDharampur
Shrimad Rajchandra Mission Dharampur	SRMDharampur
Shrimad Rajchandra Mission Dharampur	+91 7718888111

STEPS 1. Save our number to your phone contacts
2. WhatsApp us your name and city

Global Languages
Pujya Gurudevshri's discourses, meditations and SRMD Yoga videos are available in multiple languages through exclusive channels on YouTube.

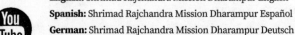

Gujarati: Shrimad Rajchandra Mission Dharampur ગુજરાતી
Hindi: Shrimad Rajchandra Mission Dharampur हिंदी
English: Shrimad Rajchandra Mission Dharampur English
Spanish: Shrimad Rajchandra Mission Dharampur Español
German: Shrimad Rajchandra Mission Dharampur Deutsch
French: Shrimad Rajchandra Mission Dharampur Français
Portuguese: Shrimad Rajchandra Mission Dharampur Português
Russian: Shrimad Rajchandra Mission Dharampur Русский
Mandarin: Shrimad Rajchandra Mission Dharampur 简体中文

www.srmd.org